C0-DAU-629

RECORD COPY
Do not remove from office

Rituals and Sisterhoods

Rituals and Sisterhoods

Single Women's Households in Mexico, 1560–1750

Amos Megged

UNIVERSITY PRESS OF COLORADO
Louisville

© 2019 by University Press of Colorado

Published by University Press of Colorado
245 Century Circle, Suite 202
Louisville, Colorado 80027

All rights reserved
Manufactured in the United States of America

The University Press of Colorado is a proud member of
the Association of University Presses.

The University Press of Colorado is a cooperative publishing enterprise supported, in part, by Adams State University, Colorado State University, Fort Lewis College, Metropolitan State University of Denver, Regis University, University of Colorado, University of Northern Colorado, University of Wyoming, Utah State University, and Western Colorado University.

∞ This paper meets the requirements of the ANSI/NISO Z39.48–1992 (Permanence of Paper)

ISBN: 978-1-60732-961-9 (hardcover)
ISBN: 978-1-60732-962-6 (paperback)
ISBN: 978-1-60732-963-3 (ebook)
https://doi.org/10.5876/9781607329633

Library of Congress Cataloging-in-Publication Data

Names: Megged, Amos, author.
Title: Rituals and sisterhoods : single women's households in Mexico, 1560–1750 / Amos Megged.
Description: Louisville : University Press of Colorado, 2019. | Includes bibliographical references and index.
Identifiers: LCCN 2019021374 | ISBN 9781607329619 (cloth) | ISBN 9781607329626 (paperback) | ISBN 9781607329633 (ebook)
Subjects: LCSH: Single women—Mexico—Social conditions. | Single women—Mexico—History. | Households—Mexico. | Mexico—Social conditions—To 1810. | Mexico—History—Spanish colony, 1540-1810.
Classification: LCC HQ800.2 .M44 2019 | DDC 306.81/530972—dc23
LC record available at https://lccn.loc.gov/2019021374

Cover illustration: Ione Robinson, *La familia*, 1991, Oleo Sobretela Acervo, Museo de Arte Moderno, INBA-Secretariat of Culture.

Contents

Figures

Tables

Acknowledgments

My first and foremost gratitude is extended to the anonymous readers who have read this manuscript cautiously and meticulously in its various stages and provided priceless comments and suggestions that have deeply impacted the present shape and essentials of this book. I would also like to commend here the editors, Jessica d'Arbonne and Charlotte Steinhardt, and the Press, who were extremely patient with my evolving drafts and numerous communications. I am also forever indebted to the conscious archivists at the Archivo General de la Nacíon in Mexico City and to those who assisted me during my stays at the Archivo Histórico Judicial, INAH, in Puebla. Curator Laurant Héricher, at the Rare Manuscripts section of the Bibliothèque Nationale of France at Richelieau, was exceptionally attentive and graceful in guiding me through their formidable Mexican repository. I also acknowledge here the assistance of the support of the librarians at the Musée du quai Branly, in Paris, in locating and identifying the African objects and secondary literature included here. Extreme gratitude goes to the anonymous librarian at the Rare manuscript collections, Van Pelt Library, at the University of Pennsylvania, without whom I would never have uncovered the previously unknown two volumes of the Mexican Inquisition on Isabel de Montoya, albeit, "La Centella," without which this entire book would not have seen the light of day. I am also particularly indebted to my postdoctoral student, the Africanist Guy Roufe, for his guiding in search of the various primary African sources that I utilize here. My research assistants in Mexico, Clotilde Martinez and Mariana Rodríguez, who worked for me at the AGN in Mexico, have labored hard throughout the years to facilitate me with the wonderful source materials contained here. My research assistant in Haifa, Ariene Cukierkon, helped enormously throughout the years. Also, the work on this book could not have materialized without the generous financial support through Israel Science Foundation grants, as well as the various leaves from teaching from the University of Haifa. Finally, my spouse, Orna, and my kids, Schahaf and May, are my daily inspiration.

Rituals and Sisterhoods

1

Mise-en-Scène

Herodotus was the first to write of the A-Mazons, placing them in Pontus near the shore of the Euxine Sea, and describing their raids against scythes, Thrace, and the coasts of Asia Minor. No men were permitted to dwell in their country, though once a year the warrior women visited a neighboring nation for purposes of procreation, slaying all male children or returning them to their fathers, and recruiting the baby girls. Their name allegedly came from the Greek *a-mazos* (without breast), from their custom of amputating the right breast to make the drawing of the bow more convenient, but a variety of other derivations have been put forward. The explorer Francisco de Orellana, at Amazonas Forest, 1541, said that women at Maranhão River threw arrows against his expedition. This myth dissipated that because of these actions the women received the name of the Greek warriors.[1] Who were those "single-breasted" maidens, and what was their role in society? And how did their sexuality defy gender relations?

Embarking on Isabel de Montoya's individual life history, and thereafter parting onto the vast landscape of singleness in early and mid-colonial Mexico, the goal of this book is to provide a fresh approach to lingering views on single, plebeian women in Latin American historiography in general, and in Mexico in particular. This book is dedicated entirely to single women of the lower echelons of society, whether they were Spanish, creoles, *mulatas*, or blacks. Indigenous single women during the period discussed amounted to as high as 39% of all mothers in rural areas such as San Martin Huequechula (state of Puebla); however, they are usually

DOI: 10.5876/9781607329633.c001

unattended to by the sources. The issue of why plebeian women remained single and established their own, female-headed households is approached here from many different angles and according to key themes that are gleaned from these women's discourses. The proportion of women in mid-colonial New Spain who never married probably rose to unprecedented level. In this present study of New Spain's single plebeian women's households, single, plebeian women either chose to dissolve their marriages, remain in alternative, long-lasting cohabitations, outside of marriage, with various male partners throughout their lives, or create alternative, women-led households and "sisterhoods" of their own. As is argued here, the institutionalization of female-headed households in mid-colonial Mexico reveals wide-ranging repercussions and effects on mid-colonial values and has particular relevance to the history of emotions, sexuality, gender concepts, perceptions of marriage, life choices, and how honor and shame were construed by the lower echelons of colonial society. Linda A. Curcio-Nagy, for example, writes about "emotional communities," within the frameworks of which "social norms, fundamental assumptions, rules of behavior, cultural scripts, modes of expression, and religious values" were formulated and articulated (2014, 60; see also Rosenwein 2015). We may take this a step further and hypothesize that ethnic groups, as well as particular *castas* (generic term for racial mixtures), operated as cultural enclaves within Spanish colonial society, which would definitely impact their attitudes toward honor, promiscuity, and gender relationships.

Why should we be concerned with rituals when discussing the social history of single women in early to mid-colonial Mexico? This book responds to this question by highlighting that embedded in the rituals crafted by single women (discussed at length in chapters 6 and 8) is the idea that the rituals reversed, as well as transgressed, the dominant relationships of power between the genders and relegated women the position of controlling the chaotic male arena. Active participation in religious frameworks within the church, such as lay confraternities, and outside it—formulating their own unique ritualistic practices and networks—allowed single, nonelite women to reaffirm and consolidate mutual interests and common grounds. They also accomplished this community outside the realm of religion. In a direct conversation with what is elaborated in this present book, Catherine Komisaruk in her book *Labor and Love in Guatemala* (2013) and Brianna Leavitt-Alcantará in her book *Alone at the Altar* (2018) have shown, in parallel, how through their own spiritual biography and spiritual networks, as well as through life of singleness, Anna Guerra de Jesús and Isabel de Pinzón, very poor single mothers and spiritual personas in eighteenth-century El Salvador and Guatemala, could redeem themselves from the abuse they underwent during their life of marriage and were able to experience autonomy and a certain independence, for the first time; they also "successfully navigated gendered tensions associated with their status as non-elite women living outside both marriage and convent." Furthermore, Komisaruk also convincingly suggests, though does not develop, that local city authorities' persecution of women's ritualistic "heretic" practices in Santiago de Guatemala should be linked with their growing role within the illicit market economy (2013, 20, 29, 30, 78; see also Leavitt-Alcantará 2018). Added to that are, obviously, the *calidad* (nature; nobility, rank) of casta women and that of their legitimate or illegitimate offspring. On the issue of how such plebeian women contested their social status (by birth), devoid of wealth, in ways that could transcend this barrier, Karen B. Graubart recently exclaimed that "but even the poorer classes found other ways to contest calidad" (2007, 105). One of the goals of this present study is to be able to identify precisely through which particular channels such a contestation operated.

Single women also assumed a far more active and central role in economic systems, social organizations, cults, and political activism than was previously thought.[2] The ritualistic facet also reveals that in spite of social barriers, they were aptly able to create distinct spaces for themselves, where they could initiate, as well as maintain, their autonomy and values, distinct from those of the general societal norms of the time. Could one, then, consider these women "marginal"? Was there a real gap between the declared norm and the social praxis, which was usually far more flexible and tolerant than one tends to think? An answer to this may be found in the precise exploration of how limited what we would call "free choice" was during the early modern era, in general, and during the early to mid-colonial Mexico, in particular, and how these women's agency was all about basic, existential choices they made on an everyday basis. Nonetheless, not a few social historians of colonial Latin America have already stressed in this very context that, by contrast with women of the elites, whether Spanish or Creole, plebeian women, predominantly castas, were somewhat more relieved of the elite economic preconditions associated with honor and shame that, otherwise, would have meant paying a heavy price for their decision to part on their own own road to independence (Lavrin and Couturier 1979, 280–304).

It is also suggested in this present study that a number of specific circumstances directly related to unique cultural patterns in early to mid-colonial Mexico should be taken together as substantially "contributing factors" to choosing a life outside matrimony. These factors have already been mentioned in many previous studies cited here. Nevertheless, what I aim to do here, in contrast to previous studies, is to try and salvage these women's words and deliberations out of the very often highly fragmented testimonies that we, as early modern historians, usually find in the archives (Davis 1987). Nonetheless, one needs to get a sense of intimacy with these women's mental gamut. In choosing to doing so, I deliberately present before the reader large, original chunks of these women's own utterances as they are, and only later do I analyze them. Through such testimonies one is, hopefully, able to obtain at least some shreds of the mental world of these women, even when such fragmented testimonies are heavily filtered through social and cultural biases and norms. Let us take, for example, the practice of elopement, as early as the age of fourteen, namely, paying the girl's parents for their consent to "kidnap" their daughter and live with her with only the intention of getting married. This practice was not uncommon in colonial Mexico. In direct conversation with this theme I highlight in chapter 4 that in many of the post-factum testimonies of single women one finds that they expressed no real aspirations when they were girls toward a long-lived marriage, full-fledged motherhood in general, or giving birth in particular. The consequences of these actions, besides obviously turning them into adolescent women who could not easily trust men in their lives, were many and diverse, and they ought to be considered by us in depth. Culpable men could easily plead "not guilty" when they stood up in court, blaming the plaintiff for trying to defame their honor, or leading licentious lives. Laura Gowing, in parallel, compares use of language in allegations filed by men against women's immoral behavior, and in parallel, women's allegations against men's sexual roles (cited in Boyer 1995, 15–33). Lawrence Stone has commented that "depositions in the ensuing litigation reveal, as no other data can, changing ideas among different layers of society about such matters as marital fidelity, marital cruelty, sexuality, patriarchal authority, individual autonomy, the expected roles of the two genders, and the rival responsibilities and claims of husband and wife." (1993; see also Phillips 1980).

Why did plebeian women increasingly resort to the channel of "ecclesiastical divorce" during the period under review? Relying upon the women's discourses, I respond to this in chapter 2 from a number of angles. Primarily, these women were no longer willing to be relegated to the "sacrificial" position of the wife, vis-à-vis her violent and negligent husband, willing instead to sacrifice her marriage. The data suggest that spousal cruelty was indeed a trigger for separations to be permitted after repeated court denouncements, if at all. In this context, Jessica Delgado writes that "Only severe abuse, or in some cases infidelity, justified a request for permanent separation, and options were limited for wives living apart from their husbands" (2009, 1:113). While judges showed sympathy for the plight of women, they also reminded women to fulfill their roles as wives; hence judges acted in favor of adhering to the institution of marriage, much more than in favor of other considerations such as curbing family violence.

Mexican colonial women, castas in particular, were indeed apt to enter into independent forms of living with spouses. As this present study aims to highlight, as informal marital arrangements, especially among the subaltern, racially mixed castas, and the practice of elopement of young girls were far more common in Mexico at that time, such commonplace forms subverted a "neat" patriarchal model in many ways. As the caste system was in effect a colonial fictive reality, the patriarchal model of subordination was also very much a fiction, and I cite in this respect Kimberly Gauderman in her study of colonial Quito in saying that "the apparent stability of patriarchal gender norms across this period is a fictive tradition reinforced by later legislation" (2003, 24). It was in fact acknowledged that sexual encounters prior to conjugal benediction were illicit and did not carry the value of a pledge between the involved parties if one of them declined to continue into formal matrimony (Covarubias y Leiva 1734, 154). The general public often reported such couples to the authorities, but also "tolerated a good deal of it" (Boyer 1995, 31, 65, 96–97). The cohabitants themselves were not always happy with this confining arrangement. Steve Stern has described how "even when a woman questioned a man's sincerity and intentions or when marriage clearly lay outside the prospective horizons of a relationship, a poor woman could not easily afford to rule out a sexual liaison" (1995, 270–71). Those among them who were more ambitious and wished to upgrade their social standing, in order to transcend the existing social and legal constraints, chose to remain single and become cohabitants of men from the upper echelons of local society.[3]

Listening attentively to the women's claims, in their own words, one is able to identify distinct milestones of a life in flux—of giving up marital life for the sake of claiming their freedom, of becoming voluntarily single. How precisely did such a decision-making process function among single, plebeian women in early to mid-colonial Mexico? And, also, what were the precise circumstances under which such women entered lifestyles other than marriage, namely, long- or short-lived cohabitations? No, doubt, such an individual process of trying to gather up forces and set out on a new road, in itself, required stamina and a strong will to challenge the diverse and extremely difficult consequences. As discussed at length in chapter 3, women-headed households in colonial Mexico, "sisterhoods" in particular, created a solid alternative to the paterfamilias and the patriarchal family model. Female-headed households functioned as pseudoconsaguinal "families" that included either biological, fostered, or adopted children, as well as functioned as alternative frameworks for the attainment of inheritance and self-sustenance. As shown, the perseverance and strength of women-headed households, as a new model for a social convention, especially in urban areas, stood up in sheer contrast to Spanish code of law represented in the Spanish matrimonial model.

THE SPANISH MATRIMONIAL MODEL AND
ITS TREATMENT OF "SINGLENESS"

During the sixteenth century, according to Spanish law, men were relegated to the heads of families and filled most of the roles within the family and outside it: the *paterfamilia* was responsible to educating his children, and he was in charge of managing the legal and economic affairs of the family, as well as the transfer of property. A woman who wished to file an appeal in court was bound to her husband's authority and physical presence in court, and women were not allowed to serve as guardians of their children. Three decades ago, the most common view was that in Latin America, family and kinship have historically served as safe havens, constituting critical institutions for social stability. Latin American family historians of Latin America, through an intensive review of the literature, now question many previous assumptions about various social realities that existed during the early and mid-colonial periods. Accordingly, patterns of living, residence, adherence to patriarchal rule, and family norms were far more flexible and accommodating than was previously thought (Lavrin 1989a, 47–95). These studies have opened up new paths that demand significant modifications to our thinking about how subaltern groups lived and died, women in particular. This optimistic, state-of-the art thinking is in sheer contrast with that of only a decade ago, when Karen Vieira Powers lamented that "after careful review of all textbooks and related classroom materials (collections of essays and document readers) on colonial Latin American history published from 1980 to the present, I found that not one devotes more than 25 pages to women's experiences, in spite of the recent production of a considerable corpus of new primary research" (2002, 9–32).

Women's norms of living, marriage, and residential patterns, as recent research undoubtedly shows, were influenced predominantly by manifestations of economic instability that impelled frequent migrations. The stable, patriarchal household model previously assumed to have been dominant has been shown by recent research to be no longer valid—certainly not in circumstances in which both formal and informal unions were in large numbers being dissolved after a period of only two or three years, leaving the family without a paterfamilias. Within this new approach to the history of the family in this continent, the place of women, and single women, in particular, is highlighted. In her influential book *The Women in Colonial Latin America* (2002), Susan Migden Socolow stresses, "as local economy deteriorated, the percentage of female-headed households tended to increase. Even in the wealthier cities as one went down the social scale, there was a growing probability that the head of the family would be a woman, probably single or widowed." Komisaruk exclaims that "Anna's biography challenges narratives about the marginalized or subversive position of women who fell outside the confines of both marriage and convent in colonial Spanish America and in the broader early modern Church" (Komisaruk 2013, 38; see also García Peña 2004, 647–92; Socolow 2000, 76).

Besides the emotional factors were the economic considerations. Perhaps the most outstanding feature in Spanish colonial formal marriage arrangements was the prevalent family law governing colonial Mexico between the sixteenth and eighteenth centuries, by which dowry payments, at least for Spaniards and Creoles of the upper echelons of local society, were expected to be transferred from the bride's side to the groom's family, which in colonial Mexico amounted to between 1,000 and 5,000 pesos, equal to the cost of the purchase of between three and sixteen slaves (Lavrin and Couturier 1979, 280–304; see also Korth and Flusche 1987, 395–410; Philips 1988). Lavrin and Edith Couturier have described the dowry as the woman's, and even returned to her upon the unlikely dissolution of the marriage. Although the husband administered the estate and the joint assets, the dowry was not his and he was unable by law to sell the dowry property. Therefore, uncertainty about the economic benefits of marriage, as well as the burden of dowry, could well have encouraged the development of attitudes favoring "singleness," especially among plebeian women. Yet another demographic factor that ought to be taken into consideration while determining what was the range of choices for these women was the dreadful marriage "markets" in colonial Mexico cities, given the tendency toward urban female majorities. In her study of Medieval England, *The Ties that Bound*, Barbara Hanawalt writes: "When a young woman, through her initiative and wages, managed to accumulate a bit of chattels and land and paid her own merchant, she could choose her own marriage partner. But the freedom in choice of marriage partners may have been a larger phenomenon, going far beyond those without property" (1986, 202). Hanawalt puts the weight on economic reasoning—so as to avoid such unmatched expenditures, such women sought alternative ways to fulfill their goal. However, in our present case, there are many other reasons to be examined. Under harsh economic and social circumstances, marriage options for single women, especially casta women, were poor, especially if they came from the subaltern groups in local society.

"Single"

For the early modern period discussed in this book, the definition of the term "singleness" is taken directly from the eighteenth-century Spanish *Diccionario de Autoridades* (1739, vol. 6): "La persona, que está sin tomar estado. Dixose de la voz Suelto, por no estar ligada con el matrimonio" (this is a person who has interrupted living together with his/her spouse, though maintaining his/her marital bonds): "Lat. *Solutus. Liber. Celebs, ibis* [Single, is the person who is in a state of not married; loose, for not being associated with matrimony]" Also, "suele usarse también por lo mismo que suelto, ò libre"; "Lat. *Solutus. Dissolut* [it is also possible to use it in the same manner as being free, A.M.]." In the same dictionary one finds under the entry *separado/a* [a person who is separated] the following explication:

"Dicho de una persona: Que ha interrumpido la vida en común con su cónyuge, conservando el vínculo matrimonial" (It is said of a person who has disrupted the common living with his/her partner, while still maintaining the marriage ties). Unless otherwise stated, all the translations are my own.

Therefore, the term *soltera* ("single" woman) applies during the early modern era to a woman who was not a virgin in contrast to *doncella* (virgin or maiden), and should include widows and spinsters, meaning women who never married, due to a variety of reasons, as well as women who, under worsening circumstances, either made a poor prospect for marriage and were unable to attract a potential husband or were abandoned by their husbands. What this present study emphasizes, in contrast to previous studies cited below, is that the status of being single or becoming single was *a permeable possibility and an ever-changing reality that could be explored and taken advantage of*, among many women, plebeian women in particular, during the period reviewed here, as attested to by the source material. Also included within the category are women, who, under worsening circumstances, remained unwed for a lifetime; and women who either had passed the normative age for marriage (between 15 and 29) or fertility (between 15 and 40) and, thus, would not normally be considered feasible candidates for marriage. Within this category also were young women who, at one point or other, had been deserted by their husbands and decided not to remarry; women who had actively sought to put to an end their unhappy, torturous marriages or seek refuge from their partners. Moreover, the term "single mothers" utilized here throughout, refers to women of the middle to lowest strata of Mexican colonial society and were raising children independently, without the economic or social backing of a stable male partner. This diapason of statuses and choices differs starkly from how Jane E. Mangan, for example, defines single women: "Though both single and widowed women were unmarried, the status of single women was distinct. Having never been married, they had no inheritance from husbands." This last part of her citation is significant when it came to the issue of inheritance to single women's offspring, as is demonstrated later, in chapter 4 (2005, 150).

"Separated"

During early to late colonial Mexico, the only choice available at the time for separation was through the process of "ecclesiastical divorce," which separated the married couple from each other, but did not dissolve the marital bond altogether. The circumstances that enabled ecclesiastical divorce were cruelty, maltreatment (both physical and emotional), threat of murder, and infertility of one of the spouses, adultery or abandonment, and failure to provide for the necessities of the wife and children, as well as proofs of heresy or paganism. Accordingly, the husband and wife would live in separate houses, but remained married until one of them died. The ecclesiastical divorce could be restricted to a distinct period of time or an indefinite time limit, or be permanent. Nonetheless, all of "divorced" persons would never remarry but resort instead to consensual relationships (Arrom 1976, 16–17; see also García Peña 2006, 71–72; Gauderman 2003, 49–50; Komisaruk 2013, 125–27). Furthermore, women who were deserted by their husbands could not marry, unless they chose to become bigamists. Legal marriage was monogamous, a formal union of man and woman of proper age and status. Aside from rank, freedom to enter into marriage meant that the parties were not bound by a previous and "undissolved" marriage, were not within forbidden degrees of consanguinity and spiritual relationship, and had not taken vows or holy orders.

Can one, therefore, interpret such a contemporaneous definition as having attributed to women who opted for such choices of living separately and on their own, a preexisting disposition toward lesser commitment to long-term relationships and trust? Ann Twinam writes in this very context: "Relationships between unmarried men and women without any commitment to matrimony were presumably more tenuous than those in which the parties vowed to wed. In most other respects, however, such affairs are indistinguishable from extended engagements." (1999, 82–83). By contrast to women of the elites, described by Twinam, our case studies below of plebeian women show that most of them actually preferred "consensual," long-term commitments to those that involved marriage.

THE GEOGRAPHIC AND DEMOGRAPHIC SCOPE OF THIS STUDY

The geographical scope of this study covers essentially the two urban metropolises of Mexico City and Puebla, and their archbishoprics, as well as a number of smaller urban centers located in between the two cities, such as Tlaxcala, Cholula, and Huejotzingo. As such, I chose to refrain from treating the rural areas, and the indigenous communities, in particular, concentrating instead on where I found the most substantial populations of single plebeian women relevant to this study, that is, in the two largest urban centers: Mexico City and Puebla. The decision that guided me stemmed from the fact that it was in those cities that I found the richest and most substantive data. Moreover, it would be quite safe to generalize that in the urban areas the degree of illegitimacy of children, as well as the extent of singleness, would be much more acceptable than in the rural areas given the distinctive social structures in the cities; the diversity of the local populace, arriving from many parts of the nation, with many of the migrants unmarried and unconstrained by former ties of kinship and societal norms; the relative flexibility of the social system; and the greater opportunities for cohabitation. In addition, cities were filled with property-less men and women, many of whom were recently arrived from the rural areas, in search of such as domestic servants, whose means of sustenance were evidently hazardous and temporary, which meant that they could not afford to set up stable economic arrangements, such as marriage and an independent household. Komisaruk suggests that the lack of balance between the male and female populace in the cities may have "triggered marital dissolutions and sizable number of unmarried women and female-headed households" (2018, 29) What J. Hanjal remarks about city life is especially relevant here: "The right inference to draw from a high proportion of single women in a city is often not so much that urban life discourages marriages but that cities provide opportunities for single women to earn a living and single women, therefore go to live there."[4]

According to Aguirre Beltrán, in 1742 the total population in New Spain stood at 2,477,277. By the mid-seventeenth century, the "Afro-mestizo" population, as Beltrán refers to it, was around 300,000, with 35,000 Africans. Between 1550 and 1750, the period reviewed here, a total of 70,195 slaves landed in the port of Veracruz and 426 in the port of Campeche. However, by the late seventeenth century the numbers had shrunk drastically: between 1676 and 1775, the total number of black slaves who landed in Mexico was insignificant by comparison to other parts of the New World: 2,586 at the port of Veracruz, while in the port of Campeche, merely 170 ("Slave Voyages" n.d.). By 1650, the *mestizo* populace constituted nearly 25 percent of the total population, blacks constituted 0.81 percent, Creoles 15.80 percent, indigenous 62.17 percent, and *mulatos* 10.75 percent, and Europeans (mainly Spaniards born in the Iberia Peninsula), 0.39 percent (Aguirre Beltrán [1946] 1972).

The demographic estimates concerning the size of the population of Mexico City during the period reviewed vary considerably. For example, in 1571, a partial survey conducted in this city included over 10,000 Spaniards and about 3,000 Africans, but the latter possibly numbered far more than truly estimated. However, this very partial survey did not include either individuals or groups of mixed origins among the castas, nor individuals without a fixed residency, namely, all those who lived away from the main towns, especially in the rural areas. Aguirre Beltrán, utilizing the Mexico City figure cited in Tomás de Torquemada in 1609 of 15,000 *vecinos* (citizen of a city, or a town; usually restricted to whites in colonial times) in the metropolis, estimates the total population to have been about 75,000 (Aguirre Beltrán [1946] 1972). The crown historian, Vázquez de Espinosa, gives an estimate of 145,000 inhabitants in the city in 1612, while Thomas Gage estimated its populace to be about 98,000 during his visit to New Spain in 1630. Gemilli Carreri cited 100,000 inhabitants for the year 1697 (cited in Vázquez Valle 1975, 86). And in 1765, Fray Francisco Ajofrín of the Capuchin Order, in his *Diario de viaje*, estimated that in Mexico City alone were at the time were "more than 50,000 Spanish, European and patricians, 40,000 mestizos, mulatos and blacks, together with other castas, without counting more than 8,000 indigenous persons within the city and in the slums" (Ajofrín [1726] 1959, 1:65). Furthermore, by 1607 the entire region of the central Basin of Mexico included 180,000 people (Denevan 1992, 370). Besides the indigenous populace living permanently within the city (except for the *traza* [boundaries of the various divisions of Mexico City, especially those separating Spaniards from the castas and Indians] area of the city), there was a regular flow of indigenous labor into the city on a daily basis, which was badly needed for a great variety of tasks, both skilled and unskilled, in the markets and elsewhere. So the casta population, as well as Spaniards, were intimately engaged with the indigenous presence in the heart of the city (Bailey-Glasco 2010, 27–28).

One striking factor in Aguirre Beltrán's analysis of the 1748 census of the Alcaicería quarter in Mexico City, and which may serve well our own purposes here, is that the percentage of women in the four major casta sectors of the population was substantially higher than that of males: among slaves and free blacks, the percentages were 62.78 and 37.21 correspondingly; among the mestizo sector, the number of adult mestizas was double that of adult male mestizos; among the castizos, the percentage of females was also much above that of males, though an exact figure is not available; and among the Spaniards, the percentages of females and males were 54.58 and 45.41 (Aguirre Beltrán [1946] 1972).

Where did castas, Spaniards, and the indigenous inhabitants interact closely on a daily basis? Primarily, in *pulquerías* (taverns), at the public fountains, from where water was carried to the homes on a daily basis, and at the marketplaces—in San Hipólito, In San Juan, in the southwestern corner of the traza, in the Alameda, and in the Plaza Mayor. The Plaza Mayor was the seat of the viceroy's royal palace, the city council, and the metropolitan cathedral. Mexico City's cathedral stood at the forefront of this huge square, on its northern side. To the south stood the lord mayor's office, the metropolitan's law-enforcing agency, the judges' residences, the public granary, and the metropolitan prison. Behind, one would come through the major storehouses of the city. The mansions of the most prosperous merchants and city officials occupied most of the western part of the square, together with five or six storehouses selling golden embroidery styled in Europe. To the east was the palace of the viceroy, the Royal Audiencia, the university and Santo Domingo College, and the Holy Office, at the corner of which stood the Casa de Moneda.

The Plaza Mayor was where during major festivities and holy days, as well as in times of important inaugurations of high appointments—such as that of a new viceroy or newly arrived archbishops—processions, and street parades were publicly staged. As Father Ajofrín likewise describes, "On 1 January, a 40-hour jubilee

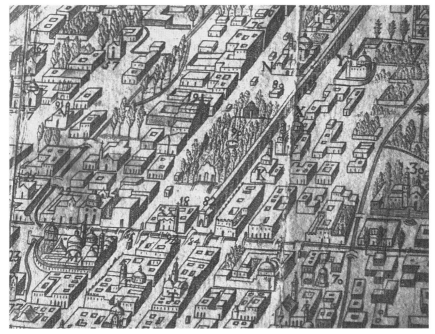

FIGURE 1.1. The Traza and the Zócalo in 1720 (a blowup of the central section), BNF, Fondo Mexicain 149, © BNF, Paris.

would take place at the Cathedral, accompanied by a lavish procession beginning at 11 A.M and lasted, with a huge crowd filling the Plaza by day and by night" ([1726] 1959, 2:35). It was there also that a bustling market was located and stalls were put up selling foodstuffs, cheap clothing, pottery, and a great variety of herbs and medicinal stuffs. The nearby Plaza de Volador, founded in 1624, was an additional bustling public area southeast of the Zocalo. Small and medium-size stores sold a large variety of merchandize there, including foodstuffs, slacked lime, and pawned garments.[5] The Plaza de Volador was also the most popular public space in the city for Spaniards, Creoles, and indigenous persons, as well as the different castes, to stroll, meet, and interact informally. It became the main arena for the *corrida de toros* (running of the bulls) and public games during festivities and holy days. During the early part of December, each year, bullfights would take place there. During the feast of Santa Cruz, bullfighting was also on display in the Plazuela de la Trinidad (Ajofrín [1726] 1959, 2:80). The Plaza de Volador also became the capital's main marketplace for castes and indigenous persons alike. Indigenous fruit and vegetable merchants reached this site from the floating markets of Chalco and Xochimilco, arriving by

FIGURE 1.2. The Alameda during the early part of the eighteenth century. © Colección Museo Franz Mayer, Mexico City.

canoe through the La Acequia Real (Royal Canal), which began in the town of Tláhuac, to the south of the capital. From there hundreds of canoes, traditional vessels called *chalupas* and *trajineras*, carried the city's supply of fresh fruit, vegetables, and flowers. The most prestigious commerce (retail merchants, imports) remained in the hands of powerful Spanish and Creole tradesmen who established themselves at El Parían market, located on the west side of the Zocalo.[6] The buildings included seven different households, with a total of forty-three inhabitants.[7] It was an area packed with vendors' stalls in which many peddlers and grocers would set up shop, sometimes permanently, throughout the archways, out onto the street, and even reaching the plaza itself. Three blocks north of the plaza was the Plaza de Santo Domingo, where the Royal Custom houses were located, side by side with the Tribunal of the Inquisition. The nearby Alameda Central, the first public park in Mexico City in the early seventeenth century, was intended at that time only for the "upper classes." Official documents of this period show that the local law enforcement agency was ordered to ban "coarsely dressed people, barefoot, beggars, or nude or any other indecent people."

Furthermore, one also needs to stress here the sheer polarity that existed in Mexico City between rich and poor during the period reviewed. Father Aljofrín, upon visiting Mexico City in 1763, was overwhelmed by the striking social divide that he had seen before his eyes, especially at the "El Baratillo"—The thieves' market—which specialized in the sale of used and stolen artifacts and clothing and other secondhand merchandise and as such was of vital service to the poor:

> Out of a hundred people that one encounters on the streets, you would hardly find one who is dressed and wearing shoes (or sandals). You see in this city two diametrically opposing extremes—much wealth, and maximum poverty, many trappings, side by side with outmost nudity, great cleanliness and much filth . . . the rest of the poor people dress as best as they are able, normally speaking, the shoeless sell shoes while the unclothed sell clothes . . . In the famous Plaza "del Baratillo," is the celebrated gathering place of all the lepers and quarrelsome persons of Mexico; it is the university of the idlers, and *zaramullos*, in which the dean of them all is the famous Pancho Moco, where they learn so many subtle devices and schemes for the sake of robbery without being indicted or identified. ([1726] 1959, 2:80)

Added to this was the poor hygiene, drainage and sanitation in this city, especially among the poor, who were living mainly in adobe, rundown houses, with an open sewage flowing freely on the streets and with piles of both private and public garbage disposed without any restraint whatsoever on every single corner, together with dead corpses of recently deceased men and animals alike (Cope 1994, 27, 34). Conditions among the poor, in particular, became obviously extremely stressful and unbearable under the dire straits of floods and epidemics, as they were fully exposed, living virtually on the street level, and with a large proportion of the population in abject poverty, subject to frequent shortages of food and other essentials. Daily life was extremely harsh, dreary, and dangerous. Numerous vagrants and beggars actually lived on the street side by side with the piles of garbage and the open sewage; bands of drunken men and women, as well as gangs of "bad sorts," roamed from place to place looking for trouble; horses galloped regularly on the streets, burglary and thefts were widespread, and bodily assaults and knife battles were common scenery (Bailey-Glasco 1910, 4, 17). Prices of rent and basic commodities soared in times of floods, bad harvests, and scarcity. Between 1691 and 1692, for example, Central Mexico suffered from a severe grain shortage, which indirectly led to the great food riots during that year (Ajofrín [1726] 1959, 121).

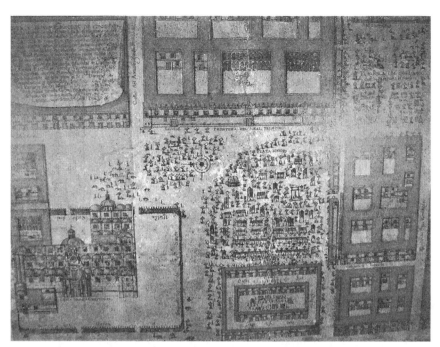

FIGURE 1.3. Portal de los Mercaderes, map in color, from *Mapas y Planos de México, siglos XVI al XIX, catálogo de exposición*, Museo Nacional de la Historia, Castillo de Chapultepec, INEGI/INAH, 1988, lámina No. 232. © Instituto Nacional de Estadística y Geografía, Mexico City.

During the last decades of the sixteenth century, the total nonindigenous population of Puebla amounted to 20,100, including 14,400, Spaniards, 3,000 mestizos, mulatos, and free blacks, and 2,500 black and mulato slaves (Martinez 2008, 144). By the late seventeenth century, the city had already become the economic, political, religious, and administrative capital of an enormous province and by then included more than 50,000 inhabitants. In 1746, this city's population was merely 50,376 (Villa Sánchez [1746] 1972, 65). Only during the first decades of the nineteenth century, and after a slow recovery, did Puebla become the second-largest city in New Spain after Mexico City. The city itself was surrounded by about 800 haciendas that were the property of its most notable Spanish residents. In addition, Puebla was the capital city for numerous indigenous towns and rural communities in its environs. As Martin Bosch describes, "With the growth of the nonindigenous population in Puebla, the houses of the mestizos, mulatos, and other castas were built within the city, between the Spanish sector, and the indigenous sphere (1999, 64)."

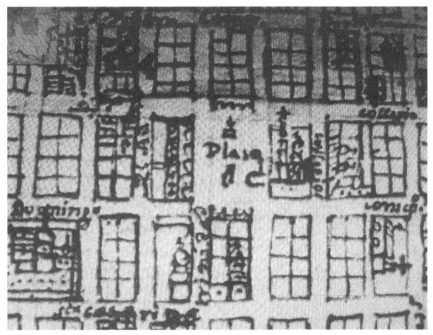

FIGURE 1.4. Map of Puebla, view of the main plaza, 1698. © Gusvel, https://commons
.wikimedia.org/wiki/File:Fundaci%C3%B3n_de_la_Puebla_002.JPG, accessed 11
February 2019.

How were these two major metropolises affected by the disastrous smallpox,
measles, and typhus epidemics that ravaged the entire landscape of New Spain
between 1520 and the middle of the eighteenth century? We are talking about
recurring waves of *matlazahuatl* (typhus), between 1576 and 1736–39—the most
notable outbreak in 1631—and smallpox, pneumonia, measles, typhus, and smallpox pandemics, between 1711 and 1748 (Ajofrín [1726] 1959, 2:145; Bailey-Glasco
2010, 51). Lourdes Márquez Morfín (1993) cites three major smallpox epidemics,
in 1711, 1734, and 1748. Peter Gerhard (1993) cites fourteen outbreaks during the
entire sixteenth century, and eleven for the seventeenth century. Between 1678 and
1746, the city of Puebla alone lost about one quarter of its inhabitants (!) due to
a number of disastrous plagues (Kicza 1988, 453–88). In addition to the plagues
and the epidemics, there was also a series of floods that critically affected the entire
city beginning on 29 September 1629, and ending in 1633; during the great flood of
1629. For example, that lasted for thirty-six hours, the only means of transportation
throughout the city was by canoes; entire houses were ruined, and food supplies
became scarce (Ajofrín [1726] 1959, 1:76–79).

Let us bear in mind that these two cities were far from being closed; they were heavily impacted by migrations from the environs, as well as from other distant areas. They were also constantly nourished from what these migrants and passersby brought over with them, whether it was germs, marriage habits, beliefs, ritualistic prescriptions, and many other influences.

THE RACIAL FACTOR: SOCIAL AND ECONOMIC CONSTRAINTS RELATED TO THE CASTE SYSTEM

In 1765, while summarizing his observations regarding Mexican society that he just visited, Father Ajofrín says:

"The castas of people, of which emerged various generations, when mixed together, have come to corrupt the customs and habits of the popular people." (Ajofrín [1726] 1959, 2:66–67)

Mexico's colonial matrix, the social and cultural infrastructure under which women grew up and into which they were obliged to integrate[,] is the subject of this section. Within the discourses of single, plebeian women, one finds the major theme of their ability and aptitude to social mobility, transcending socioeconomic boundaries and racial denominations that presumably existed within the colonial caste system. In his classic book from 1947, *Slave and Citizen: The Negro in the Americas*, Frank Tannenbaum established what is now known as the Comparative Slavery School. In 1967, evaluating the impact of the Latin American caste system upon ideas about race and racial mixture, Magnus Mörner defined Latin America as a "caste society" (Mörner 1970, Introduction). His findings helped prompt the "caste versus class" debate that continues to this very day; a theoretical framework for discussing how blacks integrated into colonial and early national societies. A major, although problematic[,] contribution to the literature that helped to shape the field of Afro-Latin American Studies, is F. P. Bowser's, *Neither Slave nor Free: The Freedman of African* (1972). This study has remained influential in shaping the trajectory of more modern studies in this field. In his study written twenty years ago on plebian society in Mexico City during this period, Douglas Cope questioned and qualified the assumption that the urban poor in Mexico sought to climb the ethnic hierarchy and to "pass" as Spaniards [Cope 1994]. Cope demonstrates that the castas were neither passive nor ruled by feelings of racial inferiority; indeed, they often modified or even rejected elite racial ideology. Castas also sought ways to manipulate their social "superiors" through astute use of the legal system. Cope describes how social control by the Spaniards relied less on institutions than on patron-client networks and intertwining individuals, a fact that enabled the elite

class to choose the more prosperous among the castas. Cope questioned and qualified the assumption that the urban poor in Mexico sought to climb the ethnic
hierarchy and to "pass" as Spaniards. He demonstrates that the castas were neither
passive nor ruled by feelings of racial inferiority; indeed, they often modified or
even rejected elite racial ideology. Castas also sought ways to manipulate their
social "superiors" through astute use of the legal system. (Cope 1994)

Cope drew upon quantitative data gleaned from the registers of casta marriages
at the Cathedral of Mexico City between 1694 and 1696 (Cope 1994). Consistent
with this, Pescador shows how, in the Santa Veracruz parish where Isabel de Montoya
lived, between 1749 and 1810, endogamy rates among *españolas* remained virtually
unchanged (86 percent vs. 85 percent), while for men they dramatically increased,
from 77 percent to 95 percent (1992, 167–69). When examining Cope's figures, this
is also ostensibly true for mulatos and mestizos, as well as "Spaniards." However, if
one scrutinizes Cope's data more carefully, it clearly show that a large percentage
of mulatos in fact intermarried with mestizos and thus did not rigidly preserve the
endogamous norm. Furthermore, when Cope draws conclusions about the second
and third generations of mixed races, he writes: "We suggest that they were drawn
into the social network of one parent or the other, whichever was more advantageous," which might possibly distance them from their own caste and enable their
children to potentially pursue outside channels of support, as the latter could rely
upon the effective mechanism of *compadrazgo* (coparenthood, god-fatherhood)
and diverse partnerships, also taking into account individual predispositions (1994,
78). Furthermore, the category *españoles* was deliberately obscured by the Spaniards
themselves, so as to avoid differentiation between Gachupins (Spaniards born in
Iberia), and Creoles (Spaniards born in the New World) in relation to the subaltern
castes, in spite of the fact that Creoles were by then already thoroughly "mixed"
with other castes (Megged 1992, 421–40).[8]

Relying mostly on qualitative sources, Robert C. Schwaller has recently furthered
the theme of racial designations, indicating that the term *mulata* might well have
come to be popularly associated with both indigenous and African descent in areas
where they intermingled, at least culturally (Schwaller 2011, 885). He further suggests that the physical attributes associated with African ancestry tended to be more
salient in racial ascription than those of indigenous ancestry, and that this is one
reason why we tend to see greater conformity in ascriptions of Africanness than in
ascriptions of indigeneity. The examples he brings are, however, more in the direction of indigenous cultural impact on Africans than not and also confirm that inter-
marriage was quite normal among them: "Francisco made no mistake in describing his wife as both the daughter of an indigenous man and as a mulata; rather,
he was using the contemporary definition of mulato which placed individuals of

European-African descent and African-indigenous descent within the same socio-racial category" (903).⁹ Schwaller's remarks on intercultural mingling between indigenous women and African slaves in the Mixteca area of rural Oaxaca does indeed convey a similar air to that of the above case of Isabel de Montoya. In rural areas near the city of Puebla, castes intermingled freely with the local indigenous populace and thus crossed the lines between the two distinct domains of the República de Españoles and the República de Indios. The latter, ministering to the needs of the former without being part of it, implied the development of two worlds, indigenous and European, linked to each other in numerous ways, but preserving their distinctive identities. Also included within the República de Españoles were the castas. Between the two, belonging wholly neither to one nor the other, were the mestizos, rapidly increasing in numbers and acquiring during the course of the seventeenth century some of the characteristics of a caste. However, in this tripartite society the República de Españoles was the one that dominated. In parallel to Schwaller, Joan Cameron Bristol indicates that "while natives could redeem themselves and enter Spanish society, the descendents of Africans could not." She further suggests that by contrast to the indigenous populace, the Afro-Mexicans were not allocated their own judicial status and were therefore inseparable from the República de Españoles but in an innate inferior designation, according to color, and not by ethnic designation (2007, 46–47, 55). This may explain, in the case of Isabel de Montoya studied below, why Isabel chose to identify herself during her inquisitorial interrogations as "partly Indian," rather than according to how friends and neighbors often designated her, as "black or mulata."

Unlike the case of Isabel de Montoya studied by here in great detail, in the case of Francisca de Acosta studied by Schwaller, one is provided with no biographical details whatsoever about the subject's ancestry. Regardless, yet another important difference between the two cases is that in Montoya's case, the latter was well aware of the need to distance herself from any supposed African affiliations, as well as from a suspected lack of a *limpieza de sangre* ("purity of blood"), as was the case with African descendance, that might be presumed by those who did not know her personally when standing before the inquisitors. However, in the cases that Schwaller brings, the persons described did not seem embarrassed by or feel the need to hide their African origins. Moreover, Schwaller's study and our own do converge with each other on mutual grounds in that, and I cite Schwaller's final remarks, "Scholarship must not further the stereotyping of the colonial period but seek to find the contradictions and contingencies which ultimately made such terms legal fictions" (2011, 907).

In *Hall of Mirrors*, Laura Lewis begins an in-depth discussion on the coexistence of *raza* (race) and *casta* (caste) within the same social hierarchy. Lewis argues that race was not always the sole determinant of social class in New Spain. Mestizos and mulatos, she finds, could be granted further rights to "Spanishness" when their Spanish fathers acknowledged them.[10] Lewis suggests "Spanishness" was, in many instances, of more importance than race itself (2011, introduction). Indeed, all of the more recent studies have effectively highlighted the fact that by the middle of the seventeenth century, one of the most conspicuous features of colonial society in Mexico was its steeply rising rate of miscegenation (Seed 1988a, 24–25).

All of the more recent studies on colonial society in Mexico have effectively highlighted the fact that, by the middle of the seventeenth century, and after more than a century of Spanish colonial rule, castes, those of racially mixed ancestry, became the dominant element, competing with the different phenotypic groups for space and a limited autonomy under Spanish colonial rule.

This is also the case for the *sistema de castas* (caste system), and its direct impact on the lives of single plebeian women; indeed, the overwhelming ramifications of race and caste make the experience of singleness much more complex than that for women in early modern Europe. At the core of the colonial enterprise, then, was a system that one may consider to have constituted an "ideal model" of how a colonial society *ought* to be organized, rather than mirroring actual realities.[11] As all recent studies clearly demonstrate, the gap between this ideal mental model and concrete social reality was far wider than those who initiated it ever imagined. In fact, this system was far more flexible and transmutable than what was previously considered by historians. Thus, the benefits of social and cultural connectedness, such as the backing of powerful and affluent patrons and godparents or partaking in social networks such as the various "sisterhoods," were even more important to one's place in society than were the color of one's skin or the other types of *naturaleza* (predisposition) of a person. This system and its attendant customs created a class of mixed-race women who, for various reasons, did not marry in equal proportions to white European women. Under such a system, largely due to race, caste—mulata/mestiza women were more likely to become or to remain single mothers.

From what will be highlighted in the chapters that follow, one may say that the social-cognitive classification in colonial Mexico included the following characteristics:

A. Raza/calidad (religion/belief; ethnic affiliation); In Colonial New Spain, the term indicated aspects of color, occupation, wealth, purity of blood, honor, integrity, and place of origin. Africans and their descendants were usually classified by their color, than according to ethnic designations (Bristol 2007, 55).

B. Naturaleza (predispositions, including the cultural environment of origins).

C. Gender.

D. Casta.

E. Civil status ("free," "slave," "single," "widowed," "married").

F. Occupation.

G. Personal competence / resourcefulness / audacity/stamina.[12]

The last, very qualitative characteristic could doubtless assist individuals in transcending many social and economic barriers of the time, as well as choose partners from social classes other than their own. One viewpoint is that of Cope, who asserts that "Mexico's social structure was based on two fundamental principles: (1) the division between Spaniards and indigenous persons; and (2) the maintenance of internal stability within each sphere. Spaniards believed that the castas threatened both principles. Biologically, of course, the castas did not really fit into either república. More important, they had no legitimate socioeconomic niche" (1994, 15). I, alternatively, tend to put far more emphasis on point G, namely, "competence," as well as on disposition. Furthermore, the core contributing factor that I believe enabled single, plebeian women to navigate within the colonial caste system and also to transcend barriers of race and class was "transmuted identities." Most, if not all, of our records attest to the fact that single plebeian women solidly navigated within this fluid and elusive caste system. In their discourses they attest to their ability to "change hats," namely, play out distinct identities vis-à-vis the church and local authorities, while at the same time using different hats, such as different civil statuses, elsewhere. The changing of hats is also depicted in the interchangeability of ethnic identities, such as that highlighted in the case study of Isabel de Montoya, allowing the transcendence of single women from one denomination to another, from one caste to another, stretching identities to the limits.

As will be observed throughout this book, a direct outcome of these phenomena was that women in general, and single plebeian women in particular, were far more flexible in their choice making than earlier assumed. As indicated above, racial/caste identities remained quite flexible and transmutable throughout the early to mid-colonial era, varying under changing circumstances and social conditions. The issue of racial identity, whether rigid or flexible, is extremely relevant here in the context of our discussion of how single plebeian women were able to operate and make their choices within local colonial society, and transcend different barriers of law and prejudice.[13] The rapidly changing social and racial equilibrium, as well as the intrusion of members of subaltern castes and their growing demographic predominance, required adjustment of the laws separating the different phenotypical groups. In those insecure times, strict measures became particularly necessary to demarcate crumbling norms, violated limits, and spoiled practices, sifting out the transgressors. Nevertheless, as shall be seen, the netherworld between law and actual social reality, between what was permissible and unacceptable by society, was still very broad and flexible.[14] Likewise, the term Creole, as used in the colonial sources, was ambiguous. At first, it seemed to designate blacks born in the Americas but later on it could also refer to Spaniards born the Americas, as well as their offspring, of mixed blood. In order to demonstrate such patterns, exemplary cases of discourses concerning social and racial identities will be analyzed.

Judith Butler has termed the phenomenon of being able to "change hats" as "performativeness," and has argued that if society defines mores in a certain way, then the individual may act in a subversive or "joking" manner against these standards and norms of conduct (Butler 1988). Moreover, if one employs here Ludwig Wittgenstein's and John Austin's philosophical analysis of language and its social functions (Potter 2001), one may emphasize the wording (cultural standards) and perceptions of racial distinctness that such women utilize to draw the line between a seemingly Spanish environment and upbringing and the "inferior" and "degenerate" world of the castas. As our study highlights, once left on their own, such young women succeeded in transcending the constraints and barriers of language and culture, deviating from the ideologically defined physical norms of both dress and language, and crossed the lines from one cultural milieu and its strict restrictions to another. Through such life stories one obtains an entire mental gamut of social and cultural biases and norms dividing the different groups and castes side by side with social realities and practices that easily transcended and even discredited those very norms and biases.

In her self-representations, Isabel de Montoya, for example, situated herself in both the República de Indios y República de Españoles (Spanish and indigenous realms) at the same time. On the one hand she associated herself with the Spanish conquistadors and their native allies, while on the other hand she linked herself with the indigenous Cuicatec nobility of southwestern Mexico, traceable back to long before the Spaniards arrived in the area. This doubling may partly explain Montoya's projected ambivalence over her caste identity, as well her maneuvering between such caste categories. Nevertheless, it is absolutely clear that she fully acknowledged the elites' tenets, or mental constructs, that blacks or mulatos "were of a different breed," that the former were assigned derogatory associations by the Spaniards, and that, accordingly, they would not yield solid or "healthy" lineages, as those created by procreation between Spaniards and Indians, especially when the indigenous persons were of noble lineage, "like herself." From the testimonies of Montoya's acquaintances, one is able to glean additional descriptive details. Petrona de Medina, wife of Pedro de la Cruz, a Creole from Tlaxcala, who resided in Isabel de Altamirano's household in Mexico City, proclaimed in court that "she did not know whether

Montoya was a mulata or an indigenous [woman]." Gertrudis de la Cruz, a mulata, and doña Isabel's slave, proclaimed that "Montoya appeared to be a morisca . . . She wore a cotton hood, an old skirt the color of pineapple; an old linen, rotten shirt; rotten shoes; she had two rings, the one with a figure of Unicorn."[15] María de Rivera, one of Montoya's "sisters" and co-practitioners, described Montoya as "una mulata libre" (a free mulata).[16] Yet another example: during Mónica de la Cruz's hearing before the Inquisition in Mexico City on 28 June 1652, she declared that "on her father's side Montoya was a descendent of Creoles, while on her mother's side, of Christianized indigenous persons."[17] The above examples and the mixed vocabulary of cultural designations, especially so in Isabel de Montoya's contradictory description of herself, clearly motion toward the fluidity of such patterns of classification, as well as of the social and cultural attributions rendered to them by the various observers, whether coming from the official, administrative sectors or from the popular sectors.[18] Patrick J. Carroll, for example, in his study of colonial Jalapa highlights the significant presence of indigenous African intermarriages during the seventeenth century (see Chance 1978, 126–27; Carroll n.d., 111–25).

One additional factor for consideration—being aware that many among the single, plebeian women came from the lower castas of blacks and mulatos—is that the latter's position in society was precarious, and therefore single women from among them may have developed special sensibilities to navigating skillfully to avoid all kinds of menaces and prejudices. Blacks and mulatos/as were likewise routinely accused by officials of being haughty, insolent, lazy, and loud, given to theft, and prone to revolt. Measures to curb their cohesiveness as a group were issued with regularity but seemingly to no avail. Blacks and mulatos were barred from holding royal, municipal, or ecclesiastical offices (Israel 1980, 64). The 1612 Uprising in Mexico City began already a year earlier with a wave of coordinated protests initiated by hundreds of blacks and mulatos right across the viceroy's palace at the plaza, from where they proceeded to the calle de Santo Domingo, and to the Inquisition's palace carrying the corpse of a dead female slave, presumably killed by the inquisitors. By 1612, when the uprising broke out, the city and state authorities had already feared a major conspiracy on the part of those two castas to put an end to Spanish dominion, and ended it with the prosecution of the presumed instigators and with the extraction of confessions through torture.[19]

In 1647, during the infamous conflict between the Bishop Pallafox of Puebla and Viceroy Salvatierra, the anti-Spanish sentiments of blacks and mulatos were revealed in their open defiance of the viceroy. The Gente vil (lowly, foul), as they were dubbed, were a special group of undesirables marked by many societal restrictions. Among the many restrictions, blacks and mulatos were not permitted to bear arms, nor could they occupy the position of owner in most artisan guilds. Yet, a far

more significant prohibition, not consistently enforced on this group, beginning
in 1623, was the ban on maintaining independent households. The viceroy of New
Spain, the Marqués de Gelvez, promulgated a decree obliging all castas to live with
Spaniards, preferably with their Spanish owners. To see to it that the ban was properly enforced, on 19 February 1633, the *contador general* (accountant; one of the four
treasury officials assigned to New Spain to look after the Crown's fiscal interests) of
New Spain published an ordinance instructing all free persons belonging to blacks,
mulatos, and Zambahiqos (one of the many categories invented and designated for
third-generation persons of mixed blood)—living either on their own or in dependent households—to report within fifteen days, for a general survey of their numbers and ages, as well as of their places of residence.[20] And in 1672, a royal decree
threatened slave owners against allowing their women slaves to sell foodstuffs or
clothes on the streets (Bristol 2007, 80).

However, the fate of those among these castes procreated by men belonging to
uppermost castas, that is, españoles—*hombres nobles*–was unquestionably far better
than that of the rest. Take, for example, Francisca de Reynoso, a free mulata, who
appealed to the Viceroy's court in order to make an exception in her case, exempting her from the new ordinance made public a year earlier (1640) prohibiting blacks,
and free mulatos, whether men or women, from living in a house of their own, as
well as from wearing silk and precious jewelry.[21] In Francisca de Reynoso's case, as in
others similar ones, the viceroy was indeed in favor of an exception being made, as
indicated in the sources.[22] In reaction to this same ordinance, in January 1641 a number of black and mulato families—headed by Domingo Perez, Francisco Gutiérrez,
Juana de Espinosa, Francisco Vázquez de Loya (and on behalf of his black father,
Antón de Loya), Catalina de Loya, and Francisca de Loya—appealed to the viceroy,
Marqúez Luis de Tovar Godines, calling him to exclude them from these prohibi-
tions and "allow them to live in dignity, together with their wives and children in
Mexico City and elsewhere, in their own independent households." However, after
submitting their plea for review to an especially commissioned councilor, Doctor
don Luis de las Infantes, the viceroy turned down their appeal, but he instructed the
justice authorities and the priesthood serving in their parishes "not to cause them
further harm concerning such mischief that they were accustomed to in the past."[23]
These restrictions merit special attention when one reviews cohabitation of single
women belonging to these groups.

EXPLAINING THE SOURCES

The qualitative facets of this study are based upon a diversity of records in the
Archivo General de la Nación (Mexico City) repository, documenting lay views of

single women's conduct, beliefs, and practices. These were found in the following sections: Archivo Histórico de Hacienda; Inquisición; Notaría; Tribunal Superior de Justicia; Bienes Nacionales; Civil; Escribanos; General de Parte; Indios; Jesuitas; Matrimonios; Ordenanzas; Bienes de Difuntos; Reales Cédulas; Real Junta; and Tierras. In the section of Bienes de Difuntos, one finds, for example, that among the richest and the most informative sources are *Cotejo de testamentos* (wills and bequests), as well as *diligencias de reclamo de herencias* (petitions and claims for inheritance) of single women and their property and those of their heirs. Within records of *hospitales, casas de misericordia* (almshouses and parish orphanages), and in parallel documents—such as letters of debt, memoranda of orphans, and affidavits given by the women themselves—I was able to locate orphans and pursue their subsequent whereabouts. Similarly, the options available to women who became separated from their spouses, or to single women who sought asylum, come to light through private petitions and public decrees related to the establishment and maintenance of poorhouses and hospitals for women of the subaltern groups (e.g., the Casa de Magdalenas and Amor de Dios, in Mexico City) and requests for the reassignment of women to these houses. These are supplemented by letters of admittance of single women into such institutions and by reports detailing their conduct in such places. Apart from this, these women are ubiquitous in parish records of baptisms and marriages, in censuses, in private letters, in legal proceedings of legitimization, and in ecclesiastical records of "ecclesiastical divorce" and betrothal, and in lawsuits over concubinage. Furthermore, appeals to ecclesiastical courts for the annulment of marriages, reports to the civil and church authorities about maltreatment, and both civil and criminal litigation filed by women against men who abused them inform us about the social circumstances behind such petitions. Within the proceedings of the ecclesiastical court of the Archbishopric of Mexico City during the seventeenth century, for example, there are many records recounting the fate of such women. Typically, the narratives relate how they had married, while still very young, men ostensibly of their own social standing, but shortly afterward discovered that their spouses had actually deceived them regarding their true background and civil status. Thus, these women sought to dissolve their respective marriages. Reports filed by church authorities and prelates of the religious orders throughout Mexico regarding the circumstances of such women who appealed to the ecclesiastical courts for help are valuable historical sources that tell why and how couples separated.

For example, in the Notaría (notary's office) section in the Archivo Nacional de la Nación (AGN), under the documents entitled *Escrituras de servicio* (service agreements), I was able to track petitions filed by either single plebeian women, or by their children, to be placed under the tutelage of a person of profession,

who would teach them a trade and provide them with room and board. Here is
an example:

> Scripture of deposit. Before Lic. Francisco de Leos alcalde del Crimen of this court,
> appeared a twelve-year-old mestiza girl, Juana, an orphan from both father and
> mother and said that she would like to be hired for service by someone who would
> treat her honestly and in a state of chastity, teach her good habits and Christian
> doctrine. And when the *alcalde de corte* [judge of the civil division of the audiencia]
> witnessed that she was without any clothes on, and maltreated, he deposited her to
> Licenciado Francisco de Figueroa Venegas, *relator* de la Real Sala del Crimen, for
> a period of six years, obliging him to keep her honest and teach her good customs,
> provide her with food, clothes, shoes, medicines for her illnesses, good treatment, and
> at the end of the six years, he should provide her with 30 pesos to be able to get mar-
> ried . . . Mexico City, 24 April, 1614.[24]

Added to all the above sources are those linked to ostensible criminality, that is,
the rationales and circumstances under which single women were detained, incar-
cerated, and prosecuted. The AGN in Mexico City holds 148 volumes of inquisitorial proceedings, which provide us with abundant references to single, unwed
women accused of *amancebamientos* (cohabitation), as well as found guilty in a large
variety of crimes and sins falling under the jurisdiction of the Inquisition. Among
these I found documented the life stories of approximately 190 single women who
were prosecuted by the Spanish Inquisition, which unfold a whole range of social
realities, social interactions, and networks of mutual trust and assistance among
single plebeian women. The inquisitorial records utilized here throughout are particularly suitable for the practice of the qualitative methodology, especially where
one is in need of applying the "interview mode." Witnesses, like culprits, were interrogated to excess by the inquisitors. The word-for-word court proceedings/minutes
left behind in the archives allow us to review both witnesses' and culprits' responses
in great detail, a fact that facilitates the application of a present-day "interview
mode" on such responses from the distant past and to be able to sort them and
classify them according to major and recurring themes as the qualitative methodology instructs us to do. However, by contrast to a present-day "interview mode,"
which poses open questions to the interviewees, the inquisitorial interrogatorium is
a closed "questionnaire" and focuses on distinct themes, mainly those that deal with
blasphemy, Devil worship, and religious and moral deviance, but also racial affiliation, including genealogical background, all of which are aimed to provide the
interrogators with a solid basis for conviction. My purpose, by contrast, is to be able
to extract from such responses/data all what interests us in particular, namely, social
networks, mutual assistance, ritual practices, genealogies, and full life histories, as

in the case of Isabel de Montoya (see appendix 1) and, if indeed possible, from how these women describe their experiences *in their own wording.*

The judicial archives of the city of Puebla house extraordinarily rich sets of the *fiscal del crimen* (Crown or city attorney attached to criminal cases) and his corps of constables' records documenting local allegations against single women, where one is able to pursue the fragmented, personal experiences of eighty-nine of such women, between 1603 and 1642. Such sources best detail the circumstances under which single women were confined to houses of seclusion or houses of correction and are invaluably supplemented by city authorities' reports on the locations and social contexts of the households in which these women reestablished themselves after they were released from such confinement. In addition, I am utilizing here qualitative sources, such as incantations and ritualistic images and paintings, for the sake of seeking social realities, that historians previously made use of for the sake of gleaning religious beliefs and practices only. I argue, for example, that ritual formula was not centered merely on the goals of "love-magic," as some historians may be inclined to interpret it but, rather more so, on appropriating spaces and its male sovereigns, in the combined social and gendered sense, not just the symbolic context, and that such ritual practices truly mirrored single women's subversive aspirations, as well as manifestations.

The quantitative database for this study is embedded in records from Mexico City and Puebla and consist of (a) a sample of baptismal records from the Sagrario Metropolitano, in Mexico City, 1672–80 and 1681–88; (b) a sample of baptismal records from the Sagrario Metropolitano of Puebla, 1650–89; (c) the baptismal records of San Martin Huaquechula (state of Puebla), San Salvador El Verde, near Tlaxcala (state of Puebla), and San Juan de los Llanos, Libres (state of Puebla); (d) the burial registry of the parish of Santa María de la Natividad, Atlixco (state of Puebla) for the years 1704–14, as well as a quantitative survey of pleas for ecclesiastical divorce and verdicts reached by civil and ecclesiastical courts in Mexico City alone concerning charges of concubinage; (e) A door-to-door, partial census, conducted between 1670 and 1678, that covers eleven different *barrios* (quarters), as well as additional residential areas, including small alleys, bridges, and squares in this part of Mexico city that I have recently unearthed at the AGN.

THE HISTORIOGRAPHICAL CONTEXT

Essential to this present study are numerous other studies. Within the context of early modern Europe, the most relevant studies are Joanne M. Ferraro's *Marriage Wars in Late Renaissance Venice* (2001); on spousal struggles in Venice between 1564 and 1650, Amy Froide, *Never Married: Single Women in Early Modern England*

(2005); on single women testators in early modern Southampton, Bristol, Oxford, and York, England, Lawrence Stone's, *Broken Lives; Separation and Divorce in England 1660–1857* (1993); and Roderick Philips's, *Family Breakdown in Late Eighteenth-Century France, Divorces in Rouen 1792–1803* (1980). Family historians of Latin America have been working hard for the past three decades or so. Historical studies of colonial society in New Spain, based on both quantitative and qualitative approaches, have questioned many previous assumptions about various social realities that existed during the early and mid-colonial periods. Accordingly, patterns of living, of residence, adherence to patriarchal rule, and family norms have been found to have been far more flexible and accommodating than was previously thought (see Lavrin 1989a). Take, for, example, Juan Javier Pescador's, "Vanishing Women," in which he examines the reality of indigenous women migrating to Mexico City to look for work and a place to live.[25] These studies have opened up new paths that demand significant modifications in our thinking on how the overall mass of the subaltern groups lived and died. Their norms of living, marriage, and residential patterns, as recent research undoubtedly shows, were influenced predominantly by manifestations of economic instability that impelled frequent migrations, for example, as we know to have been the case in particular in mining areas such as Guanajuato in New Spain. The stable, patriarchal household model previously assumed to have been dominant has been shown by recent research to be no longer valid—certainly not in circumstances in which both formal and informal unions were in large numbers being dissolved after a period of only two or three years, leaving the family without a paterfamilias.

It would suffice at this point to mention the most indispensable secondary literature that impacted this present study. Komisaruk's *Labor and Love in Guatemala: The Eve of Independence* (2013, chs. 2, 3, and 4, in particular) is one of them. Indeed, through her close study of a number of nonelite women during the mid- to late eighteenth century in Santiago de Guatemala, Komisaruk brings to the fore the very critical themes that ought to be further evaluated concerning single women, and therefore I cite her often in this book. Patricia Seed's classic study *To Love, Honor, and Obey in Colonial Mexico* (1988a) maintains that cultural changes spurred behavioral change, which in turn led to legal and institutional changes, and that three major values affected marriage: *voluntad* (will), *amor* (love), and *honor*. According to Seed, the tenet of individual consent to marry and the exercise of freedom of choice or free choice in choosing a marriage partner were embedded in the belief that voluntad was rational. However, contrary to Seed, our use of the term "free choice" theorizes that remaining single (though not celibate) should be approached from the perspective of *a conscious decision*, undertaken by single plebeian women in a variety of situations discussed in the book. What Dora Dávila Mendoza expounds in her book on ecclesiastical divorce in eighteenth-century Mexico (2005), as well as what Ana Lidia García Peña describes in her own book (2006), fit this notion only partly. And I quote from Dávila Mendoza: "The objectives that the women appealing for divorce sought on the grounds of maltreatment varied but the essence was in not wanting to keep on tolerating situations that they did not deserve nor did they wish to continue with, due to having already been conscious of what they desired [for themselves], and they knew that they were able to rely on ecclesiastical support and on legal assistance" (2005, 195) In this present citation, as in others of her book, Mendoza and García Peña both emphasize maltreatment and violence as the driving force behind such conscious decisions taken by elite women during this period, and not any other kind of circumstances. García Peña asserts that "the fear of dying during a fury of blows directed these women to justify divorce as a distinct form of remaining in peace, not being able to pursue another alternative that would resolve their situations" (2006, 196). Such a choice of either remaining or becoming single is explored in this present book from a greater variety of perspectives, including, but not limited to, violence. As such is Richard Boyer's *Lives of the Bigamists: Marriage, Family, and Community in Colonial Mexico* (1995), in which Boyer highlighted the unique strategies of bigamists in early to mid-colonial Mexico. In contrast with this study, Boyer does not discuss single women from their own vantage point, but rather as victims of abandoning husbands who formed new lives elsewhere. In my opinion, it would be constructive to reexamine resistance and diverging alliances of single plebeian women not from the dichotomist approach of "resisters" versus "subordinators," but rather from a far more multifaceted vantage point that takes into account internal factionalism within each group, as well as shifting roles. For example, Susan Gal has commented that "the dichotomy of 'we as victims' versus 'they who have the power' can be recursively applied, so that any imagined assembly of 'us can be further subdivided into an 'us' and a 'them.'" Ortner emphasizes how a single activity may simultaneously constitute both resistance *and* accommodation to different aspects of power and authority, allowing resisters to remain within the social system they contest (Ortner 1995, 173–93; Gal 1993, 407–24).

Also especially relevant to the discussion on the daily world of poor urban women are Sonya Lipsett-Rivera's *Gender and the Negotiation of Daily Life in Mexico, 1750–1856* (2012), Nicole von Germeten's *Black Blood Brothers: Confraternities and Social Mobility for Afro-Mexicans* (2006), and her other book, *Violent Delights, Violent Ends* (2013), on Cartagena de Indias; and Sandra Lauderdale Graham's study on *Brazil, House and Street: The Domestic World of Servants and Masters in Nineteenth-Century Rio de Janeiro* (1992); as well as Jane E. Mangan's *Trading Roles: Gender, Ethnicity, and the Urban Economy in Colonial Potosí* (2005). Addressing the issues of ethnic/racial identities and illegitimacy of offspring is Ann Twinam's earlier book *Public Lives, Private Secrets: Gender, Honor, Sexuality and Illegitimacy in Colonial Spanish America* (1999), and her most recent book, *Purchasing Whiteness: Pardos, Mulattoes and the Quest for Social Mobility in the Spanish Indies* (2015). The latter work focuses on the eighteenth-century term, *Gracias al sacar*, denoting a formal process, undertaken by the king of Spain and his Cámara de Diputados, of "laundering" or whitening, of applicants from the colonial elites who were standing for royal offices in the colonial bureaucracy, through the payment of large sums of money to the royal treasury. In both her books, Twinam thoroughly studies these appeals for "laundering" originating from across Latin America, and she has uncovered thirty such petitions for the Audiencia of Mexico, constituting 13.9 percent of the total number of petitions from across the colonies. Twinam convincingly maintains that the major rationale behind such petitions were "honor and property." Nevertheless, both her books are focused on men and women firmly entrenched in the colonial elite circles, between the mid-eighteenth to the early part of the twentieth century, in contrast to this present study, which examines the social phenomena "from below," as well as during the early colonial period. Take, for example, Twinam's comment that "the concealment [of a pregnancy] considered essential for an unmarried mother of eighteen might not be as critical for a spinster of thirty-six" (Twinam 1999, 62). This is indeed the case for elite women, but for single plebeian mothers in early colonial Mexico this would never have been a real concern. In addition are Karen B. Graubart's *With Our Labor and Sweat* (2007); Asunción Lavrin's and Edith Couturier's pioneering study "Dowries and Wills: A View of Women's Socio-Economic Role in Colonial Guadalajara and Puebla, 1640–1790" (1979); Silvia Marina Arrom's two classics, *La mujer mexicana ante el divorcio* (1976) and *The Women of Mexico City, 1790–1857* (1985); and Pilar Gonzalbo Aizpuru's *Familia y orden colonial* (2005), whose chapter "Los recursos familiares de adaptación" centers on the very same parishes of Santa Veracruz and El Sagrario in Mexico City, under study here, between the 1650s and 1660s. All those works converse very well with our own records on baptisms, marriages, and ecclesiastical divorce in these two parishes, during the same period. Also essential, on the issue of the assimilation of women of African origins in Mexican society of the time, especially their role in the creation of black and mulato confraternities, is Joan Cameron Bristol's *Christians, Blasphemers, and Witches*, which is very relevant for this book's treatment of the place of single African women within the domain of religious practices (2007).

ISABEL DE MONTOYA: THE CASE STUDY (SEE APPENDIX 1)

The persona of Isabel de Montoya, nicknamed La Centella (The Morning Spark)—a middle-aged, single, and a racially mixed plebeian woman who could sign her name was able to confess in "elegant Romance"—but could not read nor write, is intriguing, particularly because of the multifaceted and dichotomous sensation it sparks. Much of the time, Isabel seems to us as though she is moving relentlessly from daylight into shade; at times, she is described by her acquaintances and by herself as coming from indigenous background, at times she appears to be a mulata, at times she is very generous and warm with her friends and neighbors, at times she is both rowdy and mean. Notwithstanding, at other times, she is being portrayed as deeply engaged in the spiritually soothing, magical, and otherworldly essences. Furthermore, one can easily admire Isabel's resourcefulness and creativity that helped her greatly in gaining grounds where obstacles were unbridgeable: vis-à-vis her parents, during her adolescence, and later on in life, switching between careers when a particular one became a peril or between men she desired only to leave behind for good, as well as vis-à-vis her interrogators at the court of the Inquisition.

Where did I find the story of Isabel? I found her at the Van Pelt Library, at the University of Pennsylvania, while visiting, and by pure chance. I came across two large volumes that, apparently, were records of the Holy Office in Mexico City, of the trials and tribulations of an unmarried *castiza* (of a mixed, second-generation indigenous-Spanish ancestry), by the name of Isabel de Montoya.[26] This study strives to suggest in fact that it is precisely the multifacetedness and inconsistencies in Isabel's life story and personality that were reflective of reality, as well as replicated the anomaly of Mexican colonial society at large. Such circumstances, which are analyzed at length, obligated Isabel to accommodate her behavior accordingly, in order to "manage best in both worlds." Such a comprehension of the existential choices single women such as Isabel made is indeed essential to our understanding of the full range of choices and strategies, as well as the spiritually soothing ways adopted, by single women in order to enhance their existence in the threatening and rough environment in which they lived. Could one associate the large presence of single plebeian women in the urban scenery of Mexico to her "agency" or, rather, to the socioeconomic circumstances that impelled such a phenomenon, or, alternatively, might not better answers be found in their private life stories? I approach this theme by highlighting the possible role played by channels of mutual assistance and trust among these women. What were the reasons that may have kept plebeian women—midwives; clothing and flower sellers; seamstresses; housemaids; bread, fruit, vegetables, and stand vendors; bakers and cooks; and other servants—in a lifestyle of singlehood, outside marriage? A close consideration will be undertaken of a number of focal issues: the presence of single women in early to mid-colonial Mexico City and Puebla; the racial factor: local social and economic constraints that are closely related to the caste system;

reasons for remaining single; channels of mutual assistance and trust among single plebeian women; and caretaking of their children. But, prior to that, the following chapter introduces the major themes of concern, as they are projected from single women's discourses during early to mid-colonial Mexico, through a close analysis of the form and significance of their own words.

2

The Major Themes of Concern

According to a recent report commissioned by the Ford Foundation, an astonishing pattern still occurs in Mexico, today: of the 320,000-plus Mexican girls between the ages of 12 and 17 who are cohabiting, nearly 70 percent are with a partner who is at least 11 years their senior. The findings also show that 25,000 girls between 12 and 14 are living in "early unions." And a report by *Investigación en Salud y Demografía* (INSAD), describes how across Mexico 81 percent of marriages among girls 12 to 17 years old are not recognized legally. Heather Hamilton, deputy executive director for the charity Girls Not Brides, said: "You have a situation where a girl is perhaps choosing to be in a union, but only because she lacks other options. Perhaps there is a desire to escape poverty or a violent home environment. But we don't want a world in which girls are forced to make the least bad choice." INSAD's report on early unions in Mexico found that even when a girl claimed to be in an early union through choice, her partner was usually the one with the power and resources. The study also concluded that "many girls enter unions not because they are pregnant but for other reasons." Hamilton says that the data contested the widespread belief in Latin America that teen pregnancy is behind high rates of child marriage: "The research finds this isn't necessarily the case, at least not in half of the cases in Mexico" (INSAD 2019).

One is certainly able to trace the roots of these troubling, lingering patterns back to the early to mid-colonial period. Throughout this chapter, as well as in the chapters that follow, I utilize an emic approach, basing the text as much as possible on the women's own wording, in order to shed light on subtle tendencies and

DOI: 10.5876/9781607329633.c002

pervasive patterns of special understanding that guided single plebeian women's life histories. To accomplish this, I rely on what has been called the "ethnography of speaking," the intention of which is the pursuit of formalized frames of communicative actions and interpretations, or what ethnoscience has termed "cultural grammars, which are analogous to the grammars of linguistics" (Sherzer 1983). While anxiously scanning heavily laden, voluminous court records, historians of the early modern era usually encounter a repetitive pattern in responses to an interrogation; plaintiffs, defendants, and other interested parties largely gave the same answers to the same assortment of questions. The witnesses almost always confronted a legally determined interrogatory, established upon a determined protocol, with a certain number of standardized questions, according to precise procedural objectives. Their responses, often seemingly blurred and "empty," either added almost nothing to the questions or merely repeated verbatim what was already said in previous depositions. Nevertheless, modern scholars can use this evidence to determine variations in the testimony, first by checking the interrogatorium for the kind of information supplied by the questions and any hints about preferred responses and then pursuing the sources for more information. Scholars should also look in the witnesses' responses for original, uncontaminated views of events, through individual deviations from the common schema (Megged 2014, 163–86). By employing such a methodology, this study aims to distill certain "cognitive schemata" from the variegated testimony delivered either in the Spanish colonial civil and criminal courts or at the ecclesiastical courts of Mexico City and Puebla, arguing that the pattern established by specific verbal and nonverbal constructions reveals telling predispositions among litigants, defendants, and witnesses. Firsthand testimony is the most significant. The mental shreds and remnants of past and present experiences are the objects of such an inquest, not a reconstruction of the past in itself. Testimony is a multifaceted restructuring of occurrences, never an endeavor to represent a "true past." For example, litigants may well have shaped their testimony to "win their case." The objectives of lawmakers often concerned heavy political, judicial, and economic contexts, which should be considered with caution. Likewise, Thomas and Elizabeth Cohen caution us: "Though men and women spoke volubly, they did not speak freely, for they knew well that they were in court. As witnesses, they were in multiple jeopardy, subject on the one hand to the court's punishments for crime and perjury and on the other to retaliation from whom they hurt by what they said . . . Trials, by contrast, have competing authors and cross purposes. They often trail off into irresolution . . . What were the court, the witnesses, the suspects trying to do?" (1993, 19, 31–32).

The four major themes of concern that are repeatedly articulated in single plebeian women's discourses in this present study are as follows: (a) "Being Left on Her

Own in This World"; (b) "I Felt Deceived"; (c) "Negligence and Lack of Trust"; and (d) "Maltreatment and Cruelty." Moreover, these four themes are also often interwoven and are deeply embedded in the background of each of the chapters that follow.

A. "BEING LEFT ON HER OWN IN THIS WORLD"

In this first major theme one needs to possibly separate the "real" feeling of loneliness (being socially isolated), from the feeling of being "hollow" (being emotionally empty, thus "feeling lonely"). Lack of trust, as well as early experiences of violence and negligence, may well have led to both states and lingering emotions later in life; however, one could become socially connected as one grew up but still remain "hollow" inside. Let us listen at first to what Isabel de Montoya tells of this early phase in her life, in her own words:

> Up to the age of ten years old, I helped my mother, who was a baker. At that age a Gachupin man came and took me away with him to his mother's house, where that night he proposed to marry me, and left me under the guidance of a mulata women, Francisca Ruiz[,] and her daughter, Juana de la Cruz, where I remained for four years. The latter served as a *madrina de baptismos* [godmother of baptism] and I used to knit for her the image of Our Lady of Carmen and I accompanied her to all the feasts. When I was fourteen years old, the treasurer of the city's Casa de la Moneda had taken me as his mistress and hired a place for me, and bought a black slave who lived with me, enclosed in the house for a year where I cooked and knitted. I was rescued from that house by don Gabriel de Cabesco, a sergeant major of this city, and he had also rented a house for me and kept me for six years during which I served him. I fled that house and went to live on my own, as *mala muger* [promiscuous woman: a woman who has many sexual partners] for five more years.[1]

What does Isabel's story of her early experiences tell us? Primarily that she recounts all those early dramatic episodes and chaotic transitions from one place to another, from one partner to the next, and from one phase in life to the next, as though from a distance, as though she was far removed from the trauma. She was awfully young, only ten or eleven years old (!), when a Gachupin—that is, a Spaniard born in the Iberian Peninsula—which was the uppermost class in Mexican colonial society, came to her parents' home and took her away that very night and, thereafter, proposed to marry her. She was thus torn away from her safe environment, being unable to ever return to it. Her mother clearly consented to this act, and we can surely say that she even coerced her child to leave, out of her own personal ambition, to socially and economically upgrade herself (and the rest of her family) through her child. Isabel remains in the house of her partner's mother, under the close guidance of a mulata, who was personally involved in the religious activities of a local confraternity and Isabel accompanied her there "learning her religious lessons well, for the next four years, up to the age of 14." Already at this stage in life, she was forever removed from her parents' supervision and care. She then moved out of that shelter, being taken away from there by the treasurer of the Casa de Moneda, a high-ranking official, again presumably a Spaniard, and he made her his mistress.

So, this is when and where she was already no longer a virgin and incautious of what "honor" and "chastity" really meant for other contemporaneous compatriots in early colonial Mexico. It should be remembered that, according to the norms promulgated by the Council of Trent, under the circumstances in which either a forced or a voluntary abduction of a young, unmarried woman from her father's home was likely to occur, and the predicted outcome of which would be her deflowering and subsequent loss of honor, that woman should be taken immediately to a safe house, where she would remain until her marriage took place. The same prescription was also valid under circumstances in which a young woman had rebelled against the *patria potestad* (the father's rule) of her father and run away from home with her lover, disrespecting her parents' choice of marriage for her. Allyson Poska has emphasized recently that the lives of colonial women did not necessarily conform to the Spanish ideals according to which they were taught but interpreted according to their own, changing conceptions: "there is little evidence to indicate that any type of 'Spanish' gender norms focused on the control of female sexuality completely dominated women's lives in either Spain or in colonial Spanish America" (2012, 43).

The social practice of elopement meant that an underage partner would be "kidnapped" from her parents' house to be secretly engaged, under their parents' implicit sanction (Boyer 1995, 15–33). In Isabel's account, as in many others throughout the following chapters, one is able to notice that this norm of conduct was practiced in effect up and down the social ladder: from as high as eminent government officials, all the way down to the common people. If we borrow Stern's term "drama of virility,"—"it affirmed male-on-male rivalry between men who wished to possess the same woman, and this implied that possession of a woman was permanent unless one man robbed sexual property from another" (1995, 234)—then this is exactly what Isabel has described above: don Gabriel de Cabesco, a sergeant-major managed to "rescue" her from her first partner, the treasurer of the Casa de Moneda, and it is feasible that the two men may have known each other; perhaps one owed a favor to another or, even, money passed hands in this "transaction." Anyway, again, the parents are seemingly not involved in the affair, although, we may plainly suspect, based on previous experience, that they may well have given again their outmost consent to the act.

Of significance, in the aftermath of the Council of Trent, despite the church's formal stance during the last session of the council that discussed the issue of matrimony and subsequently insisted on the child's "free will" in choosing his/her partner for life, it was not uncommon for parents *to coerce* their child into unwanted marriage at a young age or to arrange such marriage with the groom's parents many years in advance.

A TURNING POINT

If up to this early stage in life Isabel seemingly remained blissfully unaware that anything was amiss, at this very point we can now sense, for the first time through Isabel's own words that she was now entering into a new phase, in which she was already beginning to become conscious of her own agency and gathering strength. She was now already conscience of the fact that she was being coerced and entrapped, being forced to perform various household services besides her sexual duties, all of it against her will: *enclosed in the house for a year where I cooked and knitted. I was rescued from that house*... What she describes in effect is of being completely on her own, for one entire year in that situation, and socially isolated. This time, it was not like in the first place which, by contrast, was a kind of a "safe haven" for her, where she may well have felt being cared for by her mulata mentor and her daughter, who may well have given her the feeling of an "alternative family" for a while.

Isabel was no longer raised at home, by her parents from the age of ten or eleven. In spite of all that she had undergone, she nonetheless remained in touch throughout the years with her mother. Undoubtedly her mother was the dominant figure in the house—her father is virtually absent from her life story—taught her, as she recalled, "all what she knew." She was also closely guided by Isabel Martin, her aunt from her mother's side, who specialized in popular medicine. Her parents died many years later, two years apart, first her father, in 1622, when Isabel was already twenty-nine, and, then, her mother, in 1624, when she was already thirty-one. It seems that she did not maintain any meaningful relationships with her brothers and sister, not at least that she recalls. Her youngest brother, Josephe, had died at the age of eight in Puebla. Her sister, Juana de Montoya, had died in Mexico City in 1638, that is, fourteen years after her mother had died; Nicolás, her other brother, was put in prison "because of his sister" (Isabel) and also died when Isabel was already an adult.

MARÍA INFANTE'S TALE

One remarkable story of an adolescent *castiza* and daughter of Hernando Infante, an *español* and Catalina de León (also a castiza), recounted to the ecclesiastical court in Mexico City (see chapter 3 for court cases), illustrates the fluidity of the caste system—the crossing of lines between ethnic/racial categories, and, in particular, fears by castizos of being classified as indigenous persons or intermixing with indigenous persons, as well as the crumbling barriers of racial biases. Moreover, this story also highlights the issue of the arranged marriage discussed at length in the following chapter. The cultural representations embedded in the story this castiza presented in court deserve our attention, in view of our inquiry into the true impact of social and cultural biases upon actual social possibilities open before plebeian women in local reality. Moreover, the issue of transculturation through dress that is portrayed here is significant. The indigenous couple was appropriating María Infante into indigenous settings as well as expropriating her from her "Spanish" former identity, as though contesting her former *calidad*. Graubart remarks in this respect that "clothing . . . provided visual cues, but ones that were ambiguous and malleable."[2] In María Infante's life history, from October 1643, by contrast to Isabel's life story, our protagonist remains close to her parents; however, their care and guidance of their child are deficient. At a young age the changing circumstances forced María to move away from her natural environment in Mexico City together with her mother to the minor town of Tacuba, where her father's new place of work was and where they intended to remain for at least four years. Eventually, as the picture unfolds, the father apparently was away from home most of the time, and the mother herself could hardly function as a guiding, parental figure for the pubescent girl. Let us listen attentively to what María Infante related to the court about their circumstances soon after mother and daughter had moved to Tacuba: "I was taken by Diego and María, both indigenous persons from Santiago Tlatelolco, who tried to persuade me that I should marry Diego, a pork-butcher. Having rejected the idea, having a father and a mother, and *haciendo yo resistencia porque tenía padres y era casi española* [and having resisted, myself being almost a Spaniard], they began conversing with an indigenous couple, Gerónimo and Juana, who resided in the barrio de San Juan, and convinced them to come forward and inform me that I was their legitimate daughter, and an indigenous [woman]."

Gerónimo and Juana, the indigenous couple alleging to be María Infante's legitimate parents, then began stripping off her Spanish garments, replacing them with the traditional garb of indigenous women, a *huipil* and a *nagua*, and threatened that if she would not agree to marry Diego, "they would lock her up in a convent, for life." María Infante continued to relate her story to the court,

> *Y por verme sola y desamparada y entre gente extraña, y no de mi nación, y como menos capaces, a ejecutar cualquier intento* [And having found myself forsaken, among strangers, and people not of my race, and less qualified, who could dully exercise

whatever intent they had] I felt compelled to consent, I was forced to acknowledge being their daughter, and to remain in the same clothing they put on me, and was ushered to the guardian of the Franciscan monastery in Santiago Tlatelolco. The latter, however, expressed doubts about whether it was at all justified to marry me, having noticed the dissimilarity between the persons involved finally, against my will, married me with Diego, an indigenous [man].[3]

María Infante's words do express a clear sense of distress and of *being left on her own in this world*. Once taken to the monastery of Santiago Tlatelolco, Gerónimo and Juana, the indigenous couple alleging to be María Infante's legitimate parents, were asked by the Franciscan *guardian* who conducted the ceremony if it was true that María Infante was indeed their legitimate daughter, to which they replied in the affirmative. The marriage ceremony was thus concluded. The newly married couple, Diego and María Infante, lived together in Santiago Tlatelolco as husband and wife for a period of five months. Matters, if just seemingly, had come to a presumed peaceful conclusion—the social and racial barriers and biases having dissolved when the marriage was consummated.

Apparently, while all this was taking place, María Infante did not openly express her opposition, nor her distress, despite what she later told the court. This raises the possibility that she initially consented to sharing her life with Diego, but only then, when her parents became involved, and expressed their opposition to this bond, she described the act as "having been against her free will." When María Infante was summoned to the court by her parents, she was already aware that her parents were not informed of the complete details of what had actually happened between herself and her indigenous male partner in Tacuba and of the subsequent developments that reached their climax in her marriage in the Franciscan monastery at Santiago Tlatelolco. For these reasons, and for the sake of keeping up the thin veneer of the social and cultural norms and biases to which her parents adhered, when facing them she presented an entirely different narrative suited for assuaging them.

When María Infante's parents finally "became aware of what had happened to their daughter," "it was already far too late for them to undo the act," as they explained in court. Under these circumstances, the only thing that they could possibly do that the set of behavioral norms of the time required was to rush to the ecclesiastical court in Mexico City and submit an appeal for the marriage to be annulled, and this is exactly what they did. María Infante's parents filed a complaint to the ecclesiastical court in Mexico City concerning "the illegitimacy of this marriage," asking to have it annulled on grounds that their daughter was compelled to marry an indigenous person *against her own free choice* and because the officiating priest was unfit to conduct the ceremony as he was not suited for

Spaniards, "but only for indigenous persons." Their request was granted, and the marriage was annulled.

María Infante's life story is also certainly in accordance with the social and behavioral ingredients of elopement discussed above, with María Infante still being a *doncella* and under the patria potestad of her father and with the drama of virility deeply embedded there, perhaps also between her biological father, and Diego, her partner. Furthermore, throughout her discourse María Infante reflects her enduring conflict of identity choices: she seems to have stressed that her biological parents, indeed, wished for her to be recognized by society "as a Spaniard," *like her father* and less of a *castiza* than her mother. She therefore described how, while mother and daughter traveled on horseback to their new home, a predominantly indigenous area, they wore *hábito de españoles* (Spaniards' outfit) to make them distinguishable as Spaniards. In addition, she emphasized how she constantly feared being "forcibly assimilated" among indigenous persons, *"people not of my race, and less qualified . . ."* Sometime after their settling down in Tacuba, one day María went to meet her father on the road, and there everything began to go wrong. At some stage, after having been assimilated in the new cultural environment of Tacuba, María Infante found herself effectively on her own—her father being away from home most of the time and her mother not really being able to take care of her properly. She may have first befriended Diego, the indigenous man, after meeting him, possibly, through his parents' mediation and thereafter became his fiancée, without her parents even being aware of what was going on behind their back. The marriage having been duly conducted, the young couple established their own new home. During their examination, the ecclesiastical judges undoubtedly noticed, like us, that during the wedding María Infante duly remained dressed in the traditional indigenous garb, the huipil and the nagua, and that she never once expressed apprehension when facing the Franciscan priest who conducted the ceremony and was asked to give her consent to the act of marriage. In this way, the insightful ecclesiastical judges assisted her in coming out of the ordeal, unscathed.

If we then turn to look at María Infante's tale from the vantage point of the experienced ecclesiastical judges, the only matter that they wanted to investigate in this very strange story was the issue of María Infante's "free choice," or agency, obviously being moved by the church's Post-Tridentine stance on promoting children's free choice in deciding who will be their spouse, in spite of their parents' opposition. They therefore promptly interrogated Diego and María Infante, in addition to witnesses summoned by the court to either confirm or rebuke the version of the events presented by María Infante's parents and to whether the strict norms concerning the sacrament of matrimony were respected by the parties: that the correct *palabraa de matrimonio* (words of promise) were indeed exchanged between the bride and the groom; that both parties expressed their uttermost consent to the act; that neither of them had ever been married before to any other partner; and that, at present, both of them did not wish to live apart from one another. Having ultimately been satisfied that María Infante had been married according to her "free choice," and convinced that only the formal act of matrimony was at fault, the ecclesiastical judges passed the only sentence that was possible under the circumstances, namely, they ordered a priest nominated by them to remarry the couple in church. How can we explain such "irregularities" in this conduct of the court? This is only possible if we conclude that the entire story told in court by María Infante and, in particular, the part involving her being forced by the various indigenous actors in her story, was fabricated by her in order to justify her conduct toward her biological parents. Furthermore, this fabrication of hers was insightfully recognized by the presiding judges, who fully comprehended her motives, their having fully sensed that the entire chain of events, far from being forced upon María Infante, was actually an expression of the young women's having taken hold of her own future, refuting both her parents' wishes or the tenets of society. After reviewing the various accounts, in the final analysis the true story might have appeared very straightforward to the judges.

B. "I FELT DECEIVED"

Under this second major theme are cases in which women who sought to separate from their husbands described their experiences as having been either "deceived" by their spouse or not having their initial expectations of this marriage met. We should remind ourselves that these women had married at a very young age and mostly under strained circumstances. This second major theme is directly related to the reasons provided by these women for their subsequent decision to dissolve their marriages. "Negligence and Lack of Trust" and "Maltreatments and Cruelty" are intimately interwoven with the above. Carefully reading these women's descriptions of their emotions during early, premarital experiences as a result of false promises of marriage (see also Seed 1988b, 253–76), one may undoubtedly conclude that such early experiences deeply impacted their sense of trust and disillusion from a real marriage, which under the given circumstances could never have been successfully materialized. The marriage in those cases was consequently short lived.

The story of sixteen-year-old Brígida de Arteaga, a mulata servant, is also filled with the context of deception and disillusion, lack of mutual trust and bonding, and the consequent rupture that occurs between the spouses. On 9 April 1666, the newly wed Brígida recounted to the ecclesiastical court at the Mexico City Cathedral, in the first person, how, nine months earlier, Joseph de la Cruz, a mulato, who had just arrived in Mexico City from Oaxaca, persuaded her through deception, and "by false promises" to marry him. As we are told, the couple got married at Mexico City's Cathedral on 9 September 1665. However, after the wedding had taken place, they were still living apart, as was usually the case with people of their social standing and racial affiliations. Brígida continued to live and serve in the wealthy household of don Antonio Coloma, a prominent knight of the Order of Santiago, a *maestre de campo* (senior entrada official charged with logistics, orderliness, and billeting) and corregidor (Spanish official in charge of a province or district; district magistrate) of the city, while Joseph lived and served at the household of Doctor Bernardo de Puezada Zanabría, a priest officiating in the Mexico City Cathedral. Brígida recounted: "The first thing that he had declared before her was that he had always been a free person and a descendant of free men." To confirm his pledge, he brought along with him a number of his close friends and relatives who testified on his behalf that "he was indeed free." The lack of trust and the lack of bonding led also to a maintained estrangement between the two and to not accepting the other's lack of integrity, which, otherwise, if there would have been a solid bonding between them, would possibly have been accepted by her, in spite of a possibly moderate reservation about his behavior and deeds.

Brígida ended her story by telling the court how "she had soon realized that he was not a free person." How did she realize this? It appears that not long after their marriage, Joseph took advantage of his habitual coming and going in the corregidor's house, where his wife lived and served, to commit a robbery there, for which he was thrown into prison by the corregidor's orders. After a few months and after he was set free, he was taken in as a slave by the *fiscal del crimen* and his corps of constables. When this news reached her, Brígida made further inquiries, and it came to her attention that he had initially lied to her, that he was actually a former slave of the bishop of Nicaragua, Fray Juan de la Torre, until he passed away, and that after his death the syndicate of the Franciscan Order had sold him to a *cura vicario* (a parish priest, a vicar; member of secular clergy), Doctor Bernardo de Quezada Zanabría, who served at the Mexico City Cathedral. She immediately announced that she wished to end the marriage. Hearing of this, Joseph then ran to the corregidor's house where she remained and, as she described, "He was beating the house windows, cried that he wanted her to continue being his wife."[4] On 12 May 1666, the ecclesiastical court of the Archobizpado received a letter of appeal by Joseph de la Cruz, that stated: "I urge my wife to return to live with me . . . I urge her to refrain from critically deteriorating the situation between us, and I will refrain from molesting her or causing her any harm, as I was ordered by the court."[5] Thereafter, the *vicario general* (the principal deputy of the archbishop) of the Archobizpado published a decree by which Brígida should be transferred to the house of doña María Pretel "for the sake of justice," until the court passed its verdict.

In another example, Ana de San Pedro, a free mulata, and a recent widow of Marcos Rincón, who had died a year and a half earlier in Mexico City, was married to Nicolás de Vargas, a carpenter and a free mulato from Oaxaca, for less than eight months. She appeared in the ecclesiastical court of Mexico City and claimed that Nicolás, her husband, "had cheated her by declaring himself a free person."[6]

The discourse of 8 October 1555 of fifteen-year-old Catalina Martin, a very young and inexperienced wife, throws further light on the substantial role played by initial parental compulsion and coercion to marry, "against the child's free will," on the latter's decision to subsequently dissolve her marriage. Moreover, the significant impact of such early traumatic events on these girls' self-images and later womanhood might well have been part of their reluctance to remain married. In this context, also, our first major theme also comes into play, that is, "a sense of deception" experienced by this girl that served as a catalyst to her later striving in life to remain single. We find Catalina Martin appealing to the ecclesiastical court in Mexico City against her husband, Juan Martin, an ironworker by profession, to whom she was married for the previous eleven months. She claimed through her legal representative that her own parents had threatened her and "pressured her with harsh words" to marry Juan Martin Herrero, against her free choice: *Anton mi padre y Elvira mi madre me casaron por fuerza y contra mi voluntad a Juan Martin, herrero poniéndome amenazas y temores y haciendo malos ataques de palabra y de obra*" (Anton, my father, and Elvira, my mother, married me by compulsion and against my will to Juan Martin, ironworker, threatening me and frightening me, and attacking me with evil words and deeds). Antonio de Benavente, her appointed guardian, enlightened the court that Catalina and Juan were distant relatives and that their fathers maintained close comradeship and joint interests and had thus arranged this marriage well in advance, against Catalina's will, "being too immature to resist the act."

And in Isabel's own discourse, she recalled that

> in 1619, at the age of 26 [after she had given birth to her only daughter Ana María, from Juan Serrano, with whom she was compelled by her parents to marry in church but had escaped from that ceremony] . . . I was freed from the House of Seclusion where I was placed by my parents . . . There, I became the lover of Gaspar de la Pería, who served as a cabin-boy of the Conde de Santiago. I do not know where he was born. We were married for more than twenty years, but were together for only eight days, and then he went away because he was threatened to be thrown into jail, and ever since he did not live with me.[7]

What Isabel describes for this new phase of her life history is that although she had already made a number of significant decisions regarding her life, and out of sheer sense of prowess, such as giving birth to her daughter outside of marriage, as well as marrying Gaspar de la Péria, a cabin boy, of a shady and a lowly background, against the will of her parents, the most outstanding notion that comes up in her discourse is *a sense of deception*—from her parents, as well as from her short-lived life of marriage with the wrong man, as though her choices were indefinitely ruled by fate. By comparison, Catalina's words concerning her husband's acts of both physical and emotional violence against her emphasized the lack of trust between them, an enduring estrangement, as well as radical rupture between her family and his, leading to acts of violence on both sides of the fence: "Her husband envisages her to be his most ardent enemy, and this had to do with a fight that had apparently erupted between her husband's brother, Martin and her own brother, Francisco, as a result of which the former had stabbed the latter to death."

Catalina's wording also concerned negligence on the part of her spouse to perform marital duties. She recounted how, as her husband, "who was supposed to treat her well and provide for her all what was necessary," besides vowing to be her partner for life, failed to do so "being a severe and a cruel person, of crude properties." Moreover, she described how he mistreated her throughout their living together, lashing her *como a esclava cautiva* (as though she was his captive slave), severely threatening her, and vowing on several occasions that "he should stab her to death."[8] Consequently, she said, she was under great danger and constant fear for both her physical and emotional well-being. Catalina, therefore, asked the court to deposit her in a safe place, "away from her violent husband" and that the court compel him to provide her with all what is necessary for her sustenance, including food and clothing. All the witnesses that later appeared in court on her behalf attested to her grave circumstances and described her atrocious conditions, "wandering on the streets outside her home, frightened and tired." Having fled from home, Catalina remained meanwhile in hiding in her mother's home. Juan Martin, her husband, claimed in court through his legal representative that "remaining in her mother's place, Catalina was under her direct and malevolent influence against him," and he asked the court to place her away from her mother and brothers, to which the court eventually consented. Accordingly, Juan Martin's legal representative also asked the court to prohibit Catalina's mother, brothers, and nephews from communicating with her.[9]

Consequently, the judge ordered that Catalina Martin be removed from her mother's home and deposited in the home of Doctor Pedro López and his wife. The court agreed to it and informed Pedro López's wife of the order. On 21 April 1560, almost four years after Catalina's initial appeal for ecclesiastical divorce, the case still remained unresolved; Catalina insisted on living apart from her husband and urged the court to bring her "ecclesiastical divorce" to an end. We have no further proof of the consequences.

In order to better understand the process women had to undergo, an explanation of judicial procedures is needed. As early as 1566, we find the ecclesiastical court of the archbishopric of Mexico City giving cases of marital violence reported by victimized women who sought ecclesiastical divorce, a distinct category, and cataloguing them in a separate group of documents. This new repository was entitled *Denuncias que hacen varias mujeres de los malos tratos que reciben de sus maridos y piden la separación de ellos y ser depositadas en alguna casa donde puedan estar seguras. Catalina de Covarrubias, Luisa de Porras, y Francisca Calderón. México* (Denunciations that various women make against maltreatments that they receive from their husbands, and therefore ask for separation from them and to be 'deposited' in a certain house where they could be safe).[10]

Let us be reminded that single women remained *hijas de familia* (still under extended paternal authority for remaining single) under their father's patria potestad until whatever age they married, and a woman did not return to that status if she became a widow, even under the age of twenty-five. Single men and women without fathers needed a guardian to conduct certain business until the age of twenty-five. Nonetheless, from eighteen they were already permitted to manage property, choose their place of living, and go to court; otherwise, they still required legal representation of either their father or a guardian, that latter when the court decided the father could not be considered responsible for his acts or had been exiled from the land. The church regarded both partners as equally responsible for the maintenance of the marriage; thus, ecclesiastical courts only dealt with pleas for separation initiated by either party. Other issues concerning marriage such as premarital property were dealt with by the civil courts (Arrom 1985, "Legal Status"). The civil court was made up of eight judges called *oidores*. Besides dealing with lawsuits presented directly before them, these judges also had the supreme power to review and approve (or reject) sentences that were passed on all major cases in local courts (Haslip-Viera 1999, 44). The usual pattern was that the ill-treated woman would first leave the house and seek a safe haven elsewhere, either among friends or close relatives. She would then ask the court to order the restoration of her premarital property to her, and the husband would then appeal to the court to see to it that his wife was forced to fulfill her matrimonial vows. Under such circumstances and without pursuing further inquiry, in the more unusual cases in which a full verdict was actually given, the ecclesiastical court of the cathedral in Mexico City would order that the wife return to live with her husband and comply with the sacrament of marriage. The court would warn her relatives and friends not to impede the marriage and its reunion, on threat of excommunication. The same verdict would also be applied when the husband had abandoned his wife first, after having mistreated her. It is important to note in this respect that the canonical norms established that the absence of the husband side by side with his wife was a feasible cause for separation (Dávila Mendoza 2005, 41).

C. "NEGLIGENCE AND LACK OF TRUST"

In this third theme we continue to find in single women's discourses the lingering emotion of "being left on her own in this world," combined with accusations of negligence, of maltreatments, and cruelty, as an overt, gendered strategy of invoking paternalism in the courts. In this very context, Delgado emphasizes the utilization of gendered rhetoric by women within the ecclesiastical courts for the sake of defending themselves against public defamation. The utilization of the ecclesiastical court as though it symbolizes/represents/ substitutes paternal backing for these women is in tune with what Stern has named as "pluralization of patriarchs strategy" (Delgado 2009, 113, 116; Stern 1995, 99–103). Young and inexperienced wives complained that their husband was "cold and alien to them" or that he had left them for very long periods of time, traveling far and wide, with no means for the women to sustain themselves, or that "they had stopped caring for them." Emotional negligence was a substantial reason presented in court for the sake of seeking separation. For example, Constanza Rodríguez filed a request for "ecclesiastical divorce" because, as she claimed, "her husband, Alonso López[,] had married her only for economic benefits, thereafter neglecting her altogether."[11] In as yet another example, María de Xerez asked the ecclesiastical court either to oblige Joseph de Reinoso, her husband, to feed her properly, what presumably he was negligent in doing or "she would seek the immediate dissolution of their matrimony."[12]

The usual wording in the more common cases was as follows: "*Antonia Ramos denuncia a su marido ya que desde que se casaron ha sido tan omiso que no la ha sustentado, que siempre la ha maltratado. Solicita que se le de todo lo que precisa. Posteriormente declara que su marido Francisco Javier, no ha cumplido con lo demandado y no hacen vida maridable*" (Antonia Ramos denounces her husband on the grounds that ever since their marriage he has been so evasive so as not to sustain her, and he always maltreated her . . . Lately, she declares that her husband, Francisco Javier, has not complied with what is demanded, and they do not live as a married couple).[13]

Accusations of neglect that reached the ecclesiastical court, could, however, become mutual, reflecting a basic lack of trust and matured bonding between the spouses. Usually, and under the rule of patriarchy, the husband would be the first to go to court accusing his wife for "having abandoned home and neglected her marital duties," only to cover for his own mischiefs. Diego Márquez de Vivero, for example, was accused by his wife for having abandoned her for ten years; Diego accused her in return for being adulterous, and she, in return, moved on to accusations of violence and aggravation. The legal struggle went on and on and was summarized in court in about seventy pages. Despite the hard facts, especially the ten long years of abandonment presented by the wife in court, the case was never really resolved; the judges were not convinced by both sides and at the end instructed the two to return home to continue with their life together.[14] The ecclesiastical court, on its part, tended to favor the husband's version and duly instruct the wife to return home, in spite of the overall circumstances that would not predict any apparent potential for improvement in the marital relationship. In 1604, for example, Diego, a black slave of Alonso Martinez de Zayal, *clérigo presbitario* and resident in Tenantzingo, married Clara, a free mulata, who lived in Mexico City. He denounced her in the ecclesiastical court for "having forsaken him" and "for not wishing to pursue further married life with him for the past two years." He asked the court to intervene on his behalf. On 9 January that year, the ecclesiastical court instructed his steward to fetch Clara to court, in order to explain to the judges her reasons for absenting herself from her home and from her married life.

Let us listen carefully to what Clara had to say about the circumstances. Clara appears before the court and explains that "she had lived for already many years as Diego's wife, but contrary to what he claimed, for the past four months or so, her husband had left her and moved to live in Tenantzingo." The court, having reviewed the case, ordered Clara to maintain her marriage with Diego in spite of all that, and go live with him in Tenantzingo.[15]

In 1690, in the indigenous town of Tepozotlán, Sebastián Perez, Agustina Contreras's husband, was well aware of the fact that the ecclesiastical court might sue him for negligence, so he went to court and filed an appeal to search for his wife, who, according to him, "had gone missing already a long time, without having received any news about her."[16] In as yet a very different case, Juan Ruiz of Coyoacán filed a complaint in court against his wife, Ana Pérez, with whom he had been married for the past six years, to whom he declared "he has given everything," but, in return, his wife abandoned him and had moved to live together with her mother. In this case, the presiding judge ordered that the wife's parents "not impede her return to her faithful husband."[17] No doubt, such marriage would not last long, due to the fact that mutual trust and honesty were already fatally impaired. The women's discourses reveal the fully fledged profile of such unhealthy marital bonds: physical cruelty, accompanied by emotional torment, followed by negligence and lack of sustenance. Contrary to Gowing's claims that "women's allegations of life-threatening cruelty were difficult to judge, based on subjective proofs, and hard to measure" (1996, 184), my own case studies, in this and the following chapters, suggest otherwise.

In the personal case of Juana de la Cruz, for example, she appealed before her husband in court, saying that he had deserted her for the past two years "and before that had maltreated her." Her mother, with whom she sought shelter, proceeded, at the same time, to the ecclesiastical court asking for a discharge of the marriage. In response, Sebastián López (the husband), appeared before the court and complained that "his wife and his mother-in-law obliged him to live his life apart from his wife, in another house; they maltreated him with obnoxious words and with threats, and said that he should be sent to China."

The mother-in-law contradicted him by recounting how Sebastián had deserted her daughter two years earlier, during the feast of Corpus Christi, after having mistreated her. However, through the persuasion by a few persons, she finally allowed Sebastián to enter her house and live with her daughter a life of matrimony. But, this lasted for ten days only: "He then took away from her daughter her upper dress and set it on fire, and then volunteered to serve as a soldier in the Philippines; he left this city and set to Puebla de los Ángeles, where he did not declare himself married; he later came back to her house and threatened to do away with her daughter."[18]

As materialized in this case, when the escaping wife would appear in court in person and provide the judges with a detailed account of her ill-treatment, seeking protection from the ecclesiastical court, the court would order the husband to provide his wife with all the necessities for a virtuous life and maintain her and treat her respectfully. In this case, as in others of its kind, the *alcalde del crimen* of the court ordered the husband to be imprisoned for mistreating his wife.[19]

"D. MALTREATMENTS AND CRUELTY"

In this fourth theme one is able to glimpse how physical violence and maltreatment during the early phase of marital life had an irreversible effect on the young wife in seeking to find viable, soothing alternatives. Gabriel Haslip-Viera cites a particular case in which "although Rafaela Balbuena responded to her husband's actions through retaliatory behavior, other women took even more drastic measures in order to disassociate themselves from men whom [sic] they felt were beyond redemption" (1999, 68). Komisaruk emphasizes that "most appeals were filed by women, and they portray disheartening patterns of violence. Though women who filed charges against their husbands professed a belief in notions of mutual obligation, they objected to the realities of their husbands' behavior" (2013, 128).

Isabel de Montoya likewise recounted her own, short-lived marriage experience:

He [Gaspar de la Péria] returned to Mexico City about eight years ago, and asked me if I wished to live with him again. That night he stabbed me with a knife which badly wounded my intestines.

Then he fled and she never saw him again. And she heard that he lives in a small village called Cocula next to Guadalajara, and that he had become very rich. They did not have any children together . . .

"But I had a daughter before my marriage, called Anna María de Montoya, who lives in Mexico City, and she is twenty-four years old, and a few years ago she had asked me to give my permission for her to marry. And I had had another daughter, Juana, who died at the age of a year and a half in Puebla."[20]

Such accounts vividly portray extreme acts of physical violence, enmity, and lack of basic trust that led to the ultimate separation. The direct continuity between the acts of violence and the telling about the two daughters, one still alive and well, which is a relieving presence, and the other, who had died very young, brings in some kind of an outsider's vantage point on her life story and its ramifications.

In Leonor de Toro's case from 1573, for example, during her life together with her spouse in Mexico City, for the past five years, as Leonor complained, the theme of "being left on her own in this world" clearly emerges: "He [Juan Gonzáles, her husband] would beat me with sticks, made me intentionally fall from a horse, and caused me to bleed from lashes, leaving me to die of hunger . . . It came to my knowledge lately that he wishes to expel me from this city and abandon me on my own in a remote place, where I do not have any relatives or anyone that I would be able to rely on, and I know that if I comply, I will die in his hands, stabbed to death by him."[21]

Leonor thus recounted in court how, after only one year of marriage, her husband had left her behind and traveled away from Mexico City to the Mines of Zacatecas, abandoning her and their child with very little to sustain themselves.[22] Since his return to the city, over a month ago, he constantly refused to provide Leonor and their daughter with any costs. In the Mines of Zacatecas, Juan Gonzales took a local indigenous girl as his concubine, for which he was prosecuted by the local vicar. In this case, as in many others of the kind, marital violence coincides with other themes: negligence and lack of trust, not abiding to marital obligations, adultery, and public defamation.[23]

Maltreatment was also in the background of the following case. In 1699, Francisca de San Diego, a widowed mestiza living in Mexico City, appealed to the ecclesiastical court concerning her married daughter, María de la Encarnación, who was married to Cristóbal de Ramos. She recounted how, after long days of maltreatment by her husband, and upon finding him at home together with his concubine, her daughter fetched the fiscal del crimen and his corps of constables. As a consequence of the affair, the husband found himself in prison, while his concubine was forcibly deposited in the *recogimiento* (shelter; House of Correction, seclusion) of María Magdalena, where Francisca's daughter was also deposited, for the sake of protection. Francisca recounted in court how, at the recogimiento, her daughter was suffering from malnutrition, due to the fact that she only received one *real* a day as her daily allowance and was unable to buy food for herself. In 1692, the Real Sala del Crimen (Audiencia court, which heard criminal cases) in Mexico City ordered the transfer of all the women who were staying in the old Misericordia almshouse to the new recogimiento of Santa María Magdalena (Dávila Mendoza 2005, 59). The church law stated that a betrayal on part of one of the partners in the marriage was a legitimate reason for separation via ecclesiastical divorce. In this case, the ecclesiastical judge, nevertheless, refrained from passing a decision toward ecclesiastical divorce, due to the fact that neither one of the parties involved had asked him to do so. However, he acknowledged the fact that the couple should remain apart. Thus, he ordered instead that the husband increase his wife's allowance at the House of Seclusion to one peso a week and that he should comply with his sentence and remain exiled from the city on pain of being sent to the Philippines.[24]

Gertrudis Vargas and Miguel Martines were married on 28 August 1649 at the church of Santa Veracruz, in the very same neighborhood where Isabel de Montoya lived. As Gertrudis described, on Saturday, 8 November that year, during the late evening, while pretending to help her out with taking off her clothes, her husband attempted to strangle her and then with much violence broke the small finger on her right hand. On 17 April 1655, Gertrudis proceeded to complain before the *alcalde ordinario* (jurisdiction sometimes overlapped that of the alcaldes del crimen; he presided over a court of first instance as well as over cabildo meetings when the alcalde mayor and his lieutenant were absent) of the ecclesiastical court in Mexico City, exhibiting before the judges the plain signs of his strangling on her neck.[25] Gertrudis recounted that "without her crying loudly, and overheard by the neighbor, he would surely have killed her ... Ever since, he increasingly restricted her movements, and sold all her belongings, her clothes, her mattress, and linen, that were part of her dowry," and thus, "she remained with no clothes to wear, and with no shoes either."[26] Her wording reflects a state of a total dependence on the male partner, both emotionally and economically, and the vengeful acts on the latter's part if and when the female partner would exhibit any kind of independence and perseverance. On 4 November, having heard and reviewed the accumulated testimony concerning the case, the vicario general instructed that Gertrudis be deposited immediately in the recogimiento of Santa María Magdalena until further notice. Having spent some time there, Gertrudis thereafter appealed to the court for assistance, on the grounds of poverty, "because her husband had liquidated all her assets, and therefore she cannot afford the costs of the lodgings." She then asked the court to approve an alternative shelter for her. In response to her plea, the vicario general instructed the court that she should be removed from the Santa María Magdalena House and deposited at the house of the secretary of the Holy Inquisition, Miguel de Almonazi. At the same time, and under the court's instructions from 4 November, her husband was subsequently confined to house arrest, at his father's home, in the barrio de Montserrat.

One of the more representative cases within this theme in which physical and emotional cruelty and fear are also in the foreground, is that of Francisca Magdalena from 1678. She was an indigenous woman, and the wife of Juan de San Pedro, an *español* from Mexico City, with whom she had lived for the past fourteen years, in the houses of the Marqués del Valle on Tacuba Street, very near to where Isabel de Montoya resided. She petitioned the ecclesiastical court to dissolve their marriage on grounds of "undergoing extreme cruelty and maltreatment on her husband's part, ever since their first days as husband and wife." She also claimed that her husband had never really sustained her properly nor her many children and had even compelled her to provide him with a daily quantity of two *reales*.

Throughout this ordeal Juan de San Pedro maintained a married concubine, for whom he cared, "instead of for his own children and wife." His deceived wife explained in court how her current circumstances evolved:

> And all of this was born out of a foul friendship that he maintained, and that consequently he stopped providing me with the 2 reales daily allowance, being myself so poor, with many children to sustain, and with much work, and due to all this I filed a complaint before your Highnesses judges of the court of this city, that he [my husband] was imprisoned, with the maltreatments, the threats, and all the rest described in my letter, he was sentenced to two years in a *obraje* [large workshop producing textiles and other goods], where he is at present, and now he dares pretending to ask me to accompany him there, wishing to execute, again, his evil intentions against me, and even wants to oblige me to do so, but, I would only wish to be able to live securely, because I am fearful of him, and of being tempted to experience anew his mal intention.[27]

"THE KINDNESS OF NEIGHBORS"

It is highlighted here that friends and neighbors did try to intervene and even deter husbands from acting violently against their spouses.[28] In such accounts one is clearly able to understand the role of what we could describe as "networks of safekeeping" by friends, neighbors, and responsible citizens, as well as the complex women's networks of reciprocities that undermined patriarchal gender relations, and in contra cruel and deserting husbands, was undoubtedly a crucial factor for these plebeian women in taking the initiative within the frameworks of the ecclesiastical or civil courts. Gauderman adds to this by saying that "networks of acquaintances could also aid apprehension of wayward husbands" (2003, 60). Furthermore, such webs of support would consequently serve as the basis for the establishments of "sisterhoods" of mutual trust and self-assistance among single women, after marriages have been dissolved.

Francisca Magdalena herself divulged her agony and suffering to her neighbors, and on several occasions they did come to her rescue and even succeeded in saving her life from her husband's wrath. On one of such occasions, she told them that "he planned to do away with her, and threw a wooden bench at her head, causing her severe bleeding." She was thereafter ushered to the house of a Spanish merchant and a neighbor, who took care of her and stopped her bleeding. The husband, Juan de San Pedro, was thereafter sentenced to serve two years of forced labor in the obraje de Juan de Avila, near Coyoacán. The abused wife, Francisca Magdalena, was to be deposited for safe keeping in the house of don Francisco Cortés de Mendoza, this court's clerical authority.[29] In as yet another case in which friends and neighbors came to the rescue, from 1686, is of Margarita de Porras, the lawful wife of Sebastián Cordero. Margarita presented herself in the ecclesiastical court of the Metropolitan Cathedral in Mexico City and recounted how her husband habitually mistreated her, "forcing her to flee their house from fear." Margarita requested that the ecclesiastical court annul her marriage on that basis. However, by sheer contrast to the earlier case, presented above, in which the mother of the suffering wife intervened on her behalf, and came on her rescue, in what follows, the wife's mother appears to have taken the side of the abusive husband and favored the traditional solution of urging her daughter to resume her marital life. Margarita, therefore, sought help from the ecclesiastical court against her own mother, Josepha de Porras, "because of her hatred towards her, and her forcing her to continue living with her husband." After further deliberation, the court decided to place Margarita in the home of Maestro Miguel Ortiz, a surgeon, and his wife, until the lawsuit would be concluded. Subsequently she was placed by court order in the recogimiento of Santa María Magdalena. There, we find Margarita writing to the court, in third person: "She was currently ill and with no medication, and that she is in danger of dying, and that her husband refused to provide her basic needs, such as food and clothing." So, she requested the court to remove her from there and place her somewhere else, where she could be attended to and cured. Margarita was apparently removed from the recogimiento and placed in the care of Juan de Pareja and his wife. Her husband was notified of the transfer and the court allotted one month for her recovery in this house of de Pareja. Margarita's solicitors present the court with a certificate issued by Maestro Gerónimo Guerrero, a physician, who visited Margarita and granted her *limosna* (charity) for the poor; the doctor testified that Margarita had been ill for over a year. Here, as in other cases, the long process of separation from the abusing husband takes these women from one shelter to another, a process that, no doubt, allows much time for contemplation concerning their destiny. Meanwhile, the husband came to court and claimed that "it has already been two months since my wife complained and appealed to the court against me for mistreating her and forcing her to work for me . . . since which she has already been moved three times from one place to another where she was due to be sheltered." But then comes to the fore the evidence of how Margarita is already molding her new road to recovery: we are told how, one night, when Sebastián (the husband) came to speak with Margarita at Juan de Pareja's store, "she treated him very badly, with foul words and with violence, up to the point at which Juan and his wife had to intervene and take her forcefully back into the house."[30]

In the lawsuit between Gertrudis Vargas and Miguel Martines, who lived in the Callejón de Los Gallos (the Fighting Cocks), in Mexico City, one is also able to see how existing webs of mutual aid by friends and neighbors served as intermediaries between the different spaces.[31] Let us review the testimony: a watchful neighbor, Magdalena de Abrego, was a single mestiza who lived behind the San Gregorio church. She described in the lawsuit how she "had heard loud noises and cries while she was passing beneath the house of this couple." Thereafter, she took the initiative and met the husband outside his house, while his wife was still crying loudly [inside]. When she asked him what went on in their house, he replied that he has beaten his wife, and that "as her lawful husband, he is fit to do so." The same neighbor witnessed how Gertrudis had been repeatedly beaten by her husband and that she was left with no clothes at all. Magdalena was also well aware of the fact that Gertrudis's husband, once he had acknowledged that his doings had been exposed by the neighbors in this barrio, "finally planned to do away with his wife."[32] Another of Gertrudis's acquaintances, María de la Oy, was a married mulata. When she came to her house to fetch a hat that she had borrowed from her, she found Gertrudis lying on the floor, tied up, with blood running all the way down her face and neck. When she asked her what had happened to her, Gertrudis replied that it was due to her husband's beating her. When the husband entered the room he forced María de la Oy to leave their house. The latter testified in court that she was well aware of the fact that the beatings were carried out on a daily basis by the husband. Two others of Margarita's neighbors also described to the court the situation inside and outside the home of Sebastián and Margarita. One of them, Pedro de Mesa, a tailor who lived in the same house, witnessed how "the door to the couple's house was always closed" and how he daily heard fighting between them; "he has also seen her husband playing *naipes* (cards) and betting on cocks in the *corral* (courtyard) of the house," next to the La Merced Convent.[33]

Don Francisco Bernabé, *administrador de ingenio* (administrator of a sugar mill), testified in court that the couple's *aposento* (rented room) "was virtually located on the street"; one day, upon passing next to the house, on his way home, "he heard loud voices and lots of noise coming from there; he entered the room and he saw the husband violently beating his wife." When Bernabé attempted to intervene he was also beaten by Sebastián, and the latter left the room accompanied by the witness. "He proceeded immediately to her mother's place, *which stood on the corner*, whereupon knocking violently on her door he entered the house and told the mother to go urgently to fetch her daughter because otherwise he would kill her." Don Francisco Bernabé testified how he knew that "Margarita had already been pregnant once from her husband and that during her pregnancy he had beaten her badly, and that running the risk of miscarriage, she went to an indigenous man, who took her to his mother's house, where she remained for twelve full days, during which she was left with nothing at all."[34] Doña Melchora de San Juan, testified that "to be able to go out of her aposento to the street, Margarita would ask her to lend her some clothes and a gown of hers, because her husband would not buy her clothes nor would he provide her with linen for her bed . . . and had taken away from her all that she had brought along as her dowry."

It appears from the above, as well as from many other lawsuits cited here, that public defamation of the cruel husband was in effect a public ritual of degradation that chastised such husbands even before going to court. Gauderman likewise asserts that "wives who did not publicly air their grievances with their husbands were at a disadvantage when they brought formal criminal charges against their spouses, because they could not rely on the validation of outside testimony."[35] Seeking ecclesiastical divorce on the grounds of violence was indeed the most common factor to be found among plebeian women of colonial society in Mexico. The total number of cases found is meager—only 237 cases—and can therefore represent only an extremely partial sample. Nevertheless, this figure is, indeed, compatible with the figure presented by Dora Dávila Mendoza, namely, 300 appeals for divorce. Dávila Mendoza's survey covers the period between 1702 and 1800.[36] The general scarcity of the appeals could either indicate that formal appeals for ecclesiastical divorce were far from being a widespread phenomenon, that many of the documents were destroyed during the nineteenth-century wars, or that the overwhelming majority of dissolved marriages—in particular, among the lower echelons of colonial society—never reached the ecclesiastical courts. Many women chose not to undergo the formal process in the ecclesiastical courts but separated *informally*. Moreover, the higher number of españoles among them indicates that they were less concerned about this process than the castas, the former having originated from more powerful families and with the needed connections within the church to resolve their cases more smoothly. By comparison, of the total of eighty-one legal cases studied by Arrom concerning ecclesiastical divorce, merely 17 percent involved men and women from the lower classes of Mexico City (Arrom 1995, 275). Among the female claimants in the official records whose petitions for "ecclesiastical divorce" were approved, 24 were dubbed españolas, 11 mulatas, 6 blacks, and 4 mestizas, while among the male claimants, 26 were españoles, 9 mulatos, 6 blacks, and 7 mestizos. All the rest of the claimants in our sample were not categorized according to race. Notwithstanding the size of this sample, what it would also indicate is that for a small number of women, the torturous experiences of cruelty and molestations were so unbearable that they served as a powerful reason for them to initiate the dissolution of their marriage.

If we analyze the above data, we are able to see that 69 percent of the total cases involved specified a reason from the categories established by this survey, while 31 percent did not specify a particular reason for seeking separation. One also notices that maltreatments and cruelty reported by women against their husbands constitute the highest percentage of the total reasons for seeking "ecclesiastical divorce"; that is, 38 percent and 6 percent of the cases cited direct threats and intents of assassination as the major reason for seeking separation. That is, if we combine the two figures together, then, 44 percent of all cases brought into the ecclesiastical courts may have involved alleged direct physical violence by men as an explanation for why these women chose to remain alone. The data suggest that spousal cruelty was indeed a trigger for separations to be permitted after repeated court appearances, if at all. While judges showed sympathy for the plight of women, they also reminded women to fulfill their roles as wives; hence judges acted in favor of adhering to the institution of marriage, much more than in favor of other considerations such as curbing family violence. Complaints by men against their wives that they "did not abide by their marital obligations," and therefore sought separation, constituted 9 percent. *Men's* appeal to the ecclesiastical courts to oblige their wives to return home also constitute 9 percent, while, by comparison, women's appeals for this sake constitute only 2 percent, which is clearly explainable by the fact that there were many more women who chose *not to return home* to their former circumstances, than men, and preferred instead to deposit themselves voluntarily in a *casa de depósito* (a shelter run by an acclaimed citizen). These figures are comparable to those presented by Dávila Mendoza for the eighteenth century. Accordingly, 42 percent of all cases of appeals for separation were based on "maltreatment," 14 percent on adultery, 6 percent on not complying with matrimonial obligations, and 2.3 percent due to abandonment of the house. Nonetheless, in contrast to this study, the author does not

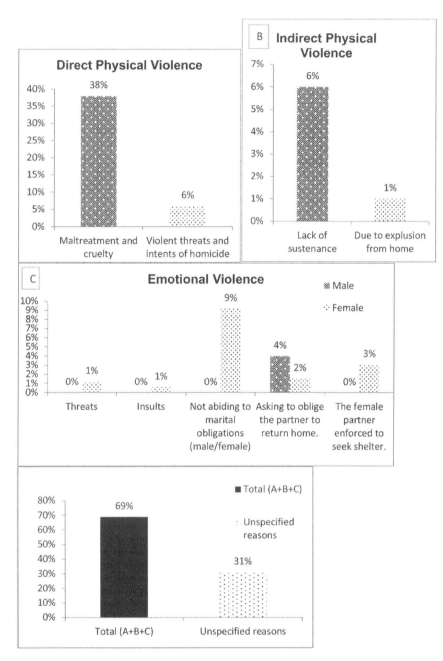

FIGURE 2.1. Reasons for seeking "ecclesiastical divorce": the quantitative facet. By the author.

distinguish among various categories within the larger term "maltreatment" (2005, 187). Separated women were also deposited in convents, *casas de honra* (households of honorary citizens), or recogimientos for their own protection.[37]

One should clarify at this point that recogimientos were houses of seclusion under the guidance of the religious orders, to where promiscuous women, both single or married, were usually sent to improve their conduct, and perform punitive works after they had been caught in illicit sexual behavior. Working in the sex trade as prostitutes was a common way to earn a living for both lower-class married and single plebeian women, if living conditions worsened. Isabel herself testified that during part of her life in Puebla, she practiced prostitution (see also Guy 1991, 1–4). Casas de depósito were, according to Lee M. Penyak, "less severe than other punitive institutions"—that is, private houses—run by "honorary citizens" in which women were housed by court order as a safe haven against abusive and negligent husbands or partners. Nevertheless, as Penyak herself concludes after a contradictory example, "Depósito, therefore, might not only be used to place women in temporary custody, but also as part of their final jail sentence . . . punitive institution into one that could protect them and provide them with the time they need to assess their best course of action."[38] Yet another alternative was the *hospicio de pobres* (poorhouse) or the household of an "honorary family," where the women would receive "proper care and education in a Christian environment," if the case was of minor concern. Nonetheless, all these houses and shelters were not regarded as penalizing institutions by the women seeking asylum. This pattern is corroborated by the presence of 4 percent of the cases in which men complained to the courts that their wives "had abandoned home" and gone to live in what they considered a safe haven, preferably a casa de depósito, or even a convent.

Let us read now a typical letter sent by a deserted husband to the city authorities:

"Juan de Soto, vecino de esta ciudad y marido y conjunta persona de Tomasa López, parezco ante V.A y digo que habrá tiempo de dos años poco más o menos, que la susodicha se halla ausenta de mi lado y compañía sin hacer vida maridable, el cual ha sido sin causa ni motivo que para ello le haya dado en cuya atención que hallarse al presente en la casa de María López, la madre de la susdicha. Por tanto, a vuestra alteza, pido y suplico se sirva de mandarse ponga la susodicha en el recogimiento de Santa María Magdalena, en donde estoy pronto a sustentarla y darle lo necesario atentar no querer estar en mi compañía en que reconozco. Merced de la grandeza de V.A, juro a Dios y ofrezco información."

[Juan de Soto, resident of this city and the husband of Tomasa López, I appear before you, your excellencies, and inform that there may have been more or less two years that the abovementioned avoided being beside me and in my company, and avoided maintaining a life of matrimony, which was without any apparent given reason or motive; she is to be found now in the house of María López, the mother of the afore-mentioned. Consequently, I plead before you, Your Excellencies, to instruct to place the aforementioned in the House of Seclusion of Santa María Magdalena, where I am available to sustain her and provide her with all that is necessary, while she attempts not to wish to be in my company, *which I do acknowledge* (emphasis added). I pledge to God and offer information.][39]

Listening attentively to these abandoned women's claims, in their own words, one is able to interpret such a changing position in life—of no longer willing to play the sacrificial role—as both an intrinsic and an implicit predisposition on the part of such women to give up marital life for the sake of claiming their freedom, of becoming voluntarily single, and heading toward the alternative household model, described in chapter 3.

3

Female-Headed Households

I first met Juana de Sossa in Cholula, in Mónica's place, where she lived for a while. She came there with her two daughters, who lived permanently in Puebla, and said she was looking for a remedy for one of her daughters, Isabel, who was abandoned by the man who had made her pregnant. (Isabel de Montoya's testimony)

While on a visit to Huejotzingo, looking for my neighbor, Marco de Siluo, to whom I owed some money, I passed by Montoya's house . . . Montoya had offered me to become a lodger at her place. (María de Rivera's testimony)

Women-headed households in colonial Mexico, "sisterhoods" in particular, created a solid alternative to the paterfamilias and the patriarchal family model. Female-headed households functioned as pseudoconsaguinal "families" that included either biological, fostered, or adopted children, as well as functioned as alternative frameworks for the materialization of inheritance and self-sustenance. As shown, the perseverance and strength of women-headed households, as a new model for a social concordat, especially in urban areas, stood up in sheer contrast to Spanish code of law represented in the Spanish matrimonial model. The basic questions tackled here are: How precisely did female-headed households form? How did these alternative families and households actually function? What was the place of children in these households and how were they perceived? The essence of this chapter derives from the three following themes, introduced in chapter 2: (a) "Being Left on Her Own in This World," (b) "I Felt Deceived," (d) "Maltreatment and Cruelty."

DOI: 10.5876/9781607329633.c003

The roots of the first theme were traced in particular to the lack of emotional and material care and guidance, as well as a subtle lack of what psychoanalysis calls "holding" during early childhood and adolescence, either by their biological parents, or by adult figures in their early life. Winnicott first utilized the term "holding environment" to ascribe the optimal environment to "good enough" parenting. He emphasized that emotional problems developed when a person had been deprived such holding environments in childhood (Finlay 2015, chap. 5). The second theme was treated within the context of bad occurrences with early male partners, and mistrust toward the possibility of leading trustful and mutually respecting relationships with men. The fourth theme dealt, in particular, with severe experiences of violence with male partners/spouses. All those, woven together with the contents below, provide us with a sensible explanation as to why these women chose to create their own sisterhoods and households, in which mutual assistance, emotional and material guidance, and sharing that they found in such frameworks versus the distrustful world outside, became so essential. There, it could also be safer to raise their own children, as well as foster other children.

In his article in the special issue of the *Journal of Family History* 16, no. 3 (1991), dedicated entirely to the issue of female households, Robert McCaa converts a quantitative-historical vantage point into a qualitative one: "The central issue for future studies of the Latin American family is no longer a matter of ascertaining the frequency of female householders . . . but rather to interpret context, perception, and change" (1991, 211; see also Kuznesof 1989, 168–86). It is argued here that female-headed households became, more or less, a stable haven for individual women, as well as for several women together. In her study of the history of the family during the early modern era, Beatrice Gottlieb illustrates how the notion of household and family in Europe tend to overlap: "Co-residence is often considered more important in defining a family than blood relationship" (Gottlieb 1993, 7). For the nineteenth century, Silvia Arrom has found that in Mexico City female-headed households were even more common among higher and lighter-skinned echelons of society than among blacks and mulatas (1985, 151–52). My own sources for the sixteenth to the eighteenth century show a different picture altogether, with the balance in favor of the latter. A possible explanation for this apparent discrepancy is that the formal data are misleading: indeed, many of these shared households were registered as being owned by women from the middling to upper classes, whereas in effect most of its tenants were poor women who could not afford houses of their own.[1] As is further argued, perhaps one of the most decisive essences in those women's decision to become single, as is gleaned from such sources, was their substantial reliance on webs of mutual aid and support by other single women of their class or of other echelons of local society in their immediate surroundings.

A "NEW FAMILY" MODEL

In considering "singleness" versus "family" and "household," one has to define better the latter terms. According to Elizabeth Dore, "the first refers to kin groups constituted by blood and/or marriage," while the second to "residence units" (1997, 101–17). However, "family" could undoubtedly also constitute an unmarried couple—whether mixed gender or the same gender, living in a long-term cohabitation, together with their offspring—or three to four single women living together in a shared, female-headed household, with their children. As for the latter case, family and household terms are merged. In this very context, I argue, single plebeian women did form new family models. To define such a model, I am tempted to "borrow" sixteenth-century Nahuatl kinship terminology because, leaving blood ties and marriage aside, such terminology resembles the arrangements discussed here in a number of ways, primarily the way in which the tenants perceived their framework of "being together." Notwithstanding, I am well aware that indigenous presence in such households, in Mexico City and in Puebla, was small. The Nahua lived in large and complex arrangements within the *calli*, which functioned as a conglomerate of couples related to one another and to the calli's head by blood or through marriage. Such complex frameworks sometimes included up to thirteen persons, who, for example, were made up of two extended families, including single young males and females, and four married couples (McCaa 2003, 23–48). In their daily confrontation with a myriad of hardships, single women in early colonial Mexico—street vendors, clothing and flower sellers, seamstresses, housemaids, cooks, and servants in their profession—appeared to opt for the creation of "sheltering" sisterhoods within an enclosed space, which in turn became their safe haven.[2] This space served many functions, binding unrelated women together in an unending chain of reciprocity. It appears from the records that alternative households headed by single women consisted mainly of matriarchal-matrilocal patterns, with the female head normally coming from a better socioeconomic background than her tenants, as caretaker of the daily needs and local arrangements. By comparison, in her study of single women in sixteenth-century England, C. Peters claims that "the headship of a household by a never married woman, and even by children, was perceived as a possible, if not necessarily ideal, solution" (1997, 330). Single plebeian women who sought shelter in such alternative kinships were predominantly deserted women, widows, and women who remained unmarried throughout their lives. I seek to elaborate on both the social and personal domains of the alternative household, as they unfold from the sources.

In Nahuatl, there is no expression equivalent to a "family," emphasizing instead the *huanyolque*, "those who live with one," or *calli*, that is, the household compound (as a structure) and those included within it, whether of consanguineal relations, or *tlacamecayotl*, namely, lineal kin relationships. In Alonso de Molina's Nahuatl-Spanish dictionary (1571), one finds a number of correlating entries:

> *cenyeliztli* = "being together," or, people who share the same household; *cencalli* = "one household," *cencaltin* = "those who reside in the same house"; *cemithualtin* = "those who reside in the same patio," and *techan tlaca* = "people in someone's household" (Molina [1571] 2001, 16–17, 92). The *ithualli* was an open patio, in which daily socialization materialized between the tenants (Molina [1571] 2001, 42), as it was in such shared female-headed households including their offspring, whether biological or fostered (see below), while the term *cihuacalli* was given to "women's house."

The common denominator of all these Nahuatl entries is that they emphasize the place and environment where shared lives are being maintained, but none of them states the origins of the ties among those living together. Moreover, they express an idea closer to a "household," rather than a "family," which is similar in this sense to what the female-headed household projected, although the single women sharing such a household were not tied to each other in any way whatsoever through kinship or marriage; therefore, it is definitely accurate to name such ties as "pseudo-consanguineal," and, therefore, they did indeed form a new family model.

The institutionalization of single women's households in mid-colonial Mexico had wide-ranging repercussions and effects on mid-colonial values, gender concepts, perceptions of marriage, life choices, and how honor and shame were construed. Steve Stern, in contrast to Patricia Seed, argued that subaltern women and men in fact developed their own ideas about legitimate gender authority.[3] Such arrangements lasted sometimes far longer than what Haslip-Viera recounts: "Despite a social environment that discouraged women from living alone or in groups, they were able to maintain this arrangement for two years, supporting themselves by spinning cloths and making candle wicks for various entrepreneurs before they were apprehended" (Haslip-Viera 1999, 97). Women's strategies for survival integrated those alternative family frameworks, their webs of self-reliance and mutual assistance, household arrangements, and childcare of their illegitimate children. Such intimate webs of interaction and reciprocity, as is argued here, definitely transcended ethnic and racial boundaries and associations (Bennett 2003, 90). Analogously, Herman L. Bennett's describes: "On 2 September 1645, the provisor and scribe perhaps unwittingly registered how household, occupational, and residential ties intersected with legal status, ethnicity, race, and a Christian consciousness. The existing social networks, forged in diverse spatial contexts, extended from their initial locus and ultimately linked specific individuals who were dispersed throughout the urban labyrinth" (90). Although the following description by Cope can represent a point of departure—"Ethnicity was a social reality in colonial

Mexico City. But race was a social label rather than a strictly economic one. The most intimate social relationships tended to occur among members of the same racial group. These, in turn, served as the basis for a branching network of less intimate links, which quickly penetrated into all sectors of plebeian society" (1994, 83).—these networks were more complex. As is gleaned from the sources utilized in this book, female-headed households, transcended class, racial and ethnic barriers, that are usually emphasized under the heading of the caste system.

On many occasions the mere existence of such alternative frameworks drove these women to part with their violent husbands, abandon their homes, and, very soon, join existing female-headed households in their surroundings. Separated women were usually first deposited in convents, *casas de honra* (households of honorary citizens), or *recogimientos* for their own protection, but shortly afterward, they safely integrated within existing networks of assistance among other single women. They usually started at an existing *casa de vecindad* (tenement house) and, later, moved to female-headed households, such as *aposentos*/cuartos (separate habitations, which will be discussed later in this chapter), rooms, or apartments for rent, or within individual houses owned by wealthy Spanish or Creole widows. It is noteworthy that all these houses and shelters were never considered by the women seeking asylum as penalizing institutions (see Penyak 1999, 84–99).

How precisely did female-headed households form? Cases involving single women living together abound in the province of Puebla records for the period stretching between 1629 and 1662. Most of them cite single, caste women, either widowed or who had never married; they usually lived together and shared strategies of survival. One of the records tells us about how such women entered a female-headed household. Isabel de Montoya recalls her phase of becoming adult and independent: she had moved to Puebla, fleeing from her violent husband, Juan de la Péria. In the nearby town of Cholula, Isabel had met Isabel de los Angeles, twenty-four, together with los Angeles's mother, Juana, who was Isabel's neighbor in Huejotzingo. Isabel de los Angeles, a single, Spanish plebeian woman, was a weaver by profession. She was born in the peripheral small town of San Juan de los Llanos Libres, near Puebla. Isabel de los Angeles was pregnant at the time from Antonio de Candias, a man from Tlaxcala, who had sexual relations with her as a young woman with promises of marriage, and then left her for good. On one occasion, while still in Cholula, Isabel de Montoya informed Isabel de Los Angeles's mother, Juana, that "her daughter was extremely weak, and that she had had a miscarriage, and then told her that she would entrust her daughter to God's will." After a few days, Isabel de Montoya went to meet Isabel de Los Angeles's mother in Puebla, while she herself was on her way back home and reproached her for not having cared for her daughter, as she had promised her earlier on in Cholula. Some months later, Juana returned to Puebla, where she was offered lodgings by Isabel de Montoya at her place. Montoya had also advised Juana that "she had sown seeds in the earth, to know whether the man who had left Isabel would come back to marry her."[4]

FEMALE-HEADED HOUSEHOLDS: THE DEMOGRAPHIC DATA

My quantitative records from Mexico City rely upon a door-to-door partial census that covered eleven different barrios of this city, as well as additional residential areas, including small alleys, bridges, and squares in this part of the city, which was conducted between 1670 and 1695. In total, there were 53,313 inhabitants (see appendix 2). The figures gleaned from this survey *are drastically lower* than previously estimated in similar studies, except for Poska's study of the Buenos Aires survey of 1767. In order to find out the exact number of women-headed households and their inhabitants, and thereafter calculate their percentage vis-à-vis the total number of households surveyed and the total number of inhabitants, I have extracted from this census only the distinct areas that correspond to locations in which those particular households were counted. The total inhabitants counted in this partial census amounted to 6,408 with 1,466 households (the third table in appendix 2). Among them, I was able to locate 278 female-headed households (19 percent of the total households) shared by single women in which there were 611 single women tenants (10 percent of the total population), belonging to different strata of society. By comparison, for the parish of El Sagrario in Puebla, Miguel Marín Bosch indicates that 1,777 (44 percent of all households) were headed by women.[5] And Pilar Gonzalbo Aizpuru's analysis of the same repository from 1777 informs us that among 4,246 households surveyed, 45 percent were headed by single women (2005, 282, table 35). In his study on Guadalajara, Thomás Calvo outlines that 163 out of the 346 households in Guadalajara for which he found data (47 percent) were headed by women. In Calvo's words, "the female heads of households were often condemned to such a status once they stopped cohabitating, due to old age, or became isolated widows." (984, 203; see also Calvo 1989, 292–93, 297). In her research on variations in family household structure and domestic residence in late-colonial Celaya, Mexico, Catherine Doenges also notes that in the urban area of Celaya, single and widowed women headed 20 percent of all households; 15 percent incorporated non-kin members into their households, mainly servants and other subaltern women; moreover, 40 percent of Celaya's 965 boarders lived in households headed by women (1993, 166–72).

The average female-headed, shared households registered, excluding tenement houses, consisted of 3.25 single women. Individual houses figured prominently in the barrio de San Pablo; there we find thirty-nine such houses, with a total

TABLE 3.1. Types of female-headed shared households in Mexico City, 1678

Area surveyed	No. tenement houses (total no. of tenants)	No. of separate rooms Aposentos/ cuartos (total no. of boarders)	No. of individual houses (total no. of tenants)
Barrio de la Misericordia	Casa de recogidas (3)	0	
Barrio de Montserrat	1 (8)	0	5 (16)
Barrio de Necaltictlan	0	0	3 (9)
Barrio de San Antonio (Coyoacán)	0	0	2 (7)
Barrio de San Pablo	4 (21)	0	39 (84)
Barrio del Hornillo	2	3 (7)	11 (31)
Barrio de La Merced	1 (3)		8 (21)
Barrio de Santacruz	0		12 (30)
Puente de Balbanera	3 (11)	6 (12)	4 (11)
Casa de la Puente de Vigas	1	4 (7)	5 (8)
Plazuela de los Gallos	3	14 (18)	16 (38)
Callejón de Jamaica	1	3 (4)	4 (8)
Callejón de Trápala	0		3 (7)
Atrás de La Merced	1	2 (4)	2 (7)
Puente de La Merced	1	2 (3)	3 (6)
Puente de la Leña	1	3 (6)	5 (16)
Callejón Dorado	1	4 (5)	4 (6)
Barrio La Trinidad	3	6 (11)	5 (16)
Puente de San Lázaro			1 (2)
Barrio Tomatlan (San Agustín)	1	6 (12)	8 (19)
Barrio de San Sebastián	4	14 (27)	13 (32)
1ª cuadra Puente de Santo Domingo	1	4 (7)	2 (5)
4ª Cuadra Aduana		3 (9)	2 (6)
5ª Cuadra. Calle de Santo Domingo		3 (4)	1 (3)
Enfrente del Portal de Santo Santo Domingo		2 (3)	2 (6)

continued on next page

TABLE 3.1.—*continued*

Area surveyed	No. tenement houses (total no. of tenants)	No. of separate rooms Aposentos/ cuartos (total no. of boarders)	No. of individual houses (total no. of tenants)
6ª cuadra		Tienda (4)	1 (1)
Portales de la Catedral	0	2 (4)	3 (12)
Cuadra del Empedradillo	0	3 (9)	1 (3)
Total	29 (46)	84 (156)	165 (410)

of eighty-four boarders (including the owners). One notable example is a house owned by Antonia de Solís in the barrio de San Sebastián, in which seven other single women resided. In the barrio de la Misericordia, in one female-headed household, for example, there were three women registered; two out of the four boarders in this house were titled *españolas* (either Spanish or Creole women), as they are named *doñas*; on the sixth cuadra of Santo Domingo, there was one single *casa y tienda* (a house with an adjoining shop, stall, or storing space, normally on the street level, with the living area on the upper floor) in which four tenants were registered as well as a total of eighty-four *aposentos/cuartos* (separate habitations: rooms or apartments for rent), in which 156 single boarders lived. In the barrio de la Trinidad, for example, we find registered doña Teresa de Santigüi's apartment, where she, as the owner of the place, lived with two other single women boarders, doña María de Perea and Ventura Benitez, from apparently different social affiliations. Residential areas, such as the Plazuela de los Gallos, in the barrio de San Sebastián in Mexico City, for example, included fourteen separate rooms, with twenty-seven single women boarders.[6]

In 1662, Isabel de Montoya lived in the small alley behind the church of San Juan de Dios, in the barrio de Santa Clara. There, she rented rooms to two single women boarders in another house she owned on Donceles Street, each of whom paid rent of four reales a month. Subsequently, some of the rooms in this house were rented to five different boarders, each of whom paid between four and six reales a month (11 reales +10 *maravedís* =1 *ducado*).[7] By comparison, around 1670, the monthly rent for a full house in Seville, Spain, was around 3 to 4 reales a month, so that by comparison, the monthly rent of a single room within a house in Mexico City was drastically higher and therefore the economic ability of an average household maid to rent a room of her own, during the mid-seventeenth century was problematic.

In the Santa Veracruz quarter, Donceles Street apparently constituted a "mixed" neighborhood composed of the affluent and the famous, living side by side with

FIGURE 3.1. The Santa Veracruz area, where Isabel de Montoya lived during the mid-seventeenth century; the church building to the right side of the aqueduct, at the center of the image, is the Santa Veracruz Parish Church, where Isabel was baptized, and the building in front of it is the San Juan de Dios Hospital. The garden across the viaduct is the Alameda. Facing the Alameda is the Corpus Christi Collegiate. Biombo de la Conquista de México y vista de la ciudad de México, Óleo sobre tela / Bastidor de madera con trabajo en blanco de España (carbonato de calcio) y hoja de oro, fines del siglo XVIII. © Colección Museo Franz Mayer, Mexico City.

more numerous humble citizens. This residence of poor and rich in close proximity was a very usual phenomenon for the time, and it was only around the mid-nineteenth century that residential areas became increasingly separated by class. Likewise, in 1647, for example, we find living in the same street the lead canon of the Mexico City Cathedral, Dr. Juan Nieto de Avalos, who in 1645 became the canon of the cathedral in Puebla and the representative of Bishop Palafox in the Holy Office, where Montoya had probably met him during one of her interrogations. Also living in Donceles Street was the priest of the parish of the Santa Veracruz, Lorenzo Vital de Figueroa (González Rodríguez 2004). In the nearby houses of the *cofradía* (confraternity) of the Santíssimo Sacramento also resided a thirty-year-old single woman named Catalina de Arcila, whose profession was to teach small girls (possibly orphans) to work, read and write, and pray.[8] Doña Isabel Velázquez de la Cueva was the widow of Capitán Juan Gutiérrez Gorilla, who resided on the parallel Tacuba Street, in the Las Brivescas houses, next to the *alguacil mayor* (town sheriff). Among them, also, were men and women of African descent, who had originated from Angola. Bennett describes how "on August 26, 1645, four individuals 'from Angola' entered Santa Veracruz's parish church to request a marriage license. Diego, a widower enslaved to Pedro Gómes de Piñeda, and Margarita, a widow enslaved to Juan García Calabe, both repeated a performance with which they were intimately familiar through their previous marriages to Cristiana and Juan. (Bennett 2003, 88)." In 1678, there were 440 households registered on this street that included a total of 1,500 inhabitants.[9] According to Sonya Lipsett-Rivera's findings, the rich and poor lived in close proximity to one another, sometimes in the same building, with the poor occupying the lower floors and the wealthier on the upper floors.[10] In the Rich Collection, University of California, Berkeley (UC BERKELEY BANC MSS M-M 1738-1743), one finds originals and certified contemporary copies of documents tracing the history from 1675 to 1815 of a particular house and lot variously described as situated in the "Hornillo" or "Santa Cruz" ward of Mexico City or "by the Manzanares Bridge" and eventually bequeathed by María Teresa Gómez Calván for charitable purposes under the administration of the Congregación del Santísimo Cristo de Burgos. Included are records of transfer through direct sale, auction, and inheritance, as well as evaluations, petitions, judicial decisions, certifications, and a floor plan of the house, and background material dating from as early as 1612.

The living quarters of female-headed, shared households in barrios such as the above, were made up of *vivendas* (a suite of rooms), which were distinguished from cuartos (single-room apartments that were usually located on the street level). Individual houses figured prominently in the barrio de San Pablo, in which we find thirty-nine of them, with a total of eighty-four boarders (including the owners).

One notable example is a house owned by Antonia de Solís in the barrio de San Sebastián, in which seven other single women resided. On the ground floor lived the servants and maids of the household and the rooms were sometimes rented out to the poor and their kin (Haslip-Viera 1999, 12). Most of the shared rooms in such households were characterized by a constant replacement of tenants, as many were unable to pay even the minimal rent (ibid., 33) We should also keep in mind that most of these women lodgers—who generally served as wet-nurses, cooks, and household servants—kept a room of their own in their master's or mistress's household; they returned home late, to their private lodgings once work had finished.[11] For example, Josefa de Saldívar, a single maid, was a subletter of an aposento in the inner courtyard of a house situated behind the convent of Our Lady of Guadalupe and owned by Antonio Ramírez, a Spanish baker. The rent was minimal—2 pesos monthly—but the conditions were accordingly: *jacales* (reed and adobe shacks), lodging mainly indigenous women who presumably served as day laborers in odd jobs throughout the city, only to return to their native towns of origin on weekends (Cope 1994). Around 1650, single, young women, such as Ana María Vázquez ("light-skinned"), who was part of a large population of labor migrants arriving in Mexico City from as far away as Santiago de Guatemala, could only afford to find a single room for rent in a house owned by Josepha, a single mestiza. The latter accused Ana María of stealing her possessions.[12] Ana María, like many others in her situation, became a servant. We are well aware that young women often entered into contractual relations with women of higher social class, to serve in their households so as to provide for their bread and mattress to sleep on. The monthly salary of a *criada* (housemaid) in charge of raising the mistress's children, which was the likely occupation of some of those women, amounted to four pesos or four reales each week (16 reales a month; 1 peso = 4 reales). During this period, María de Ahumada, for example, raised the grandsons of doña María de Quirós, for a period of thirteen months. María de Ahumada later denounced her mistress for having refused to pay her the full salary she was owed, which amounted to fifty-two pesos.[13] Usually, the contract was issued on condition that the nominee would be above twenty-five. An example is the service contract issued to Ana María—a free mulata "who was said to be above the age of 25"—to provide services for two years in the household of Juan de Rivera, a public prosecutor, during which the latter was obliged to provide her with food and lodgings, cure her of her diseases, and pay her the sum of two pesos in reales at the end of each month; Ana María, on her part, was obliged "not to be absent from service and to do all that he ordered her to do." In the barrio de Tomaclan, we find the aposento of Leonor de López del Castillo, in which two other boarders lived. In addition, there were 165 individual houses or private dwellings headed by women in which, all in all, 410 women, coming from different castes and strata, shared their living either as free lodgers or as boarders (paying a monthly rent).

Kim Phillips has argued—from the evidence of low wages—that "it is difficult to see how such harsh working conditions could have in general held a high degree of economic and emotional independence for young women" (2003, 131).

PUBLIC HOUSING

The types of public, residential units identified by us as registered in the survey carried out as a partial census between 1670 and 1678 were a casa de recogidas (house of seclusion) and a casa y tienda. Before 1585, in Mexico City there were only three religious institutions in which women could be placed for rehabilitation: the Magdalen house of Jesús de la Penitencia, the Colegio de Niñas Mestizas, and the recogimiento of Santa Mónica, which was the latest penitentiary to be established in Mexico City in 1582, and the goals of which were "coercion and surveillance of unruly women of the elite." As its founder claimed, the house also aimed to discipline women of the elites against resorting to the growing tendency of dissolving marriages and curbing excesses among the women of Mexico City.[14] During the last decades of the seventeenth century, the Casa de Misericordia was founded as a house of seclusion for young and unwed women of the upper classes or for married women who were separated from their husbands, and in which they were obliged to pay for their maintenance. The monthly rent for such casa y tienda was about twenty-five pesos *de oro común* (type of basic metal from which the coins were manufactured), basically, about 2.5 *reales*. Furthermore, there were, in addition, aposentos/cuartos, individual houses owned by wealthy Spanish or Creole widows, and casas de vecindad—tenement houses (Melé 2006, 43). In the *Diccionario de la Real Academia* of Spain, the definition for *casa de vecindad* is: "La que contiene muchas viviendas reducidas, por lo común con acceso a patios y corresponderos." Patrice Melé comments that "the tenement house, a particular form of a popular living space, had been converted into a symbol of degradation of the old household unit . . . they were not numerous in the central barrios, that were predominated by edifices for rent. Tenement houses were often the direct result of the death of their former owner, if he or she left no heirs behind" (2006, 43).[15] Convents also owned large portions of this city's rented properties. Cope notes that during the late seventeenth century, "the Convent of Balvanera alone rented out eighty-eight units (stores and residences) in fifty-three buildings" (1994, 30). Casas de vecindades were made up of several apartments located on the upper floor and internally divided into separate rooms that their owners would rent out by the room. On the street level, the ground floor was either used as a shop and for the storing of merchandize or rented out to poorer tenants (Bailey-Glasco 2010, 39). Such separate rooms were sometimes extremely small and unaired; such conditions, obviously, did not allow the possibility of a male partner residing there, nor for the woman to give birth there. By comparison, in her study of domestic spaces in colonial Tucumán, Romina Zamora finds that "the rooms for rent represented an extremely important income in the [urban] domestic economy . . . the quantity of available rooms for rent implied that city dwellers were prepared to accommodate a steady number of occasional residents that could, in turn, substantially alter the urban composition and dynamics . . . In reality, the renters were not merely occasional, but that numerous renters lived permanently or during long periods of time" (Zamora 2010: 6). Moreover, as Zamora emphasizes, more than half of the nonpeninsular population lived in such households under the status of dependents, 65 percent of which were women.[16]

Tenement houses, with multiple tenants, were originally destined mainly for paupers, but not exclusively. Tenement houses in the barrio San Pablo, for example, included nine single women sharing their lodgings. The establishment of tenement houses within the barrios was sometimes the initiative of individuals, but normally the city council was involved. In order to establish a tenement house one needed an authorization either from the city council or from a religious institution, as for example, in the case of one of those houses in the barrio San Pablo, which was opened after a certificate was obtained from a priest of the parish of La Merced. The survey includes twenty-nine such houses, distributed in all of the barrios surveyed. Although most of the tenement houses surveyed did not report the exact number of tenants in each, in each one of those that did provide the surveyor with figures, one finds between four and nine single women tenants, coming from different ethnic affiliations of local society, who also included Spanish women among them, possibly former nobles' widows who had become destitute, as the titles of some of them, indeed, demonstrate.

TOWARD AN OVERALL DEMOGRAPHIC ESTIMATE
OF SINGLE WOMEN IN NEW SPAIN

Scrutinizing and classifying sample records of registered baptisms of *castas* (namely, blacks, *mulatos*, and a few indigenous persons) in the parish of the Sagrario Metropolitano in Mexico City (the cathedral and its surrounding barrio) from 1672 to 1688, one finds 4,667 baptized. Of all the mothers of these newborns, 54 percent were registered by the local priest as "single mothers," who had illegitimate children baptized; the mothers were between twenty and forty years old. By comparison, married mothers made up 46 percent only. The records indicate that officiating clergy were instructed to set aside a special day for the administering of the sacrament of baptism to the castas, while the *españoles* and *gachupines*, Creoles, and indigenous population were told to come separately on different days. The parish baptismal books fully recorded illegitimate offspring's reception of the sacrament, adding a note that "the father was unknown." If both parents would not identify themselves, their baby could not be recorded as a *hijo natural* but was listed instead as *expósito*, meaning foundling, abandoned, or undesired. The fact that there is not an instance of a father's name listed for a hijo natural does not suggest that the church would not allow it.

The church did allow fathers' names to be listed for hijos naturales and would not force the couple to marry against their will.[17] The results have been divided into two periods for comparison (see table 3.2).[18] Note that, in order to focus on parentage, one needs to ignore baptisms of adults and orphans. In the first period (1672–80), 54 percent of the total of 4,244 baptized children with known mothers (excluding the orphans and adult baptisms) had mothers who were labeled *soltera* (single), while 46 percent had married mothers. During the second period (1681–88), 45 percent of the 2,080 baptized children were presented by single women compared to 54 by married women. Overall, 54 percent of children were brought by single women for baptism while 46 percent were presented by married women, which is a high estimate, by comparison with other studies. Our estimates from Mexico City baptismal records show that among single plebeian women, 13 percent (299) were labeled "free," while 14 percent (318) were designated as "slaves"; for the remaining entries, the status of these women was not specified. As we have no complete censuses carried out across Mexico between the sixteenth century and the mid-eighteenth century, not even overall censuses in the cities, data samples that are utilized here may overall *not* reflect the actual "civil" status of women in these cities, but only indicate tendencies and social phenomena within a particular sector of the population, namely, plebeian women. Within this particular sector, we must therefore rely on partial censuses, such as baptismal records and population surveys carried out in some of the barrios of Mexico City in which women between the ages of sixteen and fifty were registered as either "single" or "widows" or were alternatively listed as *doncellas*. Even so, the high percentage of single plebeian women still remains in effect, taking into account the number of illegitimate births that surely continued to be a widespread phenomenon among this sector of the population and the natural tendency of such women in particular to avoid registration. Regarding nonurban environments, I have also carried out a comparable survey of single women in rural areas of Tlaxcala-Puebla, east of Mexico City, among ethnically mixed populations.

TABLE 3.2. Single mothers (*castas*) in seventeenth-century Mexico City: Parish baptismal records from the Sagrado Metropolitano, Mexico City, 1672–1688

Year	Total baptized	Orphans	Adult baptism	Married mothers	Single mothers
1672–80	2,290	71 (3%)	55 (2%)	887 (46%)	1,277 (55%)
1681–88	2,377	54 (2%)	243 (10%)	1,048 (54%)	1,032 (45%)
Total	4,667	125	298	1,935 (46%)	2,309 (54%)

THE PUEBLA-TLAXCALA BAPTISMAL RECORDS

By comparison, in Puebla registered baptisms reviewed for the parish of El Sagrario between 1650 and 1689 also indicate very high rates of single motherhood. In 1678, this parish had a population of 39,000 inhabitants (Bosch 1999, 64). The highest rate of single, unwed women was indeed among the castas, or plebeian women. I found that 48.8 percent of all mothers were registered by the local priest as "single women" (Grajales Porras and Aranda Romero 1991, 21–32). In order to be able to compare tendencies and patterns between the urban and rural areas, as suggested by Calvo (Calvo 1984, 204), I have also carried out a comparable survey of single plebeian women in rural areas surrounding Tlaxcala and Puebla, among mixed populations dominated by indigenous men and women. I chose to examine the baptismal records of three parishes: San Martin Huaquechula (state of Puebla), San Salvador el Verde, near Tlaxcala (state of Puebla), and San Juan de los Llanos, Libres (state of Puebla). In contrast with the urban areas, in the rural areas the most striking phenomenon is by far the almost complete absence of any entry for the babies' fathers; that is, while in the urban areas, in most cases, an entry would indicate "father unknown," in the rural areas, in almost all entries such an indication remained blank. In San Martin Huaquechula (state of Puebla), between 1674 and 1730, among the 120 baptisms registered, single indigenous mothers constituted the highest percentage: 34 percent (41), single *mulatas* 12.5 percent, and single mestizas a mere 8 percent. For all the rest of the mothers, 46.5 percent, no racial affiliation was specified. Of the total, only five fathers were registered as "unknown," while all the rest were unspecified. Twelve of the newborn were baptized in haciendas, four in ranches, and twelve in *ingenios* (sugar mills); the locations of where the births took place were in in Chiautla, Tecpan, Xochimilco, Tecali, Santiago Tetlan, Santa Ana, and only one in the city of Cholula—Luciana María—an indigenous girl (born 1730), her designated godmother was doña Michaela.

In the small, rural community of San Salvador el Verde, near Tlaxcala (in the state of Puebla), the survey covers random years between 1654 and 1657, containing

270 baptisms by single mothers, out of a total of 580 baptisms listed, 8 percent of whom (21) were designated mulatas, 5 percent (14) mestizas, and 6 percent (17) indigenous persons. From among the 270 baptisms, for twenty-three the space for father is entered as "unknown" while in all the rest, 155 of them, it is left blank. Here is a sample entry from the rural area:

> Parish: el Verde, San Salvador, Puebla, vol. 10, Fol. 181/3, Date: 2/8/1643: Baptized name: Francisco; Mother's name: Juana, "negra, esclava de Rodrigo Dolienlan, soltera" (single); place [of residence]: "casa de Pedro"; godfather: Pedro Vazquez; god-mother: Luisa de Betancourt; race: "negro, esclavo"; father: "unknown."

In San Juan de los Llanos, Libres (in the state of Puebla), the survey covers the years between 1654 and 1705. Of 816 records listed, 178 baptisms were associated with single mothers, 13 percent (24) of whom were designated mulatas, 3 percent (5) as mulata slaves, a mere 1 percent (2) black slaves, 9 percent (16) mestizas, 28 per-cent (49) indigenous persons, and 1.5 percent (3), españolas. For 23 of the baptized children, the father is entered as "unknown," while for all the remaining 155 cases, paternity is left blank. Sixty-four of the babies were born and baptized in haciendas, 7 in *estancias* (cattle ranches), and 19 in private households, where the mothers pos-sibly served as housemaids ("en servicio de . . ." [in the service of]).

THE INSTITUTION OF GOD-FATHERHOOD

In these rural areas the institution of the *compadrazgo* (godfatherhood) was also central to the local ritual and was essential for the legitimacy of newborns, espe-cially when they were born on rural estates or farms.[19]

In his own study on of marriage choices in Mexico City during this period, Cope emphasizes the role played by the compadrazgo for social advancement: "we sug-gest that they were drawn into the social network of one parent or the other, which-ever was more advantageous," which would possibly take them away from their own caste, and enable their children to pursue outside channels of support, relying upon the effective mechanism of compadrazgo and diverse partnerships, as well as taking into consideration individual predispositions. In the parish of San Juan de los Llanos, Libres: 50 of the newly born had the two godparents present at their baptism, 57 only the godfather present, and 66 only the godmother. On only four occasions was there no godparent present at all. Ten of the godmothers were desig-nated as *doña*, indicating their either Spanish or Creole affiliations while only five of the godfathers were designated as *don*. A representative example of a baptism in which two godparents were present was performed on 26 November 1679, the slave María Matina from the household of doña María Teresa having her newly born son, Juan (a "mulato"), baptized. The child's godparents were Nicolás de Herrera, and María Teresa (the daughter of the mother's owner, doña María Teresa). In San Salvador el Verde, 15 babies were born and baptized in small indigenous towns in the area, 18 in haciendas, 4 in estancias, and 18 in private homes. Single mothers serving in these farms and estates usually opted for the landlord to be the godfather. For example, Juana María gave birth to her daughter Isabel, designated as a "mestiza" in the Botello household on 3 August 1679. A few years earlier, on 13 March 1673, Margarita, a single mulata, gave birth to her son, Tomás, at the Botello estancia; his recorded godmother was María de Borges, but the baby's father was designated as "unknown." In 209 of the baptisms, the child's godmother was present, 21 of whom were listed as *doña*, while in 114 cases the godfathers assisted, only 5 of whom were listed as *don*.

In San Martin Huaquechula, 82 godfathers attended the ceremony, 17 of whom were entitled *don*, while 100 godmothers were present, 12 of whom were designated as *doña*. For example, on 2 March 1643, María, a "single black" baptized her son, Antonio (who was recorded as being "mulato"), with Pedro de Sancedo and Ana de Alvarez serving as godparents, while the father was listed as "unknown." In yet another example, Francisca, the newborn daughter of a black slave woman Juana, was baptized on 2 August 1643 with the assistance of Pedro Vázquez as godfather and Luisa de Betancour, as godmother. Francisca was also registered as having been "black and a slave," her father listed as "unknown."

Some persons figure prominently in the registry as godfathers, possibly because they were considered important in the local area; among them, for example, was don Miguel Pérez: On 27 January 1699, he assisted together with the godmother Ana Juárez in the baptism of Juana, the daughter of Juana María; on 4 February 1699 don Miguel assisted yet again with Ana Juárez as godmother in the baptism of Andrés, son of Nicolasa Trujillo (mestiza); on 10 July 1701, Pérez assisted as godfather in the baptism of Pedro, son of María Muñoz; while on 16 July 1701 he served for a second time as godfather of a child of Nicolasa Trujillo, her daughter Ventura (mestiza); on 13 June 1702 we find don Miguel assisting as godfather in the baptism of Alfonso, son of María Muñoz, again with Ana Juárez as godmother; on 14 October 1704 he assisted in the baptism of Luisa, daughter of Agustina in Xochimilco; and on 14 October 1705 he was godfather in the baptism of Francisca Hiyarda, daughter of Francisca de la Paz (española).

COMPARATIVE STUDIES ON SINGLE WOMEN'S DEMOGRAPHY

The above estimate of single, plebeian women in both Mexico City and Puebla and its environs gleaned from both our surveys is in fact consistent with the high percentage of households headed by single women, including widows, in colonial Mexico that has been noted in several studies since at least the 1980s. Nevertheless, previous scholars typically focused on middle- to upper-class women, and neglected plebeian women.[20] Pescador's study of poor indigenous women who migrated to Mexico City is an exception, in providing quantitative data on women of the lower echelons of colonial society (1992, 167–69).[21] Woodrow Borah's earlier study of the partial census of the city of Antequera, in which Spanish single women are present, is singular by the way in which it provides us with the average number of solteras (unmarried women), with children per thousand inhabitants in terms of the same division by race for the rural inhabitants and a single grouping for the city of Antequera. As early as the middle of the sixteenth century a standard system of parish registers was initiated in New Spain, and in 1585 the Third Mexican Provincial Church Council instructed that officials separate the registers of births, confirmations, marriages, and burials, of indigenous persons and nonindigenous persons. These registers were the legally requisite evidence of legal marriage and legitimate descent (Borah and Cook 1966, 946–1008). Juan Javier Pescador, for example, estimates that 49 percent of women in the parish of Santa Catarina in Mexico City were single, 31 percent were married, and 20 percent were widows (1992, 212–24). Also according to Calvo, by the mid-seventeenth century, the percentage of hijos naturales surmounted the average percentage of births (58 percent of the total births; 1992, 291). Juan Javier Pescador (1992) calculates that 49 percent of women residing in the capital were single, 31 percent being married and 20 percent widows. Christopher H. Lutz's figures on Santiago de Guatemala, between 1770 and 1772, cite 57 percent of the 1,626 baptisms of the gente ordinaria were for babies born out of wedlock (1994, 233–39). The rates of illegitimacy were somewhat lower among infants identified as Spaniards, namely, between 26 and 37 percent of baptisms and 24 percent in each decade between 1700 and 1769. Gonzalbo Aizpuru figures confirm this, stating that half of the women in Mexico City were single (1987, 151–52). Thomas Calvo has estimated that "in the past," as many as 39 percent of both Spanish and Creole women remained single for life, while among indigenous women a third remained single (1984, 206). In the text accompanying a table appearing in Calvo's study ("Marital status of deceased persons in the Sagrario of Guadalajara, 1685–99"), he explains: "Single simply means unmarried. Such women could have been either concubines, unwed mothers, or spinsters. This applies equally to men. However, the number of women reported as single at their death is significantly high." In the table itself, contrary to what Calvo found, there is a clear division between "married or widowed" and "single." By comparison, in her study of early to mid-colonial Cartagena, Nicole von Germeten notes that by the eighteenth century, "at least one third of all residences had woman as head of household and in charge of a small family group . . . ," and in a certain low-socioeconomic neighborhood of Cartagena, "nearly 20% of the plots of land were owned by single women (usually of African descent)" (2013, 7). According to Robert McCaa's (1994) analysis of the 1777 census from Parral (Nueva Vizcaya) in Mexico City's parish of Santa Catarina, 35 percent of the women between the ages of sixteen and fifty were single. For women located in the lower hierarchy of the castas in particular, marriage options were usually restricted to either men belonging to their own ethnic group or to other non-Spaniards. If all other studies show that between 25 percent and 35 percent of the population, especially women among the subaltern castas, did not marry at all, preferred to remain single, with or without children, and maintained long-lasting relationships of cohabitation with partners of other castas, as well as the high rates of bigamy, as indeed Richard Boyer has shown, then, one cannot arrive at sweeping conclusions on the overwhelming patterns of living among the different castes, instead relying upon very partial quantitative data alone.

Pilar Gonzalbo surveyed a total of 10,735, registered baptisms of castas in the parish of El Sagrario in Mexico City, as well as 4,996 registered baptisms of castas in the parish of Santa Veracruz, between 1650 and 1669. However, there is no breakdown here into "single mothers," as is in my above sample. The number of matrimonies of castas as shown by Pilar Gonzalbo Aizpuru (2005) for the same parish, between 1660 and 1673, yields a meager sum of 1,427, which, in comparison with the baptismal data, clearly evinces the magnitude of the phenomenon. Agustín Grajales Porras and José Luis Aranda Romero (1991) found out in their survey of hijos naturales in the different parishes of the city of Puebla, between 1750 and 1759, that only 6 babies out of 908, or, 100 out of 4,000, were brought to church by both parents to take the sacrament of baptism. However, their survey of the records concentrates only on mestizos, castizos and españoles. The percentage of single plebeian women was likely higher given the tendency of such women to avoid registration. Nevertheless, one has to approach these statistical figures with caution. As for European figures of single women in Zurich, during 1632, that are very much compatible with ours—namely, 48 percent of single women, vis-à-vis 37 percent of married women—J. Hanjal thus cautions us that "large numbers who are single are thus no proof of abstention from marriage." Is it possible that in these registers not much attention was paid to the distinction between a single woman and a widow? (1965, 117). In the Puebla registers, as in Mexico City, both the civil status and racial affiliation of these single mothers are given. When asked, 61 percent of the single women identified themselves as mulatas, 15 percent of whom described themselves as former black slaves.[22]

Nevertheless, the lack of an overall, complete census for Mexico City and Puebla and the data samples that are utilized here might *not* be representative of women's "civil" status in these cities overall but, rather, provide us with tendencies and social phenomena within a particular sector of the population, namely, plebeian women. The Villaseñor census of 1742 produced valuable reports for many parishes and towns but failed to cover the entire colony. The best colonywide census was the last, that ordered by the Viceroy Conde de Revillagigedo (1789–93) and the first to use a standard format for listing individuals by name, age, sex, occupation, race, and marital status.[23] A preliminary, house-to-house census of the central area of Mexico City, which is now named Colonia Centro, studied by Irene Vazquez Valle (1975) was carried out in 1753, but unfortunately it has been only partially preserved. Two additional colonial censuses were taken, in 1777 and 1793, of which relatively large parts have survived. The only full, house-to-house survey of the entire city was carried out in 1779, and a complete census of Mexico was carried out in 1790, in which there appeared the total of 1.3 million women above the age of fifteen.

RAISING CHILDREN AND FOSTERING OTHER CHILDREN

Until recently, the most common view was that in Latin America, family and kinship have historically served as safe havens, constituting critical institutions for social stability. However, during the past two decades, both quantitative and qualitative historical studies of social institutions and living patterns in Latin America show that other, alternative frameworks may have functioned in parallel to, and even entirely instead of, such places of shelter. This section of the book also complements a great number of leading works by both European and Latin American historians on the issues of abandoned children, child circulation, and foundling homes,[24] but traces such phenomena back to much earlier times than has been recognized until recently in the historiography of the Latin American family. The study of abandoned children and orphans during the early modern period is still relatively scarce and so is a comparative study of such phenomena in early colonial Latin America. A recent exception is Komisaruk's short treatment of this theme.[25] Ann S. Blum's article on child circulation and orphanage houses in Mexico City during the nineteenth and early twentieth century is very illuminating regarding various social issues and welfare systems related to abandoned children during the Independence Period.[26] Boswell showed us how, prior to the thirteenth and fourteenth centuries in Europe, informal arrangements for these foundlings meant that through the "kindness of strangers" they were placed in strangers' households, while later, when welfare became institutionalized, convents and hospitals became the safe harbors for these children. My own study demonstrates that in early colonial Mexico, such informal arrangements of childcare described by Boswell (1988) were also very common within the parishes and, as in Europe, only later did they evolve into the formal institutions of foundling homes.

As single mothers, to create an alternative familial framework was primarily to create a viable safe haven for themselves as well as for others. One should highlight on the outset that, apparently, many single women bore only one child. Robert McCaa, in his analysis of the records of 358 single women in Parral, Nueva Vizcaya, estimates that between the ages of fifteen and forty-nine, single women would have children at the average age between 0 and 9, and that, children of 10 through 15 were far less common among them. And he adds that "having exhausted their years of fecundity, about fifth of those who survived, of each generation, did not benefit from the matrimonial benedictions, but, perhaps, they did experience sentiments of maternity" (1989, 299–325). A feasible explanation for this phenomena of one-time births by single women is based upon (a) these women's usually had only maintained transient and fragile cohabitations with different men and (b) nutritional deprivation, high rates of poor sanitation, ill health, and limited access to potable water, caused many such women to experience premature births or miscarriages (see Hanley 1989, 4–27). Isabel de Montoya's first baby, for example, had died at an early age; in 1662, in an inspection of Isabel's property, the Inquisitors uncovered inside one of her wooden chests, what would have been very likely the dead baby's blanket, which she cherished.[27] Her only living daughter, Ana María de Montoya, was exceptionally fortunate to have been able to live together with her mother, for a few years, during her adulthood. While, indigenous women, had higher fertility rates than Spanish or casta women, their life expectancy was significantly shorter. We should also take into consideration that fertility as well as childbirth depended significantly on a number of correlated factors: the age of marriage, temporary sterility provoked by malnutrition, insufficient conditions of sanitation and hygiene, the conditions of pregnancy and confinement, permanent sterility resulting from an insufficiently conducted delivery, the excessive rate of infant mortality—usually between ten and fifteen days after birth—and former miscarriages (Johnson 2002, 220–21).

Single, plebeian women found it hard to cope at the same time with the harsh circumstances in which they themselves grew up, as well as their subsequent experiences in life. As a consequence, then, single plebeian women needed sheltering and supportive "sisterhood," namely, to be actively affiliated to a close circle of mutual assistance, in order to maintain their children. Furthermore, one significant issue that comes up in our records is that female-headed households actually evolved to become effective fostering and adoptive institutions of their own merit. Co-lodgers within such households, besides taking care of their own biological offspring, took care also of children other than their own for the sake of additional income, as well as to help other single women in dire straits.[28] Usually, it was the owner of the private home, where she rented rooms for single women tenants, who was assigned the role of the fostering person, but not exclusively. In her study of foundlings in late colonial Brazil, María Luiza Marcílio notes that "the informal or private rearing of foundlings in family homes was the widest system of protection of abandoned children, present throughout the history of Brazil. It is this [system] that, in some sense, renders original the history of assistance to abandoned children in the country" (Marcílio 1998, 136) In this, Marcílio undoubtedly follows Boswell's study of child abandonment in Europe, centuries before the institutionalization of the foundling home.

On many occasions, these children had become fully integrated into such new family frameworks. Many of them were orphaned, given away to the care of these single women by the surviving parent, or the parent's benefactor, who had taken care of the child up to that point but who could no longer do so due to ill health or death.[29] The handing over of such children to other single women with whom they were acquainted, whether done voluntarily or out of mere compassion for the child, was often handled as a service the foster mother was paid for; at other times, when the biological mother was in dire straits, no such arrangement was made. One such exemplary case can be found from the court records of late fifteenth-century Britain. According to a petition brought forward by a certain Jane, when she was a single woman, aged eighteen, Margaret, the accused party, promised to treat Jane as if she were her daughter, as she had no children of her own. Jane came to Margaret with clothing, provided by her kin, and thirty ells of linen cloth. The petition then goes on to relate that Margaret became ill and, at the point of death, made her will and bequeathed to Jane some clothing and various household goods including brewing equipment and that she gave Jane first option to buy Margaret's house and the rest of the brewing vessels. Jane served Margaret for around six and a half years and left to get married. She took neither wages nor apparel from Margaret (Beattie 2006, 177–202).

In our present study, for example, Juana de las Vírgenes, a single woman who lived in the Minas of Pachuca, was given two young girls to care for, educate, and raise until they reached the age of reason. In her will Juana declared that because of the love she has for them, she is leaving most of her belongings to the two girls, and she instructs her benefactors to tell them that their parents had left them behind in her home many years earlier. The items she bequeathed to the girls included traditional cloths, necklaces, mattresses, and a significant number of images of saints.[30] The usual procedure was to seek the intervention of the civil court that would decide upon whether to place the child in the care of a reputable person (i.e., the landlady) whom the judges trusted, such as prosecutors in the Real Audiencia or professional men of esteem, for a limited period of time of up to six or seven years. During the period set by the court, boys would be given a proper education preparing them for a profession, while girls would presumably have reached a marriageable age at which stage they would be allotted a dowry in the amount instructed. In María de Armenta's will dated 7 February 1670 (and which went into effect with her death in 1691), she declared that she had put aside for many years the sum of 200 pesos that her mother, María de los Ríos, had bequeathed to Ana de los Ríos, an orphan who grew up in her home. Complying with her late mother's wishes, María instructed that this sum be granted to the orphan in addition to which she personally bequeathed to Ana another 300 pesos to be given to her in due course when she would be married. Furthermore, María de Armenta instructed that the orphan be provided with regular clothes, white clothes, a dress, a mantle, a chest with *ajuar* (bed linen), a bed, mattresses, bracelets, jewels, a rug, and a mulata slave named Jerónima who was to work for her during her lifetime and thereafter be freed.[31] In a similar fashion, in 1688 Juana María de la Cruz, a prosperous indigenous widow who lived in Puebla and was once married to Captain Felipe de Monzón, a *pardo libre* (a free, dark-skinned person of casta, and of mixed blood) left behind half of her property to twelve-year-old Felipe Monzón (named after her late husband) and to eighteen-year-old Matías Monzón, two orphans brought up by her in her home, as she herself was unable to bear children of her own. Before her death Juana María instructed that the property be bequeathed to the orphans only when they reach the age at which they are able to administer it, and, until that time, the sums due to them after the sale of her various properties should be deposited by Lieutenant Cristóbal Vidal, the guardian she designated for them, in a trust that should yield 5 percent annual interest that would be allocated for purchasing their food and clothing. She also instructed that the costs of her funeral and interment be extracted from Felipe Monzón's portion of the inheritance. The rest of her wealth was distributed among different chapels, convents, and the funding of religious devotions in Mexico City.[32]

ADOPTIONS

The term *madre adoptiva* (adoptive mother) appears for the first time in our sources in 1726. The legal terminology was applied to cases in which single women were too poor to sustain their children on their own with their former partner, the children's biological father, who already was far removed from the family and unwilling to acknowledge paternity.[33] In some cases, such women elected to give up their child so that they could be brought up and educated in the home of a respectable couple whom they had come to know. After an initial agreement was reached between the two sides, the legal arrangement between them was formalized in court. In this way Gertrudis Isidora Rodríguez, a single woman and the mother to ten-year-old María

Antonia, conceded her maternal rights to one Margarita García and her husband, José Llanos y Ortega, a painter, "para que la eduquen y mantengan como si fuera su hija legítima" (for the sake of educating her and taking care of her as though she was their legitimate daughter).[34] In the documentation, the titles *tutora y curadora* are also commonly applied to the "adoptive mother." Apparently, in contrast with today's process of legal adoption, the arrangement in New Spain did not grant the "adoptive parents" full legal rights of parenthood over the child and can be compared more closely to the status of a modern foster family. For example, in the archival sources I found the following citation from the late eighteenth century:

> Consulta hecha por el cura de Pachuca Maríano Uturria, sobre el bautismo de una muchacha llamada María Nicolasa, hija adoptada de María de la Concepción Marquinco, quien decía haber presenciado la aparición de la madre difunta de la muchacha, confesándole que había mentido al asegurarle haber bautizado a su hija cuando se la entregó.[35]

> [A consultation made by the priest of Pachuca, Maríano Uturria, concerning the issue of baptizing a baby girl by the name of María Nicolasa, the adopted child of María de la Concepción Marquinco, who has claimed to have witnessed the apparition of the child's late biological mother before her, who confessed to her that she was lying to her when she assured her that she had baptized her baby before she gave her up for adoption.]

ORPHANS

A sample survey that I conducted within the baptismal records of castas from the parish of the Sagrado Metropolitano, Mexico City, for the period between 1654 and 1664, includes a total of 3,489 baptisms, in which 17 percent are designated as orphans. However, we do not know from these records whether or not these orphans were raised by single women.[36] Nonetheless, independently from this sample survey, we have a variety of records from which we are able to identify the widespread phenomenon of single women raising children who were not their own and yet who became an inseparable part of their family and household. Many of them were orphaned, given away to the care of these single women by the surviving parent, or the parent's benefactor, who had taken care of the child up to that point but who could no longer do so due to ill health or death.[37] The handing over of such children to other single women with whom their mothers were acquainted, whether done voluntarily or out of mere compassion for the child, was often treated as a service the foster mother was paid for; at other times, when the biological mother was in dire straits, no such arrangement was executed.

Most often, such orphans were given to some close kin of the deceased who was economically able to raise them. In such cases we cannot draw a line between orphans who were informally adopted by the benefactor and cases of orphaned slaves, who were brought up in the same household and whose fates were stipulated within the will, being transferred together with the other orphans of the family to the care of close kin as free persons.[38] Orphaned servants were often given to the care of the religious orders in convents. For example, Lorenza ("de color membrillo cocho" [a red-skinned mulato was one of the extreme casta labels instituted around 1650]), an eight- or nine-year-old slave girl, was "donated" to the Jesús María Convent in Mexico City in 1693 by Fernando de Oñate, the cousin of Magdalena Leonor de San Gerónimo. According to Oñate's will, Lorenza was to remain there as a slave until the death of his cousin Magdalena, after which she was to be freed and transferred to the care of the latter's unmarried sister, María Antonia Pardo, where she was to remain as a free servant until she had reached the age of reason and by then, hopefully, had acquired a proper profession. During the same year, María de la Concepción, a sixteen-year old mulata girl, was also handed over to this convent by Magdalena Leonor de San Gerónimo's uncle, Diego de Olarte.[39] In yet different circumstances, María Estupiñán of Mexico City, the widow of Juan de la Gala Moreno, with whom she did not have any offspring, instructed in her last will that Gerónima de la Gala, a thirteen-year-old Spanish orphan who was raised in her household, should remain there until she had reached the appropriate age for her to marry, after which she should also be granted the then twelve-year-old black slave, Ana, daughter of Luciana, María Estupiñán's late slave who was also born in her household, Ana to remain in the service of Gerónima.[40]

FOSTERING ARRANGEMENTS

Once a child or children became orphaned, fostering arrangements were common among nearly all indigenous groups in Mexico. We get of glimpse of this from an example in the sources, when in 1638 a representative for the monastery of San Juan Bautista de Coyoacán, Fray Lorenzo Maldonado OP, came to court to speak on behalf of Dominga Velázquez. This indigenous woman served as a tutora y curadora (teacher and guardian) of two children, Constantino and Gertrudis, whose biological father, don Felipe de Guzmán, had been the indigenous governor of San Pablo in Coyoacán. Dominga was fostering the children who had become the sole heirs of don Felipe de Guzmán.[41] In 1740 a poor, ten-month-old baby, María Maximiliana, was at the center of a court battle between at least three persons, all of whom claimed equal legal rights over her. The first and foremost among the three was María Magdalena Bueno, the baby's biological mother, a single española who had filed a lawsuit in the ecclesiastical court of Mexico City against Caytano de Vargas, a married mulato and servant of Marqués de Salvatierra, for having deflowered her after having promised marriage and who was possibly the biological father of the still unborn baby. A few months after the initial submission of the lawsuit and upon María Maximiliana's birth, Caytano tried in vain to remove the baby from María Magdalena Bueno. Subsequently, when María Maximiliana had reached the age of ten months, her mother, who now found herself desperately in need of a safe haven, succeeded in concealing the baby's whereabouts from Caytano in the household of Lorenzo de Talavera, *maestro de sembradero* (a small-size farmer). The latter submitted documentation to the ecclesiastical court claiming to be the true progenitor of María Maximiliana, who had been conceived during a supposedly "long-lasting relationship" with María Magdalena Bueno, the baby girl's mother. Later on that year, María de la Soledad, a parda libre and Caytano de Vargas's legitimate wife entered the picture, claiming rights over the baby and asking the court to grant her custody of the child, "who was possibly the offspring of her husband and herself." Toward this end, María de la Soledad alleged that she and her husband had already possessed an infant named María Victoriana who was, she claimed, actually the same baby related to María Magdalena Bueno's lawsuit.[42]

On 15 June 1740, the court ordered that María Maximiliana be placed for fostering in the *casa de la morada* (the dwelling of) of don Agustín de Almoquera *receptor del número* (treasurer, receiving agent of funds or fines) of the Real Audiencia in the city. However, this fact did not deter María de la Soledad, who argued that she and her husband were much more capable of raising the poor, ten-month-old baby María Maximiliana than was her own biological mother, due to the latter's poor education and bad upbringing and due to "her depraved manner of living." María de la Soledad also informed the court that she had already succeeded in removing the baby from the care of don Agustín de Almoquera, on the pretext of "wishing to take care of her, educate her properly, and teach her Christian doctrine for the sake of the proper upbringing of the little baby who would become her own child. . . ." She thereafter asked the court to order the biological mother, María Magdalena Bueno, "not to accost her, nor ever to come near her house." Finally, on 31 August 1740, the court authorities ruled in favor of the biological mother and ordered that María Maximiliana be safely returned to her, warning the other involved parties to refrain from communicating with her.[43]

Other cases of persons fostering children not biologically their own come to light subsequently to the death of the caretaker, as they are recorded in parish burial records. Examining the burial registry of the parish of Santa María de la Natividad, Atlixco (state of Puebla) for the years 1704–14, one finds, for example, numerous entries of children who died at a young age. Within the registry we find a variety of circumstance recorded in more detail: (a) children who were born out of wedlock; for example, Francisca de Olivera, the hija natural of Maríana de Olivera, who was only ten months old when she died; or Miguel de Zamora, hijo natural of Isabel de Zamora; (b) children who were born to single mothers and were either entirely abandoned or deposited in the home of an esteemed neighbor, to be cared for; for example, Lucía de los Reyes, only eleven months old when she died, is said *que se crió* "to have been brought up" in the household of Juan del Castillo Grimaldes, resident of this town, "who provided this child with a proper church burial"; or María Teresa de las Dolores, a four-month-old infant when she died, who had been looked after in the household of Doctor Cristóbal Muñoz; or Francisco, who was "more or less" three years old when he passed away and who had been cared for in the home of Miguel Rodríguez; (c) children whose mothers had disappeared from their lives; for example, the doncella Isabel López, daughter of Pedro López. In this unique entry, there is no mention of either the mother's name, as is usually the case, or whether the deceased had been either the *hija legítima* or hija natural of her father.[44]

There was yet another model by which the civil court ruled in favor of transferring an orphaned child to a foster family where he or she would perform some services in return for upkeep. Under such circumstances, the transfer of the child became formal once the court signed a legal document between the parties acknowledging the relationship between the foster family and the child as "working relations." This discussion corresponds with Elizabeth Anne Kuznesof's fine study on such practices in Brazil (1998, 225–39). The civil court in Mexico City might issue to a single woman, for example, a *escritura de servicio* (work contract) in her favor, meaning that the child was obliged to provide her with services in exchange for food and care. The case of an eight-year-old mestiza named María is particularly revealing of this arrangement. In November 1612, the child, who had been wandering aimlessly in the streets, presented herself to the city authorities in Mexico City, claiming that she was the daughter of one Juan Pérez, a Spaniard, and Maríana, an indigenous woman from Huasquesaloya, near the town of Atotonilco in the state of Hidalgo. The *fiscal del crimen* submitted her case to the civil court, and, when queried about her circumstances, the child urged the judges to find her a decent person who would look after her and sustain her until her parents came to fetch her. The court ruled to place her in the household of Francisco de Sandategui, who shortly after transferred the girl to the home of a single woman named Catalina de Chávez. The latter pledged to provide the child with food and clothing and nurse her if she fell ill, until someone claimed her.[45]

There were other circumstances under which a single woman might care for an orphan or an abandoned child for some years before actually seeking legal status or acknowledgment for her or his care. For example, María de Chávez, a humble unmarried woman, had cared for Catalina, a thirteen-year-old mestiza girl in her home for a few years whereupon, to avoid the risk of the child being removed from her care, in June 1613 she presented herself in the civil court of Mexico City and asked that *escritura de depósito* (a deed of deposition) be issued on her behalf, thereby effectively granting her the legal status of foster mother. The document instructed that by court order, a monthly stipend of two pesos be paid to her from the royal treasury in exchange for her formal obligation toward the child, whereby she would continue to provide her with food and lodging, nurse her when she became ill, and teach her good manners.[46] On 13 November 1613, Luisa de Torres, a free *mulata*, similarly asked the civil court for an escritura de servicio to formalize her relationship with María Magdalena, an adolescent girl whom she began to look after from the age of twelve years. The *alcalde de Corte* (judge of the civil division of the audiencia) approved the request and ruled that María Magdalena would remain in Luisa's household for another five years, during which time the latter was obliged to provide María with room and board, a monthly allowance, and a decent education.[47]

There are also cases in which the biological, single mother of a child sought the court's assistance in obliging the benefactor under whose care she placed her child, after the foster parent did not comply with the obligations formalized in the contract between benefactor and mother. In this way did Catalina de la Cruz, a free black woman and the biological mother of Bernardino Adame, file a complaint in Mexico City's municipal court against Tomasa Ruiz, wife of master shoemaker Alonso Rodríguez, for her husband's alleged neglect of their agreed-upon duties toward the child, namely, to teach him the craft of shoemaking. It was specifically for this reason that Bernardino had been placed by his mother in the couple's household, and Catalina had actually paid them for this. In addition, the complaint alleged that the Ruizes maltreated her son.[48] In her study of indigenous women in the mines of Zacatecas, Dana Velasco Murillo (2013) gives a similar example of a single indigenous mother who, unable to sustain her son, gave him to a Spanish family so that he would work and learn a proper trade.

In other cases, single women who were infirm or close to death, instructed that their children be transferred to the care of other single women they knew or to reputable persons who had the resources to raise them. For example, Menchaca, a single mulata, sought in 1667 the assistance of the civil court in Mexico City in arranging care for her child, who was presumably about to be handed over to her by the executor of her biological father's will.[49] Similarly, Pascuala de San Juan de Dios, a free mulata and widow from Mexico City, dictated her last will on 9 February 1700. She had been married to the late Antonio de la Cruz, a free mulato, from whom she had four descendents: twenty-five-year-old Leonor de San Antonio, a mulata slave, twenty-one-year-old Antonio Sebastián, and twenty-four-year-old María de la Rosa, also a single mulata slave who in turn gave birth to Juana Theresa, also a slave. Pascuala left all her belongings to her children.[50] She declared in her will that she had brought up in her home a five-year-old Spanish orphan girl who had been left on her doorstep and that she wished the child to be transferred to the care of the bachelor Juan Pacheco Riquelme so that he would continue raising the orphan and see to her education.[51] In another case, Marta Romero Rodríguez, a widow also referred to previously, raised a number of different children though they were not her own including a fourteen-year-old black girl named Ana and a fourteen-month-old black baby, the daughter of a single black slave, Magdalena. Marta's household also included yet another small child, Nicholás Muñoz, who was apparently abandoned by his parents on her doorstep as well as Diego, a black child for whom she had much affection. The latter was only four years old when Marta requested that he be placed in the Nuestra Señora de la Merced convent in Puebla, and stipulated that he "should never be sold into slavery." On her death-bed, Marta also issued specific instructions regarding each of the other children for whom she had cared: fourteen-year-old Ana was to be transferred to the care of her neighbor Juana de Loaysa and was to serve as the latter's slave; Ana, the fourteen-month-old baby, was to be separated from her biological mother, Magdalena, and thereafter raised by Juana Bautista, a free mulata living in Puebla, while the baby's mother, Magdalena, was to be given to a certain engineer, Juan Díaz, to serve as his slave.[52]

Eight-year-old Miguel de la Cruz, a free mulato, had been given by his parents, Miguel and Isabel de la Cruz, to Ana de Santiago, a single woman living on her own in the calle Mesones in Mexico City, when the child was but six months old. Apparently Miguel's biological mother, a free mulata, was already very ill at the time the baby was given to Ana de Santiago, as his mestizo father had been forced by harsh circumstances to migrate to far-off Minas del Canela in the northernmost state of Sonora to work. Subsequently, Miguel had been raised by Ana de Santiago as if he were her own child, the two residing in a room that she rented from a certain Diego Pavón, *maestro de herrados* (master of horse shoes) in Mesones Street in Mexico City. When the boy reached six, Ana de Santiago transferred the child to the care of his godfather, Alonso Guerrero, because she apparently thought him more capable than her of providing the child with a solid education and a proper profession, teaching him good manners and preparing him for life in general until Miguel would reach the age of reason and be able to stand on his own two feet. The child was held during the hearings in the public prison of Puebla, on suspicion that he was a runaway slave, and as a consequence of the trial was released immediately.[53]

In yet another example, Lorenzina de la Cruz, a prosperous single woman living in Texcoco, bequeathed the enormous sum of 300 pesos to a one-and-a-half-year-old orphan girl named María, whom she had brought up in her house, the money to constitute María's future dowry and for her maintenance, "in case her [future] husband dies." One finds a good number of cases of gestures of gratitude toward single household servants, whereupon the person making the will left behind a sum of money to constitute in due course either the dowry for the servant or as means of taking care of her children. The sum of 300 golden pesos was apparently the customary amount expected to be given to a girl who was about to be married. In addition, Lorenzina de la Cruz's will instructed that a number of young slaves in her household be freed: Josepha, then a seven-year-old mulata was to initially remain in the service of Lorenzina's younger sister, María de Alba. Two other slaves were granted outright manumission in the will: fourteen-year-old Francisca and thirteen-year-old Lorenza, the latter being the daughter of Teresa, a single black slave who had served in at Lorenzina's household.[54] Francisca Gómez, a single mulata living in Coyoacán, had two daughters, one of whom she had placed in the convent of La Encarnación, while the other still lived with her. Unfortunately, the sources provide no explanation for Francisca's deciding at one time or another to transfer her two granddaughters, the children of the daughter who still lived with her, to the household of her sister, Maríana María, "to be taken care of."[55]

In 1689, Juana de las Vírgenes, a single woman who had migrated from las Minas de Pachuca to Mexico City, had been raising in her household three girls who were not her own—María de la Oya, María Venturas, and María de San Joseph—whose respective parents had placed them in the care of Juana, paying her in advance for their upbringing and education. In Juana's will she left instructions on how her belongings were to be divided among the three girls: To María de la Oya, she left a white mattress, a small white pillow, earrings of white almonds with its pearls, coral bracelets, and old shirts so that the three girls could distribute them among themselves; a small Santo Ecumeo (a revered saint of the Spanish Catholic church) image; and petticoats made of heron. To María Venturas, Juana left a mattress, a blanket, red silk petticoats, a small effigy of San Francisco, a savannah, a Chinese plucked string instrument, a yellow (*damascado*) *huipil*, and a small chest in which her heir should keep her clothes. To María de San Joseph, Juana left two woolen cushions, a shirt covered with green trappings, and petticoats.[56] Another woman, Josepha de Santillán, bequeathed to Josepha, a nine-year-old orphan whom she had raised in her home, a mattress, a blanket, and a chest de Peribán. Josepha's will also instructed that the orphan move into the household of her daughter, Agustina Gallegos, who received no share in her mother's property.[57]

SISTERS TO THE HOUR OF DEATH

This section discusses the patterns of the bequest of property among single women living within female-headed households, as well as outside. Those women living together for many years obviously maintained a relationship based on mutual guarantee, joint destinies, mutual care and affection, and an equal share in property, during lifetime as well as in death and inheritance, so that each one of them takes the role of a "security network" for the other. It is noteworthy that whereby single plebeian women rarely made wills, elite women are overrepresented in the repository of wills available to us in the archives. Nonetheless, I will be looking closely at such wills in order to highlight similar patterns of the transfer and bequest of property among single women, including houses, orchards, and plots of land, as well as private belongings, but under entirely different circumstances. Examining a sample of wills of single women testators in late sixteenth-century Lima, for example, Graubart writes that "the ubiquity of indigenous and plebeian wills in colonial archives makes it clear that colonial law and legal instruments were perceived as providing relief to those fearing the chaos that might ensue with their deaths." In this sense also, Stern's "pluralization of patriarchs" fits well into this context.

Furthermore, Graubart highlights indigenous women's unique and asymmetrical patterns of inheritance and division of their estate in early colonial Peru, between sons and daughters, legitimate and illegitimate offspring (2007, 103–19). Cope, on his part, describes how, in Mexico City, "Nicolasa de Espinosa gave half of her hard-earned house to her stepchildren. Juana de los Angeles Canales willed one apartment to her niece and two more to her adopted son. The mestiza seamstress Sebastiana Hernández left her house to a clergyman with whom she was a close friend but added the proviso that her indigenous *comadre* (godmother to her child) be allowed to live 'for the rest of her life' in Sebastiana's suite" (1994, 30).

On 15 September 1631, Marta Romero Rodríguez, a single and a prosperous black widow, passed away in Puebla, where she lived. According to her will, she asked to have a lavish tomb erected for her at the Nuestra Santa Hospital, where she would lie next to her only child, Miguel Domingo. Furthermore, she asked that the priest of the Cathedral of Tlaxcala accompany her body in person, together with twelve of his choir boys, and, "as accustomed," Mass was to be chanted for the sake of her suffering soul, on that very day. In addition, she asked for fifty masses for her sake, as well as the same number of masses to be said for the sake of the souls of her beloved ones who had died and are in Purgatory. She also asked for the members of the confraternity of La Caridad and Santo Rosario to be notified of her death.[58] Her more specific instructions are as follows: to bequeath to Juan de la Cruz, a free black and living in this town 50 pesos of her property; and to Ana Santos, a free mulata and her daughter-in-law, 300 pesos; and to her niece, Ana de Santiago, a free mulata and a widow, 50 whole pesos "for her love that she showed towards her." As to her real estate: the two small adobe houses that she owned and rented out during her lifetime—the one, located in the barrio de Analco, and the other, attached to some houses on the street leading toward the San Angel de la Guardia Chapel—were both bequeathed to two single black women, with whom she was apparently closely acquainted and apparently formed part of her close-knit web of support: forty-five-year-old Juliana and twenty-year-old Magdalena. In a direct conversation, Amy Froide writes, in parallel, for England: "Women created households and mutually supportive relationship with other unmarried women during their lifetime, and upon their deaths frequently made these women their heirs" (2005, 71). The priest who inspected the property right after her death commented that "the houses were in a very bad shape due to the heavy rains and humidity and the walls were on the verge of collapsing." Furthermore, Rodríguez bequeathed four religious paintings that were in her possession to the *cofradía de los mulatos* (the confraternity of the mulatos), established in the very same place where her burial should take place, in the Nuestra Señora Hospital, to be hung on the sides of the main altarpiece; an effigy of Christ the Redeemer, as well as San Nicolás, another of San Antonio, and another of the Virgen; the statues of all three were to be hung above her tomb.[59]

In the case of Leonor de Vargas and María de Vargas, two unmarried sisters, who lived together in Coyoacán, their joined will cautions that "nothing of the aforementioned clauses should be materialized before both of them are dead." They both owned together a number of houses and some lands, "with no significant value," which were to be sold, to pay the expenses of their funeral and burial, as well as the masses said for their souls. Ten pesos of the value of the houses and lands were to be granted to Petronilla, their nephew, together with a small parcel of land that they originally acquired from local indigenous proprietors. The latter was also bequeathed one large and one small wooden container, and another of those together with a short jacket were bequeathed to a single woman by the name of Francisca Xertrudis. To Luisa, another of her friends, she bequeathed an earthen pan and a small skirt; to María de la Cruz, another of her earthen pans and a wooden bed; and to María de Najara, her silken veil.[60] A neighbor of the two sisters in Coyoacán was a single mulata by the name of Francisca Gómez. When her hour of death approached, Gómez instructed that she be buried next to the altarpiece of the Santísimo Sacramento, at this town's church and that twenty masses should be said following her departure. The property she owned consisted of a small parcel of land in the barrio de San Juan de Letrán. She instructed that the parcel of land be sold, half of the value of which she bequeathed to her two daughters and the other half to be left for her sister. Her humble possessions included an old mule, an effigy of San Nicolás that belonged to her godmother, and an outer skirt, that belonged to her sister.[61]

Josepha de Santillán, a single woman who died in Mexico City in 1691, bequeathed her very humble possessions—including petticoats, a mattress, a savannah, and a writing-desk—to Juana de la Trinidad, her daughter; her other daughter, however, named Agustina Gallegos, is not mentioned as having been entitled to her belongings.[62] Pascuala de San Juan de Dios, a free mulata and widow from Mexico City, dictated her last will on 9 February 1700. She had been married to the late Antonio de la Cruz, a free mulato, from whom she had four descendants: twenty-five-year-old Leonor de San Antonio, a mulata slave; twenty-one-year-old Antonio Sebastián; and twenty-four-year-old María de la Rosa, also a single mulata slave, who in turn gave birth to Juana Theresa, also a slave. Pascuala left all her belongings to her children.[63] Thomasa de San Juan, a single mestiza who died in Mexico City in 1692, instructed that her heirs—Juana, Joseph, and Thomas—also her three grandchildren, receive the sum of 106 pesos left by her with Bernabé Fernández, a local merchant. To cover the costs of her funeral and burial, Thomasa also instructed that some utensils and jewels she had owned be sold.[64] In another case, Barbola Hernández, a single indigenous mother who lived in Mexico City had only one son, Martin López Palomo, who died long before her and had left all his belonging to his mother, his sole beneficiary.[65]

4

Raising Children

This chapter is a natural transition from the section on raising children in the previous chapter. However, in contrast to chapter 3, here I concentrate instead on the questions of paternity, illegitimacy, kinship, and the frequent relocation of children from place to place and from one form of kinship ties to another. Moreover, what is also at stake here is the myriad of experiences of single women's children, according to their varying socioeconomic conditions and circumstances under which they came to mature. Typically, the single mother would often shift lodgings, with or without her male partner, and so the children born outside wedlock would find themselves trying hard to adjust to new environments, as well as to changing family arrangements. Cohabitations with temporary partners normally did not endure, and the female partners were thereafter left on their own with newborns. Under such circumstances, they found themselves helping one another often in looking for the biological father of their offspring and, upon finding him, anxiously trying to engage him and oblige him to at least recognize his children, if not provide them with food and clothing and, even further on, become committed toward them. It was also in such dire straits that "sisterhoods" functioned as a true charitable framework of mutual support, often helping the single mother in raising funds for fighting her case in court; many of such futile attempts ended up in the ecclesiastical courts, with the mother seeking judicial remedy over inheritance and costs for the children. However, there were cases of single women who were partly compensated by their former partners, as in the case of Isabel de Montoya. Juan Serrano, Isabel's

DOI: 10.5876/9781607329633.c004

first partner, acquired for their mutual eighteen-year-old daughter, Ana María de Montoya, a small adobe house located in a narrow alley behind the San Juan de Dios convent in Mexico City. The house was between calle Donceles and calle Tacuba in the Santa Veracruz barrio, in the very area where the girl's mother, Isabel de Montoya, was born. Upon his death, Juan Serrano bequeathed the house worth 220 pesos to his daughter. Isabel shared lodgings there with her daughter and several other boarders (see above).[1] In another example, in 1689 Juliana de la Cruz, a single mulata slave and mother of two, María and Juan de Monroy, presented before the court evidence related to her children, demanding their recognition as hijos naturales of Captain Alonso de Segura y Monroy, the *alcalde mayor* of Cuauhtitlan. Juliana's motivation in approaching the court was also to obtain her own liberty, as well as part of the captain's inheritance for herself.[2] Such cases were extremely complicated, involving diverse and conflicting interests, and usually lasted for many years. No doubt, pursuing such legal channels empowered these women and might even improve their standing in society. Likewise, on a number of occasions in which the single mother was still a slave, she would appeal for recognition on behalf of her offspring as a means of securing his/her manumission, in addition to gaining a part of the estate of her children's late father. The life experience of children of African slave mothers was obviously highly different from that of children of free and unattached mothers. The laws of the *Siete Partidas* protected certain rights for enslaved individuals and provided a number of legal channels for manumission. Christian slaves were entitled to marry one another with the masters' permission, and masters were legally bound to grant permission, unless they could prove that the union posed a serious danger to their interests. Masters were prohibited from exhibiting cruel treatment, including separating family members from one another, excessive physical punishment, starving slaves, or exploiting them sexually. Masters who did not abide by these laws could be taken to court, and, if proven guilty, their slaves would be sold to another master or, in certain cases, manumitted. Slaves who displayed exceptional service to a master or the state were eligible for manumission.

Here is an exemplary registry of single women's newborns, coming from the parish records of La Asunción Santa María la Redonda in Mexico City, between 1619 and 1622:

Noviembre 13 de 1619.
Bautismo de María, hija de Plonia del barrio de Colhuacatonco.

Junio 23 de 1620.
Bautismo de Juan, hijo de María Mónica, del barrio de Tezcatzonco.

Septiembre 21 de 1620.
   Bautismo de Nicolasa, hija de Petronila, viuda, del barrio de Tezcatzonco.

Octubre 4 de 1620.
   Bautismo de Francisco, hijo de María Francisca del barrio de Copulco.

Octubre 27 de 1620.
   Bautismo de Joseph, hijo de Juliana, negra.

Febrero 18 de 1621.
   Bautismo de Magdalena hija de María, viuda del barrio de Tezcatzonco.

Febrero 20 de 1621.
   Bautismo de Blas, hijo de Lucía de Ávila del barrio de Apanoaya.

Agosto 28 de 1621.
   Bautismo de [hoja mutilada en el margen donde debería estar el nombre de
   la niña], hija de María Jerónima.

Septiembre 13 de 1621.
   Bautismo de Agustín, hijo de Francisca Crispina, viuda, del barrio
   de Tezcatzonco.

Septiembre 28 de 1621.
   Bautismo de Nicolás, hijo de Isabel.

Octubre 12 de 1621.
   Bautismo de [hoja mutilada del margen donde debería estar el nombre], hijo
   de María Jerónima, del barrio de la Concepción.

Octubre 22 de 1621.
   Bautismo de [hoja mutilada del margen donde debía estar el nombre], hijo
   de María Jerónima del barrio de la Concepción.

Abril 3 de 1622.
   Bautismo de Pascuala, hija de María Magdalena.

Abril 13 de 1622.
   Source: AGN, Proyecto OAH (GO), rollo 2205, Bautismos, La
      Asunción Santa María la Redonda DF.

INSECURE UPBRINGING

In effect, single plebeian women's children would often suffer the same fate of their
mothers. For example, in 1659, María de Segovia, a single woman living in the barrio

de San Francisco in Puebla, who had given birth to a single daughter as a result of an affair with a married man who would not recognize his offspring, was unable to bring up five-year-old Juana de Aguilar, her natural daughter. After having been convinced by Joseph de Pisar y María de Herrera, her acquaintances who lived close by, she finally decided to deposit her for a period of about four years in the house of a certain Luis Gordillo and his wife, during which time she would pay for her clothes (vistiéndola yo a mi costa). The couple, apparently, would send the small child to do errands for them, wandering the city streets of Puebla, as well as household works. A year later, and in an extraordinary manner, this five-year-old girl had managed to escape from the house, all by herself, but still did not dare to go and seek help, care, and support from her own mother, but opted instead to go to her aunt. This choice, at such a young age, may well have been due to the very circumstances under which she grew up, until she was given to Gordillo's home. She must have felt uncared for and perhaps even rejected and alienated by her mother, as she was her hija natural, and, perhaps also, her mother's sister was far more warm and loving toward her than her mother, in her own recollections that she still cherished. Thus, we find her at the home of Josepha de San Pedro, her aunt and the sister of her mother, but only for three short days. She recounted to her aunt how she fled an enduring maltreatment by Luis Gordillo and his wife and how she had suffered all throughout her stay with them. Nonetheless, the little girl was forced back to Gordillo's house, where she remained well up to the age of twelve, when her mother finally filed a complaint to the city authorities, pleading to be give her child back. Let us listen to her words:

> María de Segovia, the legitimate daughter of Pocho Nieto and Josefa de Aguilar, I say that there could have been seven years already since, after being asked to do so by Luis Gordillo, inhabitant of this city, and under the intervention of Joseph de Pisar and María de Herrera, and of my free will, I have brought over to them my four-year-old natural daughter, having provided her with clothing of my own costs until a year ago, that my daughter, Juana de Aguilar, who went to live with Josefa de San Pedro, my sister and her aunt, underwent maltreatment by Luis Gordillo, which should not have taken place, for being at the age of nearly twelve years, notwithstanding, he would not return my daughter back to me. I ask that justice will be administered in whatever necessary.

Thereafter, the fiscal del crimen ordered little Juana to be permanently removed from Gordillo's home and returned to her natural mother. One could only imagine what would have been the new situation at home, once Juana returned to her mother's home after seven years of absence and estrangement, and both mother as daughter would need to be newly accustomed to each other.[3]

One finds that single women who could not afford to provide for their children on their own opted at times for more extreme and unconventional arrangements faced with a stressful situation: for example, Ana María, a single indigenous woman living in Mexico City, went as far as the civil court to get an order obliging her own son, Juan Nicolás, to go and find work away from his mother's home, in an *obraje*. She took these legal measures after her son had vigorously resisted the idea of leaving home.[4]

MARÍA DE LA CANDELARIA: A CASE STUDY

In order to further probe the issue of what we may dub as "child negligence" during the early colonial period, I pay close attention to the following case: María Ruiz de las Ruedas, a single, light-skinned mulata, who had once been a slave, had already borne four children out of wedlock, when she found herself one day sharing her life with Joseph Velazco, a humble Spaniard in San Juan de los Llanos, near the city of Puebla. María's children were a young daughter named María de la Candelaria, a son named Sebastián Flores Perla, and another son and daughter.[5] Economically unable to raise her children when cohabiting with her new partner, and, perhaps also, the latter had sanctioned their maintenance within the shared habitation, María placed all four children in the nearby Buenavista Hacienda belonging to Antonio de los Reyes, to serve as slaves. The records do not relate whether María Ruiz de las Ruedas was herself a former slave or if the biological father(s) of her children had this status, in which case all the respective children would automatically be considered slaves; even more bleak was the possibility that the mother may have actually sold her own children into slavery. Schwaller notes that as from 1574, the general policy recommended by Viceroy Enriquez—that all children born to black slaves would automatically be considered slaves themselves—was never actually adopted, and officials in New Spain never considered its implementation (Schwaller 2011, 893).

Our utmost attention is drawn in this case study to the fate of the children, not to their mother's. What I would like to emphasize in this rather long case is the cross-generational fate and repercussions upon María de la Candelaria, in particular. While María de la Candelaria became the direct slave of Antonio de los Reyes's wife, her brothers and sister were sold to Antonio de los Reyes's father-in-law, Martin de Carrabero, who also resided at the hacienda. So at least, the four siblings remained closely together in the same environment.[6] As María de la Candelaria later recounted to her foster father, Joseph Velazco, for the first twelve years or so as de los Reyes's slave, she bore the brunt of constant molestations and lashings by her owner. Later, when she was already twenty-six, her owner made her his mistress;

she gave birth to a first child, but the infant died after only a few months. Two years later, she had another of his babies, María Josepha, who was later formally brought up by her biological father.

Cohabitation between the two went on for about six years, as various house servants later testified, during which time María succeeded in pressuring her master to manumit both herself and her daughter immediately upon his wife's death (de los Reyes's legal wife was on her deathbed at the time) and also convinced him to suggest to his wife that the issue of their freedom be included in her will. However, after his wife's death, Antonio de los Reyes refused to fulfill his oath, and María and her daughter María Josepha remained in bondage. During Holy Week of 1706, the local priest, Miguel Peres, publicly admonished de los Reyes for his evildoings and his moral transgressions.

The priest went further and actually removed María de la Candelaria from the hacienda of de los Reyes and found a haven for her in the home of his own nephew in another village. The priest also instructed that María de la Candelaria's brothers and sister be allowed to leave the hacienda.

In October 1706, María de Candelaria, was twenty-eight, alone on the streets of Mexico City, and in poor health. At this stage, she finally decided to sue her owner for all the damages she and her daughter had incurred at his hands. However, being unable to travel to where her mother, María Ruiz de las Ruedas, resided and formally present an appeal before the local judges, María de la Candelaria sent a letter to her mother asking her to submit charges to the court on her behalf. The case, initially reviewed locally, was subsequently transferred to the court of the Audiencia in Mexico City. María de la Candelaria's letter of appeal to the Audiencia, which she delivered in person, reveals much of the tribulations she underwent from a very early age, which undoubtedly had wide repercussions on her own offspring, as well as on her personal life, and begins as follows:

> I present myself before the royal audience of Mexico to seek justice against my owner, Antonio de los Reyes, for having deflowered me and taken my virginity when I was still very young, and for having made me pregnant with my two daughters, one who died and the other who still lives; and for having kept me as his mistress for twelve whole years, and having been compelled to do so, as I was when he had taken my virginity under the pain of lashes and other maltreatments and threats, reduced me to obey his will; offering me my liberty, and thereafter also that of my daughter, and all this time he would not bring this about, and that he kept me maliciously oppressed and subject to his evil friendship.[7]

Moreover, María de la Candelaria asked the court to order de los Reyes to compensate her for her many years of domestic service, as well as for her loss of liberty, and to remove her daughter from his care.[8] Again, the sources do not document the circumstances that prevented María Ruiz de las Ruedas, the mother of María de la Candelaria, from saving her four children from such anguish. Indeed, placing her offspring in a state of slavery, away from a safe home and a supportive environment, is, to us, indeed, a radical choice. Similarly, we have no testimony regarding whether, during all those years, she paid regular visits to the hacienda to see how her children were coping with such torturous circumstances. If she did in fact come to visit them, she probably would have mentioned this in her court testimony. What is more puzzling for the modern observer is that her daughter, María de la Candelaria, did not entirely break off her connections with her mother and foster father, and despite everything that had transpired sought their help when she found herself in dire straits, something which is completely absent from the accounts of María's siblings, once they found themselves on their own, wandering the streets in search of alternative owners and a new home. Throughout the ordeal, the mother, María Ruiz de las Ruedas, in fact only appeared on the scene when she was finally summoned by the judge to appeal on behalf of her daughter. On that occasion she asked the judge to provide her daughter with a stable place to live together with her daughter María Josepha where she would be protected from her former cohabiter, Antonio.

On 25 October 1706, the presiding judge instructed that María de la Candelaria and her daughter María Josepha be placed in the casa de recogimiento in Puebla until more information was presented in court, and prohibited her owner, Antonio de los Reyes, from taking possession either of her or her daughter. María de la Candelaria subsequently sent a letter of appeal to the court of the Audiencia in Mexico City saying that she would not be able to appear in person before the court due to poor health. According to the testimony submitted by various witnesses who appeared before the court, prior to her death Isabel, wife of Antonio de los Reyes and María de la Candelaria's mistress, dictated her will in which she instructed that María de la Candelaria and her daughter be set free. However, according to the witnesses, her husband, Antonio, did not abide by this request due to hostility and tension between himself and his daughter, María Josepha.

On 6 November 1706, the Audiencia ordered that María de la Candelaria and her daughter, María Josepha de los Reyes, be set free and returned to their new domicile. In addition, their owner, Antonio de los Reyes, was instructed not to accost or pursue them. Antonio de los Reyes himself was nowhere in sight when the court made its decision, and so the orders and instructions were left at his hacienda with his sons, his servants, and the rest of his family, until he would reappear. We have María de la Candelaria's confirmation in her own handwriting that she received the verdict in her favor and that "it is publicly and generally known that Antonio de los

Reyes is hiding somewhere in Mexico City because he is being prosecuted by the criminal court for his acts of violence against her."[9]

A few weeks prior to the dramatic events of Holy Week of 1706, as tensions mounted at the hacienda, Antonio de los Reyes ordered María de la Candelaria's three siblings to finally leave his household, dismissing them together with their papers to look for work at the hacienda of his godfather, Alonso de Castro, who expressed no desire to buy them as slaves. They then departed from de Castro's place, only to return to the Hacienda Buenavista during Holy Week. When the priest discharged all Antonio de los Reyes's remaining slaves, including María de la Candelaria's brothers and sister, he issued them all new identity papers. We have no further word of either their fate or their whereabouts. The usual procedure was that adolescent slaves, such as María de la Candelaria's siblings, who had already served in a household from a very young age, were often set free on the death of their owner or mistress. Others slaves were manumitted after purchasing their freedom with savings they had put aside. The will of doña Damiana de Osorio from 1653, for example, instructs her heirs to inquire whether the parents of her young slave, Antonia, wish to free her and, if so, to do all that is possible for her liberation and safe return to her parents. In addition, doña Damiana instructed that her nine-year-old slave, Francisca, daughter of her slave María, should also be freed and sent with her title of manumission to doña Isabel de Villegas, to be looked after until the age of twenty, "during which time she should be well treated."[10]

In yet another case, that of Josepha de los Angeles, a mulata and the hija natural of Diego Tinoco, Josepha was born as a result of cohabitation between Diego Tinco and María, his black slave from Angola. We are told that, up until the age of seven, Josepha was taken care of by her father in his own household and that she and her mother were then placed by him in the care of his niece, doña Isabel de Silva, who was married to Pedro de Espinosa. Diego also left a large sum of money behind for their needs, and the two thereafter became housemaids in local dwellings. Moreover, as they were subsequently told, Diego had seen to it that the two would be freed after his death. Nevertheless, in May 1643 we find Josepha in rags, aimlessly wandering the streets and telling passersby how her mistress, doña Isabel, had mistreated her, refused to set her free, "in spite of the fact that she was told to do so by her father," and how she also denied Josepha the right to address her mother, María, as such.[11] In the above case, Diego Tinoco, the male partner, possibly attempted to conceal any association with his cohabitant and their mutual child once the latter had grown up and apparently refrained from any type of attachment or open relationship with either of them in the years to come. A fate like this would leave an offspring no other choice but to grow up in a different home and family, in different surroundings and probably under harsher circumstances.

APPLYING FOR RIGHTS OF INHERITANCE

Both widows and single mothers remained legally inferior to men: neither of them could exercise *patria potestad* over their children; although they maintained the legal responsibility to support their children, they had no authority over them, contrary to rights of men (Dore 1997, 109). Therefore, rights to inheritance for children of single women were certainly closely associated with the recognition of these children by their biological father. Clearly, children who were orphans, after both their father and mother had died, stood far less chance of representing themselves in court and fighting for a share of their late father's bequest, particularly if they were still slaves.[12] Others were sons and daughters of single women who were still alive but who could no longer raise their children, either for economic reasons or because of a change in the mother's status, for example, after having entered a new relationship in which the partner would not accept the mother's offspring as part of his household. Twinam rightly remarks that "as the years passed, the traditional bonds of responsibility and affection that linked fathers with their illegitimate children stretched thinner, so that fathers became less likely to provide for offspring after their death," if ever they did so during their lifetime (1999, 174). Yet, in mid-seventeenth-century Mexico we find that, in spite of their inferior status and position in society, single women who gave birth to one or more offspring were upon their partner's death nevertheless eligible to receive a share of their partner's inheritance and property but only by filing an appeal to the Tribunal Superior de Justicia, Alcalde del Críimen / procesos *civiles*. This was so even when the civil status of such women and the paternity of their offspring were never recognized by their partner during his lifetime. We have seen that single mothers were also entitled to file an appeal to the ecclesiastical court of the Archbishopric of Mexico City, obliging their partner to recognize his offspring as his, and his cohabiter as their biological mother. Scrutinizing the civil litigation filed in the Supreme Court of Justice in Mexico City,[13] one encounters a great variety of cases reviewed by the court dealing with the fate of single women as well as their offspring. These include appeals for alimony for themselves and their children after having been abandoned by their male partners;[14] appeals by single women for recognition of their offspring as hijos naturales of their deceased Spanish progenitor; and appeals by the offspring themselves for recognition, which were aimed at obtaining child support, but also, as Komisaruk suggests, "Paternity suits also served purposes beyond attaining child support. For a woman who had been abandoned with children, the judiciary provided a forum for public declaration and punishment of the man's wrongdoing."[15]

In many cases reviewed here, the adolescent children would be the initiators of the legal proceedings. María de Valverde, for example, grew up with her single mulata mother, Tomasa de Santa Teresa. Despite feelings of lingering pain and offense by her absentee biological father—as she continually experienced, having been physically and emotionally abandoned by her father during most of her childhood and adolescence—she succeeded in mobilizing sufficient strength and courage to mount a brave fight to achieve recognition. Based on the fact that she was represented in court by her guardian, it is possible that she was still underage (older than eighteen but younger than twenty-five) at the time that her claims to inheritance from her deceased father were presented in court. Despite her youth, she persisted in her struggle to obtain her share of the property from her late father, Francisco Valverde, against the other claimants, who included his legitimate sons and lawful wife.[16] In spite of being hijos/hijas naturales (illegitimate children) of the father and therefore not entitled to part of his formal inheritance, single mothers' offspring nevertheless went to court to claim their due on the grounds that their father had acknowledged them de facto as his offspring during his lifetime; that he publicly demonstrated his care for them, sustaining them economically, providing them with food and clothing throughout their childhood; and that now that he was gone, they deserved the continuation of his support through his inheritance, despite the fact that they were not mentioned in his will. As hijos naturales in a society and age in which illegitimacy cast a pall over one's life, this status constantly permeated the children's every step and often became an inescapable legal obstacle. The significantly higher percentage of hijos naturales among black and mulato slaves in Mexico between 1670 and 1749, ranges between 72 percent, and as high as 86 percent. Such offspring usually experienced an intense and difficult struggle to gain their biological father's acknowledgment of them as his children during his lifetime. Furthermore, after his death the struggle became particularly pronounced if and when they attempted to inherit some of his property.

Perusing the huge repository of documentation at the AGN dealing with hijos naturales, one in fact finds very few cases in which the biological father was willing to acknowledge paternity. An unmarried mother had the right to claim the acknowledgment of fatherhood for her children, but this provided her only with an allowance for her children, nothing more. Having been born outside relations sanctified by formal matrimony, the children of single women found that their quest for recognition by their biological father, who was often far removed from their lives, an unending and a highly frustrating journey that lasted well after the biological father's death. At times, fathers to such hijos naturales were particularly harsh with their offspring, making this quest especially painful. In her book *Public Lives, Private Secrets*, Twinam writes that "after all, when an unmarried father and mother carried on an open and long-term affair, outsiders would have a very good idea of the natal status of any resulting children . . . Although the natal status of the infant Joseph Francisco was that of hijo natural, his parents protected their own identities and demoted him to the category of 'unknown parentage' on his 1744 baptismal certificate . . . The lifecourse of don Francisco Javier de Betancour reveals how a child raised by a mother became obsessed by his lack of connection with his father's superior name."[17]

In our records, one such deserting father, Agustín López Valdés, for example, left an explicit note attached to his will in which with razor-sharp wording he emphasized "no reconoce a una hija natural, y no dejarle ninguna herencia!" (he does not acknowledge a certain illegitimate daughter, and she should be left with nothing of his inheritance!)[18]

> *E porque no se pueda dudar quales son hijos naturales, ordenamos e mandamus que entonces se digan ser los hijos naturales, quando al tiempo que nascieren o fueren concebidos, sus padres podían casar con sus madres iustamente sin dispensación, con tanto quel / padre lo reconosca por su fijo, puesto que no aya tenido la muger de quien lo ovo en su casa, ni sea una sola. Ca concurriendo en el fijo las calidades suso dichas mandamus que sea fijo natural (Leyes de Toro, No. 11).*

If we rely entirely on jurisprudence, not on reality per se, the above Law of Toro No. 11 states plainly that biological fathers could only acknowledge their children as such on a number of conditions: when they were still in the womb or when their mothers were not "woman on her own," whom his father kept in his household. Having met these conditions, right after being born, the fathers were able to marry their mothers without bans, then, such children could be acknowledged as legitimate children of their fathers. By contrast, in common-law countries, such as in the British Islands, cohabiting couples could wait several years after the birth of their illegitimate children before getting formally married, "and yet had no further children (Adair 1996, 178–79)." One must remember that from a strictly legal stance, fathers were considered liable and indebted only for their hijos legítimos (legitimate children).[19] However, as our records reveal, in praxis, the courts would grant verdicts in favor of claims for support by illegitimate children if convinced their presumed father was indeed their biological father, although the conditions stated in the above laws were not effectively met.

In 1693, such a case was fought in the court of the Tribunal Superior de Justicia, Alcalde del crimen—procesos civiles, in Mexico City. There, Nicolás Benítez Cabello petitioned to be acknowledged as the true heir to his late father, Felipe Cabello. However, shortly before the latter's death, the elder Cabello had apparently dictated a memorandum before a witness, Juan de Valentín, in lieu of a formal will; this step was possibly due to their having been no judge in residence nearby, nor a scribe or a *corregidor* in his village, the closest having been in Coyoacán, which was too far for him to travel to in his poor state of health. In this substitute memorandum, the late father declared that he had been married to his first wife, Josepha de Heredía Vargas, but that they had been childless. Beside him as he dictated the memorandum, stood his second wife, María Calvo de Espinosa, to whom he left his possessions along with those he bequeathed to his brother-in-law, Nicolás de Heredía, the brother of his first wife, Josepha de Heredia Vargas. However, Felipe Cabello's "natural" son, Nicolás, was nowhere mentioned in the memorandum.[20] In conflict with Nicolás petition, it was heard that Cabello's legitimate wife and widow, María Calvo de Espinosa, asked that the court declare the memorandum as a valid legal document, in place of a formal will that Felipe had been unable to dictate due to his deteriorating state of health.[21] On his part, Nicolás stated in court that his father had died twenty days earlier without leaving any formal will behind and with no declared heirs and asked the court to delay all further activity related to disposal of the estate's property until the case was concluded.[22]

According to all the witnesses brought forward by the litigant, Felipe Cabello had been a humble farmer who lived on a secluded ranch on the rolling hills above the village of San Jacinto, which was under the jurisdiction of Coyoacán. The deceased had made his living from petty dealings with the neighboring *obrajes de paño* (textile mills) on the Altos de San Jacinto. Several crucial elements make this case unique. First, we know from the registry of matrimonies archived for the parish of Santa Veracruz in Mexico City that Felipe Cabello was formally married in church on 6 June 1650 to Josepha de Heredía Vargas, his first lawful wife. Second, as Felipe had himself claimed in his memorandum—and as his "natural" son, Nicolás, was finally able to testify in court during the last session of this case—Felipe Cabello had had a "second wife" well after he had first married his lawful wife, Josepha. However, there was obviously no record of a church marriage between Felipe and the woman indicated in the memorandum as his "second wife," María Calvo de Espinosa. Nor do we find any coinciding information concerning a possible case filed in the ecclesiastical courts to either terminate the marriage between Felipe and Josepha, his "first wife," or to prosecute Felipe on grounds of bigamy, which would have indeed been the case before us, under the ostensible circumstances. What is also particularly odd here is that the first wife, Josepha, was not at all involved in the case, either as a litigant, claiming to be the only lawful heir to the deceased, nor as a witness brought forward by the ecclesiastical authorities to testify against her late husband's alleged bigamy. Josepha is nowhere to be seen in our sources, nor do we have any evidence that she died before Felipe became "engaged" to his "second wife." Third, if these circumstances aren't already complicated and suspicious enough on their own, what follows just adds to the confusion: if we juxtapose the testimony with the date of his first marriage, we see that Felipe Cabello had already lived with his lawful "first wife" for ten years or so, without bearing any children of their own, prior to his starting an illicit affair with a local *doncella* by the name of Melchora María de Vargas. This affair lasted for about two and a half years until 1663, some twenty years before the present case was brought before the court and some time before his "second wife," María Calvo de Espinosa, appeared on the scene claiming to be his lawful heir. The doncella Melchora had been a tenant in the house of Juan Antonio in the nearby village of San Jacinto. That same year (1663), she became pregnant from Felipe and gave birth to Nicolás. Virtually immediately, Melchora, unwilling to raise her unwanted newborn, apparently took her newborn to the house of Domingo Benítez, an inhabitant of the village, and left him in the doorway of the house. Three days after she gave birth to Nicolás, Melchora María died from apoplexy and was buried in the churchyard of San Jacinto. Nicolás, the newborn orphan was raised by Domingo Benítez, who did not formally adopt the child but kept him in the family household for the next fifteen years. According to one witness, two years after Melchora's death, Felipe, the father, apparently "attempted to seize Nicolás" and take him away from the Benítez home and bring him to his own home and "become his true parent." However, the occasion quickly turned violent. Domingo Benítez reacted to Felipe's illegal entrance into his domicile and his attempt to abduct Nicolás by delivering a blow with a silver ball to the biological father's head. Felipe escaped from the scene, bleeding and without his son. On the next day or so, after his escape from Domingo Benítez's home, Felipe admitted to a friend to his having "regretted the fact that he did not marry Melchora. Had he done so, he would have avoided all the risk, and would have legitimated Nicolás as his true son."[23]

This case has additional significant points worthy of attention. Primarily, we do not know the racial affiliation of Nicolás's single mother, Melchora. While some of the court witnesses claimed that she was "a reputed doncella and of Spanish origins," this testimony appears highly unreliable, given the fact that her surname, Vargas, was the same as that of the second surname of her partner's first and lawful wife, Josepha de Heredía Vargas. This leads us to suggest the possibility that Melchora was perhaps an ex-slave of this wife who had taken her mistress's name, a very common practice among freed mulatas. Also, when reviewing the testimony, one should also be particularly attentive to standard phrases used by both the litigating parties as well as by the witnesses. For example, the principal litigant, Nicolás testified: "siendo los dos ambos libres, para poder contraer matrimonio, y como tal, me nació y nombró el susodicho siempre he hestado en opinión de tal por tanto" (Both being free persons, they were able to be engaged in matrimony and likewise I was born and the above-mentioned named me, and I was always under such an opinion for a long time.) It is essential to note that masters of slaves usually discouraged formal marriages among their slaves, and thus most of slaves who married did so outside Christian marriage in church (Thornton 1998, 180).

Felipe Delgado, a fifty-year-old muleteer, who became the brother-in-law of Felipe Cabello (he was married to his sister, María Cabello), testified that he was well aware of the illicit relationship that Felipe was conducting with the doncella Melchora as a consequence of which Nicolás Benítez Cabello was born. "In order not to lose her reputation and honor, she gave birth in secret, and left her newborn near the doorway of Domingo Benítez, where Nicolás grew up."[24] Isidro López de Bocanegro, an administrator of obrajes de paño in the Altos de San Jacinto, testified that he had known Felipe Cabello for many years and that the latter had acknowledged the fact that he was having an amorous relationship with Melchora María de Vargas, *española* and unwed, who resided in the houses of Juan Antonio in town . . . It was public knowledge that Nicolás was indeed their natural son . . . and he also confirmed the fact that, "had she not died, Melchora María de Vargas and Felipe Cabello would have been married thereby legitimizing Nicolás as their heir." This last witness added that the mother was "of good repute" and an "reputable person in this town." Franco de Villagómez, yet another witness, recounted in court how, ten months before Felipe's death, he accompanied Nicolás to see his father, above the village of San Jacinto, where he lived, and "saw both of them mount horses and gallop off together and then dismount and have dinner together at the house." And there, the father asked the witness: "how does this fat man [*gordito*], who is my son, appear to you?" "And that it was public knowledge that Nicolás was the natural son of Felipe and another single woman, whom he did not know."[25]

Such standardization of language can be attributed to the goals of dispelling suspicion, "laundering" illicit habits, and reaffirming the social order. Nevertheless, under the circumstances outlined above—in which the deceased had taken another wife without having first applying to the church to annul his lawful marriage with Josepha, compounded by his illicit relationship with a single woman during his marriage that resulted in the birth of a "natural" son—the conditions set by the Laws of Toro No. 11 were not met and the court was unable to pronounce the judgment in favor of Cabello. Thereafter, Nicolás Benítez Cabello claimed that the memorandum supposedly dictated by his late father had been forged (!) so that ultimately the ecclesiastical court was forced to transfer the case to the supreme civil and criminal court in Mexico City for further investigation of the evidence presented before them.[26] Of course, the single woman, Melchora, was the true victim of this case, as in other instances, since even if she survived the ordeal she could never have expected to be compensated by either of the litigating parties.

In cohabitations between a single mother and the biological father that were long-lived and lasted as much as between eight and twenty years offspring were sometimes partially raised by their semiabsent biological father, thus allowing the development of intimate and caring relationships between the children and their father, which could also make the lingering pain of the absence more acute. For example, during the 1670s, for between eight and ten years, Joseph Bravo Díaz maintained an intimate relationship with Josepha Muñoz, his sister's *mulata* slave; their relationship was carried on openly both on the premises of the hacienda and in the city of Puebla. Out of this relationship apparently three children were born: Juan Carillo Bravo and his two sisters, Manuela and Francisca. The father never formally acknowledged them as his true offspring. Francisca was the eldest among the three, having been born on the premises of the estate, and, as her mother remained a slave in doña Leonor's household, the daughter resided there from the time of her birth. Francisca was later transferred to doña Leonor's widowed daughter, doña Manuela Carillo Muñoz, where she remained a slave even after her father's death. Francisca's younger brother and sister, Juan and Manuela, were subsequently born in the town house of Leonor Munōz in Puebla's barrio de Analco, to where doña Leonor had moved soon after the death of her husband, Diego Carillo. It is very likely that there, too, Joseph Carillo Bravo had routinely reunited with his illicit spouse, Josepha Muñoz, with the consent of his sister, doña Leonor. Also, during his visits to Puebla, Joseph was able to spend time with his two natural children, Juan and Manuela, without outside interference. Occasionally, the two younger children were allowed to visit their mother at the hacienda where they were seen in public, as was testified to later on by Cecilia Baez, a free mulata and first cousin of Juan Carillo and his sisters, who lived in Puebla but would frequently visit the hacienda to spend time with her relatives there. During these visits, Cecilia was accompanied by her mistress, Isabel Munōz, sister of Leonor Munōz, owner of the hacienda. Cecilia testified in court how, on her visits to the hacienda, she witnessed how Joseph Carillo Bravo openly hugged the two children, treating them "as his own children . . . These children played freely, all over the hacienda's premises, and were treated affectionately by everyone."[27]

The negative decision of the court regarding the Josepha Muñoz's children's case represents, indeed, the futility of suing for rights of inheritance, when there was no firm substantiation of the father's full acknowledgment of his "natural" offspring during his lifetime.[28] Later in life, extremely poor and with no one to help them, the Carillo Bravo (Muñoz) brother and sister were seen by others, dressed in rugs, peddling in the streets of Puebla and in the main square, selling cheap iron trivia. Children unable to depend on adults for food had several ways to get bread. The very young turned mostly to begging, particularly for leftovers at the doorways of inns and wealthier homes. They hung around the markets, where they begged for leftover bread or partly spoiled produce that wouldn't keep for the next day (see also Perry 2007, ch. 9). The fate of their sister, Francisca, who remained enslaved at the hacienda, was presumably far better than their own, considering how she was at least able to avoid destitution and starvation while living in the household of her widowed mistress, Manuela María, and in close proximity to her own mother, also a slave up until the point in which she was transferred from the hacienda to Puebla.

Shortly after her partner's death, Isabel de la Cruz, a free mulata and single mother to Beatriz de Carvajal, did all that she possibly could to ensure that her daughter would be able to inherit some houses that had belonged to her biological father—a sizeable property in the San Sebastián barrio of Mexico City—in due course. The father, a Spaniard named Juan Carvajal, apparently had acknowledged his paternity just before his death.[29] There are also cases in which single mothers fought for part of the biological father's inheritance that, the mothers would argue, was due to their mutual offspring even through the descendant was already deceased. María Inés de la Vega, a *mestiza* and single mother of the late Antonia Felipa, had given birth to the daughter as a result of sexual union with Miguel Díaz de Cienfuegos. After the latter's death, Antonia Felipa's mother went to court to claim part of Cienfuegos's inheritance, seeing as her deceased daughter had been his hija natural. María Inés brought with her a copy of her daughter's death certificate.[30]

In cases in which the biological father had indeed recognized his offspring while still alive, the mother could appeal to the ecclesiastical as well as the civil courts to seek part of his estate.[31] Such recognition was deeply embedded within the social fabric in which these children grew up and constituted the terms and conditions by which their mothers sustained themselves. There are cases in which children went to court on their own initiative to seek part of their biological father's inheritance, while in other cases they were represented by their single mothers. In the follow-up to the case I cited above, Beatriz de Carvajal, the free mulata and mutual hija natural of Isabel de la Cruz and the late Juan Carvajal, did eventually go to court herself to claim part her biological father's estate consisting of houses located in the barrio de Santiago, in Mexico City. Unfortunately, we do not know how old Beatriz was when she approached the court or whether she succeeded in acquiring what she claimed.[32] Andrea de Rivera, a single woman and mother of the child Agustín de Useda, went to court herself to represent her son against Álvarez de Hinostroza, the executor of the estate of the late Agustín de Useda, whom the mother claimed to be the "natural father" of her child. The elder Agustín de Useda bequeathed their mutual offspring the considerable sum of 500 pesos, but, according to the mother, the estate's executor never transferred the bequest to her child as specified in the will.[33]

THE EXTRAORDINARY CASE OF BARBOLA DEL MORAL

An extraordinarily detailed case, 140 pages in length, which could well serve as a test case for modern times, can be found in the appeal of Barbola del Moral (or,

Barbara de Morales) to both the civil and ecclesiastical courts, calling for the recognition of the late Lucas Gonzales as the biological father of her two young daughters, Juana María and María as his hijas naturales. The story takes place in the small indigenous town of Tlalnepantla, under the jurisdiction of Tacuba, and in the nearby village of San Francisco Tizapan, among cattle and mule owners and middle-size farmers. The petitioner's appeal demands her own recognition as the *madre natural* (biological mother) of the two girls and her right to inherit part of Gonzales's estate on behalf of her daughters.[34] The inheritance at stake, located in the nearby town of San Francisco Tizapan (Tlalnepantla), consisted of a midsized cattle and mule ranch with an estimated value of 5,505 pesos. Appearing before the ecclesiastical court, Barbara de Morales argued that the two girls were the biological daughters of the late Lucas Gonzales and that, at the time of their births, both she and the deceased had lived together out of wedlock and that Lucas had in fact acknowledged them as his own daughters, providing them with all their needs as long as he was alive. Barbola claimed that she had already been widowed to the late Juan de Quiñones before entering into a relationship with the late Lucas Gonzales and that she had remained with him until his death from a leg complication two months earlier. In contradiction to Barola's testimony, some of the witnesses on behalf of the defendant Gonzales described in court how Barbola had already maintained an informal union with yet another man, Juan de Castañeda from the town of Tepozotlán, prior to her relationship with Lucas Gonzales. However, Lucas's cousin, Francisco de Herrera, a Spanish silversmith from Mexico City, testified on behalf of the claimant. This witness told the court that he was convinced of the two girls' *being the mutual offspring of his cousin and the claimant* and that in fact the late Lucas and Barbola also had had a mutual son, Miguel, who died when he was a year old. Francisco furthermore told the court that he always encouraged his cousin to provide these two girls with food but that "he had never encouraged him to continue this illicit relationship." According to Francisco's testimony, on other occasions he would ask his cousin Lucas why he wasn't attending to his girls' needs now that they had already grown up, and Lucas would respond by saying—"Andando el tiempo las remediaria . . ." (Time heals everything . . .). On another occasion, when the witness was visiting Lucas, who was already sick, he saw how Lucas's mother, María de Contreras, picked up one of the girls, Juana María, "giving her much affection, and that she recognized them as her own granddaughters." Another witness on behalf of the claimant, Antonio Sánchez, a Spaniard and painter at a company producing playing cards in Mexico City, served as Juana María's *compadre* "under Lucas's instructions," adding that when Barbola was pregnant with Juana, Lucas persuaded him to go and fetch her from Tlalnepantla, where she resided, and bring her to a house which Lucas had found for her in Mexico City; there Lucas himself provided her with all her needs.[35] Another of Lucas's first cousins, Andrés Bressera, also a silversmith, said that Barbola and Lucas remained together for eight or ten years; that he himself had served as compadre to Lucas when he baptized his son Miguel, who later died; and that the second girl, María, was almost born in his own hands. He further recounted how, when Barbola was already pregnant with Juana María, Lucas brought her to Mexico City from their ranch in Tlalnepantla and set her up in a house he had rented for her in the barrio de Santa Inés. Like Lucas's other cousin, Francisco de Herrera, Andrés Bressera also claimed to have encouraged Lucas to take care of the two girls and forced him to help them out of troubles and provide their mother with money and other necessities. This witness added that "he was sure that, having died without repentance, Lucas would leave behind a portion of his estate to the two girls and that Lucas's mother would also recognize them as her granddaughters."

Don Agustín de Cervantes, a native Nahua lord and an appointed confessor in the Archobizpado (!), who lived in the calle Santa Teresa in Mexico City in houses owned by Francisco de Zarate, testified that he was present at Lucas's deathbed and how the latter whispered to him that he had left behind no will and that he was unable to confess to him, but could only hold up his hand.[36] In January 1676, the representative of the defendant Nicolas Gonzales asked his witnesses if they were aware that when Barbola del Moral was pregnant with the two girls, she had been living with Juan de Castañeda in Tepozotlán where they were born and thus apparently were *his* daughters? María de Contreras, Lucas's mother, agreed that the girls were *not* the children of her son, Lucas Gonzales, because during the time of her pregnancies Barbola del Moral was indeed cohabiting with Juan de Castañeda in the town of Tepozotlán. This witness further asserted that her late son Lucas had never recognized the two girls as his own children, nor did he include them in his will; nor, in fact, did he have any property of his own, "because he lived in his mother's s house and at her expense."[37] In September 1677, Barbola del Moral interrogated her own witnesses, asking them whether they knew that Lucas was a capable farmer who had accumulated property of his own but that his mother and brothers had expropriated most of his estate, leaving behind only a few belongings of little value. All Barbola's witnesses testified that Lucas indeed possessed a large quantity of mules and mares and that he had sold two slaves, one mulato and one black, in the Plaza Mayor of Mexico City. One of these, Nicolás de Espinosa, a Spaniard and an ironmonger in the Plaza Mayor of Mexico City, testified that he had witnessed the birth of María, the younger of the two girls and that it was when Barbola was pregnant with Juana María that she had moved from Tlalnepantla to Mexico City, where she gave birth to the new daughter. On many occasions, when this witness visited Barbola's lodgings, he saw Lucas "holding and fondling his daughter María," and he told how Lucas would always declare that "these were his two daughters, together with the other son who had died." Although Lucas remained living in San Francisco Tizapan together with his mother, most of his days he spent in Mexico City, where he would reside in Barbola's house. By 1678, the prosecutor of the Supreme Court was for granting Barbola del Moral her share of the estate of the late Lucas, but doña María de Contreras, his mother, continued to file litigation *in contra*.

MEAGER PROSPECTS FOR SOCIAL MOBILITY

Clearly, in a society based very much on honor and pedigree, the offspring of single women found it hard to climb the social ladder. Such values no doubt also influenced their choices regarding marriage later in life. In the repository of sources available to us, there are many cases of single plebeian women who were slaves most of their lives but who were freed by their masters at some point in time, either as a result of the latter's death or as an act of mercy. Some of these slave women mothered children, and the latter were therefore automatically considered slaves themselves. A few of the records we have relate the endeavors of such single mothers to liberate their children from slavery. Such an example was that of Clara Rosa, a free mulata living in Mexico City. After the death of her mistress, doña Gertrudis Bravo de Agüero, in 1726, Clara's benefactor became doña Juana Lorenza, doña Gertrudis's adopted daughter. Because the latter was still underage, she was placed under the guardianship of doña Patrona Bravo de Agüero, who also became the guardian of doña Juana's inherited property, which included Clara Rosa's fifteen-year-old daughter, María Micaela. The latter was in effect raised by doña Patrona Bravo de Agüero from the age of three to fifteen, at which point her biological mother, Clara Rosa, began doing everything possible to set her daughter free. Clara Rosa actually went to court, claiming that her daughter was being maltreated by her mistress and therefore should be freed. Taking into consideration that the case involved a young slave, whose own mother was ready and eager to care for her outside her enslaved situation, the judges may well have pressured doña Patrona Bravo de Agüero to endorse their inclination and free the girl. However, the latter agreed to do so only on condition of being reimbursed to the sum of 200 pesos, which, she claimed was equivalent to the work value of María Micaela, the slave, for doña Juana Lorenza, her underage mistress. The two contesting parties then proceeded to hire *corredores de Lonja* (professional evaluators), who could determine the exact market price for the girl, which was finally set at 175 pesos.[38]

Social mobility by offspring of single plebeian mothers was usually restricted to formal engagements with prospective partners originating from "upper" racial groups only if the latter came from very humble socioeconomic backgrounds. Juan Galindo, for example, was a free mulato and the hijo natural of Alonso Galindo Morillo from Cuernavaca and Ana Maña, his single mother. Juan had moved with his mother to live in Mexico City when he was a small child, and found himself constrained due to his civil status when he wished to get married. His best prospective bride was forty-year-old Francisca del Castillo, an española, with whom he became acquainted in their mutual parish of the Cathedral in Mexico City. Francisca del Castillo herself was of very humble background. Francisca had been widowed only a month-and-a-half earlier when her husband, Baltazar de los Reyes, died suddenly in the Hospital de Nuestra Señora de la Caridad. The widow, Francisca, was indeed eager to quickly remarry, most probably due to her advanced age and her expectations of possibly still being able to become pregnant. The couple's request to be married in church was approved despite so little time having elapsed since the death of Francisca's first husband. The approval of the church authorities can only be explained if we assume that the ecclesiastical judge was already convinced that due to Francisca's advanced age and her desire to give birth to a child, the case indeed justified urgency, usually exercised only in cases of ill health. Furthermore, men of the church, including the present judge, have long thought that the role of marriage was indeed to restrict sexual licentiousness; therefore he would not have thwarted or even delayed Francisca's subsequent marriage.[39]

5

Singleness and Sexuality

Doña Melchora had overheard Magdalena one day advising her "sisters" there to "refrain from marrying men who pretended to become engaged with them . . . Lorenzo [her husband] was seized by an uncontrollable desire to have sexual relations with Magdalena." (Doña Melchora's testimony)

In the background of the contents and context of this chapter is the second theme: "I Felt Deceived." Acutely embedded in the life history of these women are the early adolescence experiences of sexual harassment and the loss of virginity to young men and elder partners who had promised to remain with them forever and then had forsaken them. As a direct result, the women's matured sexuality provided them with the arena for vengeance: through the unwinding of this early feeling of deception, they turned lust into their weapon against such men.

In Ana Lidia García Peña's essay on the phenomenon of single women in Mexico City during the nineteenth century and the first decades of the twentieth century, based on 217 cases found in the Juicios por Alimentos (court cases concerning petitions for alimony) of the Archivo Histórico del Tribunal Superior de Justicia in Mexico City, that author takes a different stance than this present study regarding these women. She writes: "The present investigation explicates how those women experimented and utilized excessively their sexuality as much as their fertility for the sake of establishing illicit relationships within which they encountered pragmatic solutions for their lives, more than a romantic love." García Peña explains that these

DOI: 10.5876/9781607329633.c005

women "adopted" the posture of victimization and "a certain theatrical behavior in order to turn the judicial authorities' reasoning in their favor." Their "playing the victim" was accordingly an intentional choice on their part, aimed at gaining alimony from the partners who had deserted them as much as welfare from the state. García Peña also explores the lives of single mothers and the circumstances of the endemic poverty and social isolation that often characterized their lives. While gender constraints often cast women as victims, there were also many ways in which women wielded agency, albeit within the period's restrictive social constraints and discriminatory laws: "Presenting themselves before the public authority [the civil court] they created a socially-construed discourse, that of seduced victims who were deceived, and who were now seeking protection . . . they were at one and the same time victims of their poverty and survivors of their strategies." As García Peña interprets the attitudes of single women regarding their remaining unmarried, she points out two significant patterns or "strategies," which she identified in their behavior: (a) "they established relationships of concubinage moved by economic interests more than by personal preferences," and (b) "they knew how to take advantage of the assets that they held in having illegitimate offspring." Accordingly, as she expounds: "Their first strategy was to maintain relationships of concubinage or adultery with the hope of coming across an option of subsistence, a masculine assistance," while after a few months, when abandoned by their lovers, all alone with their babies, they would then pursue their second strategy: "the utilization of their newborns via the judicial channels" (2004, 647–50). Nicole von Germeten also pursues a similar direction of thought when she says: "non-elite women organized their sex lives with economic goals in mind," but, in contrast to Garcia-Peña, the latter refutes "proscriptive moralizers on the sexuality of Spanish, indigenous, African and racially-mixed women" (2013, 232). García Peña's interpretation is indeed radical in that she places intentional agency upon these women, in a manner much more pronounced than what Steve Stern originally meant when he asserted that "Women mobilized the patriarchs of the local infrastructure—village authorities, priests, local elders" so that they could use the legal system to their own advantage (1995, 101). Our own assessment of these women is far less conclusive than that of García Peña, and in contrast to her I prefer to avoid viewing them through a perspective of "victimization" or intentioned "strategies." It may be possible that some savvy women have known how to "work the system"; most, however, were really in desperate straits.

The goal of this chapter is, nevertheless, to be able to provide some insights into single plebeian women's treatment of honor, chastity, and sexuality from a number of vantage points, as well as how their sexuality was viewed by the church, the colonial authorities, and the people around them. Stuart Schwartz's treatment of "sexuality and thought" and on "simple fornication" in his book *All Can Be Saved* corresponds perfectly with what I am trying to elaborate upon here. Accordingly, in Spain, the notion was that only long-lasting concubinage, of over seven years, was said to be a mortal sin. Schwartz's historical actors, as he describes, "defended the more stable unmarried relationship," and viewed "simple fornication" "as a lesser sin" (2008, 26–34). What does this tell us about moral norms and sexual attitudes of the time? Indeed, it tells us much about the unbridgeable gap between subaltern norms and attitudes, and the church's stance on monogamy.

THE DUAL MODEL OF CHASTITY

Throughout the Middle Ages, two opposing models of marriage were prevalent in Europe. The first was essentially civic, its function being to preserve the social order; the other was essentially ecclesiastical, serving to maintain divine order. By AD 1140, Gratian set forth the tenet that bonds of marriage were "determined by mutual consent and not by the consummation of marriage, because where there is to be union of bodies there ought to be union of spirits" (qtd. in de Moor and Van Zanden 2010, 5). In 1215, the Fourth Lateran Council stipulated marriage as a consensual, voluntary act, in which the woman, in an equal manner to that of the man, could freely choose the partner who best suited her. By the first decades of the thirteenth century, the Western European doctrine of consensual marriage was already widely disseminated across entire church structures, from the highest echelons down to the parish level, by means of the parish priests' sermons to the laity. Matrimony was considered a sacrament in the Catholic Church when Pope Innocent IV insisted on challenging the opinions of the Valdesians. In 1239, the decretals of Gregory IX stated that marriages were made by God and that the priest's role was only to proclaim God's will post factum. In 1439, the Council of Florence, in a decree to the Armenians, established matrimony as the seventh sacrament, a sign of the union between Christ and the church (Tanner 1989, 550). The teaching of matrimony as a sacrament was confirmed by the Twenty-Fourth session of the Council of Trent, between 3 February and 11 November 1563, devoted to the traditional doctrine on matrimony.[1] The Church thus reestablished its dominion over marriage, confirming it as a sacrament (Goody 1984, 157–82; Duby 1978). Among the prescriptions (*Tametsi*) that the Council of Trent approved, was one dictating that marriage was to be made public and accompanied by public pronouncement of the relevant bans; that consent of the parents was to remain a precondition, but that the marriage without parents' consent remained legal. The wives were called to accept the authority of their husbands, and to win them over to the faith without speaking a word but solely by good conduct, purity, and reverence (Bell 1999, 237). Sexual conduct in marriage was an inseparable part of this package.

In the mid-sixteenth century, Ignacio Loyola, the founder of the Jesuit Order, wrote: "The whole foundation of Christian Society rests upon the peaceful and honorable conduct of married people . . . In respect to matrimony, there reign disorders and a bad example flourishes like a weed. Married women live with no fear of God . . . [those who have separated from their husbands in open sin]."[2] Thus, the immoral behavior of married couples and the dissolution of marriage were among the main points to which the Jesuits directed the spiritual attention of noble women, as had Loyola himself (Blaisdell 1988, 244). The Tridentine model of marriage was not enforced in New Spain until 1588, and even then much ground was still left for local norms to prevail. The Third Mexican Church Council of 1585 raised the penalty to automatic excommunication for anyone interfering with the free choice of partners to marriage, ordering punishment of informal unions in which one of the partners was already married or otherwise barred from legitimating the union by going through a church ceremony.

What were the widespread concepts in early modern Spain concerning a married woman? To be complacent with her husband, always faithful, between submissive and enamored; to be resolved in character, however, tender and kind toward the children, vigilant over the servants and maids, so that they would perform one's duty, and diligent with the affairs of the house and of the property. Likewise, in 1523, in his famous treatise, *Instrucción de la mujer christiana*, Juan Luis Vives prescribed a set of rules and norms of conduct that should deter virgins, adolescents, young ladies, married women, and widows from transgressing their assigned roles in society; he claimed that such infringements would bring the institution of the family to a ruin, and recommended restricting sexual behavior and misrule, and enforcing female obedience through distinct penalties, from the admonitions to corporal punishments (Elena Martinez 2004, 482–485). His compatriot and the contemporaneous Fray Antonio de Guevara conveyed this in his prose: "The properties of the married woman are that they should consider with gravity going outside, with sanity to govern the house, with patience to endure the husband, with love to raise the children, with affability towards the neighbors, with hasten to keep the property, with fulfillment in things of honors, a friend of honesty and an ardent enemy in the company of indolent young woman" (qtd. in Vigil 1986, 45).

The Hispanic Catholic worldview of the relationship between body and soul stemmed from early Christianity's dichotomy between the two. Accordingly, from the times of St. Paul onward, sex and freedom became interrelated issues: the early Christian Fathers vehemently admonished the Roman world's utilization of male and female slaves to satisfy their (free) sexual lust and instructed instead that free choice is the will to overcome lust, which was considered to be a repugnant sin, one of the seven deadly sins and an infringement of the Ten Commandments. In consequence, early Christian morality, by contrast to Greek and Roman morality, alienated itself from nature and the cosmos, and returned to God (Harper 2013). Lustful thoughts, feelings, and actions had to be overcome; therefore, people must disconnect themselves from their own bodily senses (Curcio-Nagy 2014, 48). Women played an ambivalent role of women as mothers and at the same time as the objects of sexual fantasies. Analyzing the Arapaho myth cited by Claude Lévi-Strauss, Chris Knight has meticulously described how, according to the phases of the moon, a woman possesses two complementary identities: "During the seclusion phase she is a sexually unavailable, ritually unattractive sister or mother and, during the marriage phase she is an attractive, sexually available wife" (1997, 133–53). It was further thought that under such a constant state of transition, the power relations among the genders were not as encapsulated as we thought them to be and that there were recognizable beneficences to it for "women on top." In this very context, the various practices of single plebeian women, the subjects of this book—such as the choosing and changing of different male partners, their exploration of their bodies, and "sinful lust"—could well be interpreted to be different forms of recalcitrance, vis-à-vis the prevailing structural modes of repression, to "dominate" male virility through both mundane and magical means.

During the peak of the Catholic Reformation, the church norms surrounding marriage and extramarital cohabitation in colonial New Spain brought to the light the insidious image of women living together in "free spirit" and free love. As I wish to highlight here, during the early to mid-colonial era, single plebeian women enacted a free choice contradicting contemporaneous church teachings, in the ways in which they were able to, and chose to, forsake matrimony, explore their bodies (and lust), and turn their bodies into a power mechanism. In this context, free choice could be associated with the distinction between body and soul, reality and ideology. Seventeenth-century authors, such as Antonio de Molina, advocated that virtuous people shun bodily desires and allow only reason and the soul to reign over their behavior (Jaffary 2004, 160).

One other substantial phenomenon that could clearly be associated with the above is the pervasiveness of the institute of cohabitation among the mixed castes in particular and the fact that the church and state were unable to restrict this phenomenon in actuality. This last point is in direct conversation with what Martha Few writes: "Furthermore, body images began to shape discourses of violence in colonial Guatemala, as men and women from all social groups in the capital connected community conflicts to monstrous, leaky and malleable bodies, transformed by women's sorcery practices. In addition, some women used their own bodies and body parts as instruments and expressions of ritual power . . . The use of body parts linked specifically to female sexuality spoke to many people's fears about women's ability to control men through witchcraft and magic" (2002, 4, 54). Therefore, such single women of color were viewed as a real menace to the theological-ideological teachings emphasizing chastity over lust, as well as to the model of life of matrimony and to the patriarchy. Contemporary theologians portrayed single women as leading an evil way of life, immoral, and dangerous to their surroundings, especially those who reached menopause. Our own records from Mexico City and Puebla, around the same period, abound with references and citations concerning the moral and behavioral conduct of unmarried, deserted, and divorced women, as well as listing instructions and ordinances recommending their reeducation and punishment within city recogimientos.[3]

Throughout the period reviewed here, it was believed that "evil socialization" could certainly take place among women living on their own, who were usually without male guidance. They were, likewise, described as living in sexual promiscuity and fornication and as practicing deviant and heretical rites. The generating evil was also claimed to occur under circumstances in which transgression against the Christian model of the patriarchal, holy family was the outcome of an intentional revolt against it, through the total abandonment of the discipline of family life by women for the sake of pursuing different alternatives of pseudoconsanguineal relationships. These women were thus portrayed in the records as having relinquished family life and chosen instead to partake in sisterhoods and quasi-consanguineal relationships or bonds.[4] Let us look at Fray Agustín Farfán's famous treatise on medicine in New Spain, *Tractado breve de Medicina* (Mexico City, 1592). The author describes how the most common maladies of the unmarried, those living away from their husbands, were *mal de madre* (or vaginal pains) and ulcer of the abdomen. According to Farfán, both were related, to the peculiarities of the menstrual cycle among unmarried women, due to the fact that their menstrual blood is "particularly warm, humid, and corroded" and could flow from parts of a woman's body besides her vagina. He goes on to provide the symptoms: "'Having suffered from the withholding of the semen, together with an irregular menses, they are in such pains that they feel like dying. They are a vessel of extremely dangerous venom . . . their intoxicated blood is mixed with melancholy, and its vapors reach up to their brain, causing great agony, and sometimes a condition of madness.' The Mal de Madre could originate either from the withholding or the abundance of semen, but in any of these circumstances, *estando el mal en su rigor y fuerza*. [evil being his arduousness and potency]."

Prescribing the appropriate measures to be taken, Farfán advised refraining from extracting blood from the patient until the corrupt semen contained within the blood had diminished to its normal quantity and quality. "Otherwise, this act could cool the vagina too much and cause vapors to accumulate and ascend to the heart and head of the corrupt semen, but in case the patient is pregnant this should never occur" (Farfán 1592 [1944], bk. 1, ch. 11; bk. 2, ch. 18). A single woman's menstrual blood was, therefore, the most polluting and poisonous and her mind "most prone to vice."[5] The English Protestant missionary and traveler Thomas Gage, whose testimony we should approach with caution and reluctance, visited Puebla during these years. He attested how it was "an accepted norm" among attractive black and mulata young women to become the courtesans and cohabitants of rich and powerful merchants and public officials there. They were also depicted as "dressed in their particular seductive style, with abundant jewelry and silk pieces, which led the Spaniards to deprecate their own wives" (*Thomas Gage's Travels in the New World* 1969, 69–70).

Handing promiscuous women over to the authorities was the most convenient outlet for fending off anxieties and redressing and adjusting the threat, especially in small, racially homogeneous, close-knit inner circles of men related by marriage and by common interests in mid-seventeenth-century New Spain. In the records, the malevolent side of these women was also strongly associated with the act of polluting the household, thus leading to a final separation between married couples and even causing the death of the deserting partner. Julio Caro-Baroja's study of Pierre de Lancre's investigations into Basque witchcraft in the early years of the seventeenth century clearly indicates the French judge's view of such transgressions of family life as the major cause of the outbreak of witchcraft and Devil worship in this area in particular. In her study on witchcraft and marginalized women in India, Ajay Skaria concluded that by "depicting women as practitioners of gratuitous violence and by treating them all as potential dakans [witches], men vehemently criticized the female exercise of power . . . among Adivasi women, their image of themselves as dakans [witches] was very intimately and quite directly connected to the combination of their power and its marginality." (Caro Baroja 1965, 151–65; Skaria 1997, 108–37). In his *Night Battles* Carlo Ginzburg concluded that "the witches took the place of her family and legitimized her feelings of intolerance and revolt against her real family, sentiments she could not express and which she ascribed to convenient inventions" (1986, 136). In her study of the Inquisition of Toledo, María Helena Sánchez Ortega cites a far more extreme case, also in 1648, of an intentional revolt against and replacement of the moral and cultural code of the "disciplined family." In this case, a woman nicknamed "La Lobera" [the "wolf-woman"] was accused of having made a pact with the Devil while living a semisavage life in the wild, "with a pack of wolves, controlled by her commands, after the father of her child had refused to marry her" (1986, 207). The "process" was alleged to occur especially within "disturbed" family structures and in particular among kin living away from society, to whom the discourses of the church and the Inquisition always attributed the nature of a secret lodge or cult as well as the explicit practice of incest.

What, then, were the contributing factors and incentive for single women to adopt modes of living in "misrule"? In 1639, for example, Juan de Espinosa, single, and María de Rivera, a widow, were formally charged with cohabitation. The unusual punishment for both was severe and exemplary: banishment for two years to the Philippines. Their return to Puebla was preconditioned upon their marrying in church and undergoing Communion.[6] The Post-Tredintine ecclesiastical courts, backed by local city authorities, took into their purview the prosecution of single male and female cohabitants.[7] The other ordinance concerned "women, whether married, or single, who publicly live with adulterers, or with concubines. If they are threatened three times and still remain disobedient, they should be punished severely by the local church authorities, and even driven out of their diocese" (*El sacrosanto y ecuménico Concilio de Trento* 1785, sess. 24, ch. 8, 413; Seed 1998a; Stern 1995). Friends and neighbors were likewise encouraged to publicly denounce such illicit relationships, as well as provide information to the court. Unmarried couples were put under much stricter surveillance.[8] Beginning in 1606, one of the most elaborate cases to be found during these years in which rigorous actions were taken against fornicators by both the church and city authorities in Puebla was that of Maríana de Ojeda, a single mulata from Puebla. Furthermore, this specific case was intended to serve the authorities as a good example of demonstrating single women's promiscuity and limitless sexual craving, as well as the evil incurred by single women who have already reached menopause, and especially when they grouped together "to commit carnal sins." The court records of the criminal process against Maríana de Ojeda, initiated by the alcalde mayor of Puebla, and thereafter transferred to the criminal court of the Archbishopric in Mexico City, are 155 pages long and strikingly detailed. They included the testimony of tens of witnesses. Altogether, her trial lasted for eight years, from 1606 through 1614. Maríana de Ojeda, a single mulata, born in Seville, Spain, arrived at the Mexico shores, after the death of her husband, Gaspar de los Reyes, a surgeon. She settled in Puebla, in the vicinity of Los Portales, on the Mesones Street, and next to the Plaza Pública, where she became the owner and manager of a public pastry shop, below her house, where she also sold wine and beverages.[9] The court records of her case highlight the fact that Ojeda's shop became a crucible for single women, who interacted and exchanged valuable information concerning the possibilities and prospects of both married and single men. Numerous scandals arose from these exchanges, resulting in denunciations to the city authorities and the church authorities by the betrayed wives. The interrogation pursued by the criminal court of the Archbishopric of Mexico City is of significance to our observation of how such women were persecuted and what concerns were echoed in the questions posed to them.

The questions were the direct outcome of the denunciations that had arrived on the desk of the prosecutor. Asked by the public prosecutor if while selling cakes and wine in her pastry shop, "many men came to her house and have had communication with her?," Maríana de Ojeda replied that "many people would arrive at her house to buy these commodities, and then left without her having any contact between them." Asked thereafter if "each day she would let many single and married women enter through a camouflaged doorway, and from there they would climb up to her rooms, where men awaited them in her bed and slept with them, and thereafter, had afternoon tea together?," She denied it all. Asked by the prosecutor if "one day, she came to the house of a married woman, whom she hated for having denied her a relationship with her husband, she scolded this woman and told her that her husband would ordinarily arrive at her house, and saying other evil and dishonest words to that woman?," again, she denied it all. Asked whether she "was ordinarily the cohabiter of Pedro Alferes Troya, who supported her with food, lodging and money by which she rented her house?," she refuted the information. Asked if "on many occasions, she would use foul language with her neighbors, standing by the doorway of her house?," she denied it. The next question posed to her was, "if a year earlier, she went to the Portales de los Mercaderos, below the *casas del cabildo* [municipal council's buildings] of the city, and there, approached one honorable, married man, who was working by the doorway of one of the stores, and said to him publicly, foul words, without any reason and caused him disgrace?"[10] In the same manner, on 21 September 1609, forty-year-old Gonzalo Peres Troya *alférez* (ensign), the owner of a silver mine, was accused of having maintained concubinage with Maríana de Ojeda in 1603, for a period of two years, during which "they slept and ate at the same bed and same room" in her house; there he had been caught by the alcalde mayor. He admitted to having had a relationship with Ojeda but claimed that he had never been imprisoned for this and that "it is already three and a half years that he does not have any contact with her whatsoever."[11] This wording, no doubt, accentuates a style of living that mimics a real matrimony, but nonetheless ridicules it.[12] On 21 August 1609, Maríana was brought to court to respond to the accusations of cohabitation filed against her. She was already forty years old by that year, and a widow. Asked if she has had a relationship of cohabitation with the above and "slept and ate at the same bed and same room," she responded by saying that she has known him for more than two years and that for a year and a half they maintained a carnal relationship. He would not come to her house, but she went to his, and that on that day and night he came to her house for a short while, and seeing the alcalde mayor at the door of the house, he hid himself in one of her rooms, and it was then that the alcalde mayor found him. Cohabitants usually spent a few weeks in jail before being warned against ever meeting one another again.

During much of August 1608, Maríana de Ojeda was kept under house arrest in a *casa de depósito* (a safe house for depraved women) at the alguacil's lodgings. Thereafter, she was sentenced to one year of exile from the city and, in case she did not comply, was threatened with a fine of 200 pesos. On 18 September 1609, the prosecutor, Pedro López presented the formal accusations filed against her. These included denunciations by several married and respectful men and women who lived on her street, concerning bad and promiscuous behavior and foul words, made in public by Maríana de Ojeda and directed against them, as well as charges concerning cohabitation.[13] Married women were usually treated discretely by the court, and thus their names were not disclosed in the records.

Let us review the exact wording utilized: "una mujer que no conviene declarar su nombre . . . Or, Joseph del Castillo y una cierta mujer que por ser casada no declara su nombre, están públicamente amancebados de seis años a esta parte conociendo y durmiendo juntos como si eran marido y mujer conosiéndose carnalmente" (a woman whose name should not be mentioned . . . Or, Joseph de Castillo and a certain woman, who, for being married, would not declare her name, publicly fornicated for already six years until these days, knowing each other and sleeping together as though they were man and wife, knowing each other carnally).[14]

How did single women coming from the plebeian classes treat "honor" and "chastity," as well as vows of marriage, and "concubinage"—as yet from a very different angle and mentality than that of their contemporaneous compatriots from the uppermost echelons of colonial Spanish society? Poska (2012) proposes that even Spanish women, who migrated to the colonies, with time, have changed their attitudes toward honor and chastity, as they assimilated into the local environment and mentalities. As is gleaned from the primary sources cited here, Spanish women of all classes indeed shared with plebeian women in the colonies much more than was previously portrayed, in sexual behaviors and practices. Nevertheless, in this debate one needs to separate the issue of sexuality from the more mundane socioeconomic considerations, such as the difference between the marriage prospects of Spanish women and women belonging to the lower *castas*, in case they lost their virginity prior to matrimony, or, the future of these women's inheritance, if they cheated on their male partners during marriage (see also Schwartz 2008, 22–37).

Until the age of twenty-one, and at the end of a long period lasting six whole years, Isabel de Montoya was Gabriel de Cabesco's mistress, and by then she had already completed her transition into womanhood. She was now mature enough to make her own choices in life, and thus she took the initiative and ran away from that house and from those circumstances. Nonetheless, the depraved circumstances lingered on, following her trial, thereafter impacting each direction she had taken in life. The main elements and ingredients were already ingrained there: the lack of a moral guidance, the lack of care and parenthood, and sexual promiscuity, from a very early age. She likewise *chose* to become a *mala mujer* (a licentious woman), for five more years.

THE IMAGE AND PRESENCE OF WOMEN IN THE PUBLIC SPHERE

In early modern Seville, as Mary Elizabeth Perry describes, there were special spaces destined for women who transgressed the norms and who were found wandering in the streets, seeking easy gains. Called *mancebías*, these public spaces especially assigned for concubines were institutionalized for the sake of all those dubbed by the Laws of the Siete Partidas of Alfonso X as those "que están en la putería e se dan a todos cuantos a ellas vienen" or, simply, prostitutes, who hung around inns and taverns accompanied by *gente de mal vivir* (thugs), whose presence was a threat to law and order and peace. Perry cites a contemporary Spanish economist, Martinez de Mata, to have acknowledged the fact that changing economic circumstances, mainly foreign competition and monopolies have caused a decline in the institution of matrimony: "wives were frequently abandoned by underemployed and unemployed husbands who left to seek their fortunes in the cities, the army, or the Indies" (King 1993; Perry 1998). By sheer contrast with chaperoned, white, honor-burdened women across the Atlantic, in contemporaneous Mexico City and Puebla, unmarried women, especially black women and other members of the castas, were omnipresent, performing nearly every task imaginable in the cities. Moreover, their omnipresence was also visible on weekends and during feast days, in the colonial, Spanish-dominated plazas, streets, and public parks, such as the Alameda, originally created as a strolling park for the elite, which was predominated by male pedestrians. There, they lingered, seeking amusements, arranged occasional rendezvous with men, met acquaintances, chatted and drank together, bartered with other street vendors, and brought charms and amulets, as well as learned new crafts from local indigenous herb sellers. Sandra Lauderdale Graham writes in this context that "the church—or better, the open place in front and around the church—rivaled the tavern or corner store as a second meeting place. Unlike the tavern, though, the space near the church was dominated by the presence of women. Young women held rendezvous here with their lovers" (1992, 64). In the city of Puebla, in the local market place, single plebeian women would stroll or take their sumptuous afternoon luncheon. They could also meet men of the upper classes at the public baths of Atoyaque or, during festivities at the plaza, when blacks and mulatos wearing their traditional clothes mounted theatrical representations and other amusements such as dances and music. Nevertheless, all such pursuits, amusements, and "public scandals" virtually ended upon the inauguration in 1640 of the new and repressive rule of the new archbishop and ex-viceroy, Juan de Palafox y Mendoza. Under his rigorous moral and ecclesiastical reforms in Puebla, all dances, music, and games enjoyed by blacks and mulatos, and women and men on Sundays and holy days were suspended indefinitely. Prostitution, as well as other lesser immoral transgressions of the strict observance of the norms of proper behavior and living, were severely punished.

One needs to emphasize here that single women did not transcend their assigned roles in society, but, to the contrary, *they were fulfilling their assigned roles as poor women of color who had to scramble to make ends meet.* Their goal was to survive, not to reweave the social fabric. Nevertheless, their potent presence on the streets was viewed as a menace by the colonial elites. And as Bailey-Glasco puts it: "Popular pastimes for the elite were marked by restraint and composure, and through official legislation and unofficial pressure, elites would try to force this Bourbon style and aesthetic onto the plebeian classes" (2010, 38). Andrea Vicente adds on nineteenth-century Guadalajara that "the negative stereotypes that surrounded them focused on their roles as working women, their presence in public space, and the questions it raised about their overall character" (Vicente 2012, 97). In 1671, viceroy of New Spain, Marqués de Mancera, described to his councilors the situation of disorder and criminality created by the multiplicity of *pulquerías* (taverns) in Mexico City and their becoming the centers for mischiefs and drunkenness by both men and women, especially the poor:

> As for the plebeian Spaniards, mulatos, mestizos, and all others of lowly quality, of either sex, they have dedicated themselves to such vices with such an excessive liberty that, perhaps, they do not believe this to be a sin, or, that they are self-persuaded that they can freely commit it being immune of punishment; as it is, they already perform this [abomination] in the public squares and in the streets, causing disturbances in their neighborhoods, especially during feast days and festivities of the city quarters and more frequently in the immediate surroundings of the taverns and quarters. And upon the reoccurring state of drunkenness, they should be given 50 lashes in the public square and their hair should be cut . . . Whenever males and females are encountered together [in a state of drunkenness] in whatever part of the city, in certain places or neighborhoods, their hair should be cut, and they should be lashed a 100 times, as well as be incarcerated for one month; if they are found in the same state the third time, their hair would again be cut, they should be lashed again a hundred times; mulatos, mestizos, lobos, and all others belonging to lowly quality will be banished to a mill to perform forced

labor in the course of three years . . . and Spanish women will be placed in *recogidas* [houses of seclusion].[15]

In order to curtail public drinking, especially by women, and restrict the free mingling between both sexes, the city authorities of Mexico City and Puebla issued a decree limiting the number of taverns selling pulque in the city to merely thirty-six, twenty-four of which were for men only, while the remaining twelve for women only. In addition, *fiscales del crimen* acting under the Audiencia appointed special inspectors in charge of paying regular visits to assure obedience to the law, as well as prohibit disturbances.[16] Immediate and severe punishments were inflicted upon all those who were disobedient and who drank to excess. The colonial instructions could be compared to the pre-Columbian ones, cited by the Spanish lawmakers:

> "In ancient times, people who drank in excess and committed sins were punished by (a) cutting their hair or burning them with *ocotles* [pine sticks]; (b) by ruining their houses; (c) capital punishment. In some places, like Texcoco, they would throw them into the river." (Para que se llenase de agua muerto, quien tanto bebía vivo y muriese bebiendo quien por beber vivía sin excepción de personas, pues Motecuhzoma castigó a un sobrino Netzahualcoyotl Rey a su tía, y uno de los reyes de Texcoco a su muger hermana de Motecuhzoma. [So that the one who while living drank to excess, should drown, filled with wáter, and the one who lived to drink will die drinking, with no exception of any person; Motecuhzoma castigated his nephew (for that); Netzahualcoyotl, a king, (punished) his aunt (for that), and one of the kings of Texcoco (punished) his wife, Motecuhzoma's sister.])[17]

IMMORAL GUIDANCE

Guido Ruggiero recently claimed that "crucial was the disciplining power of a complex web of concepts that turned on honor and reputation and their association with female sexuality" (1993, 59). This was, perhaps, valid in northern Italy. Nevertheless, in New Spain, as all of our records attest, we can be assured that there was no single code of honor and shame in colonial Mexican society.[18] The case of two widowed mulatas and traveling vendors of clothes from Puebla, Luisa Franco and Inés, may have served as an exemplary model for the city authorities at the time. They were both accused in 1629 by the city's criminal court of "dressing like indigenous persons and causing public scandals." Forty-year-old Luisa was the widow of Juan, an indigenous stonemason and subsequently the pregnant cohabiter of Pedro Juárez, the indigenous *alcalde* of the San Francisco barrio in Puebla. Her friend Inés is described as having unlawfully lived with another man, an indigenous tailor. The

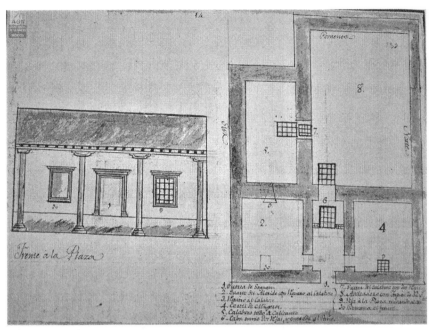

FIGURE 5.1. A Women's public prison (space No. 4 in the drawing), facing the Plaza Mayor in Mexico City. © AGN, MAPILU, Mexico City.

two women were eventually detained by the fiscal del crimen for innkeeping, for leading immoral and scandalous lives, and for cohabitation. They "violently resisted their arrest" and were sent to prison.[19]

The litigation records describe how they regularly sold the forbidden pulque liquor from their homes: "They made many of the indigenous persons become drunk every day, and encouraged them to avoid work, and not to go to mass on feast days. In addition, they lived unmarried with two indigenous persons." We have ample evidence that from around 1643, municipal city authorities in Puebla, as well as the ecclesiastical court, became much stricter in the measures they adopted against those who sold Pulque, and in effect people who were found guilty of selling it ran the risk of excommunication.[20] This exemplary case of the two women is, in fact, multifaceted, including as it does charges of immorality and promiscuity in addition to the crossing of racial affiliations and ignoring restrictions on dress. Special instructions were commonly made public against blacks and mulatos, including restrictions on dress, such as the prohibition from 1614 against wearing silken veils, like Spanish ladies, or wear European costume or dress like indigenous women. The usual penalty in Puebla for women such as these was to be sent to the

Magdalena *casa de recogimiento*, "to improve their lives." Even though it was first established as a recogimiento for noble married women when their husbands were away or had abandoned them, it later became a recogimiento for "mujeres malas," a forced refuge for women who diverted from the prescribed sexual and moral behavior (Myers 1993, 63–87). Between 1606 and 1609, the house first served as a hospice for noble women of Puebla. Its founders were Francisco Reynoso and Julian López. Such women were those who were unable to support themselves economically, were under other poor circumstances, such as having been abandoned by their husbands who went to Spain or for other reasons. In 1677, the house was turned into a place of forced seclusion for "lost" women, under the advocacy of Santa María Magdalena Penitentiary. Being nearly empty the whole year or "caused many scandals" by the women put there by the justice authorities of the city, as the bishop of Santa Cruz put it, the house was finally shut down in 1681. It was replaced by a college for young women, girls and widows, for poor women, virtuous and notable. Its penitents were now transferred to another house on the same street, by the same name of Santa María Magdalena. It was opened on 11 June 1680, under the protection of Santa María Egipciaca, until it held fourteen girls, at which point its name was changed to Santa Mónica.

VIRGINITY VERSUS "SEXUAL PROMISCUITY"

Generally speaking, young maidens belonging to the plebeian classes sought refuge in the prevalent norms of colonial society when it came to the issue of their virginity and to the barter between promises of marriage in exchange for sex. Cultural constraints and norms were evidently very different among the various ethnic groups in Mexico; nonetheless, young women among the castas were no less preoccupied about their reputation than doncellas (young women of Spanish descent), coming from the uppermost strata of Spanish colonial society as, for example, described by Nicole von Germeten in her study of colonial Cartagena de Indias (von Germeten 2013, ch. 1). The mothers of these young women were even more concerned about exempting the price from their perpetrators.

Let us begin with Pedro de Heredia, a mailman who traveled daily from Mexico City to the town of San José del Parral to deliver packages. One day in February 1663, he made his way together with his old friends, Francisco Gómez, and Pedro de León. The three traveled together that day and decided to stop on their way at the local baths. Having arrived in San José del Parral, Pedro de Heredía persuaded his friends to give him the address of Inés de Parea, whom they knew. Having gone to her house, he induced her "with love and affection," as well as with a proposal for marriage, and thereafter deflowered her. When the two friends came to her later that day, Inés de Parea complained of Pedro de Heredía's misconduct toward her, and that he had left her behind, "dishonored and humiliated." Thereafter, Francisco Gómez calmed her down, promising that he would see to it that Pedro de Heredía would indeed come back to marry her. The latter returned to Mexico City, where he subsequently confessed to his sister that he had indeed proposed marriage to Inés, took her virginity, and was therefore committed to her but could not fulfill his promise, and thus he refrained from traveling back to that town, as he had up until then on a regular basis. His sister apparently was aware of the fact that her brother was planning to marry an entirely different woman, without the knowledge of his parents and that he had deliberately changed his surname to Gutiérrez, declaring himself an orphan, in spite of the fact that he was the legitimate son of Francisco de Heredía and María Álvarez.[21]

As we learn from this story, Inés de Parea's troubling experience fell under the colonial category of *estupro*, meaning "the seduction of a virgin," not a violent rape (Von Germeten 2013, ch. 1). She was jilted but may well have consented to sex by Pedro de Heredía believing in his professions of love, and in his false promise of marriage, rather than having been actually raped by him.[22] Likewise, in yet a very different example from 1673, Marta de San Pedro's mother filed a complaint to the fiscal del crimen in Puebla against Juan de los Reyes, an indigenous man, "for having violated and taken the virginity" of her daughter.[23] Agustina described her daughter as being between fourteen and fifteen years of age, and as "quiet, honest, and withdrawn at the time." The mother related how Juan de los Reyes had repeatedly tempted her daughter with promises of love, and one day he entered their house situated in the barrio de Analco in Mexico City and, when alone with her daughter in one of the rooms, persuaded the girl to go with him to a lonely, isolated, and uninhabited spot outside the city, where he "deflowered her of her virginity, with the gravest of consequences." The daughter herself described how Juan de los Reyes took her from her house, and "lured her by pretending to tell her some secrets to go with him to a lonely site behind the convent of La Encarnación, where he laid her down and took off her petticoats, and being a virgin and honest she tried to force him back and tried in vain to get up from the ground, but he raped her." An indigenous woman by the name of Marta María, who served in that household, said that the day of the incident was All Saints' Day, a public holiday. Early in the morning of that day Juan entered the house, and when she warned him that he should not be there, he became infuriated and pushed her aside, entering the daughter's room by force. Upon leaving the house, she again warned him that if the girl's father saw him, he would kill him. "And he took her away with him by force and compulsion and violated her in a field outside the city." On 4 January 1674, Juan de los Reyes was finally imprisoned in the prison at Puebla. Likewise, twenty-six-year-old Agustina

Espinoza, a single mestiza, also filed criminal charges against an anonymous culprit, who, according to her claims, "deflowered her by pretending to marry her in the near future, made her pregnant, and left her with a small daughter." She told the court, in his absence, that "the only thing she wished for was to be left in peace, after he would pay her 50 pesos as compensations for her emotional damages."[24]

In another serious incident reported to the authorities near Coyoacán, on the outskirts of Mexico City, an indigenous woman named Luisa María, the mother of sixteen-year-old Juana de la Cruz, filed a complaint in court against Lucas Miguel, a young indigenous man and a carter by profession, accusing him of having "robbed, beaten, and sexually assaulted her daughter" along with other culprits who could not be located at that point but one of whom was Juan Gabriel, a lime burner.[25] What is striking in many of these stories is that conformity to the rules of the *patria potestad* were not necessarily observed. As Asunción Lavrin noted in 1978, "the pressure to conform to accepted modes of behavior were great, but adherence was not as strict as has been assumed, despite the constant supervision of the Church." (37). Furthermore, that the church and city authorities could have sanctioned punitive actions initiated by the parents of single women that affected the fate of their offspring, completely disregarding their mothers' standing; however, they neglected to do so.[26] Among the upper echelons of Spanish colonial society, as was in Spain at the time, in cases of ravishment or defloration, and in particular when the girl/woman became pregnant, the latter was financially compensated through the payment of her dowry by the male offender, and the latter, who had promised marriage in return for sex, "were not forced to continue their relationship with their deceived partner."[27]

CLASSIFYING ADULTERY

As we shall see below, appeals to the court on the grounds of either violence or adultery did not necessarily end up in a final separation; often, the couple was either advised by the court to return to live together after a certain time was given for reconciliation, during which the wife would lodge at her mother's house. Generally speaking, during the period reviewed—that is, between 1559 and 1750—the word *adulterio* appears scarcely within the documentation, in sheer contrast with the word *amancebamiento* (see also Alberro 1991, 155–66). The former is sometimes replaced by the expression *amancebamiento con una mujer casada*. The likely wording for more moderate cases involving *adulterio*, in which there was only a proven intent on one part, without the open consent of the other, would be in the following manner: "Juan Domingo casado con Alejandra María contra el mercader Felipe Montefar, por querer tener amistad ilícita con ella" (Juan Domingo, married to Alejandra María, against the merchant Felipe Montefar, for having wished to be engaged in an illicit friendship with her).

Adulterio meant sexual acts between a married woman with another man, who was not her husband or, alternatively, between a married man and a woman who was not his wife. The Canon law distinguished between two types of adultery: "simple," and "double." The former, when both offenders were not married, while the latter, when either one of them was married (Dávila Mendoza 2005, 68n7). On the other end of the spectrum, in the more "clear-cut" cases of adultery by both sides accompanied by a direct denunciation in court, the usual wording would be "Pleito que presenta doña Ana Bravo, vecina del Pueblo de Ajosingo, contra su marido Antoinio de Leite y una india de nombre Juana, por adulterio, México" (A denouncement filed by doña Ana Bravo, inhabitant of the town of Ajosingo, against her husband, Antoinio de Leite, and against an indigenous woman named Juana, for adultery).[28]

On the more extreme end of the spectrum, there is the following case of adultery, in which one of the partners was married while the other was a widow but who both maintained cohabitation for more than twenty years. Melchor Muñoz, mulato, and Rapahela de Castro, *morisca libre* (blood mixture: Spanish and mulato), both from Tepotztlan, Cuernavaca, and the latter thirty years of age, were thus immediately arrested by the ecclesiastical authorities of Mexico City, after having been denounced by their neighbors.[29] In indigenous areas, by sheer contrast with city life, cases of adultery or even concubinage were rarely reported to the Spanish authorities, or such cases were discretely resolved within the confines of the local community. Indeed, scanning through the multitude of sources available on this theme, one finds few examples of indigenous women ever seeking separation from their husbands, on the grounds of any of the reasons listed above, and among the indigenous nobility this was especially true, except for such rare examples as in the following: in 1632, for example, doña María de la Cruz, a noblewoman and the *cacica* (female noble ruler) of Xochimilco, went to the ecclesiastical court in Mexico City and sought separation and divorce from her husband, Francisco Caballero, which was highly unusual for indigenous society at the time.[30]

In Fray Alonso de Molina's Nahuatl-Spanish dictionary from 1570, one finds the following entries concerning concubinage: (1) *chahuacocoya* ("the woman is tormented because her husband has a concubine"); (2) *nochahuanan* ("my stepmother," or "my second mother"); (3) *chauapilli* ("the child of one's former woman"); (4) *tlacpahuitectli* ("previously begotten") or, *mecapil* ("*hijo de manceba*") (Molina [1571] 2001, 19, 81). All these four forms allude to polygamous traits still practiced among the Nahua nobility, but transliterated now into Spanish-Catholic terminologies, which does not necessarily mean that the former woman/wife has died, or had been permanently abandoned, but that a second wife exists and even gives birth to heirs, and that those heirs could well be adopted by the second wife as their own. Referring to the latter, Fray Bernardino de Sahagún, in his *Calidades de parentesco*, writes, "ieplitzin teconeuh intepiltzin tlacopilli" (*half son or daughter*), "*calitic cunetl chaneca*" meaning "among these people, there are legitimate children, and bastards" (Sahagún 1982, 13–40).

Julia Madajczak suggests that "the term *-chauh* was used within the polygynous family for a male partner not married in a ceremony, who also had other wives of higher rank" and that the term *chahuayotl*, which Camilla Townsend interpreted as "concubinage" would rather fit "cohabitation"—"from the point of view of a woman" (Madajczak 2014, 309; Townsend 2006, 347–89; see also Dehouve 2003, 94–106; Raby 1999, 203–29). During the early part of the seventeenth century, Torquemada already had transcribed extramarital relationships in indigenous society, and the fate of concubines, into a pure Spanish-Catholic term—*tlacallalcahuilli*—which means, someone who deserted, as if to say, a person who could leave, without an insult to the marriage, as opposed to one's own wife, which they called *cihuatlantli* ("desired woman," from *ciuhatl* = woman + *tlantli* = teeth). In the case in which there was no need to claim the daughter from her parents, so as to take her as a concubine, they named such a woman by the common and general term, which is *temecauh* (concubine of a single person). The custom for the most part was that after the male concubine had begotten a son from his female concubine, then he would be obliged to abandon her or take her as his legitimate wife, which was required by her parents. There was another type of permissible concubine, which either the lords and nobles would request prior to their marriage or after they have already been married with their lawful wife, whom they called *cihuapilli* (noble woman) (Torquemada 1723, bk. 12, ch. 3; bk. 15, ch. 15).

Nonetheless, there were indeed cases in which Spaniards committed adultery with a local indigenous woman while living within a traditional indigenous town. In such environments, nothing could escape the scrutinizing eyes of elders and women. Such circumstances and local social pressure often forced the offended side to come forward and bring the case out in the open, even against his/her initial tendency to keep this in secret. For example, doña Ana Bravo, Antoinio de Leite's wife, both residing in the town of Axotzingo, came to file a complaint against her husband for having committed adultery with an indigenous woman by the name of Juana.[31] Likewise, in the indigenous town of Tomatlan, María Josepha also denounced a local married indigenous woman, for having "deserted her own husband, and came to look for the former's husband, for him to become her lover."[32]

CLASSIFYING AMANCEBAMIENTO

Amancebamiento was a term used during those times for the state of a partnership/ cohabitation between two mature partners, what we would call today strictly in

Anglo-Saxon terms "common law spouse"—outside of wedlock, as opposed to "adultery" or "cheating" on one's partner within marriage. Let us look at the different wording utilized at times when *adulterio* was involved and at times when *amancebamiento* was the case. *Amancebamiento* was a term used for the state of a partnership/cohabitation between two mature partners, what we would call today "partners for life." Moreover, during the period that this book deals with, the phenomenon became so common and widespread that in 1674 that the church initiated a special edict for the sake of encouraging matrimony.[33] Furthermore, to prove this point I hereby cite as yet another example, in which the two partners came forward to the ecclesiastical court and declared themselves voluntarily as "common law spouses," who now wished to be married and asked the court to help them to achieve this goal: "Declaran ser amancebados. Contrayentes: Diego Márquez, 26 años; Mariana Pérez, Mestiza, 34 años. Santa Catalina Mártir."[34]

In the more extreme cases, however, in which the partners created havoc, the ecclesiastical court was left with no choice but to prosecute both and exert harsh punishment to satisfy the public outcry. In such cases, parish clergy censured illicit, informal unions of any duration and pressured the couple to either separate or marry, especially when "the couple's conduct was thought to be a manace to morality," as Martinez-Allier asserts,[35] and as our own records clearly show. The likely wording would be "viven escandalosamente amancebados," or, as follows: "Denuncia de Miguel de Perea Quintanilla, promotor fiscal del Arzobispado, contra Pedro de Urquiza y Ana García por vivir públicamente amancebados durante mucho tiempo dando escándalo a la gente. Pide se ponga censura agravada" (Denouncement by Miguel de Perea Quintanilla, prosecutor of the Archbishopric, against Pedro de Urquiza and Ana García, for cohabiting publicly during a long time, creating a public scandal. Asks to reprimand the two culprits).[36] Another example for the wording utilized: "Alonso Jiménez de Castilla, fiscal de Arzobispado y Provisor y Vicario general, denuncia criminalmente Juan de Meneses español e Isabel, Castiza, sobre que están públicamente amancebados, viviendo y durmiendo como marido y mujer" (Alonso Jiménez de Castilla, prosecutor of the archbishopric and vicar general, denounces criminally Juan de Meneses, a Spaniard, and Isabel, Castiza, on the charge of cohabiting publicly, living and sleeping together, as though they were husband and wife).[37]

From about 1600 onward, friends and neighbors were promptly encouraged by the parish priests, as well as by city authorities, to publicly denounce such illicit relationships, as well as provide information to the court. In theory, at least, unmarried couples were put under much stricter surveillance by the fiscal del crimen, as the records from Puebla demonstrate; however, lacking the figures of how many such couples were never denounced, only to maintain their relationships, the degree of

TABLE 5.1. Incidence of cohabitation between 1555 and 1649

Year	Frequency	Percent (%)
1555–1559	161	36.34
1600–1649	277	63.97

TABLE 5.2. Incidence of endogamous cohabitation between 1555 and 1649: A Sample

Race	Years	Frequency	Percent (%)
Mulatos	1555–1599	3	50
	1600–1649	3	50
Creoles	1555–1599	79	45.93
	1600–1649	93	54.07
Indigenous persons	1555–1599	3	75
	1600–1649	1	25
Spanish	1555–1599	2	11.11
	1600–1649	16	88.89

Note: Compare with Komisaruk (2013, 141, table 4-2).

effectiveness of such curbing remains a mere speculation.[38] Searching thoroughly through the AGN sections between 1555 and 1599, and between 1600 and 1649, I found altogether merely 438 cases of denunciations of concubinages, and by contrast, merely 80 cases involving adultery (table 5.1). The first period, 1555–1599, comprised 36.76 percent of the total occurrences of unmarried spouses, while the second period, 1600–1649, comprised the remaining 63.24 percent. The significance is clear: until the second time period, the church usually ignored the phenomenon of cohabitation, until those partners came forward and asked the ecclesiastical courts for permission to be formally married in the church. And then, also, they were usually urged to do so. If they bore children out of this union, their children were not legitimate but considered *hijos naturales*, "with the least stigma attached to the term" (Borah and Cook 1966, 950).

There were also very few cases in which both charges of amancebamiento and adulterio were applied to the culprits. Likewise, in 1692, Alonso Meléndez, a single mestizo, and Cathalina Rodríguez, a local indigenous woman, who was apparently married at the time, both from the indigenous village of San Francisco near Puebla, were accused in the ecclesiastical court of Puebla on both charges.[39]

Between 1600 and 1649, and especially between 1606 and 1630, at the height of the Counter-Reformation era, one is able to observe a drastic intensification of the ecclesiastical courts in Mexico in their surveillance and policing of cohabitation, either between single men and women or in extramarital unions. Formal prosecution of concubines and bigamy increased, mainly due to the need to reinforce the sacrament of the holy matrimony and curb the widespread norm of cohabitation without marriage. But, at the same time, the higher frequency could be attributed to an assertive church official. The Mexican Inquisition, established in 1571, also intensified its persecution of sexual crimes during this period, leading to a drop in more than 20 percent of all cases in this category (Holler 2010, 120). From around 1630 onward, by contrast, one is able to notice a drastic decline, followed by noticeable pattern of moderation in the number of cases reviewed, meaning that after a relatively short period of curbing such practices, the Mexican Church reinstated its traditional stance on the issue. Throughout the two periods reviewed—that is, between 1555 and 1599 and between 1600 and 1649—the incidents of adultery remained very low. Still, Stuart Schwartz is absolutely right in saying that "the illegitimacy statistics, of course, can tell us about practice, but not about how people felt about what they were doing . . . While fornication and toleration were two quite distinct activities, the evidence for the continual practice of fornication should at least make us wary of interpreting the sketchy documentary record of toleration as evidence of absence rather than absence of evidence or as proof of orthodox belief" (2008, 32). Similarly, Allyson Poska comments that "marriage's location at the intersection between human desire and heavenly virtue often made it the crux of conflict between parishioners and the Catholic Church" (1996, 871–82).

If we compare the two periods according to race, and we draw our attention to denunciations of endogamous cohabitations among Spaniards, in particular, then, for the first period, such cases comprised 11.11 percent of the total cases involved, while for the second period, they comprised 88.89 percent of the cases prosecuted. Cases involving mulatas and Creole males, that is, exogamous cohabitations, comprised 26.92 percent for the first period, and 73.08 percent for the second, which means that the curbing of such informal unions focused especially on interracial unions and, in particular, on cases in which Spanish/Creole men and women were involved with other racial groups. This pattern is also explainable by the fact that we find among mulatos, for example, the total number of cases persecuted involving endogamous cohabitations remained equal during the two periods reviewed.

By comparison to Gowing's findings, in the AGN, I was able to locate, between 1540 and 1750, eighty-three cases involving adultery (illicit relationships with a married woman or man) that did not necessarily result in ecclesiastical divorce. Out of these eighty-three cases reported, thirteen of which the plaintiff was the male partner, the ecclesiastical court was asked to oblige the man's wife to return home, while the same appeal was reported in only five of the cases in which the woman was the plaintiff. Although the ecclesiastical courts usually granted separation on grounds of either proved adultery by either partner, or on grounds of extreme cruelty, many of the cases reviewed by the court involved the husband's desertion, leaving his family behind with no means to support themselves. As in early modern England, many among the claimants were left with no final sentence in hands and were thus forced to seek out their own unique solutions for their present state of distress and for the unwanted domestic circumstances in which they were living. Meanwhile, the deserted wife sought other means of support, having previously exhausted all possible legal channels in order to compel her husband to provide for his family whom he had left behind. In ten of the eighty-three cases found, the female partner was forced to seek shelter for the family's personal safety, away from home, predominantly in city houses of seclusion. Writing about late Renaissance Venice, Ferraro describes how "bad marriages forced women to make poor choices. Some refused to avail themselves of the city's asylums, viewing them as institutions of control rather than of protection (Ferraro 2001, 109)."

CLASSIFYING CONCUBINAGE VERSUS COHABITATION

The oldest reference to the meaning of concubinage according to the Laws of the *Siete Partidas* (No. 4:14) (published between AD 1252 and 1284 [Madrid 1807, vol. III] under the reign of Alfonso X of Castille) is as follows:

> Barraganas defiende Santa Eglesia que non tenga ningún christiano, porque viven con ellas en pecado mortal. Cá según las leyes mandan aquella es llamada barragana, que es una sola, e ha menester que sea tal que pueda casar con ella si quisiere aquel que la tiene por barragana

> [Barraganas the Holy Church should protect itself against, so that no one among Christians should maintain, because they live with them under mortal sin. This (person) according to the laws (of the Church) order that the barrangana, who is on her own (unmarried and unattached), and (the one who lives with her) should be capable of marrying her, if he wishes to do so, the person who has her as a barragana.]

The Third Mexican Church Council, of 1585, raised the penalty to automatic excommunication for anyone interfering with the free choice of partners to marriage, ordering punishment of informal unions in which one of the partners was already married or otherwise barred from legitimating the union by going through a church ceremony. Among the lower classes informal or free union was common and tended to be prominent in racial mixing. The church viewed children born to a couple who were living together unmarried, but who could be married if they wished, as potentially legitimate. Such children automatically became legitimate if their parents got married in church. Spanish concepts of illegitimacy of children born outside of a registered church marriage were strictly imposed by both Spanish ecclesiastical and civil courts concerning issues of inheritance (Borah and Cook 1966, 946–1008).

Well up to the first decade of the seventeenth century, the Mexican Church concentrated its efforts on "preventing priests and married men from taking partners or concubines and toward urging that partners in informal unions remain together for life," as long as the partners did not create "a public scandal" concerning their "immoral" way of life. Unless they caused scandal, we would not expect the church authorities to initiate surveillance or prosecute partners. However, if one assumes that social and cultural classifications are indeed rigid sets of behaviors that are dictated by society in the very same manner as gender, then they should be similarly subject to constant challenges, adjustments, and modifications, as well as to transcending experiences. Likewise were the societal definitions of concubinage (see Borah and Cook 1966 on this theme). Our goal in this section is to try and salvage from single, plebeian women's discourse what were the contributing factors that led them to adopt such alternative lifestyles to marriage.

In the *Diccionario de Autoridades* of the Spanish Royal Academy, published between 1726 and 1729, under the entry *Concubina*, one finds the following definition:

> *"La manceba o mujer que duerme en el mismo lecho con quien no es su legítimo marido. Es voz puramente latina"* [The woman who sleeps in the same bed with someone who is not her husband. From Latin: *concubus*, a carnal act].

Furthermore, the early modern Spanish dictionary defines the term *Barragana* in the following manner:

> *"Antiguamente se llamaba así a la amiga, dama o concubina que se conservaba en la casa del que estaba amancebado con ella, y para serlo era preciso fuese libre y no sierva, soltera, única, y que no tuviese parentesco en grado conocido con el galán que le embarazase casar con ella si quisiese."*

Concubine: *Manceba* or woman who sleeps in the same bed with someone who is not her legitimate husband. (Barragana was formerly called the friend, lady or concubine who remained in the house in the house belonging to the one who cohabited with her, and to be that [in that status] precisely, she should have been free and nonservant, unmarried and unattached, and who was not related by kinship in any known degree to the man who would have been too embarrassed to offer her to marry him if she wished to do so).[40]

What I intend to highlight in this section is that short-term, as well as long-term forms, of cohabitation/concubinage were an inherent part of a choice-making process carried out by such women described in this book. Emphasized here is that on the one hand, due to the lingering, limiting circumstances of the terrible marriage markets in Mexico City and Puebla, and with a female majority, and, on the other hand, earlier, unhappy marriages and lingering, bitter sexual experiences, many plebeian women of all racial origins found their safe haven in both short and long-term cohabitations and concubinages in which they were able to play the powerful role of the dominant sexual partners. Herman L. Bennett shows that especially among slaves, long-lasting forms of concubinage were extremely common (Bennett 2003, 87–88). Writing on Brazil, Muriel Nazzari comments in this respect: "I will not be using the term *consensual union* to describe long-lasting relationships outside of marriage because it implies a certain equality between the partners. I wish to emphasize those relations between men and women outside of marriage that were highly unequal, including relationships between masters and slaves in which force might have been applied" (1996, 107–24). Nazzari concentrates on the asymmetry between sexual partners. Otherwise, however, in cases in which the single woman seeks a partner and finds one of her choice, this could be the case for "free choice" as numerous abundant life stories cited below inform us. My position here, contrary to Nazzari's, is to try and trace power and resourcefulness in those women who are inaccurately viewed *only* as victims. Let us take, for example, how Graubart phrases this from the vantage point of subaltern indigenous women in early colonial Peru: "Because I am female and very old" was not only a statement of victimization, however. Although women recognized the constraints and limitations placed upon them as subalterns, they also identified and utilized the institutions that could act on their behalf (119). The choice of becoming a cohabitant can presumably be explained by the fact that single, "racially inferior" women of the castas found themselves, at about the age of thirty, situated at the bottom of the social hierarchy vis-à-vis their available marriage options. Therefore, for many among the unwed blacks, mulatas, and mestizas without pedigree or dowry, the only "better" option was to become a cohabiter.

Was cohabitation ever considered by single women during the early modern period as even *preferable* to a legal marriage or a substitute for it? In answering such queries, one should indeed seek the true meaning of such practices in the contemporaneous attitudes and mentalities of mid-colonial Mexico. McCaa, for example, emphasizes the central role played by concubinage in colonial society: "The historical presence of concubinage in all three societies, the ease with which it was adopted in the Americas and its affordability were central to its persistence in Latin America, particularly amongst members of the lower class. Unfortunately, there were no registers to record this practice therefore it is difficult to determine the exact number of illicit unions that took place in society and their durability. It should suffice to say that it was prevalent throughout the period" (1994, 38; Kuznesof 1995). In his study *Families in Former Times*, Jean-Louis Flandrin defines concubinage in a rather raw manner: "In contrast to marriage, which was a social institution by which families of the same standing entered into an alliance to perpetuate themselves, concubinage was a personal union, an affair of love, at least on the part of the man. It could become established at all social levels . . . Other unions could not be transformed into marriages because one of the partners was already married . . . concubinage was adapted to the inegalitarian structures of society, and allowed the bastards to survive" (1979, 181, 182).[41] Living as cohabitants did not necessarily imply "living in sin" for unmarried women and single mothers of hijos naturales. However, the main concern over the unruly lifestyle of unmarried girls remained throughout as that of preserving honor and confining overt sexual promiscuity. In his book *Crime and Punishment in Late Colonial Mexico City, 1692–1810*, Haslip-Viera describes how "In the early eighteenth century, fornication and concubinage by unmarried persons was judged to be a serious problem. Hundreds of persons were apprehended for 'these sacrilegious acts' and subjected to certain corrective measures." And he cites a figure of 12 percent of all those arrested during 1740 to have been associated with unlawful partnerships and having avoided marriage in church (Haslip-Viera 1999, 67). Schwartz estimates that "rates of illegitimacy in the Spanish colonies in the Americas were of a different order all together, often doubling the levels of Spain," which he cites to be around 3 and 7 percent of baptisms, "although in cities like Valladolid they were as high as 20 percent." He adds that "the sociology of accusations indicates complex patterns that reflect factors other than a conflict between popular acceptance or rejection of simple fornication as a mortal sin."[42]

Yet another spectrum that we ought to consider here is the duration of cohabitations and their impact on child rearing. In his book *Courtship, Illegitimacy and Marriage in Early Modern England*, Richard Adair writes: "Often it is unclear from the records exactly how long cohabitation had taken place, especially when the relationship was very long-term." He also describes how contracted couples who had children lived together in the male spouse's parents' house while others without children opted for a long-term arrangement in which the female spouse was to remain in her father's home, where her partner would visit her on a daily basis (1996, 178). In this context, therefore, we should take into consideration also the cumulative aspect of cohabitation, over a considerable period of time, let's say, over five years or more, whether in an uninterrupted sequence of years or, during different periods, of long durations. By contrast with what Ana Lidia García Peña suggests, cohabitation was on many occasions a long-term arrangement. Take, for example, Diego Ruiz, a married man, who cohabited with Maríana Sánchez, a single mestiza, "for more than twelve years"; as one of the witnesses in their trial described, "*they sleep together in the same bed and share the same table*, and as a result of this carnal acts, they now have between three and four children together, and due to this Diego Ruiz does not maintain a married life with his wife, and both of them have been imprisoned three times already and they have been threatened not to reunite, and they have ignored these warnings and continue living together."[43] Also on trial during 1606 were Jerónimo de León, a married man, and María de Miradeles, a single woman, who cohabited *for at least fifteen years*, had two children together, and as a consequence, both his wife and his mother-in-law "found themselves in a state of impoverishment."[44]

By comparison to what Komisaruk comments, that "most of the unsanctioned couples who entered the archival record appear not to have formed households together, or to have done so only for short periods," my study brings to the fore that long-lasting consensual unions (concubinages) involved, in effect, the establishment of a full-fledged nuclear family patterns. Twinam writes in this very context: "Relationships between unmarried men and women without any commitment to matrimony were presumably more tenuous than those in which the parties vowed to wed. In most other respects, however, such affairs are indistinguishable from extended engagements." (1999, 82–83).

And by contrast to Schwartz's cases cited for the Iberian Peninsula (2008, 32–37), women from across the Atlantic considered concubinage to be a better choice than marriage. In 1574, for example, in the heart of Mexico City, we find thirty-year-old Ana López, a mestiza and single mother to a fourteen-year-old daughter, haughtily declaring in front of some male companions that "it was a much better choice to become a concubine, than to be badly married." Shortly afterward, she was arrested and tried by the Mexican Inquisition for having propagated in contra to the Holy Sacrament of Matrimony.[45] In as yet another example, in July 1626, María de Morales, a humble Spaniard living in Tlaxcala and married to a farmer (they were about to move to a farm located near the small town of Cholula), confessed to the inquisitors that "due to her husband's bad behavior towards her" she had said to him on a number of occasions that "she remained married to him only for the love of God, but that now God should take His vengeance on him," and "que mas valía estar amancebada que casada, para recibir mal tratamiento del marido" (it was a better choice to live in cohabitation than be married and suffer an appalling treatment from one's husband).[46] It would also be important to cite here Mexico City's councilor, Guillén Brondat, who around 1583 claimed in a direct connection to the growing tendency of misrule among the city's women that "there was so much looseness and license among most of the married women." Such women, "to be able to attend with freedom to their evil intentions and lewdnesses," sought to divorce their husbands "in exchange for wandering loose and with license and free of [their husbands'] dominion" (qtd. in Holler 2001, 25).

I believe that a deep reading of women's discourses opens up a vantage point into the moral arena and sexual behaviors of these women and provides ample reasoning for their behavioral patterns. No, doubt, individual endeavors by plebeian women to try to gather up forces and set out on a new road of one's own, in the aftermath of bitter and unrewarding marriages, required stamina and a strong will to challenge the diverse and extremely difficult consequences. In her book on the domestic lives of servants and masters in nineteenth-century Rio de Janeiro (Brazil), Sandra Lauderdale Graham writes: "The poor did not choose the features of their existence; poverty imposed or exaggerated the problems with which they coped. But in their manner of coping, they built up their own store of meanings and ways of acting that oftentimes differed from those of the better-off . . . Thus their fragile independence, with its elements of assertiveness and adaptation, was insurance against vulnerability" (1992, 62). Ferraro also writes, "Yet, the actions of these two unhappy wives demonstrate how women who sought personal satisfaction found ways to change their life circumstances." Ferraro, indeed, presents before us a number of women who took their destiny in their own hands. Lucretia, for example, "preferred sinning to an unhappy marriage; and she took the steps, though not without a price, to change her life circumstances" (Ferraro 2001, 90, 121). And I cite Gabriel Haslip-Viera on this: "A review of the documentation reveals that most women who were involved in these cases [concubinage] had a strong sense of independence, and a rebelliousness that was in total contrast to the submissive ideal promoted by educated ideal and the law" (1999, 69).

THE CHURCH'S STANCE ON COHABITATION

In what follows we are able to observe how church policy and church decrees addressed the issue of cohabitation prior to marriage, as well as the predominant presence of clandestine marriages outside the church. By the end of the fifteenth century and the beginning of the sixteenth, the church synods established different sanctions against the omission of nuptial benedictions, so that "those that will be newlywed would not lead a married life without receiving first these nuptial blessings in church. That is to say, the obligatory nature of the liturgical celebration of the marriage under the threat of serious sanctions prevailed. The alleged reasons provided for this were that the couple should not live together before they were sufficiently observed by the ecclesiastical authorities so as to avoid the doubts concerning the question of whether they lived together before they were married, or not . . . many among them do not avoid that, and thus, as soon as they are newly-wed, they exhaust this marriage, which causes a great scandal especially among the simple people, that they do not have them by, that they did not see them receive blessings." Or, as was affirmed in the synod of Osma, "Many marry by offering common words such as what a husband should do with his wife without the customary solemnity, and according to this doubt if those that do that achieve happiness with their wives or by concubines." The sanctions established against the partners who did not celebrate the *velaciones* (covering the face with a veil) of their marriage were excommunication and a series of penalties. The synods also set forth other coercive measures in their attempt to eradicate clandestine marriages.

The more specific problems addressed by the synods concerned mainly the consent of the partners to the act of marriage: cases of bigamy or promises of marriage to one partner and an actual marriage contract with another one, as well as the lack of the paternal or familiar consent.[47] Therefore, in Post-Tridentine New Spain, diverse examples of transgressions against normative family bonds, especially by women reaching menopause and beyond the age of fecundity, were retold by theologians and inquisitors based on the testimony presented before them in the inquisitorial interrogations. The exposition to the public eye of such cases served as an obvious means of propaganda for reestablishing societal norms. The Tridentine model of marriage was not enforced on the population of New Spain until 1730, and even then much ground was still left for local, informal norms to set the tone. Thomas Calvo cites in mid-century Guadalajara a "rising tide of cohabitation and illegitimacy," with 58 percent of all children being registered as illegitimate. Thus, Calvo concludes, "more than half of the offspring in such society could not be, in any way what so ever, described as 'marginal'" (Calvo 1992, 293–95; see also Gonzalbo Aizpuru 1987, 44–47; Seed 1985, 284–93; 1988a, 24–25, 64).

If the deflowering of young women of "racially inferior" origins by men of "superior" status and race was an accepted norm, then the general rule for such women was to become cohabitants, until the promise of marriage was presumably obtained. Nonmarital unions or flexible marital patterns were commonplace, especially among racially mixed communities and members of the lower echelons of society. The populace across New Spain tolerated these acts, as well as those of such women, only to the extent to which immoral living combined with supernatural transgressions became a real menace. Nevertheless, during sixteenth- and seventeenth-century Mexico, the church's repudiation of such a practice did not mean that such cohabiting couples were not encouraged "to amend their ways" and to get married under church rites, and thus there were not a few examples of cohabiting couples going together to the ecclesiastical court, declaring themselves living in cohabitation, and seeking approval for their formal matrimony in church, but the court remains suspicious on such cases.[48]

For example, Juana Cicilia, an indigenous woman from the town of Ixtlahuaca (Valley of Toluca), and Hernando de la Torre, *morisco* (blood mixture: Spanish and Mulato), from Toluca, wished to get married, after a long time of both living together and apart as cohabitants. The ecclesiastical court declined to approve their marriage, on the grounds that Juana Cicilia was the cousin of a woman with whom Hernando de la Torre had already lived, without marrying, before her time. Nevertheless, as the documentation of this case shows, the court thereafter received a sealed letter that "indicated that for the neophytes [indigenous persons], it is permitted to marry outside any limits of consanguine affinity." Thereafter the permission was granted.[49]

A different case altogether that, nevertheless, also proves this point, is that of twenty-year-old Agustín de Dorates and sixteen-year-old Juana de Saldívar, who asked the court to marry them. Then, however, Juana de Saldívar's Spanish family came along and declared their opposition to the act (that is, banns, *amonestaciones*), due to their having lived together openly as *amancebados* (concubines).[50] In the same manner, Diego Solano, the brother-in-law of Francisco de Herrera, asked the court of the Archbishopric to put the latter in the archbishop's prison, and deposit his sister in a recogimiento, to put an end to their illicit communication and carnal relationship.[51]

In her study on nineteenth-century Cuba, Verena Martinez-Alier distinguishes between two major patterns of elopement, that is, consensual abduction. She explained the first as "elopement was also a way of commencing concubinage, common among the lower strata . . . Elopement with a view to premarital concubinage was fairly frequent." The second was "to overcome social inequality as an obstacle to marriage" (1974, 103–9). It was in fact acknowledged that sexual encounters prior to conjugal consecration were illicit and did not carry any value of a pledge between the involved parties if one of them would refuse to continue into formal matrimony (Diego de Covarubias y Leiva, *Opera omnia* [Geneva, Fratrum de Tournes, 1734, 154]).

CONCUBINAGES IN PRAXIS

On 15 May 1690, very close to his hour of death as he lay bedridden in the barrio de Analco in Puebla, the rancher Joseph Carillo Bravo Díaz dictated a memorandum to Miguel Martinez de Massarón, the vicar of this parish and an ecclesiastical judge, before five witnesses. To ensure that he would be promptly absolved by the priest and receive Extreme Unction, Díaz manipulatively utilized María Ramales's name, falsely claiming to have once been married to her in church, according to the laws of the church "but, alas, with no offspring." By this time María Ramales was

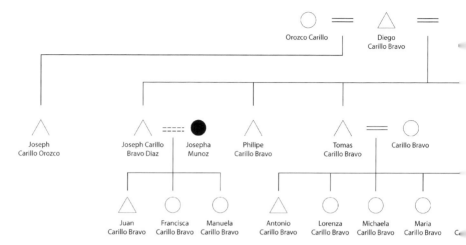

FIGURE 5.2. The Carillo Bravo family tree in the Hacienda San Juan Tepalcahuican emphasizing Josepha Munõz and her children's place there. Drawing by Noga Yoselevich.

already married to Lorenzo López and lived in the same town of Nuestra Señora de Asunción Amozoque. Needless to say, no registry of such a marriage was ever attached to the memorandum.

What Bravo Díaz did not mention in his testament was his ongoing, long-lived intimate relationship with Josepha Munõz, who served as a slave in the *hacienda de labor* of the household of doña Leonor Munoz's, known as San Juan Tepalcahuican. During the 1670s, for between eight and ten years(!), Joseph Bravo Díaz maintained an intimate relationship with Josepha, his sister's mulata slave; their relationship was carried on openly both on the premises of the hacienda and in the city of Puebla.[52] Out of this relationship apparently three children were born: Juan Carillo Bravo and his two sisters, Manuela and Francisca. I further pursued their fates in chapter 4, "Raising Children." The hacienda stood on lands in the valley of Amozoque, 2.5 kilometers from the small town of Nuestra Señora de Asunción Amozoque, which was itself located some 18 kilometers east of Puebla, being part of the *corregimiento* of Cuauhtinchan. Around 1675, the hacienda and its members consisted of seven different households, belonging to three married brothers, their unmarried brother Joseph Carillo Bravo Díaz, their unmarried sister María Manuela, and their half brother Joseph Carillo Orozco. All told the extended Carillo-Díaz family included thirty-three family members, all of whom, with the exception of the half brother Joseph Carillo Orozco, who was indeed the father to natural children but had never been married,[53] were direct descendants of both

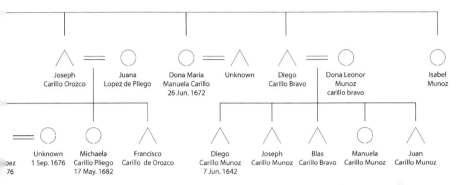

Joseph Carillo Orozco	Juana Lopez de Pliego	Dona Maria Manuela Carillo 26 Jun. 1672	Unknown	Diego Carillo Bravo	Dona Leonor Munoz carillo bravo	Isabel Munoz

| ⟶ Unknown ⟶ 76 | Unknown 1 Sep. 1676 | Michaela Carillo Pliego 17 May. 1682 | Francisco Carillo de Orozco | Diego Carillo Munoz 7 Jun. 1642 | Joseph Carillo Munoz | Blas Carillo Bravo | Manuela Carillo Munoz | Juan Carillo Munoz |

don Diego Carillo Bravo and doña María de la Encarnación Díaz Carillo, both of whom were Spaniards (see Carillo-Bravo Family Tree, below, in which Josepha Muñoz is depicted). One of the four full brothers, Joseph Carillo Bravo Díaz, himself unmarried, maintained his own separate household, on an *estancia de Ganado mayor* (cattle ranch) next to the hacienda. It consisted of one and a half *caballerías* (unit of agricultural land measurement equivalent to 105.8 acres in Mexico) of land and bordered the lands of his half brother Joseph Carillo Orozco, his full brother Felipe (depicted as Philipe in figure 5.2), and that of a neighbor, Juan Ramales, on another side of the cattle ranch.

Apparently, Joseph Carillo Bravo Díaz maintained ongoing working relations with a neighbor who was also another of his half brothers, Joseph Bravo Orozco. Four years prior to Joseph Carillo Bravo Díaz's death, this latter Orozco's son, Francisco, rented some land from him. Joseph Carillo Bravo Díaz himself was also in debt for some time to the elder Orozco as is seen from his will in which he bequeathed to the latter the considerable sum of ninety golden pesos to cover this debt. Joseph Carillo Bravo Díaz lived on his ranch together with a sixty-year-old slave, Teresa. Also sharing his lodgings was Antonio Carillo, the elder son of his brother, Tomás Carillo, who lived on the hacienda with the rest of his family and whom the rancher Díaz raised and trained for Tomás's future livelihood as a farmer. An additional lodger was María Ramales, the daughter of one of Díaz's neighbors, whom he also raised "as though she was his own daughter."

UNWANTED PREGNANCIES

In 1556, in an edict was published in France against clandestine marriage, after a companion edict addressing a "serious and detestable" female crime also appeared: clandestine pregnancy and childbirth. The edict complained that women who conceived children by "dishonest means" (out of wedlock) often disguised or hid pregnancies and delivered newborns secretly and sometimes suffocated and murdered them, disposing of the bodies in hidden places. The edict forbade women to hide pregnancies or to deliver babies secretly without witnesses. If they did so and delivered a dead child (or said they delivered a dead child), they could be charged with murder and punished as an example to others. Following this extraordinary edict, pregnant women, whether single or widowed, were required to make official *déclarations de la grossesse* (statements of pregnancy) at local civil registries and to submit to interrogation (1989, 11).

All throughout the early to mid-colonial period reviewed here, there was a widespread phenomenon of single women choosing to abandon unwanted babies. One should take into consideration that during the implementation of the Post-Tridentine decrees in New Spain, as in Europe, single mothers were more inclined to abandon unwanted children—the fruits of broken cohabitations, or, brief sexual liaisons—so that they would have more prospects of getting married in the church if they planned to do so in the future. Jean-Louis Flandrin notes on this point that "often, the seduced girl was driven away as soon as the pregnancy became evident, and it was in isolation, in the country, or in a big town, that she gave birth to and then abandoned her child" (Flandrin 1979, 184). Let us remind ourselves that the Tridentine model of marriage was not enforced in New Spain until 1588, and even then much ground was still left for local norms to prevail. Young women, especially those coming from the more prosperous echelons of society, were eager to avoid further damage to their reputation and honor, which would put their future prospects for marriage at risk. For them, it was essential to give birth in secret, and then to immediately abandon the newborn somewhere away from their neighborhood and transfer the baby to the care of responsible single woman. Usually, such "natural" offspring would be abandoned on the doorway of a randomly chosen house in another section of town and would possibly be adopted by the family who found him or her and who formally declared the child to be an orphan. On other occasions, such unwanted babies were placed in the care of other single women living in tenement houses, or in female-headed private homes. It was also not uncommon for illegitimate children raised by distant relatives or by strangers to reappear later in life on their biological mother's doorstep, the mother having hidden her unwanted pregnancy.

Many such women, already with younger children in the house, would try to conceal the birth of an illegitimate child from friends and neighbors, including their own children, by going outside their own immediate environment and placing the newborn for fostering. But, somehow, the information was sometimes revealed to her offspring.[54] Some of these women may well have been positioned between the old marital relationship and the establishment of a consensual union, and this may have encouraged them to keep the child if they believed that the creation of a stable cohabiting relationship was imminent and that there were sufficient economic prospects to set up a new, independent household.

SEXUAL INCOMPETENCE AND STERILITY

In cases in which sexual impotence or frigidity of either one of the spouses, as we learn from the cases reviewed in the ecclesiastical court of Mexico City, the marriage would not be annulled, unless the couple was found to be barren for a period of three years, though the ecclesiastical judge could shorten the waiting list for the case to be reconsidered, during which time, one could imagine that the male partner's honor and respectability shrank considerably, the wife interpreted his impotence as lack of love and consideration towards her needs, and both partners "experienced hell."[55] In one of those extremely rare cases for the period reviewed, Gertrudis de Soto asked the court to dissolve her marriage to her husband, Manuel Vázquez de Aranda, due to the fact that "he suffered from a perpetual impotence, and could not make her pregnant," that is, the marriage has not been consummated.[56] In 1609, in as yet another example, Antonio de Añas claimed that his wife "was impotent and cannot copulate, and that there is no remedy for it." She, in turn, complained against her husband that he was leading an evil way of life but could not bring herself to enlighten the court on the apparent contradiction between her description of his perpetual impotence and his copulating with lowly women; but herself, with whom he has had children, he has also maltreated with words and insults, the result of which is "a state of detestation between them." Thereafter, the wife conceded in acknowledging her sexual incompetence in court and to her husband's demand to dissolve the marriage, but the judges were not convinced by their claims and provided the following reasoning for their doubts: (a) it is improbable that the two were living together as husband and wife, in public and in private, for as long as twelve years, being aware of this fault, without having pursued such proceedings much earlier on; (b) her condition "is likely to be healed"! Antonio de Salinas, Francisca's legal representative, responded to the judges by saying that "it is the truth that Francisca Rosillo is not capable of becoming pregnant, nor giving birth, nor becoming a mother, which is the most significant cause for the flouting of this matrimony, for the impotence on her part, and in view of the observations made by both matrons and surgeons, time will not be able to heal this defect, nor additional cohabitation between them could make it valid." One is able to interpret such a sacrificial position, as both an intrinsic and an implicit tendency on Francisca's part, to give up life of marriage of such value for the sake of claiming her freedom. She was well aware that at the end of a three-year period of observation, whether or not the couple was barren or not, the ecclesiastical court would undoubtedly reach a verdict annulling this marriage, which had not been consummated. Thereafter, she would finally be able to become voluntarily single.[57] Joanne M. Ferraro, in her fascinating book *Marriage Wars in Late Renaissance Venice*, treats in-depth comparable attitudes towards cases of impotence that resulted in the woman partner's seeking annulment of marriage: "Camilla reached a point where she was no longer willing to save her marriage." In such cases, the marriage would not be annulled, unless the couple was found to be barren for a period of three years, although the ecclesiastical judge could shorten the waiting list for the case to be reconsidered, during which time, one could imagine, the male partner's honor and respectability shrank considerably, the wife interpreted his impotence as lack of love and consideration towards her needs, and both partners "experienced hell."

SINGLE WOMEN'S SEXUALITY CHALLENGES
MARRIED WOMEN PAST MENOPAUSE

Reanalyzing the myth of the Wawilak Sisters, from northeast Arnhem Land, and the mythological explanation of menstruation and progeny, Chris Knight has suggested that "the cultural logic of menstrual synchrony itself . . . undergoes structural inversion through the agency of male rituals of pseudo-procreation" (1983, 35) Describing the Australian aborigine Kunapipi ceremony, Berndt has written: "two or three nights before the finale of the Kunapipi at Yirrkalla, after the boys have passed through 'the core of their Kunapipi experience' (in being swallowed into the Uterus of 'the Mother') all the women make their way to the men's sacred ground dancing. Some are ochred and decorated 'to dance for coitus'" (1951, 50). To this, Knight comments that "it is the women themselves who now hold the power, invading the men's 'secret' ground and forming into a 'snake' of their own. The women have their own secret name for the Snake, with which they are supposed to deceive the men, and as they call out this name ('*Kitjin*') they warn the men not to get too near 'or your bellies will come up like pregnant women'" (1983, 45). Thus, on the one hand, the ritual displays the theme of symbolic, mutual appropriations of exclusive spaces and roles assigned to both the men and the women by the ritual, and, on the other hand, it depicts inversions of power relations between the two genders. In the context of the structural inversion proposed by Knight, I suggest that we may interpret the dramas presented below concerning shared spaces between single, fertile women and married women who have reached menopause as significant to our understanding of the threat posed by single women to marital harmony.

In times of growing mistrust and alienation between husbands and wives past menopause, the issue of sexual prowess of single women could become a menace to the stability of the household. Under such circumstances, particular spaces appropriated by single women within the household would often become "melting pot" for transgressions and tension between the competing women, namely, the mistress and the housemaid. In the sources one is able to distinguish particular accounts concerning two spheres—(1) comestibles, cooked and uncooked food in the household, and (2) sexual fluids —in which single women's magical arbitration indeed operated vis-à-vis married women. There is, of course, a rather straightforward explanation for this. In their role as household maids and servants, the single mestizas, mulatas, and blacks had easy access to the family kitchen and intimate corners of the household. Family comestibles and the matrimonial bed of the deserting partner would therefore become the natural arenas for their magical operation in the event that these women's aspirations were not fulfilled (see Phillips 2003, 140–41; see also von Germeten 2013, 32–35). Furthermore, single women such as Magdalena, below, dared challenge and compete with married women already past their age of fertility over sexual agency—though they were both their dependent and of inferior social class—as well as propagate in contra the normal family model.

Fifty-year-old Lorenzo de Torres, a royal accountant, lived next to the Cruz de los Talabarteros ("saddle-makers") at the Santa Veracruz barrio in Mexico City. In 1673, he and his wife, forty-year-old doña Melchora Cortés, took under their care a single woman, Magdalena, who was the daughter of a mestiza, had originated from Puebla, and was also over forty years. Magdalena had been raised by doña Melchora Cortés's aunt, doña Francisca Rico, ever since she was a child and an orphan, who suffered from a tumor and was thereafter hospitalized at the Amor de Dios Hospital.[58] She recovered there from the tumor. She was taken to doña Melchora Cortés's home after she had asked her to let her live there, "for the love of God." Magdalena, who was born in Atlixco, was the daughter of astrologers, and was capable of divining and telling fortunes through a "philosophyzing with a stone." She had one upper-front tooth missing, was of medium height, was thin, and was dark skinned. She stayed in their house for eight months. Throughout the days that Magdalena stayed in their house, doña Melchora constantly reported to have suffered from terrible headaches, and her husband from stones in his kidneys.

Magdalena's distinguished space in this household was a unique corner leading from a corridor. Doña Melchora had overheard her one day advising her sisters who came to visit her there to "refrain from marrying men who pretended to compromise with them." It was also in this corner that Magdalena would unfold a bundle that she carried with her, filled with various green powders, potions, and herbs.[59] Subsequently there followed a series of incidents/occurrences between Lorenzo de Torres and his wife, doña Melchora. Lorenzo was seized by an uncontrollable desire to have sexual relations with Magdalena. After this materialized, he revealed the affair to his wife, who, in turn, quarreled with Magdalena, who called doña Melchora "an old woman who could not satisfy her husband." Furthermore, doña Melchora thereafter succeeded in finding Magdalena's bundle, seized the powders and burned them, and then hid the ashes. For what purpose? We would not know.

PORTRAYING "STREET BATTLES" AS SEXUAL ARENAS

Katarzyna Szoblik describes the expression in Nahuatl, *tlachinolxochitl*, in Ancient Mexico, meaning "Warfare Flower" as denoting "a sexual act, in the form of a struggle between the man and the woman, united within the concept of the carnal act and war. I think that such a conceptual merger reflected, on the one hand, the common sexual affairs of the *Ahuianime* with the warriors and, on the other, the custom that they maintained, for which according to Torquemada, they would risk their lives, going to war together with the warriors" (Szoblik 2008, 196–215).

The competitive relationships, filled with sexual violence and the utilization of magical formulas, between single women and men are strikingly depicted by a unique series of mid-seventeenth-century anonymous popular drawings I found at the AGN in Mexico City. These drawings, entitled *sobre curación y hombres hechas por mujeres*, are sometimes accompanied by handwritten texts in the genre of popular ballads; on others, they are devoid of accompanying texts.[60] I argue that such drawings may serve as a convincing qualitative, primary source for us by which to decipher contemporaneous cultural/mental representations of common attitudes toward sexuality, as well as women's views of their subversive role in society, and of women trying to regain the male's chaotic environment through their sexuality, in sheer contrast to Nicole von Germeten's emphasis on "where men asserted their dominance through their control over their dependents' sexuality" (von Germeten 2013, 54).

The first among these drawings (figure 5.3) is entitled *Casamiento* (Marriage).[61] On the upper left side, we see an indigenous male figure wearing traditional tunics, urinating on a public phallus-style stone pillar; to his right is the figure of a woman facing him and holding a flowery branch in her left hand. To the right of the woman is yet another woman tending to two male bulls. Below, in the middle

FIGURE 5.3. *Casamiento* (Matrimony). © AGN, MAPILU, Image No. 04904-1.

of the drawing, are public fountains/water basins equipped with phalluses jutting out toward women, who are washing clothes or combing their hair; next to the last woman stands an indigenous youth. The drawing is thus characterized by an abundance of male phalluses invading and "violating" the moral space of Marriage, as well as the space of women and their bodies, claiming appropriation drawn in a number of ways and positions.

To my mind this drawing represents a double-mirrored, contrasting view and interpretation of gender relationships, in a similar manner to that of Bruegel the Younger's *The Fight between Carnival and Lent*. Likewise, it is an overall representation of, and statement about, the multicultural facet of Mexican colonial society, being subverted and repudiated. On the one hand, it represents the realities of lust of the unmarried from the vantage point of popular culture (and perhaps, also, from the vantage point of single women), and on the other, it offers a religious-moral-didactic discourse on the conquering of lust through the image of a "Marriage-of convenience" and "tamed love," represented here by the coat-of-arms of the unified crown of Castile and Aragon. Marriage could, consequently, "tame" the battlefield over space between the genders and redeem them of lust, by offering them a "peaceful environment conducive to personal realization" (Curcio-Nagy 2014, 51, 59). The obvious aim of the latter was to propagate the moral and religious ideal skillfully discussed by Curcio-Nagy, that marriage can overcome lust and that "lust could be contained through conjugal love." Why double-mirrored? Because, the two contrasting facets of this drawing remain overtly balanced, like Carnival and Lent, each of which maintains its own raison d'être. This analysis is also in direct conversation with what Jaffary interprets in his *False Mystics* of the Aramburu caption: "Marriage suits you; my God told me so." And as Jaffary interprets the caption, "These allusions to matrimony may relate to societal suspicion of Aramburu, who was a married woman living apart from her husband, or they may refer to her public reputation for working as a spiritual and social counselor to women in her community" (Jaffary 2004, 167). Besides its moral facet, the earthly reality described on this scene can also be attributed directly to what Sharon Bailey-Glasco emphasizes in her book *Constructing Mexico City* about the water infrastructure in Mexico City, as well as the public fountains as a place of social disruption during these times: "Water came from a variety of public fountains throughout the city, but they were often in a state of disrepair, or more commonly in use as laundry and bathing facilities. In addition, most of these fountains were located in the city center. People living in outlying barrios (e.g., Santiago Tlatelolco) were often forced to spend large portions of their day getting water themselves, or pay a water carrier" (2010, 40). Public fountains were also the sites where "young girls and women risked verbal and physical harassment" and where vagrants and other "lowly sorts" established themselves regularly (71, 90). So fountains were therefore among the public places where men and women met on a daily basis but also an important stage for dramas of virility enacted by men and boys, vis-a-vis its challenges by women, as well as its scenes of appropriation by one or the other competing genders.

Figure 5.4, possibly deals with female formulas utilized for appropriating the street (the male arena) through ritual magic, as the wording and the terminology employed in the captions suggests, while its main theme is the power relationship between men and women. The drawing is partitioned along a horizontal into two reverses sections: (a) in the lower half of the drawing and to the left are a naked man and woman beginning to "harmoniously embrace," presumably signaling aspirations for "espousing," represented by the caption *esposo* (spouse, husband, consort) between this couple, followed by an act of an intercourse, most probably on the mattress depicted below them in the drawing. To their right is a female figure "run through" by a long dagger or sword, presumably piercing her heart and exiting at her back; the act presumably describes "disillusionment" from the above futile aspirations for a proper espousing. Beneath, she holds forward in both hands a huge phallus with the caption *simiento* (semen), which might signal this woman's move away from disillusion toward empowerment: she decides to take hold of her destiny by choosing to control and subdue men to her will by way of her sexual prowess. This context is clearly connected with what ensued in the beginning of this chapter,

FIGURE 5.4. "This Is Home." AGN, MAPILU, Image No. 04904-1.

that is, how lust becomes a weapon of vengeance for these women against men who betrayed them or disillusioned them. A skeletal figure of death shot with arrows is depicted collapsed beneath this, which may signal a final subdual of the male figure. To the right, in the same scene, is yet another female "run through" by two long daggers or swords, one in the stomach, the other in her lower abdomen, being fatally wounded in the "battlefield" between the sexes.

To the right of the second women is a blooming tree, possibly representing "creation," and to its right is a framed caption reading: "El hombre está obligado a meter la luz a Dios por lo obscuro, más no está obligado meter la luz por el culo que es gran porquería" (Man is compelled to hold a light up to God who is so obscure, but he is not compelled to hold a light up to the anus which is extremely filthy), which may insinuate the ritualistic use of the two binary elements of defilement and cleansing by the women to emphasize their complex and ambiguous treatment of their struggle with men.

Below this caption, a light beam enters via an open door, next to which is another caption: "luz no le falte a mi Dios, en lo que obscura se hallare" (Light will not be lacking for my God, and through darkness I will manifest), which can clearly be associated here at once with the women's ritual acts on the doorway, described below, and directed toward the Street (in its animated form). Further to the right, actually the rightmost scene in the bottom half of the drawing, are a naked man and a woman positioned harmoniously, again, motioning toward aspirations for an idealized "espousing" and the creation of a proper home for themselves and for their children; the caption above them thus reads: *cas[s]a* (house/home).

Above this last couple is the following caption: "a las dos en una pieza por Dama, la corona. Y yo entro por su grandessa—digo Señor, que la Ce——ella señor, no es doncella—que un dedos por sí passo—digo que dormí con ella y a Vos señor atrasso" (for the two, in one piece, by the Lady, the Crown. I am entering her greatness—I say, Lord, that the——she, my Lord, is not a virgin, that I go through with two of my fingers, I say that I have slept with her, and to you, my Lord, I retract).

This last text are the words of an anonymous male who describes an act of an intercourse, how he has violated a young woman, who was no longer a *doncella* (virgin) when he entered her. The wording here includes references to the Virgin Mary, as well as to God Almighty, so that the person involved is depicted as performing an act that simulates Catholic rites and dogma, within a framework of ritual magic, utilizing similar divine substances, such as the Light of God, for the sake of a ritual enactment. What is also familiar here is the depictions of "male" and "female" substances, which are common in Mexican "love-magic," for example, the utilization of "male" and "female" peyote plants, that comes from Huichol culture of the North, all of which might be connected to the magical acts related to the Lord of the Street (see more later in this chapter on love-magic).[62]

On the upper half of the drawing, appearing to the viewer as being upside-down, and to the extreme right is an exotic bird, which I believe is a hummingbird (*tleuitzillin* = fire hummingbird), which in Nahua/Aztec culture symbolizes the soul of the departed (the souls of the warriors accompany the sun on its daily journey from the east. At the end of this journey, they are transformed into hummingbirds and butterflies), is hovering; to its right (the viewer's left) stands a woman by herself next to which is an caption reading "no es cassa" (It is not a house/a home, which could also mean "it is not harmonious!"), meaning, perhaps, that the aspirations depicted on the lower part of the painting are unfounded; to her right (again, further to the viewer's left) stands the figure of a naked man with the caption "es coral" (*corral*?) that may be deciphered as meaning "It is an enclosure/an impediment," or, alternatively, "It is an open space, in front of the house." The significance of the two captions taken together may be associated with the positions of both men and women on their own separate existence, while the figures to their right (the extreme upper left of the drawing) again represent, to the contrary, clinging still to the aspirations of "harmonious relations between the genders," ideally defending one another against any malicious intent.

Figure 5.5, possibly created by the same anonymous author as figure 5.4's, begins with a citation from the fourth article of the Seven Corporal Works in Catholicism:

FIGURE 5.5. "Works of Charity Provide a Lodging to the Pilgrim."
AGN, Mapas y Planos, Image No. 04904-1.

"Las obras de caridad dan possada al peregrine (the works of charity provide a shelter for the pilgrim)." Below, is a continuation of the mental frame that appears on the caption:

"Que quiere decir, pelegrino es una forma de hombre que no es nacido ni conocido del lugar, y hasi ai disconfianza en que no se sabe si tiene forma de hombre y en sus dentros es algún lobo que quiera destrozar la obeja, aniquilar la casa, o destruirla—y por no faltar a la caridad, se le atan las manos, mientras que tiene possada hasta que el se quiera un libre para su destino"

[That is to say, a pilgrim is the sort of a man who was neither born at nor is familiar with a place, and likewise there exists mistrust towards him, since while outwardly he has the form of a man, inside he may be some kind of a wolf who wishes to devour the sheep, to annihilate the house or destroy it; and not lacking in charity, they will tie his hands while he is therein sheltered, until the time comes that he wishes to be released to pursue his destiny/destination][63]

What is the exact relation here between this particular citation from the scriptures and the illustration? As I interpret this, the utilization here of the Catholic dogma of the Seven Corporal Works of Mercy is intended to provide a canonic literary framework, in the form of an allegory, for the ulterior, magical formulas inserted within the subtext, which is within the text itself and the depicted metaphor. The subject matter of the subtext is indeed the possible violation of the sense of harmony, shelter, and home provided by the woman, the latter's natural sense of mistrust toward the man's intents, and the means that the former utilizes in order to defend herself against such violations. Therefore, the most clear-cut depiction of such a defense is "the key" held by the woman and her taking control of, or her subjugation of, the man's virility. The pilgrim is the ideal-type male matching, who "finds his way" to the woman's safe harbor but who is eventually taken hold of by way of luring.

Beneath the title are the figures of an upper-class man, to the left, and a city woman holding a large key in her left hand to the right, which can be deciphered, again, as representing an ideal-type male for single, propertyless, plebeian woman of the city striving for a proper matching and preparing the "key" for a better future, with a spouse and a home to live in. However, as the above, when the circumstances do not provide for such a future, the only way left for her is to regain control over her men through sexual prowess: the woman is subduing what seems to be a "disorderly" phallus in her right hand.

Figure 5.6 (below) advances beyond the previous one, in the direction of fully manifested magical formulas. The instigator here describes his acts in the first-person, masculine:

No hago el cuchillo en mujer—lo hago sobrenatural—y si me lo pongo hacer—para poder trabajar—es obra que con las manos—me lo pongo a fabricar—por impulsos soberanos á quíen debo benerar—el general lo pidío, no selo puedo negar—porque ami me defendió de todo bruto Animal—más le advierto no entré a dentro de mi propia formación—y solo fuera del cuerpo—es con esta condición, este no lo hago en el culo, es fuera de mi mujer, que ni a mi ni a ella le[oc] cupo—este mi proprio saber—justicia tengo que hacer—sí en mi própria forma entraré—y yo lo sabré poner—en dónde a mi forma es de venado, el hombre se haya de los pies a la cabeza, todo por el cuerpo passa—más de Dios es la Grandesa—soy muy feo y mí corona—yo lo tengo de tomar—que dos coronas es broma en la

FIGURE 5.6. Male Incantation. AGN Mapas y Planos, 2100/5225, Image No. 04908-9 BIS.

cabeza aguantar—darle a cada cuál lo suyo—es la justicia mayor en oficio que en mi [oc]cupo—es tesorero mayor—pues como repartiré—a la formación del cuerpo—más por probe alcanzaré—lo que fuere más acepto.

[I will not use the knife on a woman—I do this supernaturally—and if I am about to do this—to be able to work—this is done with the hands—I get them to do it—due to superior impulses which I am obliged to venerate—the General asked for this, and

I cannot deny it—because he protected me from all the savage animals—moreover, I warn him not to enter my own corporality—but only stay outside my body—thus under this condition, I will not be doing it in the anus, outside of my woman, neither in mine nor hers will I take charge—this is (due to) my own awareness—I am obliged to do justice—and if I will enter in my own form—and I will know how to take this form—where my form is that of a deer, the male will be complete from feet to head, all of which is his own body—more of which is due to the Greatness of God—I am very ugly (aggressive) and my crown—I will have to take hold of it—that (with) hold-ing two crowns on my head, this is a joke—to give each one what is his—this is the utmost justice in the office of which I am in charge—a High Treasurer—according to which I will distribute (justice)—to the bodily form—I will be able to conclude (this creation)—that which will be more acceptable].

Beneath this lengthy caption, a male figure is holding a sword. The formula here is clearly shamanistic/magical: the male author, perhaps a male role-reversal assumed by a shamanistic woman, by way of supernatural powers that enter the form and body via God, whom she/he calls "the General," and she/he takes hold of these powers in the form of a supreme being "administering justice." The figure of the deer mentioned in the caption here also appears in the following figure 5.7. There, too, one discerns similar ritual formulas related to the ambiguous relationships that exist between men and women, depicted here in the forms of *cartilla enferma de sas-tres*; *cartilla saludable* (letters of cure). We know of the practice from this period, of writing a prayer on a piece of paper called a *Carta de tocar*, which would be folded and which single plebeian women would pass on to one another for protection, as well as for the casting of "love magic" spells with the aim of luring upper-class men. Such practices may have originated with African slaves in Portugal, such practices having also been very common among Africans in Bahia, Brazil.[64]

Letters of cure or protection are frequently mentioned as part of the supernatu-ral means employed by women to subdue men. Other such ingredients, learned mainly from indigenous practitioners, include objects concealed in wardrobes (see Magdalena's story, above), natural artifacts and fluids, pubic hairs, menstrual blood, a man's spent semen, men's clothes, shoes (borrowed), church objects such as holy water, the words of consecration, altar stones (appropriated from a church and placed in the home), and *abas, bejuco* (natural ingredients).[65] The bodies of black slaves and servants are also mentioned in the sources as representing and possess-ing supernatural powers. Similarly, touching their naked body with the *carta del tocar*—as seen in the lower left part of figure 5.7—engenders the acquisition of such supernatural powers. The women figures in figure 5.7 are seen in various domestic roles in which they practice magical cures, while the mounted men figures above

FIGURE 5.7. "Curing Practices." AGN, Mapas y Planos, 20100/5200, Image No. 04903.

them (all of whom are Spaniards) dominate the public space, most especially as a *caballero*—"a nobleman riding a horse." On the upper left side is a woman whose caption reads "Congo," which might refer to her origins. She is extending her hand to the male figure to her right.

Finally, figure 5.8 depicts two sets of ideal-type male and female couples: the first is a "poor woman" and a "rich man"; and the second a "poor man" and a "rich woman." The figures are facing forward, not each other, but they are nonetheless engaged in *luring one another*. The male figure, second from the left, appears to be about to launch an arrow to snare the woman to his left; while the second male figure, to the right of the first, is passing a pledge of engagement to the woman to his right, so that here, as in the first two illustrations of this series, the author and instigator wishes to represent binary situations or circumstances that are interchangeable through the will and prowess of such women-shamans.

SEXUALITY AND MAGIC

In a direct conversation with the above, what is argued here is that sexuality, combined with magical practices, provided single women with effective channels for experimenting subtle resistance vis-à-vis the male-dominated world around them. To make my point, I am utilizing here materials extracted from the far-removed

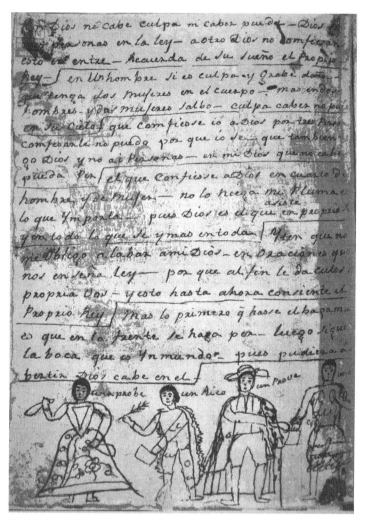

FIGURE 5.8. "Human Fortunes." AGN, Mapas y Planos, 2100/5200, Image No. 04903.

region of the Minas de Guanajuato, that which will also be applied in chapter 6 of the book. On 17 March 1650, the Edict of Faith was pronounced at the local parish church in Las Minas de Guanajuato. At four o'clock in the afternoon of that same day, thirty-year-old Roque Muñoz appeared before don Francisco de Sotomayor, the commissioner of the Holy Office in Santa Ana de Las Minas de Guanajuato, and was asked to confess. Domingo Nuñez, a forty-year-old Creole, reported to the Guanajuato inquisitorial commissioner a number of interconnected incidents related to a Marí Rodríguez. Choices of marriage for single women such as Marí Rodríguez from the Royal Mines of Guanajuato, were obviously poor. Their best option was to live independently in the "alternative household" or to live as a boarder in another home, next to a local hacienda or ranches. They were single women of mestizo descent, sharing lodgings in the household of Gaspar de los Reyes, the majordomo of the hacienda of San José, belonging to the widow doña Ana de Godines. These women had apparently lived together earlier on, in the town of León, some twenty kilometers north of Guanajuato, where they were renowned for their proficiency in midwifery and supernatural crafts.

Four years earlier (1646), while staying at the cattle ranch of Rodrigo Pérez, a farmer of Irapuato, the nearby rural community, said that he was having an affair with this woman, whom he strongly suspected of using love magic procedures to subject him to her will. He claimed that, one morning, when he woke up to gather his mares, he encountered in the service kitchen of his house one of his indigenous servants carrying in one hand a cup of chocolate and, in the other, some blood spilled on a plate. Pérez asked this servant what the blood was for, and she replied that her "mistress," Marí, wished him to drink it. Her mistress extracted blood by placing *guijuela* (leeches) on the lower parts of her body, and being filled with blood, she tore them off, and then took the blood. Domingo Nuñez had heard other men testify that they had actually experienced the same practice performed by Marí, who added leeches in their chocolate drink, and they had interpreted her intentions as directed toward "subjecting their love and affection to her powers."[66] Another of Domingo Nuñez's acquaintances in the Guanajuato area, don Antonio de Cueva, narrated to him that he had kept Marí as a cohabiter for a while, but that "he thought very badly of her." Therefore, he planned to pass her over to don Juan de Molineros, "whom she had already turned out of his senses, placing together with one of his black slaves, a broom and a hoe under his pillow." Domingo Nuñez himself recounted on one occasion to his daughter-in-law, doña Isabel Márquez's daughter, that he had heard from Cristóbal Rodríguez Correa, resident of the mines of Santa Fe, near Mexico City, that Marí "gave don Juan in his meal the brains of an ass, to defraud him."[67]

In her book *Hall of Mirrors*, Laura A. Lewis argues that in comparison with the Old World, in Mexico, ideas about gender and race were inseparable from ideas about witchcraft.[68] Mexican ideas about witchcraft and its power were similar to European witchcraft beliefs, but the cultural situation in Mexico made things far more complex. The imposition of Spanish culture onto indigenous territory in the sixteenth century led to the creation, in the minds of Spaniards and indigenous persons alike, of two dueling domains of power. The officially sanctioned domain was Spanish, masculine, and Christian. This domain exercised authority through both the secular courts and the ecclesiastical courts of the Inquisition. In contrast, the unsanctioned domain was indigenous, feminine, and non-Christian. It exercised authority through the magic of witchcraft. Ironically, both domains were created and fostered by the hegemonic Spanish culture, which "spoke both to power and to the subversion of that power." Indigenous persons, who were seen as feminine and weak, were believed to have "a special relationship to the devil . . . because of their gullibility." Women, regardless of race, were also believed to be easily tempted into making use of the unsanctioned world of magic. Lewis argues that witchcraft in colonial Mexico was not merely seen as a form of religious deviance, but also as a form of social deviance, considered most dangerous when it threatened the Spanish hegemony (Lewis 2011, introduction). Single women often used native techniques and substances and appropriated church rites and its monopoly over nature's pow-ers. In her studies on women's spirituality, Caroline Bynum has emphasized that nonorthodox religious activities exercised by women in autonomous frameworks during the high Middle Ages originated in the church's denial of their celebrating Mass. Such autonomous frameworks, as in the case of the beatas, remained on the edge of the church rites, but assumed growing grounds of expression and popularity, by ways of mysticism, dreams and apparitions, which, in times, was viewed as rival-ing the almighty authority of the church hierarchy. It was then that such women were directly associated with heresy, as well as with witchcraft and magic and, thus, compelled to an ongoing persecution. Nevertheless, similar to the whores whom they reformed, the beatas enjoyed more freedom of expression and operation than most other women of their time. In her compelling study on gender and disorder in early-modern Seville, M. E. Perry highlighted the central role performed by women in the field of healing, in spite of the "growing determination of men who domi-nated official culture to control the women working within a popular tradition." This was evident in the private, as well as in the public, spheres, where they did much of the work in hospitals and prisons (Perry 1990, Chaps. 9 and 10). In this very context, Baily Glasco rightly remarks that "women also held an important posi-tion within the ranks of curanderos. Unlike the structure of professional medicine dominated by men, curanderos could be commonly found treating patients, offer-ing medical advice, and generally taking on a more significant role in the popular arena. This is partially reflective of a tradition in Mexica medicine that encouraged women to participate in the medical sphere, beyond the role of caretaker" (Baily-Glasco 2010, 65).

By the end of the sixteenth century, however, women healers, particularly those serving as midwives, were increasingly associated with sorcery and immorality. They were, likewise, accused of using their houses as shelters for other women, where, presumably, they facilitated, among other services, illicit sex. Writing on the Inquisition in seventeenth-century Mexico, Solange Alberro has thus described how the collective practice of love-magic became for women the force for belonging, for the sake of security and coaffirmation. In the situation of permanent inferiority, women and slaves in colonial Mexico sought alternative means other than those barred by social norms, "to attract the superior, the one who is unattainable in reality" (Alberro 1988, 290-91). In direct conversation, Martha Few describes how in Santiago de Guatemala, "many attributed certain illnesses to the activities of female sorcerers and magical healers, working alone or with the aid of supernatural beings at the behest of the sick person's enemies" (Few 2002, 77). A most important point raised by Solange Alberro in this context is the role of these women as cultural intermediaries.[69] For black and mulata women, who were situated in the lowest racial and social rankings of colonial society in Mexico, and even more so when they were still slaves, the subordination of supernatural powers that they brought over with them from their lands of origins in western Africa provided effective channels to transcend their inferior status, and to dominate those of the ruling classes who sought their assistance.

During the first decade of the seventeenth century (ca. 1606), in his unpublished manuscript *Etiopia Menor e Descriçao Geografica da Provincia da Serra Leoa*, the Portuguese Jesuit missionary Manuel Alvares S. J describes:

> Maleficium is the art of doing ill to others by the power of the Devil. The ways in
> which the ill is done are called maleficium. They can be divided into two types. The
> first is amatorio. It is employed in order to generate sensual feeling in individuals, so
> that they will wish to perform the sexual act with certain partners and will refuse to
> do so with others. This gives rise to strife between married couples. This art is widely
> employed among the heathen of the Serra [Leon] by means of love potions, and
> they are skillful at it. They concoct potions from different herbs, and it is sufficient
> for them to carry these around with them to be loved, not only by women who lack
> self-control, but by those who normally possess it very strongly . . . in one of the Cape
> Verde Islands there were two women skilled in the diabolic art. The Devil never tires
> and is always finding new ways in which he can be worshipped. So it was in the house
> of the Jolofa woman. In the apartment properly dedicated to rest and repose at night,
> she entertained him, the enemy of all peace, seated on his throne in fine robes. In this
> place she kept a large bowl of water, around which a number of candles were kept
> burning on special days.[70]

We are told by L'Abbe P. D. Boilat, in his *Esquisses sénégalaises* (1856), that the use of a variety of very effective charms and magical formulas to lure much-wanted male candidates for marriage was indeed common among Walo women in Senegal, for example. He likewise describes how, in 1841, in one of the towns of the Walo

Kingdom, a young female slave was owned by a rich lady. When the former reached a marriageable age, she found herself sought after by two rival candidates, the one whom she desired mostly and the other whom her mistress desired for her. In order to lure the one she wanted, the young slave went to seek the powers and intervention of a "spiritual man." She asked him to make a *grigri* (similar to Carta de Tocar) so to be able to materialize her marriage with the one she wanted and turn away the other candidate. She paid him in advance, and the man proceeded to the local cemetery, where he collected the human remains of a shoulder blade. He thereafter "wrote upon it his evocations" and went back to present this grigri to the young slave. He instructed her to prepare a tasty dish of beef and rice and put the bone inside the dish and to invite her lover in to eat it. He promised her that after this meal, he would become so in love with her that he will marry her without delay (Boilat 1853).

In Mexico, the daughters of Luis Díaz living in a ranch, half a league from Cholula, fasted nine days prior to San Juan's day to foretell whether their marriages would be good or bad and practiced the superstition of grinding bones in cold water on the eve of San Juan's day and seeing in those bones "reflections of what will proceed."[71] (On an elaboration of African origins of Mexican beliefs and practices, see chapter 7).

6

Sheltering Sisterhoods

To be able to go out of her aposento to the street, Margarita would ask her to lend her some clothes and a gown of hers, because her husband would not buy her clothes nor would he provide her with linen for her bed. (Doña Melchora de San Juan's testimony)

This chapter is dedicated to deciphering the modes of socialization and reciprocity among single women in early to mid-colonial Mexico. Such reciprocities involved a myriad of aspects including helping one another in finding jobs, renting rooms, acquiring municipal licenses for putting up stalls in the marketplace, exchanging goods, provisioning food, assistance in finding a male partner, and childcare, as well as the exchange of knowledge, and "gifts." Especially relevant to the reasoning behind corporate experiences among single women is the quest for empowerment. The latter can be linked directly to earlier emotions of weakness and of being alone in the world. Therefore, the two major themes of concern that are looming this chapter are themes A and D: "Being Alone in This World" and "Maltreatments and Cruelty." As the discourses below will show, interactions among these women centered on helping one another in dire straits, as well as in daily travails, as well as in acquiring and disseminating all sorts of common knowledge. Such women were intimately involved in one another's lives. Their process of socialization would take place at the patios of the female-headed households to which they belonged, while working in the markets and on the streets, and within various penitentiaries, as well

DOI: 10.5876/9781607329633.c006

as within the framework of being part of a clientele that frequented Isabel's abodes of healing. Let us hear these contents as they are voiced by these women.

THE NATURE OF RECIPROCITIES

In 1648, Juana Bautista, a free mulata and a widow, sold the house that formerly belonged to her late husband, located in the barrio de Analco in Puebla, in the street behind the parish church of San Ángel de la Guardia, and next to the Jewish baker's houses, for the price of thirty golden pesos. She then moved to share a new household with a few of her "sisters."[1] Single women were intimately and intensively involved in one another's lives in a variety of aspects, including help in finding jobs, renting rooms, and acquiring municipal licenses for putting up stalls in the marketplace. The Plaza Mayor, and the Volador Markets, for example, were filled with such portable stalls, named *mesillas*, that were usually owned by women of the mixed castas. The owners of these stalls paid between one half and one and a half reales per week for putting up these stalls (Cope 1994, 31). Such owners of stalls, alas, were usually barely able to support themselves and their offspring (Haslip-Viera 1999, 28). Single women also exchanged goods, provisioned food, provided assistance in finding a male partner, and provided childcare, as well as bequeathing property in the hour of death.

Who were Isabel's "sisters," and how did they describe their encounters?

"SISTERS"

Isabel's web of mutual help and assistance with her "sisters" materialized during their daily works at the stalls on the marketplace, on the streets, as traveling vendors, during births and social engagements, and, finally, on their deathbed. Her "sisters" also came from among her most loyal clientele, who were extremely variant and heterogeneous, originating from all echelons of colonial society and from diverse racial and caste affiliations. In order to fully grasp the mental gamut of social interactions of the time, in this section I have chosen to stay with Isabel de Montoya's own words in describing her "sisters," how they met one another, and what their most immediate concerns were in seeking both material and spiritual support from one another.

Certainly, most of the contents available are directly related to what the inquisitors were interested in forcing these women to confess to and what they were substantially seeking out, namely, diabolic practices and, to a lesser extent, "love-magic." It is also important to note that what is described below are practices found among a certain group of single women, of various backgrounds; it would be far-fetched to even presume that such practices were a common "norm" among *all* single plebeian women of a certain background or racial affiliation. This information is only what was found in our distinct sources. However, reading carefully between the lines, one is able to salvage some meaningful clues that can offer direction toward deciphering social realities, as well as the means by which these women communicated with and helped one another in times of need. Furthermore, I am utilizing here corresponding qualitative sources, such as incantations and ritualistic images and paintings, for the sake of seeking social realities, that historians previously made use of for the sake of gleaning religious beliefs and practices only. I argue that ritual formulas was not centered merely on the goals of "love-magic," as some historians may have been inclined to interpret them, but more so on appropriating spaces and its male sovereigns, in the social and racial sense, not just the symbolic context.

It is significant to note that during the actual treatment, these upper-class patients underwent a symbolic social leveling that lasted only as long as they were in the actual dwelling place of the healer (see my elaboration on this point in the section treating the animated essence of the Street in chapter 7). Thus, such practices clearly challenge the simplistic "high"-"low" social scheme embedded within the caste system.

Isabel's "sisters" were doña Ana Machorro; María de Rivera, a mulata and a bread seller; Margarita, the daughter of a milkwoman called Constanza, who lived next to her daughter; Juana de Sossa; another Gachupin, doña Juana, a friend of the mulata; doña Luisa, who was nicknamed La Prieta ("blackish"), in Vera Cruz; and María Josepha, a shopkeeper from Huejotzingo; and Mónica de la Cruz, who has been her close friend for over twenty years.

ANA MACHORRO

Isabel visited doña Ana Machorro at the Santo Domingo Convent in Puebla, where she lived, and then the latter recounted that she had great affection for a certain man, who did not want her, and asked if she had any remedy for making him want her. Doña Ana declined to help Isabel directly but insisted that she go see an indigenous herbs-specialist, one among many who sell herbs in the main square. The indigenous man advised Isabel to grind some *puyomates* (poyomatli, in Nahuatl, is an Aztec mixture of aromatic, excitable drugs that one smoked or drank. Wimmer 2004) and give the powder to drink in a chocolate cup to that man. And he gave her four of them, for which she paid four *reales*.[2] Five days later, Isabel was introduced by Ana to a mulata, Isabel de Vibanco, who lived next to the Alameda in Mexico City and who was knowledgeable "of many matters of the kind." The latter asked for a table, and opened a cloth in which she had some dry Ava (originate from Sandwitch Islands, leaves cordate, acuminate, many-nerved) leaves, a piece of carbon, a piece of silver, a piece of mineral salt, and a piece of brimstone, all spread on a taffeta cloth.

The mulata pretended to be able to perform the miracle and bring back the man, but in the end, the man returned to Spain and doña Ana lent the mulata bracelets of pearls, a golden reliquary, some shits, a cloth, a silken veil, a decorated plate, and some woolen cloths, all worth more than 200 pesos. The mulata instructed Isabel to serve as a godmother to a baptized child, but by then Isabel had already fled the town, back to Mexico City. Isabel also remembered how, one day, when she came over to see doña Ana, there was a Creole woman with her, by the name of doña Maríana, who had two black women together with her who sold pork sausages for her on the streets. On that occasion, the mulata recited for them the prayer of Santa Marta on the four corners of the neighborhood. Later on, she handed over to Isabel the prayer, written on a piece of paper, and advised her to say it by a window. Later still, the mulata appeared at her house and demonstrated to her and to Mónica de la Cruz how to perform the magic, which she did at doña Ana's house. She then foretold Isabel that "she should leave that town and go to the town of Vera Cruz, where she should be able to establish a successful trade." To Mónica de la Cruz she advised "to stop chasing men, who only used her and then deserted her, and go and serve in someone's household." De la Cruz then left them and returned to sleep late at night, with a broken skull. "Isabel cured Mónica with maguay and some lime and then she left for good." Once in Puebla she also got to know a certain doña Luisa, married to Balasteros, a muleteer, "who had had an affair with a local physician, who abandoned her. So, she sought remedy from Isabel." "And doña Luisa was also very fond of buying green stones called Chalchihuitles by the indigenous persons. She gave these precious, curable stones to an *alguacil* of Puebla and to a sentinel who belonged to a regiment in Puebla." Finally, "her husband threw her out of their house, and forced her to leave town . . . In Huejotzingo, another woman, by the name of María Josepha, a shopkeeper, asked her for a remedy to attract the man she loved." So Isabel gathered some *yerba buena* and ground it, and gave it to María Josepha to place in the man's food. In return, she asked for two reales worth of chocolate, two of bread, and two of sugar.

Three other women, nicknamed Las Tlaxcaltecas, came to her to ask for remedies: They were, Isabel Suárez, and her two daughters, Ana and Isabel. Their mother wanted her daughter Isabel to marry a notary, while for the other, she wanted that her lover, a canon, should return to her. Isabel provided her with a fumigator for that purpose. About twelve years previously (1650), a mulata, Catalina Cortés, doña Ana Machorro's godmother and the wife of Joseph Cortés, a free mulato, came to Isabel to seek remedy to attract her husband back to her. She said that she would have gone to a mestiza called Bernardina, but she had already been tried by the Inquisition. So, Isabel gave Catalina some portion of the bone marrow of a mamey and some powder of ground avocado pit. Another time, three years prior, Catalina had come to her and asked for black magic against a mulata neighbor of hers, whom she wanted to avenge. Another old woman, Clara, the wife of the cattle dealer from Puebla, Felipe de Segovia, once sent for her, to cure her from her permanent indisposition. When she arrived at her place, she told her that she was also looking for a remedy to attract her husband back to her, for he had a concubine.[3]

MARÍA DE RIVERA

Fifty-year-old María de Rivera describes herself as an unmarried free mulata and a bread seller by profession, who was born in Puebla and lived later in the barrio de San Piscah in Mexico City, next to San Juan de Dios Church. On 22 May 1652, María was accused of having practiced *echijos y embustes* and other superstitions. Up to July, she was summoned three times to confess, but could not remember more. Isabel had first befriended María de Rivera while imprisoned in Puebla's House of Seclusion, where María was one of the regular visitors. In the course of her sentence, María de Rivera habitually provided Montoya with provisions of food and clothing, which Montoya badly needed: "She first met her in Puebla, where the latter, for reasons of charity provided her with food—because of her poverty, and then came to see her in her house and stayed there for a day and a night, and when they realized that they liked each other, Montoya promised her to give her a vapor maker" ("para que tuviera ventura").[4] In return, Montoya had taught her new friend a body of supernatural crafts: "And then, after four days Montoya returned with some green rosemary in a colored cloth and a grain of rue and other yellow powders which seem to have been exerted out of brimstone saying to María de Rivera that she should spread incense inside her house with the burner *y al echarle en la lumbre, dixese con el nombre de la Santissima Divinidad* [and while throwing it onto the fire, cite the name of the Holy Divinity] and she incensed her house . . ." "On that occasion, Montoya entered her house and instructed her to leave behind some *naguas de la yeta colorada* [colored petticoat] and to hand them over to her, which she did. Montoya spread them open on a small table and beside them she placed *una semilla de ruda o cosa que le parecía* [a seed of rue or some alternative that appeared to her as efficient], and counted the seeds and then moved them from one side to the other, and muttered a few unintelligible words, and then handed over the *naguas* [petticoat] to María while praying. From then on, for a few days, María took care of the naguas and washed them, and then gave them to a small orphan, whom she had adopted, to wear . . . Montoya also provided her with *flor de la doradilla* [bot.], to place in the water and let the man she loved to drink . . . Four months later, while on a visit to Huejotzingo, looking for her neighbor, Marco de Siluo, to whom she owed some money, she passed by

Montoya's house . . . Montoya had offered her to become a lodger at her place."[5] She goes on to say, "I communicated these matters to a Gachupin woman, who had recently arrived in Puebla and who brought with her a great quantity of white cloths—some of which she gave her as a token for her help, to make shirts. On one occasion, when I became 20 years old, Andrés de Solorzano, the treasurer Manuel de Sobremonte's cousin, came to me and told me about a rich widow, doña Bolonia, whom he wished to marry, and promised her a considerable present if she should make this come true . . . To which I responded by saying that I had friends who could help him. I then went to Montoya, who was imprisoned during that time, and the latter instructed me to get it from her gachupín friend an ounce of green silk, some golden lace and a bit of civet [a perfume] and musk, and a pint of water *de hazahar* [orange blossom water] which she brought with her to the prison, and in one corner Montoya placed the civet and the musk in a thimble in the orange blossom water and gave it to me to grease the widow's pillow, by which the latter would become engaged, and the silk and golden lace and the gallon of the water, Montoya said was for the Owner of the Street . . . But, due to the fact that she cared much for that widow and that she was a sick person who could easily fall into Mal de Madre, Rivera did not prescribe her that ointment but only the scent." And to Andrés she said, after having taken the money, which she shared with Montoya, that because of the "works of the Devil, she could not bring about this marriage." Once, when Montoya stayed in the house of seclusion, where Rivera had first become acquainted with her, "she told her that there was an indigenous woman who knew much more than her (of healing) and with corn grains she achieved great fortunes. She first knew Mónica, a single mestiza, when they were girls. Mónica lived in Cholula, and there she was a cook. And she had another friend, María de Salazar, a mestiza who had taught her to use a small purse of grass which she showed to Montoya in the House of Seclusion. And once María had asked Montoya to provide her a medicine to attract her man back, and the latter asked for two chicken and two pesos . . . And Montoya convinced her to become devoted to Santa Marta and asked her to ask a mulato painter, called Pancho to paint an image of the saint for her . . . Montoya once directed her to go to a mulata who lived in Puebla, called Josepha de Miranda, who had a wax heart and who had cured a friar with that heart . . . When Montoya came from Huejotzingo and Mónica from Cholula to Puebla, they used to meet in Juana de Sosa's house." Margarita de Palacios was never on good terms with Juana de Sosa "because she had once persuaded don Francisco de Montealbuo to kill her brother, Juan de Palacios, and that is why she had thrown her out of her house."[6]

Isabel, on her part, recounted her own version of how she first met with María de Rivera:

She first met María de Rivera at Puebla's House of Seclusion, where she came to visit. María had helped her on several occasions, giving her bread, chocolate de atole, and a small portion of meat. In return, she asked her to teach her how to perform magic with herbs; how to seduce men; how to make her bread rise better; how to cast lots from Ava leaves, as well as on how to foretell by the glazed earth wear pans. All of which she herself had learned from the mulata, Vibanco. María de Rivera remained at her place at the House of Seclusion for eight days, after which Isabel had finally left the House for good. She then moved to live in the barrio de Guajaquella [or, Oaxaquella].[7]

In 1650, Isabel de los Angeles appears on the registry of the Inquisition in Puebla, as having been put on trial on the suspicion of love-magic; she was possibly put on trial on the very same day as her acquaintance Juana de Sosa.[8] Isabel and Juana shared life in Puebla. They both were, evidently, under the constant danger of being exposed by the local city authorities or the Holy Office for their illegal activities: Juana continued to sell her pulque, clandestinely, to a growing clientele, while Montoya extended her treatments, often using a variety of hallucinogens, such as the forbidden peyote. She passed her knowledge to Juana.

MONICA DE LA CRUZ

Another associate, Fifty-year-old Mónica de la Cruz, a single mestiza, made her living preparing doughnuts and tamales as a cook in Cholula's market. "She was born in Puebla, there, she used to live in the bishop's Palace . . . on her father's side, she was a descendant of Creoles and on her mother's side, of Christianized indigenous persons." She first became acquainted with Isabel when they were still girls. In the auto-de-fé of 16 February 1653, Mónica was publicly flogged on the streets of Puebla, wearing a coronet with the insignia of a witch and then placed under the custody of the majordomo of the Hospital of Our Lady in this city for three years.[9] Isabel recounted how

> she, herself, recited the prayer of Santa Marta six times, two times with Mónica de la Cruz, once in Puebla, another in Huejotzingo, and the last time in Cholula. Mónica, herself, recited the prayer on the streets of these towns, while selling different foods, and as a result she had met one man who then abandoned her, and another man at María de Rivera's place . . . The prayer of Santa Marta was first given to her [Isabel] by the Creole woman, Doña Maríana, nicknamed La lagartija [a small lizard]. María de Rivera wished to have an image of Santa Marta, so she referred her to indigenous artists in Cholula, but she never went there. Doña Maríana told her that the prayer could "also save lives of women being threatened to be murdered by their men."[10]

JUANA DE SOSA

Fifty-year-old Juana de Sosa, a single Creole, was another of these "sisters." Juana de Sosa, also a native of Puebla, was a seamstress by profession who also worked as a cook in households of local Spaniards. She was apparently also as a balladeer, who recited popular prayers on the streets, while selling different foods and intoxicants, such as yellow *pulque* (a liquor produced clandestinely and sold in the local market place) until 1648, when she was finally put under surveillance by the Holy Office. Fearing that she would soon be arrested by the Inquisition for trading intoxicants, she fled to Cholula. There, in Cholula, during the same period, Juana de Sosa, presumably, got to know Montoya while trading in the same marketplace of Cholula, on the feast day of Our Lady of the Mountain. Montoya also traveled especially for the feast, hoping for easy gains by selling her yellow peyote to the crowds gathering at the marketplace.[11] The two women had met there, at Juana's stand, where the latter sold Montoya some silver lace that she has exposed in an open cart to the gathering by standers. Later in life Sosa shared lodgings with Margarita de Palacios for a year and had been Margarita's close friend for over twenty years. Juana de Sosa also lived in Mónica's place for a while, where she had met Isabel. She came there with her two daughters, who lived permanently in Puebla, and said she was looking for a remedy for one of her daughters, also by the name of Isabel, who had been abandoned by a man who had made her pregnant.

Isabel recounted her own version of how she met Juana de Sosa:

> I first met Juana de Sossa in Cholula, in Mónica's place, where she lived for a while. She came there with her two daughters, who lived permanently in Puebla, and said she was looking for a remedy for one of her daughters, Isabel, who was abandoned by the man who had made her pregnant. I offered Juana to go to an indigenous acquaintance of hers in Cholula, who could help her. I have also advised her, a year later, in Cholula, that she should go and live with her daughters in Huejotzingo, there they could be soon married, and she could also make a good living out of selling tepeche. A year later, in Puebla, she gave Sossa a fumigator, to fume her clothes, her bed and house, to be able to sell the *tepache* [Tepache is a popular drink of Mexican origin made from lightly fermented pineapple, spices, sugar, and beer] better.[12]

MARGARITA DE PALACIOS

Forty-year-old Margarita de Palacios—a single Spanish woman, also from Puebla—was once married to Gaspar de Morales, a lime burner; she had one daughter from him, Nicolasa, as well as a small grandson by Nicolasa. In 1654, when she had fallen ill with malaria, she went to María de Rivera, who offered her some remedy in the form of a winter vetch, which she had said to dissolve in water, pour some of it on the heart, and drink the rest—"by which she would be cured of that habitual lack of integrity." Two days later, very early in the morning, passing through the Rivera's lodgings, the latter invited her in, and there she met Isabel, who offered her some dry, green herbs. When Isabel came from Huejotzingo and Mónica from Cholula to Puebla, they used to meet in Juana de Sosa's house.[13] In the following year and a half we find Margarita sharing the same household with Juana de Sosa, whom she dubbed "sister-in-law" because she had relations with Margarita's brother, Francisco de Palacios.

CATALINA MARÍA

Catalina María was a single indigenous practitioner who sold herbs and other medicines at the Plaza Mayor of Mexico City. In 1652, she was called in by the inquisitors to identify the qualities, substances, and efficacy of the herbs and lotions and other items left in Isabel's room in the small adobe house where she had lived before her arrest. And in 1653, when Isabel was publicly flogged through the streets of Mexico City, on the way to the prison of the Holy Office, Catalina was apparently one of the bystanders. In 1658, after her release, Isabel recounted how she met Catalina again, at the raw silk stalls, in the marketplace, near the Santa Clara convent in Mexico City.

THE NATURE OF "GIFTS"

As one can also infer from the above discourses, the most substantial relationships that Isabel maintained throughout the years with six of her closest "sisters" were deeply embedded in what is highlighted here as a chain of "gifts," which were both transmitted and shared among them. Unfortunately, I was unable to find a full-fledged account of such interactions in the immediate surroundings of this study, namely, either in Mexico City or in Puebla. To corroborate my hypothesis, I was therefore bound instead to rely on the rich materials that I found as far off as the Mines of Guanajuato, though during the same period of time reviewed here. In his classical essay on the meaning and symbolism of *le donne* (the gift), Marcel Mauss links the ancient custom of the exchange of gifts in north European societies with an overarching principle: first, social bonding, and second, ritual reciprocation and mutual obligations, which bind the parties together and forever. In northern European societies, the creation of new bonds between clans and lineages were carried out through marriages. As a consequence, daughters-in-law and sons-in-law, grandsons, cousins, nephews, and the children born from both

lineages are maintained by others, and therefore, the two sides in the social binding require reciprocation of gifts. Those are, accordingly, "gratuitous gifts, usurious
loans returned or to be returned." Relying upon Samoa and Maori customs, Mauss
explains that through the gift the donor and the recipient are becoming spiritually
bound to each other, through the law of reciprocity, and that by this action the
former is permeated with power over the latter, "who accepts it." Every giver of a
gift obliges repayment. The principle of reciprocity, according to Maori customs,
was as such: "*Taonga* and all strictly personal property have a *hau*, a spiritual power.
You give me a *taonga*, I give it to a third party, the latter gives me another in return,
because he is forced to do so by the *hau* of my present; and I am obliged to give you
this thing, for I must give back to you what is in reality the product of the *hau* of
your *taonga* . . . Upon repaying, the original recipient assumes power in turn over
the first donor, hence, he accepts something of the donor's spirit" (Sahlins 1997,
71–72). However, as Mauss highlights, gifts can also turn to be poisonous, in the
case that one of the parties in this ritualized reciprocity "would fail to honor the
law [of repayment/reciprocity]" (Mauss, [1924] 1997, 28–31). By sheer contrast to
Mauss's assertion that marriage ties are the basis of such exchanges, here, the ritual
gifts exchanged within such "sisterhoods" reinforced mutual bonds and obligations
among *unwed, single women* who chose to remain single, and between these women
and their prospectus male partners. So that, in a way, the principle of circulation of
gifts between women and men was bound to remain incomplete; in this sense, men
would not reciprocate with such women. Without doubt, the hypothesis most relevant to our present theme of the gifts is that of Genevieve Vaughan and her feminist, "alternative market" approach to the gift-giving economy, where she writes:
"Unilateral gift giving produces mutual inclusion and recognition mediated by the
gift, a knowledge of the needs of the other and a response of the receiver to the giver
and the gift" (2004).

One of the most illuminating cases dealing with the exchange of gifts is to be
found within the Inquisitorial Index for 1650. It describes gift-giving ritual practices
performed among single plebeian women, household servants and midwives, in
the Royal Mines of Guanajuato, in northwest Mexico. Guanajuato, a mining community of merely 150 permanent inhabitants, was characterized by basic calami-
tous traits and patterns of unstable socioeconomic conditions, combined with the
persistent inversion of the patriarchal, stable household structures in the form of
cohabitation. From the late sixteenth century, the most predominant demographic
and cultural phenomenon in the mining area of Guanajuato was the heavy infil-
tration of nonindigenous persons and the gradual abandonment of the closed
community by the local indigenous populace in favor of seeking alternative employment outside in the nearby mines and haciendas (large rural estates) (Alberro 1992,

342–51). In 1649, the royal mines of Guanajuato, founded as a miners' camp back in 1557, underwent harsh crisis, after silver production drastically fell, and with it Spanish settlement in the area, which in 1570 numbered 600 Spanish miners. By 1649 the population had been reduced to only 150 Spanish *vecinos* (citizen of a city, town or a real de minas; usually restricted to whites in colonial times) living in the three mining camps of Santa Fé, Santa Ana, and Marfil, many of whom lived outside the camps in the adjacent farms (Brading 1978, 8). An additional 1,330 single men and women belonged to the lower castas, while the indigenous individuals among them were predominantly landless and village-less Otomí and Tarascan indigenous immigrants who replaced the dispersed original Chichimec population. They all served as *operarios* (workers) in the mines and as household servants and slaves at the farms and Creole cattle-raising settlements nearby (Gerhard 1993, 122–23; Brading 1971, 224–27).

Spaniards, mestizos, free mulatos, and blacks established themselves in cattle ranches, wheat and indigo farms, and then in the haciendas situated near the silver mines and on indigenous lands. With the drastically rising rate of miscegenation in these areas, the castas, those of racially mixed ancestry, now became the dominant element (Seed 1982), competing with the different phenotypic groups for space and a limited autonomy under Spanish colonial rule. Local dynamics in the mining community of Guanajuato were thereafter very much dictated by the worsening economic prospects. There were also pressures over land appropriation and use in the mining area of Guanajuato. These pressure had obviously mounted after 1645, when the formal procedure of the *composiciones de tierra*, that is, the official sale of the right to land titles to both farmers and hacenderos all over New Spain, became the rule (Torales Pacheco 1990, 84–101). Under such harsh economic and social circumstances, in which men usually choose to emigrate in search of occupational betterment, choices of marriage for single, plebeian women such as Marí were obviously poor. Their most apparent alternative was now to remain in their own in the "alternative household," next to local haciendas and ranches or to share as boarders. The use of such ritual gifts, therefore, seems to have aimed at trying to dictate their own ways to local men, who remained behind and chose to refrain from either free love, cohabitation, or marrying outside their race and class during these hard times.

They were single women of mestizo descent, sharing lodgings in the household of Gaspar de los Reyes, the majordomo of the hacienda of San José, belonging to the widow, doña Ana de Godines. These women had apparently also lived together earlier on, in the town of León, some twenty kilometers north of Guanajuato, where they were renowned for their proficiency in midwifery and supernatural crafts. But then, due to the fact that small communities of origin such as León in the mining territories of the north would not accept extramarital cohabitation, frequent emigration for such women remained the only option. One of them, Marí Rodríguez, a mestiza and a once-married woman living away from her husband, came up in the testimony as the main actor and instigator in the women's deviant rituals. She was known to be skillful in both love-magic and witchcraft and, together with her mother, was later prosecuted by the Holy Office as a witch.

Let us listen carefully to the accounts.

On 17 March 1650, the Edict of Faith was pronounced at the local parish church in Las Minas de Guanajuato. At four o'clock in the afternoon of that same day, thirty-year-old Roque Muñoz appeared before don Francisco de Sotomayor, the commissioner of the Holy Office in Santa Ana de las Minas de Guanajuato, and was asked to confess. He began his confession by describing to the commissioner his sinister transgressions, such as his worship of a bleeding figure of the Devil (instead of the Wondrous Christ) that he had painted on the feet of the image of the angel Saint Michael. The next theme that came up in Roque's confession was related to a number of single plebeian women, most of them household servants in this community. Witnesses of the women's acts appeared before the commissioner either voluntarily, or summoned by the commissioner's clerks in the course of the six-day interrogation that followed in the community, between 18 March and 24 March 1650. Their accounts were presented to the commissioner in such a way that the sum of the various ingredients would make a powerful case for a final implication on the basis of both moral and religious deviance. The male witnesses intimately involved with these women in extramarital affairs were highly offended by their malevolent gift, and seeking to relieve their kin and colleagues from infamy were especially vociferous. It is therefore important to consider the circumstances under which such gifts possessing supernatural properties, as well as their ritual enactment upon men, turned sour and were conceived as polluting and a real menace to the stability of the contemporary, commanding model of the family. Roque Muñoz's associates and colleagues all emphasized in their testimony acts of alluring, seduction, and defrauding on the part of these single women, household servants, and midwives. They had all experienced a similar sense of subjection of will in their attempts to resist the situation and dominate it, and the upper hand was clearly that of the gift donor, who had owned both their bodies and their souls, leaving the recipients more than bewildered.

BENEVOLENT GIFTS

As attested, the women were among an inner circle of associates who believed in the supernatural powers and good fortune attained by those possessing as *manto* o *tela* (an amulet or, the caul) of a newborn baby from a woman of a superior casta.

The membrane had been removed from the baby by the midwife, who was usually one of the household servants attending to her Creole mistress's labor. The caul, believed to possess supernatural properties, then became an amulet, associated with good fortune and then transferred to either single or married women of higher status, preferably from the same class and casta as their mistresses, for the sake of protection, social advancement, and possible matrimony. Likewise, the caul could be associated with what the Maori of Polynesia named as the *hau*, meaning, vitality, fertility, fecundity (Sahlins 1997, 82). Two of these women, a black woman named Michaela and a mulata called Lucía, were both house maids, living in a hut adjacent to the household of the Creole widow doña Isabel Velásquez. It appears that after a baby was born to their mistress's Creole neighbor, one of these two maids would remove his caul from the placenta and take it away to their hut. They thereafter kept the membrane in their possession for a period of at least two months, during which time they periodically smeared it with honey to keep it moist. Being single and of a higher social and racial standing, Roque Muñoz was apparently regarded as a perfect "match." His own household maid had thus given him one such caul for safekeeping with instructions to lubricate it. He did what was expected of him, believing in the powers of this gift, which he retained in his possession for another ten days, "until finally, moved by a bad conscience he buried it in the grounds of his house."[14] As explained in Roque Muñoz's testimony, the caul covering the fetus, as one could glean from doña Isabel's description, was a gift originally granted to the household servant and midwife by her Creole mistress, or mistress's friends, as a ritualized act of gratitude for the delivery of their babies.

The burying of the umbilical cord in the ground possibly comes from a sacred practice maintained among Nahua women during pre-Columbian times, although it was also practiced in ancient Greece (Hanson 1995): after birth, the midwife would bury the umbilical cord of a female baby in the grounds of the household, while that of the male baby was interned in the local battlefield.[15] Among the Aztecs, after parturition a number of ceremonies were carried out by the midwife. First she cut the umbilical cord and, if the child was a boy, gave the placenta to a soldier to be buried in a battlefield; if a girl, she buried the placenta near the fireplace. Afterwards she bathed both mother and child and attended to the baptism of the child, a ritual very similar to the Christian ceremony. Within four days the child was given a name, usually that of his birthday. The exceptions were for children born on unlucky days of the Aztec calendar; also, on certain occasions the name of an outstanding event occurring on the child's birthday was selected, for example, the sighting of a comet. The horoscope of the child was of great importance as were certain beliefs about the births of *coati* (twins) or *tenamnatzin* (triplets) on the same day, which were thought to augur the imminent death of one of the parents.

Visitors to the household of a newborn child would rub its bones and joints with ashes with the idea of promoting strong bone structure. But underneath all these folk practices, the primary sources indicate the keen clinical observations of the Aztec midwife. She recognized the great value of preserving the amnion intact during labor in order to obtain smooth and progressive dilation of the cervix and delivery with the minimum of trauma. As Bernardino de Sahagún points out, only a clumsy midwife allowed a premature breaking of the amnion (Sahagún 1989, vol. 2: nos. 27 and 28; see also Overmayer-Velazquez 1998).

Sahagún mentions that an embryotomy of the dead fetus was performed by Mexican midwives: "The midwife well experienced and knowledgeable in her craft, as soon as she realized the fetus was dead in the mother's womb because there was no movement and the mother was in great distress, readily inserted her hand through the channel of generation and with an obsidian knife cut the body of the creature and took it out in pieces." For this operation, the consent of the patient's parents was required; otherwise the suffering woman was left alone to die and was very highly regarded as a *cihuaopipiltin* (goddess) in the hereafter. There is a section in Sahagún in which certain gynecological diseases are clearly described. The secretion of a purulent exudate of the vagina, "like white *atolli*" is one; sexual intercourse, late in the pregnancy, is given as the cause of uterine infections and puerperal fever leading to the death of the mother (Sahagún 1950–63, vol. 6: no. 27).[16] If we, tentatively, consider West Africa as the place of origin of such practices, in Senegal, the burial of the placenta and umbilical cord was believed to restore the woman's fertility and help heal her womb (Hallgren 1983).

Roque Muñoz's disclosure on the 17 March 1650 was entirely voluntary. The Holy Office had no prior knowledge of his deeds, and it is therefore doubtful that he acted out of just having a bad conscience after hearing the Edict of Faith. More probably he had acted out of being afraid of the consequences if his own Devil worship were to be divulged to the commissioner by one of his neighbors. To cover up for the weight of his own sins, and to be honorably released, he had to give the commissioner something in return. His selection of what to divulge was by no means capricious.

Seventeenth-century European ideas concerning the menses clearly associated them with a cyclic act of shedding the placenta and with fertility (Crawford 1982, 47–73). The caul was regarded as inseparable from the life-giving substance of the placenta, and therefore contemporary medical treatises in Spain instructed the midwife to be cautious with "using moderate exercises in order to delicately rapture the sheaths (*telas*), which contain the baby within them."[17] If so, why was menstrual blood of unmarried women then considered a menace and a powerful symbol of pollution for the proper family model? The answer may lie in medieval beliefs as

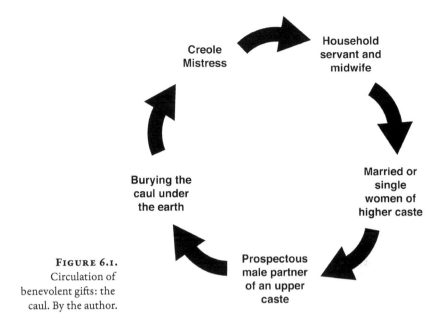

FIGURE 6.1.
Circulation of benevolent gifts: the caul. By the author.

much as in the medical literature of the time. Medieval Christians tended to view menstruation as a "curse" and physical affliction. Although medieval theologians and physicians depicted female menses positively as a natural means for purging a woman's body, they nevertheless identified menstrual blood as a pathogenic and poisonous substance. Women were believed to develop a kind of immunity to their own menstrual blood in the same way that venomous animals are not harmed by their own poison; however, if women do not purge themselves regularly through menstruation, it is thought that they will begin to display symptoms of poisoning. It was also thought that amenorrheic women represent a particular danger to children. Because the venom of the menses is usually borne by the eyes, the retention of menses creates in them an "evil eye" that may poison and potentially kill a child. This condition is especially common in women who consume "gross" or coarse foods, it was said, since these render the body's bilious humors more poisonous. Intercourse with a menstruating woman also posed a grave threat should conception occur. Although menstrual blood retained during pregnancy was understood to nourish the flesh of the growing fetus, when conception occurs during a woman's menstrual cycle this same blood, it was thought, will afflict the progeny with leprosy and other congenital deficiencies.[18]

The use of love magic in general, and menstrual blood in particular, by women across Europe is extensively documented as early as the eighth century. Rabanus

Maurus (AD 780–856) illustrates the uses for this blood when he inquires, "What sort of penance should a woman perform who has mixed her menstrual blood in food or drink and given it to her husband to consume . . . in order to overcome some weakness?" Similarly, the canonist Burchard of Worms (ca. 965–1025) remarks, "Some women . . . collect their menstrual blood and mix it in food or drink and give it to their husbands to eat or drink so that they would desire them more. If you have done so, do penance for five years on proper feast days."[19] In 1531, Heinrich Conelius Agrippa von Nettesheim wrote in his work *Of Occult Philosophy* (Chapter XLIII): "Now I will shew you what some of the Sorceries are, that by the example of these there may be a way opened for the consideration of the whole subject of them. Of these therefore the first is menstruous bloud [blood], which, how much power it hath in Sorcery, we will now consider; for, as they say, if it comes over new wine, it makes it soure, and if it doth but touch the Vine it spoyles [spoils] it for ever, and by its very touch it makes all Plants, and Trees barren, and they that be newly set, to die." (1531, ch. XLIII). Published research on the theme of love-magic in the New World is comprehensive and could not, of course, be fully listed here. Nevertheless, like their European counterparts, such studies did not challenge this practice from our own point of departure associated with gift-giving ritual action.

Yet another way of looking at it would be from the standpoint of the midwife, a role filled by not a few of the single women reviewed in this study. As described above, our Isabel de Montoya also fully exercised this expertise during a number of phases in her own life history; so did her mother, grandmother, and aunt. As Luz María Hernández Sáenz indicates, midwifery was an extremely respected profession in pre-Hispanic Mexico. Midwives served as intermediaries between the newborn and the deities.[20] In her study of the medical profession in colonial Mexico, she writes that "the midwife, *partera* or *matrona* was more than a medical practitioner. The superstitions and magical world surrounding childbirth and the important role she played in it made her a powerful figure in colonial society: someone who many saw as having almost supernatural powers," which is exactly what is being described by our witnesses here. Forbes cites anonymous instructions to midwives, prohibiting them from using either witchcraft, charms, sorcery and invocations, or herbs and potions in their treatment of patients. In eighteenth-century Mexico, Mexican surgeons and protomédicos echoed these complaints, decrying also the matronas' lack of qualifications, ignorance, and questionable racial background.[21]

One should point out that the two gifts, the caul and the menstrual blood, certainly shared much in common, the most obvious being their place of origin. There are obvious similarities between Mauss's interpretation of the dual aspects of the gift, and the stories told here: the ritual gifts—namely, the caul, the placenta, and menstrual blood—utilized by single plebeian women could be either benevolent or malevolent, and even become lethal. For single, plebeian women, who are the focus of our study, there were two major gifts that they would give: one was the gift of the umbilical cord and/or the placenta of a newborn; and the other was that of their own menstrual blood, a dangerous gift strongly associated by any male recipient with both reproduction and destruction, and which was granted to the same partner, covert or overtly, for the purpose of gaining his or her commitment. The "polluting substance"—the menstrual blood—in Mary Douglas's words, was indeed utilized by these women to inflict harm on elite men and married couples, who would not be part of the natural chain of reciprocity. We contend that the latter was closely tied with the rules of cohabitation, honor, and shame, in light of local realities (Douglas 1975, 51).

In 1606, in a treatise on the virtues of pregnant women, *Diez privilegios para mugeres preñadas*, Alonso de las Ruyezses de Fonseca devoted a lengthy section to the description of the duties and properties of the ideal midwife. Much of the material was extracted from Latin translations of diverse classic and medieval sources—such as Galen, Plato, and Albumazar—combined with some solid observations made by the author himself from his own medical experience. But the most proficient literature on the subject comes from late medieval Moslem sources that provide evidence concerning the phenomenon of female doctors/midwives in Moorish Spain (Savage-Smith 1996, 3:94). In 1406, "with striking familiarity and in great detail, probably the result of extensive and meticulous reading in medical manuals and/or information he had collected from female informants, Ibn Khaldun described female anatomy and physiology and outlines the techniques of midwifery." Ibn Khaldun concludes by saying that "this craft is necessary [essential] to the human species in civilization. Without it, the individuals of the species could not, as a rule, come into being" (Giladi 2010, 186). Yet another task midwives carried out in Muslim societies was to purify women's bodies before burial. In Islam, "midwives were granted exceptional legal status and consequently enjoyed a number of social privileges, most significant among them their role as witnesses in court" (193).

Going back to Fonseca's treatise, the midwife, in addition to being prudent and attentive to the body's signs and needs, should also be calm, diligent, and industrious and not avaricious. The powerful knowledge possessed by the midwives was, however, their ability to state, or declare, whose bodies were ready for labor and to know how to distinguish which men were sterile and which women were barren and to forecast from the membrane clinging to the umbilical cord of the newborn a woman's future fecundity. Such midwives in New Spain engendered, according to this treatise, the belief in their proficiency to foretell the destiny of both men and women. Therefore, as Fonseca warns us, their knowledge and expertise in the body and soul of women could cause them "to transcend their assigned duties."[22] Midwives were, therefore, duly instructed to refrain from using charms, sorcery and invocations, or herbs and potions in their treatment of patients, in case their special talent could indeed become polluting or "sour."

7

Representational Spaces

> In the Waters, the Street was viewed through a Yorubacentric lens. It served as the "forest" space juxtaposed with the terreiro's urban zone . . . Sacred space was therefore never left, rather the street was itself made a sacred grove. (Paul Christopher Johnson, *Secrets, Gossip, and Gods*)

This chapter is dedicated to distinct spaces and their weighty role in the lives of single women. In this context, the major theme of concern is definitely associated with both marginalization and gaining-back-power, by reappropriating space. Therefore, the intertwining of the four major themes of concern is most relevant here in the sense that the conjunction of the circumstances that gave birth to such lingering emotions served as a catalyst for the desire to claim the spaces in which these women were located. Single plebeian women, especially *castas*, who were perceived by the colonial elites as being "marginal," and their voiced social expectations and ambitions to attain men from the higher echelons of society, were indeed viewed as "transgressing the internal lines of the [caste] system" and were therefore seen as a constituting a true menace to both men and married women of the elites (see Martinez's 2008). Thus, they suited perfectly the classification made by Mary Douglas in her book *Purity and Danger* (1966), where she writes: "It seems that if a person has no place in the social system and is therefore a marginal being, all precaution against danger must come from others." Douglas illustrates four kinds of social pollution: the first, "Danger pressing on external boundaries; the second,

DOI: 10.5876/9781607329633.c007

danger from transgressing the internal lines of the system; the third, danger in the margins of the lines. The fourth is, danger from an internal contradiction" (121–22). Douglas's remarks are most germane to the discussion that develops in this chapter, vis-à-vis women's insidious image as well as colonial institutions' policing of women.

PUBLIC SPACES, PRIVATE ABODES

As the sources attest to, public space was becoming ever more restricted for the lower castas, especially women on their own, whether indigenous persons, mulatas, or blacks. This was also becoming evident in initiatives taken by city authorities to limit trade activities outside the supervised, assigned space. For example, in 1692 we find a decree handed over by the city authorities of Mexico City to the *juez de policía* (judicial administration under the jurisdiction of the local municipality) to see to that indigenous food and fruit sellers would not set up stalls on the streets' sidewalks, but only in the Plaza Mayor, where each one of them should be assigned a particular compartment according to the product they sold, and their activity should be carried out in correspondence with the particular market days given to each one of the indigenous barrios of the city.[1] In the city of Puebla, as from 1640, Juan de Palafox y Mendoza strictly restricted all public pursuits, amusements, dances, music and games, and all other social phenomena leading to "public scandals" enjoyed until then by blacks and mulatos, women and men, on Sundays and holy days. In Mexico City, similarly, from 1671, single women were inseparable part of the categorization of social elements that threatened peace, public stability and public order, especially in marketplaces and around inns and taverns. Prostitution, as well as other lesser immoral transgressions of the strict observance of the norms of proper behavior and living, were severely punished.

We could also view these restrictions from the socioeconomic vantage point. While Isabel and her "sisters" made their daily income mainly from being fruit and food sellers, managing stalls in the city markets, I suspect that the products themselves were not theirs but belonged to Spanish, male wholesale traders, who employed such women as street and market vendors on their behalf and gave them a daily income, with the net earnings from the transactions going straight to their own pockets. In 1625, for example, we find a certain Francisco Maldonado, a wholesaler from Mexico City denouncing two women who worked for him in this manner—Isabel, a free mulata and Luisa, a mestiza, who commonly sold for him jícamas, camotes, tómate and chilequillo, and other fruits in the public plaza—who he claimed never handed him over the income from the transactions. Isabel owed him the substantial sum of fifty pesos de *oro común*, while Luisa owed him thirty pesos.[2]

We can also assume that once such women managed to become known and formed their own trade ties with stores and wholesalers, as well as with owners of permanent stalls in the markets, it is most likely that such women, in their assumed roles of "cunning operators," would want to become independent, as well as aspired, consequentially, for more gains and social advancement. Marcel Detienne and Jean Pierre Vernant have subtly defined "cunningness" in their book on Greek culture: "It combine(s) flair, wisdom, forethought, subtlety of mind, deception, resourcefulness, vigilance, opportunism, various skills and experience acquired over the years. It is applied in situations which are transient, shifting, disconcerting, and ambiguous, situations which do not lead themselves to precise measurement, exact calculation, or rigorous logic" (Detienne and Vernant 1978, 3–4).

The dominant position and role of women in petty trades, such as clothing and foodstuffs in the street markets, or as *pulquerías*, discussed here, is certainly comparable to what Jane E. Mangan describes for sixteenth-century Potosí and how such single women traders "nurtured credit networks with women for petty loans and with men for larger extensions of credit." Single Women, such as Juana Payco, in seventeenth-century Potosí, "built extensive social networks that helped her succeed in petty enterprises" in the very same manner as our Isabel de Montoya, and she was also, as Montoya, from mixed Spanish and indigenous ancestry. As Mangan brings to the fore, extensive social networks empowered single women traders and allowed them to establish their own petty enterprises. Furthermore, their urban networks with other women were also accelerated by shared religious practices, within the frameworks of the *cofradías* (Mangan 2005, 150–51, 154). In our case, the establishment of what is named here "sisterhoods" was also deeply embedded in both shared economic interests and religious/spiritual affiliations and practices, as shown below.

However, they remained very much restricted by a number of overlapping aspects that became increasingly conflictive with the prospects they envisioned for themselves compared to their possible accessibility to more powerful trading opportunities, as well as in their choices of future partners. Economically independent women, who owned shops and traded across the commercial spectrum, obviously belonged to the upper-middle-class echelons of Mexican colonial society and were either Spanish or Creole. Second, accessibility to more professional circles of trade and crafts was strictly controlled by the *gremios* (the trade and professional guilds); between 1560 and 1750, the period reviewed here, Mexico's infrastructure of gremios had become highly developed. By the mid-seventeenth century, there were already guilds of tailors, shoemakers, cobblers, physicians, barbers, druggists and surgeons, butchers and bakers, hat makers and *gorreros* (cap/bonnet-makers). All of them were wholly male institutions that commonly excluded women from their ranks; therefore, women stood little or no chance at all to ascend the socioeconomic ladder.[3] Perhaps, this can be linked to what Luce Irigaray says about the futile exchange of commodities between women and men in a patriarchal society: "A socio-cultural endogamy would thus forbid commerce with women. Men make commerce with them, but they do not enter into any exchanges with them" (Luce Irigaray 1985, 175). We are able to see that public space could be transformed into a real battleground only when single women became daring enough to challenge men in their own environments. And this point leads us to what follows within the context of defining spaces of interaction and collision.

The philosopher Henry Lefebvre has described "representational space" as the space of inhabitants and users. It is a passively experienced space, which the imagination seeks to change and appropriate. Representational space overlays physical space, making symbolic use of the latter's objects (1991, 39). In this section my intention is to relay the distinct spaces in the colonial Mexican urban scene in which gender and race relationships closely collided, something I analyze from the vantage point of both symbolic anthropology and ethnohistory. The issue of private/public spaces raised in this section also corresponds to Susan Gal's posture that "the semiotic form of the public/private distinction is politically consequential; it disguises power relations, evokes characteristic anxieties, and sometimes shapes novel political imaginings" (Gal 2008, 23–37; see also Low 1996). And Setha Low also writes: "By spatializing, I mean to locate, both physically and conceptually, social relations and social practice in social space . . . how public space in urban society becomes semiotically encoded and interpreted reality . . . The enthnographic illustrations highlight socio-political forces, spatial practices, and efforts at social control that provide insight into the conflicts that arise as different groups attempt to claim and define these urban spaces. Furthermore, these processes elucidate the ways in which the forces and limits of social production of space and social construction of space are engaged and contested in public arenas" (Low 1996).

In her study of daily life in Mexico during the eighteenth and nineteenth centuries, Lipsett-Rivera converses with this present study by taking a close view at the spatial and symbolic meanings of the threshold while, at the same time, adopting Victor Turner's definition of liminality (liminoid). She distinguishes between the semiprivate domain, the façade of the house, and the street itself. As she meticulously describes, morals, behaviors, and attitudes of the different ranks in colonial society, and of women in particular, were very much determined according to what was appropriate outside the threshold and inside the house/patio. The latter could well be considered a liminal space, from which noise, marital quarrels, and violence could be overheard by neighbors and called for outside intervention, that is, switching from one space to another. "The threshold and the division between interior and exterior was a moveable line that depended to a great extent upon the relative ranks of those involved and their perceptions of the attitudes of those involved and their place within the ranking" (2012, 82–88). Such an in-between space was the *zaguán*, a covered space located within the house, normally, by the doorway. In the sixteenth-century Sevillian houses it faced the patio, allowing passage to the inside of the house. However, in our early sources of the sixteenth and seventeenth centuries, this term is nowhere to be found. Lipsett-Rivera describes the zaguán as follows: "The Zaguán was not just a threshold. Because of its size and depth, and definitely its dark corners, it was also the place for assignations and for meetings . . . It was not the moral space of the courtyard in which all was observed but rather a dark place of mysteries where loving fumbling could lead to more serious amorous activities" (93–94). Apparently, a whole web of neighbors, spouses, and friends were closely involved in one another's lives within the spaces described. Let us remind ourselves that houses at the time were facing an inner courtyard where neighbors could easily overhear one another, and subsequently get involved in one another's intimate affairs. Lipsett-Rivera comments that the doorways of houses were a liminal space, from which young women/girls were often abducted; however, there were also the acts of elopement, which were, in fact, consensual actions to override parental disapproval and choices for marriage partners (Lavrin 1989b, 63–70; Lipsett-Rivera 2012, 92–93). Lipsett-Rivera also describes how "people moved in and out of buildings and within the residences, and they had close neighbors who were present in different parts of the edifices" (2012, 92–93).

TRANSGRESSION AND APPROPRIATION OF SPACE

I utilize here the information revealed in the sources to emphasize how single women plotted their private and public spaces of engagement, established the limits between them, and transgressed and appropriated them, all via specialized ritual activities carried out in what I define as "corridors" that connected one physical environment to another. One such space was the enclosed spaces of household patios, which served as safe havens, where men did not dominate, where violence should not have occurred, where harmony supposedly prevailed, where women could feel at ease and secure, and where women shared space and experienced spiritual bonding with one another. At the other extreme was the space of the street and the marketplace, where competition and daily challenges and struggles persisted. In this sense doorways and windowpanes seem to have functioned as "thresholds" or as intermediary penumbrae connecting the distinct niches ruled by women with the outside world of the street, with outdoor life and its various loci. For example, the terms "streetwise" and "port wise" both express women's need to adapt to the rules of the spaces ruled by men; to gaze over the street from a hidden vantage point, for example, from the windowpane above; to develop strategies—even dressing like men—in order to survive. In 1602, for example, in the barrio de Santa María la Redonda in Mexico City, we find Maríana Pérez putting on a male dress, mounting a horse, and riding off—a definite transgression of the male's domain—to look for Pedro Bravo at his house. When Maríana was on his doorway, Pedro's wife came out "and accused her of having besmirched her." Bystanders heard Maríana saying to young men at her doorway: "For God's sake, I have nothing else to do with this." There, we learn of trouble erupting on the street of Maríana's neighborhood and how married women were involved in street fights with Maríana using knives.[4]

In 1603, Maríana de Ojeda was brought to court in the city of Puebla, where it was accused by the *fiscal del crimen* that "she would regularly go to the Portal de los Mercaderes [Mechant's Portal], below the Casa de Ayuntamiento [Municipal Palace] in the Zócalo of the city, and there approach honorable, married men who were working by the doorway of one of the stores, and would utter foul words to their faces without any reason, and cause them disgrace."[5] In this context it worth noting that the Portal de los Mercaderes, beneath the Casa de Ayuntamiento, located on Mexico City's main plaza, was also the site where Isabel de Montoya instructed her "sisters" to go "if they wished their men become rich." During the seventeenth century, the Portal de los Mercaderes, where women like Montoya and her "sisters" had set up their stalls, was a place where mostly silk and brocade were sold, as were fruit and medicinal herbs. The buildings included seven different households, with a total of forty-three inhabitants.[6] It was an area packed with vendors' stalls in which many peddlers would set up shop, sometimes permanently, throughout the archways, out onto the street and even reaching the plaza itself. The portal, made up of three large structures, had four corners (see figure 1.4).[7]

José Peres Gonzales, testified how on 15 January 1603, at eight o'clock in the evening, he passed through the street where Sebastián de Espinosa lived, in the Morada de Esteban de Génova. There, in front of de Espinosa's doorway, he saw Maríana de Ojeda fighting with the former, accusing him of being "an old Christian," to which Espinosa responded by saying that he was indeed an Old Christian, but not old "of an old age" (like herself) and that "she was a New Christian...." Later on that night, Gonzales saw the *alférez* Gonzalo Peres Troya, the lover of Maríana de Ojeda, forcibly enter Sebastián de Espinosa's house and stab him with a dagger.[8] Maríana de Ojeda, on her part, accused her own neighbors of trying to kill her, while she was seated on a chair by her doorway; they hurled bricks at her, one hitting the ceiling just above her head. She claimed that as a result of this violence directed at her she fell ill and was in need of medical treatment.[9] Of Maríana de Ojeda it was also told how "each day she would let many single and married women enter through *a false/ camouflaged doorway and from there they would go up to her rooms*."[10]

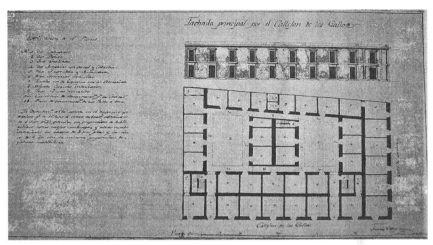

FIGURE 7.1. Principal façade of the Callejón de Los Gallos, Mexico City. AGN, Mapas y Planos, Image No. 04792. © AGN, Mexico City.

In the lawsuit between Gertrudis Vargas and Miguel Martines, who lived in the Callejón de Los Gallos ("Fighting Cocks"—what a symbolic name!), in Mexico City, in the witnesses' discourses we are able to identify the various spatial expressions and denominations that serve as cues within the text. In this view, I have intentionally italicized the different spaces and their relationships to the "inside" and to the "outside." According to the local architect's plan, Callejón de Los Gallos consisted of two patios, three flights of stairs, eight single offices, a store on the corner of the house, twenty interior rooms, corridors allowing communication between the inhabitants, and a direct passage between one inner patio and another (see Figure 7.1).

Don Francisco Bernabé, administrador de ingenio, testified that the couple's rented room (aposento) "was virtually located on the street." This battleground thus encompassed the courtyard surrounding the household, where husbands would control the space by playing naipes and betting on fighting cocks, an activity that in itself was significant, for example, at the Portal de Los Gallos, in Mexico City.

THE ANIMATED ESSENCE OF THE STREET

What is highlighted in this present section is that embedded in the ritualistic facet is the essence of gender relations. What I try to highlight is the idea that the rituals crafted by single women reversed, as well as transgressed, the dominant relationships and relegated women to the position of controlling the chaotic male arena, as is exposed in chapter 5, where the illustrations were analyzed.

During the mid-seventeenth century, cities such as Mexico City and Puebla were overrun by healers, sorcerers, and witches, who cured every sort of malady or provided supernatural devices through the use of ointments and poultices accompanied by magical prayers. Furthermore, in Mexico, in contrast with Spain and other parts of Europe at this time, magical and fertility rituals were still very much a living reality, particularly within the traditional enclaves of indigenous communities, as well as among minority groups such as blacks and mulatos. While mulatos and blacks, as ex-slaves, brought from the Iberian Peninsula by their Spanish and Portuguese owners, were the cultural carriers and proselytizers of Spanish-Morisco magical traditions, indigenous men and women served as mentors and introduced single plebeian women into the autochthonous "natural" resource of all substances. Men and women, but many more women than men, belonging to the three indigenous ethnic groups, were sanctioned by local society to manipulate the supernatural and activate nature and the abode of the underworld (caves, mines, and enclosures), that were considered to be dark and rotting but powerfully fertile. They used native techniques and substances and appropriated church rites and the church's monopoly over nature's powers. For black and mulata women, who were situated in the lowest racial and social rankings of colonial society in Mexico, and even more so when they were still slaves, the subordination of supernatural powers provided effective channels to transcend their inferior status and to dominate those of the ruling classes who sought their assistance. Men and women of the ruling classes often came to seek spiritual guidance from these women.

During the summer of 1662, Margarita de Palacios and Juana de Sosa, both of Isabel's "sisters," gave testimony in the inquisitorial court of Mexico City about certain recitations and ritual actions taught to them by Isabel that could be directed to the Lord of the Street, who, according to what the inquisitors pressured them to admit, "was the Devil in person." They both acknowledged to have participated in nocturnal offerings to the Lord of the Street, using a vaporizer made of violet silk and golden lace and into which rosemary was placed and with which Isabel would diffuse the haze it produced toward the four corners of Street—"for the Lord's Dinner." Throughout this present section "Street" is intentionally written with a capital S, so as to emphasize that the Street described in the discourses and incantations of these women was, for them, an animated entity, thus invoking his name as such: "En el nombre de la calle, señor, compadre" [In the Name of the Street, Lord, Godfather].[11] Mónica and María de Salazar participated in these nocturnal offerings. Another time, María de Rivera also used the vaporizer mentioned above to spray the Street for the "Lord's Dinner."[12] Why has the Street become a symbolic "battleground" between the genders, and what is the supernatural context attached to this space in the time and location of our current study? Was it because single, plebeian women contested the male's predominance over the street, and the market, where commodities of all types were exchanged and circulated by men? Or, was it because, as Martha Few says, "Men and women often linked accounts of violent acts to beliefs about evil and the supernatural, experienced in intimate, physical terms" (Few 2002, 42)—as the drawings, interpreted in chapter 5, indeed, represent? By contrast with the circulation and exchange of ritual gifts, described earlier on, the rituals performed by single plebeian women in Mexico City, on the thresholds of the Street, were definitely performed to appease the wild, violent spirits of this domain, so that they could partake in this space and even subdue it for their own ends.

Let us listen to how they described their actions: Asked by the inquisitorial judges about the goals of these recitations, the women responded that they were for "relieving these women from their harsh social position, and enabling them to fulfill their aspirations of finding a man of a higher status of wealth and power." The chants and prayers performed in the form of Santa Marta, "the wicked," or the Lord of the Street, were also prescribed to them by Isabel, for protection "against vengeful men who wished to do away with their women or hurt them."[13] Once, when María de Rivera was staying at Mónica's de la Cruz's house, the latter saw her guest going out at night into the Street, where she provided the Lord of the Street with dinner—bread and cheese.

Throughout all the above ritualistic actions, the door facing the Street had to be kept closed. Following the completion of the ritual, the house should be swept thoroughly and the garbage disposed of, and the bottle in which the holy water is kept should remain for a while next to the hearth. Then, all the refuse should be thrown out of "the women's door," and the bottle in which the holy water is kept should remain for a while next to the hearth. According to our reading of the above incantation, the ritual formula was centered also on appropriating the Street and its male sovereigns, *in the social and racial sense, not just the symbolic context*. Thus "the heart of wax" should be understood as being intended to (a) provide nourishment for the Lord of the Street, and (b) serve as the Lord of the Street's effigy, representing as well as manifesting the powerful presence and supernatural powers of those women in subduing possible male partners. Also, based on this reading, the Lord of the Street is invoked here as the Godfather/protector.

In a further elaboration of the above testimony, Mónica de la Cruz was instructed to "place the heart of wax between the palms of her hands" and say the following words, imitating the behavior of a barking dog: "*En el nombre de la calle, señor compadre, donde quería que estuviese fulano, el cual nombre por su proprio nombre, no las dejas parar ni posear hasta que me venga a buscar, y para ver si esto es verdad me des una sena, la de un perro, cante un gallo, o passe un caballo, o llaman a una Puerta."* (In the name of the Street, Lord Godfather, I who would wish where a certain fellow shall be, one whose name is his own name; don't let him stop somewhere or tarry until he shall come by looking for me; and to see if this is true, give me a sign: a dog, or a rooster crowing, or a horse passing by, or someone calling from a doorway.)

Isabel taught Mónica de la Cruz to wash her genitals and, with the same water, to wash the floor from the patio of her house into the room and under her bed, saying: "As I give you to drink, bestow food upon me."[14] When another woman was competing for the same man, salt would also be taken into the house of the competitor and buried by her doorway to neutralize her jealousy.[15] And as Leonor de Isla explained, in order to ensure that the efficacy of an object (a leather thong) would be retained, she had to keep it with her for nine days, after which she would return to the client from whom she had borrowed it and instruct her to bury it near the doorway, facing the Street. As Leonor further elaborated in her testimony, salt, incense, and unconsumed ashes from the hearth were utilized for either absolving disgrace or receiving redemption from it.[16]

The following testimony sheds further light on this practice: Isabel reportedly gave Margarita de Morales a heart of wax so that the latter would be able to bring back Andrés de la Cueva, with whom she was badly in love. For this object Margarita gave Isabel four pesos to be paid to Mónica de la Cruz, who owned the wax heart. Isabel thereafter gave it to de Morales to carry around with her so that she would be able to "see" a man by placing it on the doorway of his house. The sought-after gentleman would then exit via the door and stumble over the wax heart, at which point de Morales would incant: "In the name of the Street, *compadre, te pongo aquí para que él es de la calle, te trayga aquí por el ayre, que se asomaría a la ventura."* (Godfather, I hereby place you because He is of the Street, I bring you here to take a walk and breath the air, so that your presence will become visible for good fortune.)

Leonor de Isla, another single, plebeian woman, from the coastal town of Veracruz, also testified before the inquisitorial judges that every Friday she would place ground herbs behind the doorway, facing the Street, saying that "it was necessary [to do it] that way." Leonor also told how she would use a piece of half-dead lizard, placing it upon a piece of bread, and then hang it on the doorway, explaining that it was "to attract men back to her." Another woman, who had been abandoned by her partner, came on many occasions to Leonor de Isla to seek her assistance; at midday the two of them would go out together to one of the Street corners and, walking in circles around the place, "address the devils" (reciting "el diablo conjuelo, el diablo de la car-nicería, el diablo del matadero, el diablo del cuerpo de guardar, el diablo de los escrib-anos and el diablo del cárcel" [the Devil is the Teaser, the Devil of slaughter, the Devil of the slaughterhouse, the Devil of the salvaged body, the Devil of the public scribes, and the Devil of the prison]) to bring the man who had deserted the client. Leonor de Isla also testified to having in her possession an image of Santa Marta rolled in paper, an image that she would take with her at night and place on the Street surrounded by three small wax candles. Leonor related as well how once she borrowed from a client (the person "challenging") a lacing thong with which she would conjure, explaining that in order to ensure its efficacy she had to keep the thong in her own possession for nine days, after which she would return the leather strip to its owner. She then instructed the client to bury the thong near the doorway facing the Street and while doing so to call out to Barabbas (the insurrectionary whom, at the behest of the crowd, Pontius Pilate freed at the Passover feast in Jerusalem instead of releasing Jesus) and to Satan and other devils, and that all of this should be done on a Friday. However, in the end the client did not carry out her instructions.[17]

Beatriz de Valdés, one of Leonor de Isla's apprentices, testified at the Holy Office that she had learned from Leonor that in order to perform love magic on a man one wished to attract, a woman had to possess a small portion of wax, a piece of blue cloth, a piece of paper or colored cloth, mineral salt (alum), salt and carbon, a small brass coin, and "masculine" and "feminine" vetches (flowering plants belonging to the genus *Vicia*). During Holy Week, one would spread all the materials on a table. From one of the masculine vetches, the skin has to be removed, after which it was given the name "friar." Yet another half of a vetch, "which represents a sacred burial, or church," would then be mixed with the rest of the materials and conjured together "in the name of the Holy Trinity." The women participants needed to swallow two vetches, one "masculine" and one "feminine," while "uttering the prayer to Santa Marta and throwing away all the rest." While placing the vetches in the mouth to enact this ritual, the participants would utter the following: "I do not conjure vetch but someone's heart, with God the Father, with God the Son, with God the Holy Spirit, with the sky and the stars, with the meadow and the grass, with the sea, and the sands, with the sun, and with its beams, with the good-fortuned lord, Saint Cyprian, who buried his fortunes in the sea and certain truths came out." Again, the entire act was to be done during Holy Week, "and through these 'judgments' they knew to foretell things that occurred in Spain."[18]

Although it was quite common throughout the colonial period to follow precontact traditions by turning inanimate objects into powerful living beings, as is shown below, the utilization of a female saint's name (Santa Marta), as converged here with the male Lord of the Street, represents the possibility of a more nuanced reading of gendered relationships. Santa Marta, the sister of Mary and Lazarus, was one of the many virgin saints adopted in Mexico to replace the local preconquest patron gods. The usual Catholic symbolism is that she is the saint of housekeeping and cooks, and, most interestingly, she is designed to question Jesus, thereby requiring him to convince her of his status. She was also commonly regarded as typifying the "active" Christian life in contrast to Mary, who typifies the "contemplative" mode (Livingstone 1982). The image of Santa Marta was utilized in sixteenth-century Spain in a paper tied with a ribbon, inside which were enclosed some magical substances; adherents also tortured a toad by nailing it, burying it below a bed, or throwing it from a window, by which it was considered that the evil was then passed on to the person who wished to cause evil. Also figures of lead or wax on which nails were attached were enclosed in prearranged sites; conjurations to Marta "la Mala" and prayers to Santa Marta were uttered, as were conjurations and prayers to the souls of the departed.[19] The Santa Marta prayers predominated in the domain of the supernatural utilized by these women. Isabel had originally acquired the prayer of Santa Marta from a Creole black woman by the name of doña Maríana, alias "La lagartija" ("The small lizard"). Doña Maríana told her that "the prayer could save the lives of women who face the threat of being murdered by their men." Doña Maríana had two black women who sold sausages for her on the streets. The latter recited the prayer of Santa Marta for de Montoya and her female colleagues. When doña Maríana began to be more confident in her trust of Isabel, she gave her the prayer written on a piece of paper, and advised her to say it by a windowpane.[20] Following is the Santa Marta prayer that she gave her:

> Santa Marta,
> en el Monte Tabor entraste,
> con la gran sierpe encontraste,
> con el escupo del agua bendita
> la arrastraste,
> con el cordón la amarraste,
> credo y cerdo que sea amante,
> el que conmigo estuviere tirado.[21]

> Santa Marta,
> In Mount Tabor you have entered,
> [There], the great serpent you have encountered,
> [There] you were drawn to the sputter of Holy Water,
> [There] with the cord you have tied [the serpent],
> The Credo and a pig, so that he should become [your] lover,
> The one who with me will be cast off.

Now, if the figure of the Lord of the Street is, indeed, double-gendered, as it may well be conceived, then gender relationships may be treated through the channel of such ritualistic practices simultaneously as equal and reciprocated. Likewise, if the single women practitioners of these rites may clearly have identified with the figure of Santa Marta while approaching and conversing with the male figure of the Lord of the Street, they were also under the alleviating sensation that this time (away from their living reality) it was on equal terms, providing them an opportunity for experimenting with subtle channels of resistance to the male-dominated world around them. Furthermore, as is emphasized here, the curative traditions that these rituals represented were disseminated through *all social classes*, because their utilization was prevalent among people coming from different ethnic/cultural backgrounds. Thus, within this ritualistic mode we may be able to identify "an added layer of complexity" to the already complicated and ambiguous facets of the colonial caste system in operation during this period, a system that already defies overly simplistic interpretations of class relations.

THE AFRICAN ORIGINS

This section concentrates on the ritualistic antecedents and African origins that are identifiable in ritualistic acts and the offerings propitiated by Isabel and her "sisters" to the Lord of the Street (albeit, "the Devil"). It is therefore an endeavor to try and pursue specific similarities and continuities between African traditional practices and those described above, as well as the social "carriers" of those traditions across the Atlantic, namely, African slave women. There is no doubt whatsoever that the cultural repository that they carried over with them to the Americas varied greatly from one place/culture of origin to another and that some of this cultural distinctiveness lingered on for some generations after the slaves' landing in the Americas; nor did this repository evaporate entirely under the colonial mechanism of homogenization.[22]

In a recent article on the impact of African traditions on colonial Brazil, James H. Sweet inquires: "How can we 'read' Atlantic histories through an African lens, and how would these histories be transformed through such a reading?" (2014, 148). This is precisely my goal in this section. Between 1650 and 1770, the major ports of embarkation of slaves in West Africa were Senegambia, Sierra Leone, Gold Coast, Bight of Benin, and Bight of Biafra and Gulf of Guinea islands, including the islands of São Tomé and Fernando Po. As early as 1580, Spanish slave merchants had already acquired access to the coast of Guinea, and thus a new influx of slaves from this region reached directly the ports of Veracruz and Campeche. Many of them originated from the area extending between Senegal–the Gulf of Guinea–Cameroon and belonged to the Kpelle, Kpwesi, Toma, Bassa, Mende, Baga, and Wolof ethnic groups.

FIGURE 7.2. "Negroland and Guinea with the European Settlements, Explaining what belongs to England, Holland, Denmark, etc." By H. Moll Geographer (Printed and sold by T. Bowles next ye Chapter House in St. Paul's Churchyard, and I. Bowles at ye Black Horse in Cornhill, 1729, orig. published in 1727). University of Florida, George A. Smathers Libraries, historic African maps: 1729 Herman Moll (#ALW1663).

The practices discussed above may well have originated from the abovementioned West African coastal area, the Guinea coast, and down to the Bight of Biafra, and disseminated by African slaves, mainly by women, in the areas where they disembarked and established their living, as far away as Brazil. In the latter context we find Brumana and Martinez explaining that "the term Voodoo has several directions: one is the religious system: the Umbanda cult in general; more broadly, all the religions of possession; of intermediate form, only the Umbanda and Candomblé" (1991, 345). But I also realized that: "it is quite often that the Umbanda talk amongst them of your worship as Macumba, although it can also be used for a lot of them just like what they do: as a synonym for sorcery, left, works of quimbandeiro, the evil end that Umbanda in your pretense of social legitimation intends to segregate you.... Macumba is also offering the order so commonly see the streets or gates of cemeteries" (345–46). African Brazilian ceramic folk figurines, measuring 14.7 centimeters by 7 centimeters—depicted in black, red, and white with their huge mouth wide open—represent the Devil in its feminine form. These figurines are to be found dispersed in the State of São Paulo and are named "Exu"; they are part of the paraphernalia of Macumba or Umbanda rituals associated also with candomblé cults (Ortiz 1976; see also Bramly 1975).

Ramon Sarró called the Baga of the Upper Guinean coast "invisible landscapes" (2009, 6–7). Sarró argues that despite rigorous iconoclasm and religious conversion in the 1950s and 1960s, traditional sacred sites and religious objects of the Baga are still present in local customs because those sites are conceived as invisible locations that are merely "removed from the senses" (6–7). The "power of absence," as Sarró calls this, is based on "the relationship between visible and invisible realities"—an experiential sense of belonging to something that once existed, the imagery of which stands "behind" observed things and by means of which Baga persons develop the ability to see both visible and invisible landscapes simultaneously, "the feeling that things are not as they appear and that the real ground is elsewhere: *behind* what we see or *underneath* it" (8–9). I would like to "borrow" hereby Sarró's wording, by treating the African roots of Mexican, single women's rituals as "an invisible landscape" to be uncovered by us.

During the sixteenth century, African slaves from Western Africa were far from adaptive to Christianity, though many among the slaves boarding the ships to the Atlantic, especially in the Bissau region of Guinea in Sierra Leone and in the kingdom of Benin, were already proselytized (Bristol 2007, 70–71). The Wolofs of Senegal believed in a number of spiritual beings, whose natural abodes were the sacred forests but who otherwise were an inseparable part of one's kinship. These spirits could make themselves either visible or transform themselves into animal forms: they were able to reside inside houses, with their own wives and children, but otherwise they were in charge of protecting the inhabitants within the household or people in the fields, out at the sea, or in the rivers or streams (Boilat 1853, 355–56). The spirits for them were, and are still today, living objects, anthropomorphized by way of ritual masks and figurines, as well as by amulets, and imbued with a soul. Their change in status depended on the rites and rules, that is, on how to perform these rites. For the Toma of Guinea, the village was the world of humans, while the forest was the realm of the spirits. Here is where we find the African origins of Isabel's ritual practices devoted to the Lord of the Street:

In his *Relação de Diogo Gomes* and *Descripcam* (1506–7) the printer and translator Valentim Fernandes describes in the first part of his manuscript, entitled "De prima inuentione Guinee": "The idolators of the country of Gyloffa take an old pot of clay and they throw in this pot of the hen blood, the feathers and salted water and cover the said pot at the entry to the door, in a miniature structure made of straw and glaze and hurl around it much flour, rice and other substances. This is what they do each morning during their prayers and ceremonies."

More than a century later, one finds the Spanish Jesuit Alonso de Sandoval in his famous treatise, *De instauranda Aethiopum salute: Naturaleza, policia sagrada i profana, costumbres i ritos, disciplina i catecismo evangelico de todos etíopes* (1647), writing about local customs in the area of the Gulf of Guinea, which he possibly heard about from the African slaves who have just landed in Cartagena de Indias (Colombia): "Wishing to drive out the Devil from their homes, the local inhabitants prepare a special meal for Him, a *mazamorra* [a typical dish], accompanied by a whole load of feathers of diverse birds, as well as some small effigies of their idols. They, thereafter, go out to the street, singing and chanting, where they hurl upon the earth the dishes prepared for Him to eat. After all that had ended, they gladly return to their houses." (53–54).

In addition, during the same years as Alonso de Sandoval wrote his treatise, André Donelha, in his account of Sierra Leon and the rivers of Guinea and Cabo Verde (1625), wrote: "They do not possess a cult nor a faith. They adore pans, put needles inside them, and on them they kill hens, and they dip their blood in grease, and the empanada pan is positioned either on the inside or on the outside. Also they make many bread idols in the figures of men, oxen and other animals, that they name *corfis*, and they put them upon poles on the sides of the road, the ones close to the village, others afar. They say that they thus protect the villages" (1625, 133) (see Figure 7.4).

Latter accounts coming from the Waalo group, inhabiting the area next to the mouth of River Senegal, document the persistence of such practices in this area, as late as the early part of the nineteenth century (Boubacar 1972, 91–92). All the aforementioned accounts highlight the use of foodstuff, pots, and deity and spirit effigies. In addition to that, there is an act of sacrifice as an obligatory phase, followed by the spilling of blood on the foodstuff. The spilling of sacrificial blood is considered in West African societies to be an act of transfusion of energy: the sacrificed hen becomes devoid of its living substance, which is henceforth spread on the object, the receptacle, consequently generating energy. The described space, where the act of placing the offerings took place, was on the sides of the street / the door / the port entrance. The ritual's claimed purpose was to ward off malignant spirits (albeit, "the Devil") who must be appeased. The transfiguration of the persona of local, both benevolent and malevolent African gods and spirits into the Christianized/Islamicized figure of the Devil had already occurred in Africa by either Christian or Muslim missionaries who penetrated these areas. It is, however, most likely that in naming these spirits "Devil," the missionaries were clearly influenced by the appearances of native masks, imbued with the spirits, such as the Toma

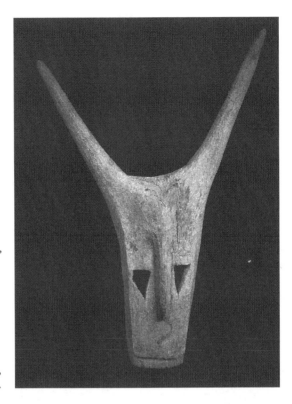

FIGURE 7.3. A "Na" zoomorphic mask in the image of a cow, for the funerary ceremonies in commemoration of the dead (Dama), Mopti region, Mali. Photo © Musée du Quai Branly—Jacques Chirac, Dist. RMN–Grand Palais.

masks in Guinea, named Angbai, or the Kore hyena masks from Mali, who had flat faces and convex foreheads topped with horns, evoking the world of nature, who bears resemblance to a "horned god," namely, the Devil, for them.

The formulas for performing ritual practices dedicated to the Lord of the Street, as attested by the sources before us, were apparently transferred from one spiritual repository, that of the Atlantic African coast, onto an entirely alien environment, peopled by a diversity of peoples and castes, whose members assimilated such practices into their new, distinct amalgam of faiths, which allowed assimilation without eradication of the old contexts. As we are told in the Mexican sources, "a certain mulata servant" (who also gave Isabel the prayer of Santa Marta written on a piece of paper, and advised her to recite it "by a window") instructed Isabel and her "sisters" on how to perform the ritual, on the street, and on how it should be carried out, on the four corners, where they lived, and directed toward the "Devil." Furthermore, such transfer and sharing of ritualistic knowledge can also be associated with the gift-giving mechanism described above. By granting these "gifts" of

FIGURE 7.4. "Kafigeledjo" godly figure smeared with blood, Ivory Coast, nineteenth-twentieth century. © Musée du Quai Branly—Jacques Chirac, Dist. RMN–Grand Palais / Claude Germain.

secret knowledge, the African women envisaged such a reciprocity as being part of what they were accustomed to back in their countries of origin, to the modus operandi of African secret societies, associated mainly with rites of initiation, in the course of which secret knowledge about the names of the forest spirits, the masks and effigies in which they were incarnated, and the magical ingredients and the distinct powers possessed by the masks, was passed over to the initiates (Snoep 2014, 32). Furthermore, as Sarró exemplifies in his book about religious iconoclasm in Guinea, women were considered traditionally the guardians of customs and sacred knowledge, and women's secret societies in Western Africa are known to have maintained covert knowledge and ritual practices vis-à-vis processes of annihilation and destruction of the old cults. In their own particular way of performing this ritual, then, Isabel and her "sisters" managed to maintain most of these ingredients, ritual contexts, and formulas, as well as the significance of the attributed space—namely, the street, the doorway, and the port—but supplemented it now with their own unique goal: warding off the powers of men over the assigned space, while empowering the Lord of the Street to appropriate this space, the street, and make men available for their own social design of enhancing their socioeconomic prospects. We may as well link this to how the Toma of Liberia, for example, conceived Afwi, their great spirit of the forest, as being able to be conjured for the sake of transforming men who disobeyed him into stone statues. Afwi, for them, was invisible but also more feared than ancestors. He appeared through masks, which were sometimes considered to be his "spouses," sometimes his "nephews." "Awfi's authority is also expressed through the *afwiti*—objects that are imbued with some of his power, for example, amulets—through which people can experience his benefits and be protected from his anger" (2009, 6–7).

On the Ivory Coast, a divinatory godly figure by the name of Kafigeledjo, incarnated by the spirits of nature and covered by sacrificial blood smeared on the feathers on his headdress, the same as in the above descriptions, would preside over Poro rites of initiation. The name of this figure signified "the one who is telling truths," and its function was to detect/reveal lies or false truths told by the initiates (see figure 7.4). For Isabel and her "sisters," thus, conjuring the spirit in the form of the double-horned African god (albeit, the "Devil"), the Lord of the Street, was directly related to such contents but in an entirely different environment and culture, of being able to inflict fear and vengeance on disobedient males, through the activation of such supernatural forces.

The metaphor of the Street as an animated entity is also in direct conversation with what Paul Christopher Johnson meticulously analyzes of the impact of West African religious conceptions brought through the nineteenth-century to Brazil by Jeje and Nagô slaves on contemporary Candomblé rituals in Bahia. Nagô is a term applied to Yoruba-speaking people, who were funneled into slavery in Brazil during the beginning of the nineteenth Century (2002, 63–64). Jeje refers to Ewe-speaking groups, mostly from the Kingdom of Dahomey, that stretched across today's Benin and western Nigeria (Thornton 1998, 261–64). One of his most significant findings in this context, one that certainly helps us in our endeavor here, is the link he describes between West African religious conceptions of the spirits of the forests and those of the Street (in Bahia): "In the Waters, the Street was viewed through a Yorubacentric lens. It served as the 'forest' space juxtaposed with the terreiro's urban zone . . . Sacred space was therefore never left, rather the street was itself made a sacred grove. The street became an extension of the terreiro's grounds, just as the forest of the largest terreiro in Bahia actually lies within their compound. Yet the two movements, out from the terreiro to the street, shared much in common as well: both relied on the street as a repository of the wild force" (Johnson 2002, 141).

Furthermore, when we delve into Isabel's medical repository found among the rest of her belongings confiscated by the Inquisition during her first arrest in Huejotzingo in 1652, one finds the following items among the rest of the repository, which attest to the African roots of the ritualistic practices: a rough cloth, covering bits of a snake or of a viper; some powders from Congo; and another small sack containing different powders, herbs, and some bones (linked perhaps to love magic practices originating from Africa that utilized bones of the dead).[23] All such items may well have been given to Isabel by her black and mulata acquaintances as practical "gifts." The sheer initiative on part of such black and mulata single women to transfer their faith, ritualistic knowledge, and paraphernalia to other single women coming from different *castas* and cultural backgrounds can be interpreted as an endeavor to keep these traditions alive, in spite of the changes, and imbue such traditions with additional vigor via Isabel's social resourcefulness.

REMOVING THE RELICS

Among the sixteenth-century Toma in Guinea (Faranah and Nzérékoré regions: Macenta, Kissidougou, and Guéckédou Prefectures, between Macenta and Kissidougou towns) and the Temne in the northwestern and central parts of Sierra Leone, as well as in the Upper Guinea region, the Temne were one of the ethnic groups that were victims of slave capture and trading across the sub-Saharan and across the Atlantic into the Spanish colonies. Among the Temne, the belief was that if women might behold the secret masks, "they will likely become sterile." Among the Temne, we also find the expression *contumbeira* meaning "an occasion on which the [masked] spirit comes out and passes through the town or the village, all the women are required to remain within their houses, avoiding sight of the spirit" (de Almada 1982; see also Thornton 2003, 273–94).

David Ames further elaborates on this with regard to the Wolof of Gambia during the first half of the twentieth century:

Of the numerous taboos and magical precautions steadfastly employed in daily life, by far the greatest number are designed to ward off *doma* . . . *Doma* inherit the power to do evil through the maternal line . . . Doma usually attack at night, though they can attack at any time during the day. They definitely prefer younger people, particularly initiates at the bush circumcision school, a mother or child just after childbirth, and new brides. And this is the main reason why at all life-milestone ceremonies, except funerals, there are elaborate and often costly precautions to ward off *doma*. If a woman has a miscarriage, her child is said to have been eaten in her womb by a *doma* . . . Miscarriages and barrenness are often ascribed to *doma* by medicine men-diviners.

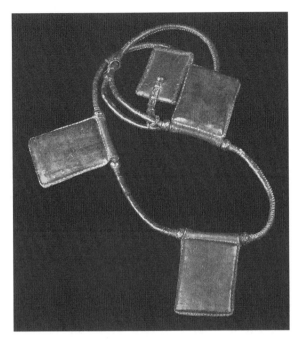

FIGURE 7.5. A Wolof amulet neckless, twentieth century. © Musée du Quai Branly—Jacques Chirac, Dist. RMN–Grand Palais / Claude Germain.

Amulets covered with leather, cloth, or brightly colored plastic were invariably worn around the neck, arms, chest, waist, or in the hair by persons considered especially vulnerable to attack—boys, mother and child before and after childbirth . . . When a child is born, branches of a *dogut* or *wen* tree are laid in the compound entrance, and a branch of the *rat* tree is kept in front of the door to the hut of the mother and new-born child for at least seven days after child-birth. (Ames 1959, 263–73).

Rhonda M. Gonzàles notes that in Spanish Inquisition records focusing on African and mulata (Afro-Mexican) women in seventeenth century Mexico City, "their testimonies reveal evidence of Bantu-derived religious understandings that had deep, sinuous roots in Bantu-descended populations of people whose ances-tors had for millennia prior to the eventual Trans-Atlantic slave trade lived in the regions of West and West Central Africa" (Gonzàles 2012). How widespread and effective were African beliefs and practices on women in colonial Mexico, in par-ticular, is further evident from what follows, which is linked directly to themes that were already discussed earlier in this book, namely, midwifery, fertility, and progeny.

During March 1627, in a get-together of between eight and ten pregnant women held in one of those women's houses, near the *tianquiz* of San Juan in Mexico City, they warned each other against evil spirits entering their homes, or any other homes, in which pregnant women, babies, or children lived. In order to counter those evil spirits, they recommended to one other that "in the course of twelve consecutive nights, they should place some brooms and a hoe, in addition to old shoes and sandals in the doorway, as well as on the windowpanes." All of them were apparently taught to do so by an old mulata midwife, who had assisted them in their previous births, and who herself would hang up some small packages (amulets?) on her windowpanes.

Inés Osario, the host, who later denounced to the Inquisition all the guests for their sins, defended her own practice before the inquisitors by saying that "es cristiana y reza a Dios pero el amor de mi criatura y que tener de defenderla de las brujas uzo que oio que era buen remedio" (I am a Christian, and I pray to God, but for the love of my fetus, and being obliged to defend it from the witches, I utilize what I hear about to be a good remedy).[24]

Furthermore, in the far-removed, northern region of Culiacan (Sinaloa), we are told how three mulatas and a black slave, all of whom were apparently very active as midwives in this area, would commonly instruct all of the women who were about to deliver their babies, to remove from their homes all the saints' relics as well as the Agnus Dei that they possessed, "so as not to hinder the delivery of the baby" and that "it was a good remedy for this sake," and in case that they forgot to do so, the abovementioned midwives would come in advance and remove the relics from the walls, and only thereafter help deliver the baby.[25] If we interpret this accurately, according to the aforementioned black and mulata midwives, the Catholic saints' relics were alleged to be in fact counterprotective and, even more so, harmful for pregnant women, as well as to their newborns. In this sense, the saints' relics impersonated for them the sacred, dual essence of the masks from their lands of origin. To counter the malevolent influence of the spirits, then, the old mulata midwife from Mexico City would "hang up some small packages, namely, amulets, on her windowpanes."

THE WOMAN AND THE SNAKE

We have no idea whatsoever who the person was behind figure 7.6, though there is a good possibility that the destitute black woman depicted here is indeed the artist, a first-generation African slave. She is envisaged locked up in a cell of the inquisitorial prison, facing a powerful supernatural African entity, in the form of "a devil," alluring perhaps to the spirited mask—an Angbai mask from Guinea, imbued with a godly spirit, that resembled the form of a devil, described above, though also representing immersed church teachings concerning the Devil. The figure of the "Devil" here is holding a thin rope rolled in his hand, which he offers her, perhaps, as means

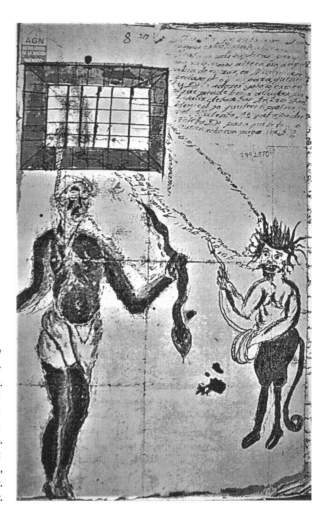

FIGURE 7.6. A black/ mulata prisoner holding a snake. "Dibujos en expediente contra blasfemias herejes." AGN, Mapas y Planos, Image No. 4887, 1764. 31 × 21 cm. AGN, Inquisición, vol. 1136, fol. 215 r. ©AGN, Mexico City.

to redeem herself from her state of misery and loss of hope, and likewise the text that is described as emerging from his mouth, saying: "para que veas que ayudote bien para que no padezcas, toma esta soga para taparme, dio y va manos . . ." ("this is for you to see that I help you well, so that you will not suffer, take hold of this rope with your hands . . .").

Moreover, simultaneously to this first supernatural figure, in figure 7.6 she is also depicted as seeking also the powers of a Snake figure, held by her in the middle of his body with her left hand as his head is held downward, in the direction of the earth; he possibly represents the figure of the great god Idem-Efik. Describing

Kalabari religion during the early part of the nineteenth century, Thomas Joseph Hutchinson, highlights the role and personification of the major god: "Idem-Efik is the name of the god who is supposed to preside over the affairs of Kalabar, and who is connected mysteriously with the great Abasi; sometimes represented by a tree, and sometimes by a large snake, in which form he is only seen by his high priest or vicegerent on earth—Old King Kalabar" (Hutchinson [1858] 1970, 145).

Although it is tempting to attribute this figure entirely to African traditional gods, one should also be aware of the possibility that the Devil herein may (also) be the classic Spanish figure, painted in such a genre of "pardon letters" from the earliest colonial times.

The text on the upper-righthand part of the drawing reads like a covert communication that she wishes to convey to another "sister," inside the prison, or outside it. She is telling her of her suffering and loss of hope. It is likely that the two women in the above "dialogue" may well have been slaves, who originated from this same area of Baga Wolof, Mandinka, Fulbe, and Kalabari cultures—the Gulf of Guinea and Senegambia—described by William Snelgrave and others (below), arriving on the shores of Veracruz or Campeche not long before that, bringing over with them a whole repository of local beliefs and customs of which the above description was an inseparable part. What reinforces the transatlantic connection with this region is that most African slaves who disembarked in the ports of Veracruz and Campeche during these years originated from this region in West Africa ("Slave Voyages," Trans-Atlantic Slave Trade Database [slavevoyages.org/voyage/search]). The message is as follows:

> Maríana, y has visto como estamos Christianos/herejes, eran, lamentado mis suplicas, pero como no lo somos, allí te envío a el que havia de entrar en mi alma ese pedazo de oblea [wafer], para que si es tu Dios, lo adores, yo solo creo en el que me ha de venir a ayudar, para salir de todo esto, hambre, y también te digo que esto es el postrero papel allá te cito, a ti y a tu pacto ante tu Dios para que se vea lo que han echo conmigo y a Dios.

> [Maríana, and you have witnessed how we exist, we Christians/heretics, lamentably those were my pleadings, but as we are not alike I deliver to you, the one who should have entered my soul, this piece of wafer, so that if it is your God, then worship him; I only believe in what has come to help me, to escape all this hunger; and I also say to you that this is the last piece of paper that I send to you, to you and your covenant with your God, so you can see what has been done with me and God.]

The prisoner's message to Maríana, thus, reveals precisely the inner spiritual conflict that she had undergone; however, she was now at the point of being fully convinced that she was bound to rely on the African gods only in order to save both her body and soul, while her "sister," Maríana, was apparently not as convinced as her to abandon Christianity.

During the first half of the seventeenth century, the Jesuit Alonso de Sandoval also describes how there were "Ídolos particulares en sus casas, a quienes reverencian y adoran y todos juntos adoran culebras, y caimanes" (Distinct idols in their houses to whom they offer reverence and adore them, and all together they worship snakes and alligators) (de Sandoval 1647, 133). And in his *A New Account of Some Parts of Africa and the Slave Trade* (1726), Snelgrave describes some "curiosities" that he met regarding local religion in the area of Dahome—the Gulf of Guinea. Among them we find the divine figure of the Snake playing a central role in the local pantheon: "And as worshipping a snake may seem very extravagant to such as are unacquainted with the Religion of the Negroes, I shall inform the readers of the reasons given by the People of Ouidah [Benin] . . . the conquerors found many of them in the houses which they treated in this manner: They held them up by the middle, and spoke to them *If you are Gods, speak and save your selves.*" (1733, 11–12; see also today's highly cherished Temple of the Pythons, in Ouidah, Benin, converted into a museum).

And yet in another chapter of his book, devoted to his impressions of the rites of initiation he has witnessed in the Island Fernando Po, Hutchinson writes:

FIGURE 7.7. *A-mantsho-ila-Tshol* Serpent Headdress, for the *bansonyi* initiation rites, Baga culture, Guinea. Photo © Musée du Quai Branly—Jacques Chirac, Dist. RMN-Grand Palais / Patrick Gries / Bruno Descoings.

As soon as the ceremonials connected with the operation are completed, all children born during the past year are carried out, and their hands made to touch the tail of the snake's skin. This species of snake, styled by the Portuguese residents of the island[,] is believed to be their guardian deity—to possess the power of good or evil towards them, to be able to confer riches, or inflict sickness, even to cause death, therefore needing to be propitiated ... Maan is the title given to the devil, and the Botakimaaon—his high priest—is supposed to have influence with him through communication with the cobracapella, the Roukarouko (the snake). The placing of a snake's skin here is an annual ceremony. Their faith in God, to whom the name of Rupe is given, is a loftiest aspiration than that of the devil; but they believe that the Deity's favour can only be obtained by intercession through the Botakimaaon with his master. The ceremony of coronation, the Botakimaaon steps into a deep hole, and pretends to hold conversation with one of the Roukaroukos at the bottom, the candidate for regal honours standing alongside ... The Botakimaaon then delivers to the king the message from the Roukarouko for his guidance in his high station, shakes over him a quantity of yellow powder, entitled Tsheobo ... collected from the river. ([1858] 1970, ch. 13, 196–97)

And last, in his study of the Wolof of Senegambia during the early part of the twentieth century, David P. Gamble describes: "*Ninkinanka*: This is a fabulous snake of immense size dwelling in the depths of the forest or swamps. Anyone who sees him dies ... Belief in these beings is also found among the Mandinka, Fulbe, etc. while the devil and *jine* are shared with the Muslim world ... Spirits of the village or specific localities (*rab*), which may manifest themselves in visible form e.g. as a large snake. c. The devil (seitane) who makes people mad, and who may steal a child and substitute a deformed or abnormal infant. d. Spirits (*jine*) Wolof stories tell of humans who were taken to the spirit world (e.g. the story of the midwife related by Equilbeck)." (1957, 73–74, 79).

The figures and spiritual associations of such snake gods and spirits were subsequently transferred via the slaves to the islands of Haiti and Cuba, where they were assimilated into renewed Bizango secret societies—small groups of slaves who had escaped from the plantations.

No doubt, all those three African practices described above, once in Mexico, devoid of the original context, were now accommodated into an entirely new ritualistic amalgam, consisting also of Mesoamerican religions, as well as adopted into an urban surrounding, with entirely different material goals, conceived by single plebeian women, coming from various backgrounds and ethnic origins. Such an ethnic and a religious amalgam also developed within the new framework of the African *cofradías* in Mexico City and Puebla. Black confraternities in

FIGURE 7.8. A "Bizango" figure in secret rites of Haiti. Photo © Musée du Quai Branly—Jacques Chirac, Dist. RMN–Grand Palais / Michel Urtado / Thierry Ollivier.

Mexico City were originally founded by Africans belonging to the Kpelle, Kpwesi, Biafra, Bañol, and Wolof ethnic groups, but became increasingly heterogeneous, accepting members from diverse African groups as well as those already born in the New World (Creoles), and mulattoes. According to the Spanish *Diccionario de autoridades* (1732), there existed a differentiation in the New World between the linguistic usage of the term Bozal, referring to the recently arrived African slaves, and *rústicos*, that is, those who remained native lands. In her study of black confraternities in colonial Mexico, von Germeten argues about their nature, "The mix of Spanish religious practice and Afromexican public ritual expression is far too complex to argue that confraternities were institutions entirely imposed upon slaves or, on the other hand, that confraternities were nothing more than an expression of African communal identity . . . Most confraternities did not begin by organizing around plebeian identity; instead, they focused on race as the factor that determined membership and especially leadership" (von Germeten 2006, 12–20, 188).

One of the earliest such confraternities was that of the Augustinian saint Nicolas Tolentino, established as early as 1560 in the parish church of the Santa Veracruz barrio in Mexico City, the very church and parish where Isabel de Montoya's entire family were to be baptized and married over several generations. Around 1599, the most important black confraternity, that of the Morenos de San Benito, was initially established at the church of Santa María la Redonda, but was later relocated to the San Francisco Convent, and was renamed the brotherhood of the dark-skinned San Benito (Benedict of Palermo), an African holy man, "who fit all the Spanish requirements for colonial subjects" (von Germeten 2006, 21); it was the brotherhood of the Coronation of Christ. The confraternity was headed by a rector, himself a black, and it accepted as members only those who belonged to the castas of *mulatos*, blacks, and *morenos* (free blacks).[26] Joan Cameron Bristol describes the black Cofradía de Nuestra Señora de la Merced, in 1611, and emphasizes the role of such black confraternities in providing their members with mutual assistance in the burial of their dead, as well as helping in buying slaves' freedom from bondage (Bristol 2007, 94–96). Our sources mention that in 1645, a certain black woman, a slave of the city treasurer don Diego López de Curate, officiated as *hermana mayor* (elder sister) in this confraternity.[27] Similarly, von Germeten also states that "advocations of confraternities with black and mulato leadership and membership demonstrate an emphasis on penitence and humility, African identity, and the importance of women members" (2003, 24–30). Another active member mentioned in the sources is Francisca Ruiz, who served as a *madrina de bautismo* (godmother for baptisms) for not a few black and mulato newborns in the parish. She instructed them in the Catholic religion as well as in the practice of local folk religion and kept watch over their moral education. A devout member of the parish, Francisca Ruiz was also in charge of knitting clothes with which to dress the image of the local patron, Our Lady of Carmen, and taught Isabel de Montoya this craft. Montoya also accompanied her on all parish processions during feast days carrying the saint's image to the metropolitan cathedral in the Plaza Mayor.[28]

It is attested in different recent studies that women, single in particular, were relegated central positions in newly established confraternities, "because they enjoyed greater freedom in devotional activities and public alms collecting" (Komisaruk 2013, 80). As mentioned in this this study, black and mulato women's leadership and important positions in lay confraternities can certainly be linked to African traditional roles assigned to women. In this context, Bristol emphasizes the fact that "urban residents would have been familiar with Afro-Mexican women who played important roles in the leadership of their confraternities" (Bristol 2007, 51).

In addition, there existed a number of other confraternities: the brotherhood of Our Lady of the Sorrows, founded in 1628, the confraternity of the Precious Blood of Christ, initiated in 1665, at the church of Santa Catalina (Masferrer León and Verónica 2011, 85–87), and the confraternities of Charity and the Holy Rosary, all of which functioned as viable channels for ex-slaves, especially women, of "moving beyond the dichotomies of assimilation and integration."[29] Moreover, as John Thornton has outlined, back in Africa "African religions produced many societies devoted to religious affairs, which nevertheless provided a good set of flexible organizational principles outside the bounds of kinship." Thornton provides us with an example of *kimpasi* society in Kongo, which was a religious organization for the lower echelons "in which kinship was specifically abolished among its members, who kept in touch with each other as a special society, once they were initiated" (Thornton 1998, 219–20). Such a trait clearly allowed their flexibility and assimilation to extend to, and thrive, within the existing cultural patterns of the New World, that transcended casta boundaries, as we could see in the case of Afro-Mexican single women's rituals.

8

Comforting Rituals

THE RITUAL PARAPHERNALIA

This chapter deals with the interplay between the material, symbolic, and cosmological contexts of single, plebeian women's ritual practices in mid-colonial Mexico. Here, it is my goal to reconstruct as well as classify these women's spiritual worlds by accumulating "forensic evidence" of diverse elements and traditions. During the past two decades or so, symbolic as well as the ritualistic aspects of archaic cultures and civilizations have been given increasing attention within the field of archaeology. In this context, in a review of Bruno David's book on the archaeology of aboriginal rock art in Australia, Tim Murray remarks that "broadening our focus to a concern with the lives of people *in all their complexity* has the potential to consider archaeological phenomena not just as evidence of subsistence or of environmental change, but as key documents for writing social history" (Murray 2008, 80). This phenomenon comes to the fore especially in the analysis archaeologists now make of mortuary rites and the deposition of the dead in the ancient world. Ever since the 1980s, these perspectives have been augmented by social, symbolic, and ideological interpretations.[1] Building upon these perspectives, recent studies have emphasized the role of mortuary practices in constructing identities and social memories (Symonds 2009). The most common questions asked in such exemplary studies are: How did past communities and individuals remember through social and ritual practices? How important were mortuary practices in processes of remembering and forgetting the past? Ian Morris, one of the leading archaeologists

DOI: 10.5876/9781607329633.c008

dealing with the study of symbolism and ritual action through material culture, argues in favor of adopting a symbolic, "performative" approach to the material analysis in which "the analysis of burials is the analysis of symbolic action" or "the objects themselves have little inherent meaning; their expressive force comes from their ritual context" (Morris 1992, 18). Andrew Jones takes us further and stresses that "social practices are mediated by material culture" and that "rituals are critical in creating and reworking cultural narratives" (A. Jones 2003, 72; see also Williams 2003a, 89–128; Andrén 1993).

The Inquisitorial index, entitled: "Voluntary depositions and testimony presented before this tribunal from various parts of the district of this Inquisition according to the general edicts of faith published during 1650" was compiled by the different tribunals of New Spain between March and August of that year. It is comprised of 25 folios and 107 denunciations, classified in alphabetical order.[2] The testimony was collected mainly from the Holy Office's tribunals extending between the mines of Zacatecas, northwest of Mexico City, and down to Puebla, Tepeaca, Cholula, and Huejotzingo, situated on the eastern axis of Mexico City–Veracruz. The different cases were presented before the commissioners on the different stations of their grand tour of inspection between March and August 1650. Alberro, while studying the inquisitorial process in this area between 1626 and 1650, has chosen to concentrate on the persecution of strangers accused of practicing Jewish rites and customs, especially those of Portuguese origin (Alberro 1998, 342–51). The usual typical program included the pronouncements of the Edict of Faith by the commissioner upon arrival at the parish, followed by confessions to the local clergy, and denunciations to the inquisitorial commissioners during the period of grace granted to the parishioners, which lasted between three and four months. The tour of inspection that year was initiated by the commissioner of Puebla, in the town of Cholula, on 2 March, ten days before Holy Week, the first case appearing that same day, and the last in this town on 29 May, following the period of grace. The present tour ended at its uppermost station by the commissioner of the royal mines of Ostoticpac, Nueva Galicia, on 9 August 9. Between 30 May and 8 August, at the peak of the rainy season, no inspections were made.

Scanning the inquisitorial index itself to investigate the presence of single women in the records brings to light an entire corpus of ritual paraphernalia, chants and prayers, and "chains of knowledge" among single women, between the early and mid-colonial Mexico. Combined with other supplementary sources from the same years, the index provides a solid basis for deciphering these artifacts as well as the rites attached to them. In 74 of the 107 denunciations cited, the "race" of the culprits—whether Creoles, mestizos, mulatos, blacks, or indigenous persons—was clearly implied. Likewise, 41.8 percent of the women indicted were of mestizo descent, while 32.5 percent of the total cases involved women of black and mulato descent.[3] The remaining 25.5 percent were of Creole descent. Creole women appear in the testimony as passive recipients, having received "evil" substances and recipes for the sake of personal gains from other "racially inferior" women. The role of the two former groups of mulatas and blacks among the actual instigators, as emphasized in the records, is therefore drastically heightened.

If we summarize the first half of this index, sixty-seven cases concern women. Of these sixty-seven cases, twenty-two concerned love magic per se, while the others involve witchcraft (15 percent), sorcery (4 percent), and superstition, together with the use of hallucination-causing substances (10 percent). Reviewing specific individual files indicates that in the majority of the cases, accusations against the same culprit were often extremely variable and even tenuous. They ranged from blasphemy and simple fornication, to Devil worship, superstition, and magic, all voluntarily denounced by those bearing witness or admitted under duress by the culprits. Therefore, there may be some overlap in the categories as well as the figures. This may serve as a criticism of the quantitative approach to the study of the inquisitorial records. The inquisitorial authorities were actually more inclined to identify and indicate the more modest indictments, such as love-magic, magical healing, and amorphous superstitions, than to charge Devil worship (see, e.g., Dedieu 1989, 317–28; Sánchez Ortega 1988, 102–4). Likewise, in the more tolerant areas such as Spain, and later its colonies, individual cases classified at first by the inquisitorial *calificador* (the officer in charge of assessing the severity of the crime) as "pure witchcraft," could shift into far more modest indictments. Frequently, culprits could be denounced under the entire range of indictments, as our own research suggests.

CHAINS OF KNOWLEDGE

In mid-seventeenth-century Mexico, as the records suggest, the substances and formulas that single women utilized on a daily basis originated from diverse but detectable sources and ethnic environments, which we should be able to discern. Natural knowledge and ingredients may have been sought inside the household, for example, from among black servants and slaves. Outside, a promising source were the city markets, where indigenous herbalists and healers were commonly found; farther afield, visits to the countryside, the shores of lakes, or the coast offered much potential, and the materials found during these outings could be brought back home to the domestic space and thereafter "domesticated." Natural environments—such as caves, lakes, and the seashore—which one could approach and where natural ingredients and substances (such as *abas* and *bejuco*) could be obtained, were places where communication with the world of the wandering dead took place, and nocturnal hordes were practiced. Such spaces could be appropriated by these women and thereafter be utilized by them for the sake of "pacifying" the nonarbitrary natural world lying, as it did, outside the limits of the ongoing struggle between the genders. The know-how they acquired was attained mainly from indigenous practitioners whom these women regularly met next to the Alameda in Mexico City and who themselves had obtained the ingredients from the same natural environments. This know-how was passed on from one woman to another. And at times, this know-how was not restricted to women, as we saw in the case of Juan Miguel mentioned below.

The following accounts enable us to trace a chain of ritual knowledge and praxis among single plebeian women originating either from African traditions or from indigenous roots, such as the Aztec sweeping ceremony, as well as the Nahua ritual of burying the umbilical cord in the ground and the eating-earth ritual, described earlier on. Regardless of their precise cultural sources, such beliefs and practices were subsequently disseminated among a great number of single women practitioners who shared such knowledge among them, as transferrers of this knowledge. It is probable that such knowledge was also disseminated by way of migrants from the rural areas into the cities. Fifty-year-old Isabel de Alarcón described to the Commissary of the Inquisition how she had learned from a certain Lorenzo, a black slave belonging to Andrés Hidalgo, how to remove a spell cast by certain "conduits": "One should light four Paschal candles inside these conduits." Fifty-year-old doña Juana de Peralta, an unmarried Spaniard and the daughter of Esteban Gutiérrez de Peralta and doña Francisca Jara de la Serda, recalled that when she was eight years old and living in Mexico City, she saw María, a mulata servant in her parents' household, eating a peyote, "in order to be knowledgeable of certain matters"; she was also aware that Marcos, a Creole slave, who assisted at her parents' house, "also swallowed peyote for the same purpose."[4]

Thirty-year-old Isabel Pérez de Zamora, a mestiza, began her confession before the Commissary of the Inquisition by recounting how she was able to foretell by the bubbles caused by a certain herb "if a man was upset with her." The herb was apparently given to her by an indigenous woman, Augustina, the wife of a black slave of Juana Mateos; the latter had acquired this knowledge from María, a free mulata, and the housemaid of Juan de Robles Delgado, and also from a certain Michaela, a mulata slave of María Hurtado and resident of Minas de Ostoticpac, who administered roots to foretell whether men were angry or not. Michaela also used other superstitions when fasting Saturdays, as was her custom, including lighting wax candles on the foot of the altar of the Virgin at the local church. She told Isabel Pérez that "in order to learn the properties of this herb she must fast during the upcoming Saturday, buy a wax candle, and light it in front of the altar of the Virgin at the parish church."[5] Six years earlier (in 1644), Michaela gave the late Alonso Sid some powders to drink in a cup made of a *tecomatl* (gourd) so that he would marry her. She was given these powders by Juana Bas, a free, black woman who lived in the hacienda de Santa Ana, two leagues away from the town, "and it was four years had already passed since she first acknowledged that Juan Miguel, an indigenous servant of Hernán Vásquez, a miner of the town, used to administer herbs to different persons." He gave her some white roots and instructed her to mold them in water, and then to wash the entrance to the house of the person she wanted. He also gave her some small yellow roses, which she cast onto the Street when she became ill. She also called Juan Miguel to cure her of an inflammation she had in her throat; on that occasion he told her that he was unable to cure her because an indigenous woman from Guadalajara, Juana Paula, had turned some indigenous persons from Sinaloa against her, and "having applied sorcery, they sent her many thorns into her throat."[6]

Isabel Pérez de Zamora confessed before the Commissary of the Inquisition how in 1639, being in the company of Josepha de los Santos and Isabel, a midwife, the former called in Juana Vivas, a free black woman, who brought along with her a small, protective charm-bundle, which she placed on the bosom of Isabel de Gustida, the twelve-year-old sister of Josepha de los Santos. The confessant Isabel suspected that "what was given by the black woman was some sort of a herb or a witches' root, to be very much desired by men and to have expertise in such arts from then on." Two years later, when Isabel Pérez de Zamora had finally unwrapped the protective charm-bundle in her house, she discovered a white root in it. She then showed the root to María de Herbas, an indigenous woman, who told her that "it was the masculine *patli* [*patli*= 'medicine,' in Nahuatl; *coapatli*: medicinal herb]—as it was called among the indigenous persons." Juana Vivas then gave Isabel yet another type of a herb, which she claimed to have acquired from an indigenous servant of Pablo de Castro. Two days later, María de Herbas, the indigenous woman, visited Isabel Pérez de Zamora, bringing the servant along with her. On that occasion, Isabel asked the indigenous woman to provide her with some herbs, and he replied that "they cost a fortune." In many other cases of the kind, indigenous expertise in the utilization of local herbs was merged with African knowledge.[7]

Leonor de Isla, for example, was able to name before the Inquisitors the thirty-three angels of the court of the sky and the earth, of the fields and the herbs, the sea, the sands, "and all the rest."[8] Inés de Miranda taught Beatriz de Valdés about a certain herb to be found only near the seashore in La Havana, called *cordia concordia*, which one had to crush inside a new stone bowl, while facing the first rays of the sun at dawn during three consecutive weekdays and with which menstrual blood could be drawn while reciting an indigenous conjuration. Inés also named another efficacious herb, *aba-voz*, an indigenous Cuban shrub, with twelve leaves, used to cure paralysis.[9] Also mentioned by her are the *Rhoicissus tridentata*, a scandent shrub or woody climber, whose roots are an ingredient used for producing a poison applied to arrows by the Nyarwanda in northern Rwanda. The Masai in Tanzania drink a cold decoction of the root for gonorrhea and as a stimulant; the stem sap is dropped onto fresh spear wounds to promote healing. Warmed roots are applied to swollen parts of the body (Neuwinger 1996, 37–38). If applied by these women as is implied here, the utilization of poison may have provided them the means for experimenting with less detectable and dangerously subtle channels of resistance to the male-dominated world around them.

On weekends, Leonor de Isla and Inés would travel together to the countryside. There, Leonor would look for male and female bejuco (a climbing plant of the tropical forests, *liana* in Spanish) that originate from the tropical regions of the Caribbean Islands. The plant is generally strong and flexible and served mainly for making knots and ties and was used in the manufacture of walking sticks distinguished by their lightness, resilience, and endurance. Yet another species indigenous to the Caribbean, called *Clitoria ternatea* = *bejuco de conchitas* = butterfly pea, had clear sexual associations. This plant is also in use in Angola, Guinea, and Ivory Coast, from where most of the African slaves destined to the Caribbean Islands and Mexico came, so that it is quite likely that black women were particularly acquainted with the plant and its uses. Leonor would habitually apply different herbs when performing her ritual practices, including *junquillo ó bejuco*, masculine or feminine, which she picked up near a lake in Veracruz and which she ground into powder while verbally conjuring. She would place *avas* (an intoxicating plant) on a table while reciting:

Holy Trinity, God the Father, God the Son, and God the
Holy Spirit, with the sky and the stars, with the sea and
the sands, with the meadow and the grass,
with the sun, and with its beams, with the well-
adventured Lord, St. Ciprian and his riches which he
threw onto the sea, and great wealth emerged.

Leonor also acquired her expertise with this plant from Beatriz de Valdés, whom she saw selecting specimens near a lake outside Veracruz. One night, a man came over and stopped by their doorway, accompanied by a black servant who was carrying a bowl "filled with the plants that Beatriz was looking for."[10] In 1622, while living in the city of Veracruz together with Beatriz and doña Juana, Leonor de Isla overheard them one night exchanging ritualistic information. Beatriz informed Juana that what one should do when distressed was to take a small bottle, together with a cup made of a *tecomatl* (gourd), and set out very early on a Friday morning to the San

Francisco, San Agustín, and La Merced Churches. In each of these churches, the cup should be filled with holy water from the baptismal font, and then some of it should be poured on ground outside the church while reciting: "Agua bendita, voy a buscar para mi bien y no para mi mal" (Holy water, I will go and search for my good, not for my evil.). Thereafter, after returning home, the baptismal water should be poured into another small bottle and then placed inside an *alrrafe con brasa* (from Arabic, a container filled with charcoal) in the middle of the house; next, inside the bottle or around the hearth, a bit of incense (male) should be placed. All of these steps had to be performed exclusively on Fridays, between 11 and 12 AM (the time of High Mass). While attending to the water, the Marta La Mala had to be recited. Then, just after midday, one had to look for the *limata del fuego* (lime, *Malus citrea*), and wash with the holy water around the ears and the hands, being careful that not a drop be wasted on the floor. The link between indigenous and African ritual practices is also extremely traceable, thanks in large part to the excellent work done on this theme by Aguirre Beltrán back in the 1950s (1955, 73–76, 275–77).

"HIGH" AND "LOW" MEDICAL PRACTICES

Isabel was born into a family of healers; the knowledge and practice of healing was strictly matriarchal, and passed down in this family from mother to daughters for three generations. Medical practice, as is clearly evident from Isabel's own family background and their access to both "high" and "low" medical practices, was never the monopoly of the educated classes in Mexico City and Puebla; such knowledge extended well into popular embryology and popular medicine.[11] No doubt, popular medical practices in Mexico were under Morisco influence, as much as by African influences, brought over by slaves from West Africa. Accepted medical notions in late sixteenth- and early seventeenth-century Spain and the New World, regarding the reproductive system, pregnancy, and motherhood, relied heavily on Galenic and medieval-Muslim medical practices (Sánchez Ortega 1988, 121). In her book on popular practices in sixteenth-century Seville, Mary Elizabeth Perry describes the following regarding Morisco practitioners:

> Moriscos practiced a medicine that appeared very similar to magic, curing through water baths and burning an article of clothing of the sick person. They also used fumigations that were closely connected with a demoniacal concept of illness. Moriscos believed not only that the fumigations created a suffocating atmosphere for demons, but also that the vapors of vegetable remedies could cure illnesses . . . The Inquisition took a great interest in these medical practices because it saw them as proof of heresy and sorcery. . . . They found them especially among women of the villages and rural areas around Seville. (Perry 1990, 28, 29)

In Isabel's family, the initiator of this medical practice was Isabel's grandmother, renowned in the neighborhood for her skills; she had passed on her knowledge to Luisa, Isabel's mother, as well as to Isabel's two aunts. One of these, Isabel Martin, had, moreover, bridged a wide gap in the medical services hierarchy of that day by marrying a Spanish surgeon thought to be the best in the city, and it was she who served as Isabel's principal mentor in the craft. This fact might well highlight the "dialogue" that developed between "high" and "low" medical practices in Mexico by the early seventeenth century. For example, Isabel recalls at one point that when she was still a child, an Italian physician, who visited New Spain, once came to her aunts' place, "and wrote down on a piece of paper the names of herbs for healing: *la yerba buena, la salvia* (sage), *el romero* (rosemary), *la palataría*, and many others."[12] This aunt, on her mother's side, Isabel Martin, had learned the craft of healing from Isabel's grandmother, Catalina Martin, a *mestiza blanca* (a light-skinned person of mixed European and Indian blood), who was also a healer and who lived and died in the barrio de Santa Veracruz in Mexico City. Isabel Martin was apparently very successful in popular medicine and acquired fame in the city; she was also the one to have initiated Isabel de Montoya into the crafts of popular healing, later in life. Isabel Martin was married to a Portuguese man, "who was the best surgeon in Mexico City, who came from Spain very poor," as Isabel recalled. She witnessed her mother as well as her aunts and her uncle cure the same way as she had learned from them: "No one had given her license to cure, but in these kingdoms everyone cures with no license . . . she had learned to cure, using herbs, since the age of eight years old, when both her mother and aunt had instructed her to grind them, when they went to heal someone, and also to prepare the potions and lotions and against all sorts of burning fevers."[13] Nonetheless, especially after 1620, *curanderismo* (popular medicine), utilizing Aztec and African traditional knowledge of plant medicines, became particularly prevalent among all classes of Mexican colonial society, with no apparent distinction between "high" and "low," in the socioeconomic as well as the praxis contexts, as is clearly reflected by the large variety of the clientele that frequented Isabel's practice (see below). This is by contrast to what Solange Alberro described: "Women accused of witchcraft are of marginal social origins, which cause them to associate with other groups of lower strata blacks and indigenous persons. The love-magic is their force for belonging, for being sought after and appreciated in their permanent status of inferiority and insecurity. They, then form a collectivity for the sake of security and co-affirmation" (1987, 34–54). This collaboration resonated in the manner whereby forms and usage of herbs and medicines traditionally employed by the indigenous persons of Mexico for magical-curative purposes were increasingly appropriated and accommodated into the formal medical practice of the Spanish-controlled colonial institutions of the Protomedicato.[14]

Beliefs concerning a woman's reproductive system (as we have already seen above), disseminated among subaltern midwives such as Isabel and her kin, no doubt converged with what was passed on to them by the normative medical practices of the time. But they were also extremely influenced by what they saw and learned and from what patients reported, as well as from the appearance of the fetus as it emerged enclosed in its membrane from the patient's womb after a premature seven-month/thirty-two-week birth or natural/spontaneous abortion.

The knowledge acquired during their routine medical practice also had an impact on what other women of the same class and background thought and knew. However, "the learned culture," imposed upon them its own unique attributes and stigmas concerning the reproductive system of unmarried women. In 1567, in Spain under Philip II, midwives and grocers dealing in spices and aromatic drugs were excluded from the *protomedicato*'s (the supreme council authorized to inspect and license medical practitioners during colonial times) jurisdiction, and in 1588 the king authorized specific licenses for empirical healers such as those who set bones, couched cataracts, removed bladder stones, and reduced hernias. These persons, however, were only allowed to carry out their activities in consultation with licensed surgeons (Risse 1987, 15–16). Luis Garcia-Ballester informs us that after 1646, and under the reforms made in the profession of the protomedicato, "only qualified applicants with university degrees were allowed to practice legally, especially outside the larger urban areas; this prompted the development of an extensive illicit practice of medicine by empirics and curanderos, especially in rural areas," and the vacuum was filled up by a small number of licensed physicians and surgeons (qtd. in Reyes 1912, 1:511–73).

"FORENSIC EVIDENCE" ASSOCIATED WITH SPIRITUAL INCLINATIONS

Using the terminology of "archaeology of rituals," reconstructing the multifacetedness of the spiritual world of single women is an endeavor that may be initiated from the inventory of their belongings seized by the Inquisition. An examination of such material evidence may bring to light the vital relationship between visual representations and religious thought and Creed; between ritual practices, and both their material and spiritual sources and resources, as well as the personal symbols of religious piety. Within such an inventory, one is able to classify spaces/environments where knowledge, materials, and ingredients were originated and kept. Furthermore, it can provide us with concrete cues of how certain objects were carried over from afar into the shared, domestic space of these sheltering sisterhoods, appropriated, domesticated, and utilized for their own ritualistic purposes. One is able in fact to "map" the distinct environments from where these objects were acquired. For this purpose I shall now examine the belongings of Isabel that were confiscated from her rooms in Huejotzingo when she was arrested for the first time in 1652. I compare these with the list of belongings found in her prison cell in Mexico City in 1662, as well as from the three wooden chests taken from her house after her death in the Amor de Dios Hospital in this city.

Let us begin in the town of Huejotzingo, back on 23 June 1652, whereupon the commissioner of the Holy Office certified that he had entered the small adobe house where Isabel lived and confiscated her assets. These included a small casso-wary, found in Juan Sebastian's house; a conch; some powders rolled in a rag; ox testicles (*criadías de choto*); a small amount of agave plant; two combs; a scorpion's head; a string of yellow beads; a riding bridle; glossy-silk sleeves; an old shirt; two chocolate loaves; chocolate drinks (believed to be extremely efficacious means for delivering spells in cases of sexual witchcraft in colonial Mexico);[15] small mirror; some spurs; three castanets; a folding knife; a rough cloth, covering bits of a snake or a viper; pieces of glass; eighteen buttons; two pairs of scissors; a bronze spoon; some powders from Congo; some roots; an earthen pan, and in it a sack made of a deer hide, containing roots and a pita bag with gall nuts of mammee tree, bark, and an avocado grain; a deer hide containing herbs; another deer hide containing powders and herbs; another small sack containing different powders, herbs, and some bones; a *chocolatero con un j/suente* (chocolate maker); three soup plates and a large-mouthed jar for catching rain; five gourds and a jug; a mattress and two pillows and some old flannel under-petticoats; five wooden boards, painted with different forms; an old *quesquemil* = El *quexquémitl*: [keʃ'ke.mitl], del náhuatl; *quechquemitl* (which signifies *punta del cuello*), which is a typical traditional indig-enous skirt; five plates and an earthen pan; an old black hat; an old blue tablecloth; two *metates* (grinding stones) with handles; a spit; eleven mats; and two pumpkins.

What does this long list of belongings tell us about Isabel during this phase in her life as a professional practitioner? First, it is noteworthy that the list *lacks any single item related to Catholicism*, or to her later intimate devotion to such objects of piety. Second, there was a strong presence of items pertaining to both African and indig-enous contexts. Third, a very large part of her belongings at this early point could be associated with her healing practices. The objects and their quantities lead us to believe that while in Huejotzingo and Puebla, Isabel acquired fame as a popular healer, that she must have had a good number of clientele by then, and that her heal-ing practices were influenced by both African and indigenous domains. They point to her leading a very modest lifestyle. Also, as attested to by her clothes and her place of living adjacent to an indigenous neighbor, as well as her kitchen items, it is most probable that she identified herself then as an indigenous woman, not a *castiza*! Let us recall that in 1662, she testified before the court of the Inquisition in Mexico

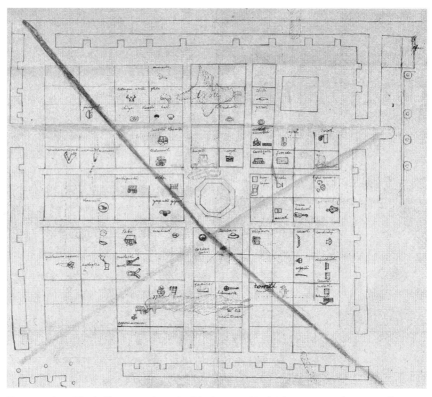

FIGURE 8.1. The indigenous *tianquiztli* in Mexico City's Plaza Mayor, depicting the locations of distinct stands where major trade items were sold (an eighteenth-century reconstruction of the conquest period layout). Manuscrito pictográfico. Tinta sepia y negra. Dos hojas de papel europeo, 37 × 46 cm. y 18 × 31 cm. BNF Fonds Mexicain, No. 106. ©BNF, Paris.

City that Pedro Martin de Guzmán, her supposedly Spanish great-grandfather on her mother's side, was married to doña Elvira, an indigenous (Cuicatec) noble lady (during the 1520s?), in charge of the communities of Teutila [or Dobahucú in the Cuicatec language, meaning Adobe House; San Pedro Teutila, on the northeastern side of the present State of Oaxaca].[16]

In 1662, now in Mexico City, after Isabel's second trial before the inquisitorial tribunal, Juan Domingo and Catalina María, indigenous practitioners, who sold herbs and other medicines in the Plaza Mayor in Mexico City with whom Montoya occasionally consulted, were called in by the inquisitors to identify the nature of the substances and the efficacy of the herbs and lotions and other items found in Isabel's room in the small adobe house where she had lived before her arrest.

The items "forensically" examined by these two experts constituted an entire repository of contemporary popular medicine and religious knowledge. After examining each one of the items laid out before them, regarding one of the herbs they both commented that "it was for curing the beverage pulque *and not to cause evil*." Examining other herbs they called *guaiesla*, they indicated that "these were for healing ulcers," while herbs identified as *talayotl* "were applied to treat gout." There were other varieties of powders and other substances (no specific names appear on the list) that they identified as "remedies for babies' indigestion." What is revealed from these findings was, indeed, the versatility of Isabel's profession, as both a midwife and a healer.

The following inventories were subsequently found in three old midsized wooden chests:

> *First chest:* An old Chinese bedspread, lent to de Montoya by Doña Nicholasa del Castillo, a widow who lived next to the Balvanera Convent; a folded piece of a woolen cloth; an old *tompiate* (pouch of woven palm leaves), together with different dry herbs, and ropes, usually applied for healing habitual indispositions; three or four colored glasses belonging to María de Rivera and given to de Montoya for safekeeping; six miniature woodcuts of a *mecoatl* (large maguey roots) made by an indigenous artist.

> *Second chest:* An old silken veil; different rags, knotted together with various herbs; various hawkweeds similar to nutmeg, which were applied to heal flatulence.

> *Third chest:* A broken chocolate-maker, rags rolled up with herbs.

> *Also found in Isabel's room:* A painting mounted on wood of Our Lady of Mercy; a blue cotton shade; a woodcut of San Diego; four additional woodcuts depicting various personalities; two small cotton mattresses of white cotton, together with her bed.

When we compare the above list from Huejotzingo with the latter inventory from Mexico City, ten and twelve years apart, we see that the presence of Catholic devotional objects increases dramatically relative to the healing items. At the same time, Isabel de Montoya's indigenous identity is increasingly fading away and being replaced by her *castiza* persona, attitudes and beliefs. The list of items that Isabel brought with her to prison on 24 July 1662 shows a much greater variety of devotional objects, and attests to a completely different lifestyle in which there is a continuous accumulation of what we could characterize as luxury or prestige items.[17]

CONFLICTING PATTERNS

What do we reckon of all this? On one hand, single women such as Isabel and her "sisters" were active practitioners in local confraternities and religious processions—for example, the confraternity of the Holy Sacrament in Puebla, reenacting the burial of Jesus, and wearing black tunics, ropes on their necks, and a crowns of thorns on their heads; they acquired and cherished saints' images and prayers and routinely partook in the sacraments. Images of the saints, no doubt, figured prominently in Isabel's list of belongings. In contradiction, perhaps, to our impression of the obvious Catholic piety reflected in the above inventory, it should be stressed that in the Holy Office's denunciations against Isabel, one finds a number of significant remarks related to her mastery of and appropriation of church "sacramentals": holy water, broken pieces of altar stones, and so on. The inquisitorial denunciations against Isabel listed the selling and use of unguents mixed with "sacramentals" in the form of small loaves of bread and soil, which Isabel had gathered from the holy relics of San Diego and Saint Michael, for the purpose of healing her patients. Thus, as the inquisitors described it, "she committed grave offences just like real witches, mixing evil with the pure and benevolent." In her defense, Isabel emphasized that "in the medicinal potions that she prepared for her patients, she mixed *cosas de santos* [saintly substances]," "for additional help." In addition, she recounted that the potions were made of ointment and "very holy" ground herbs, about which she commented: "God grants to only a few virtuous persons in order to heal bewitchments in this form, and not in any other, and likewise God has bestowed these powers upon me."

Furthermore, the overall list of items listed below, let alone the fact that she chose to carry them with her to her prison cell, certainly indicates Isabel's deep devotedness as a full-fledged Catholic, and her intimate emotional link with these objects—*objects that significantly were absent in the previous list of objects from Huejotzingo*. And no less significant, this list also manifests the body and scope of diverse knowledge that Isabel had already acquired by then vis-à-vis the spiritual essence of the Street worshiped by Isabel and her "sisters" during this period:

> 1. A cotton cloth; 2. a black *inquente* wrapped in an old cloth; 3. a black rosary,
> with a variety of numbers, some round, others angled, and ten beads between each
> coiler pardo, and from which dangled a alchemic medal which bore on one side
> the insignia of the Holy Sacrament with two Angles and below it the inscription
> "Rome"; the other side of the medal bore the insignia and image of Nuestra Señora
> de la Concepción; 4. a leather belt related to San Augustin; 5. two small pieces of
> cloth, one of which was decorated with an image of Our Lady of Carmen (commonly
> worn by people in Spain beneath their clothes); 6. small plates embossed with the

image of San Diego and his cross surrounded by luminous beams; 7. a *toston* coin, with an image of Niño Jesús; 8. a rectangular plate bearing the image of San Antonio holding a branch in his left hand; 9. a scapular on which a cinnamon-colored wooden cross is depicted; 10. a copper plate with an engraving of Our Lady of Solitude alongside a tattooed male; 11. an image of the adoration of Saint Mary Magdalene holding the cross, with a glass; 12. six pairs effigies of young cows or bulls, with male and female saints; 13. Agnus Dei painted on a cloth; 14. a roll of bread on which St. Nicholas holds a small cane; 15. a paper with the image of Christ; 16. a bull of the Holy Cross, with no names; 17. a bovine effigy of St. Anthony, with some inscription in a foreign language; 18. two small iory images of San Francisco and Saint Mary Magdalene, rolled in paper; 19. some new shoes "de quatro suelos de cordoban" [the measurments of the skin of a billy goat utilized for shoe-making]; 20. some old cotton shirts; a head kerchief made of Chinese silk; 21. a wooden walking stick.

Furthermore, as evident from their own testimony, Isabel and her "sisters" frequented the churches, prayed for their beloved saints—Our Lady of the Rosary, Carmen—and attended confessions in El Carmen, San Antonio, and the Franciscan monasteries in both cities. Their ongoing interaction with local priesthood in these two cities, undoubtedly, enriched their knowledge of the liturgy. Moreover, regular interactions with the church and the priests also provided Isabel and her "sisters" with additional channels to the supernatural, besides the rich African-linked and indigenous-linked interactions discussed above.[18] In what ways? Church objects such as holy water and Catholic formulas of consecration, as well as brokenpieces of altar stones, were commonly "appropriated" and "domesticated" by these women and utilized for their own purposes in overlapping spaces or environments. For example, the utilization of holy water from the baptismal font, for other purposes and in different environments and settings other than the church became a common practice for them. Juana de Ochoa, a twenty-five-year-old free mulata born in Puebla, who resided in Mexico City and served in Isabel Porto Carrera's household located next to the San Gregorio Church in Coyoacán, testified in court how Isabel would use a *lignum crucis* (a relic of Christ's Cross) and holy water to cure her patients.[19] Small pieces of the alter from the Franciscan monastery in Puebla would also be utilized for the sake of subjugating men; Leonor de Isla would thereafter transfer the altar stone to a different environment and space—to its "natural space"—on the seashore, disposing of the stone in the water, which could be indirectly associated with some of the above African uses. These women who appropriated church objects were also made to return them to their place of origins. For example, Beatriz de Valdés, mentioned above, possessed a cotton cloth tied to a friar's lace strip, and inside which she stored a piece of a red stone the size of an egg.

During Easter, she was asked by her confessor, Father Bonilla, if she had touched the stone, to which she responded "no"; the priest instructed her to "return it to the San Franciscan monastery where it belonged."[20]

Isabel was examined on several occasions by the inquisitors for her proficiency in the Catholic faith. She was likewise asked if she was a true Christian—baptized and confirmed, if she went to Mass, and if she confessed and was absolved on holy days. In response, Isabel was able to recite, in part or in all, the four prayers, some sentences from the articles of faith, and some of the ten commandments. It appears that her knowledge of the Catholic faith was somewhat better than the usual to be found at that time among Mexico's popular classes. She testified to have known parts of the four prayers ever since she was a child, "together with other prayers for the saints."[21] She added that she was confirmed in the cathedral of Mexico City. The last time that she confessed was "a month and a half ago, to a priest in Huejotzingo, don Nicolás de Villanueva, in the parish of that town." The inquisitors thereafter concluded: "She was able to recite the Credo [Ave María], very well, some sentences from the articles of the faith, the Salve, and some of the Ten Commandments. She confessed in a 'well spoken Romance,' but did not know more about Christian doctrine."[22] We should also remind ourselves that by the age of eleven, and during the following four years, Isabel was already under the close supervision and spiritual guidance of a mulata woman, Francisca Ruiz, who served as a *madrina de bautismos* (godmother of baptisms) in a black confraternity in Mexico City and that during these years she accompanied her to all the Catholic feasts. And it was this particular mentor who taught her to become a devotee of Our Lady of Carmen. Furthermore, a certain acquaintance of Isabel, Doña Luisa, had once heard her tell don Miguel, her cousin, how, "one night, while sleeping together with other women, she was dreaming or else, she saw an handsome man appear, dressed in green beams, with all the signs of a San Miguel."[23]

When asked by the inquisitors how was she able to identify that the apparition that she often envisioned was indeed Saint Michael and not of the Devil, and when they insisted on asking how could she determine whether it was a dream or a revelation and "that it was St. Michael and no other angel" who appeared to her, de Montoya replied that she knew him well "because she was his long-time devotee and that the fact that he carried a spade signified that he was not the Devil." She described the Saint Michael that she saw "as dressed in an orange-colored jacket with majestic green sleeves, and above it wearing an open, green-taffeta cloak with golden buttons." She claimed that "below his white tunic, he wore a woolen cap on his head. Each night, as she recounted, when appearing before her, the saint urged her to take up the curing of the sick and needy." The deep conviction and devotion that Isabel showed toward this particular saint could well have been associated

FIGURE 8.2. Juan Correa, *San Miguel Arcángel*, Escuela mexicana, seventeenth century, oil on cloth, 164 × 103 cm. © Museo Franz Mayer, Mexico City.

with what Madre Juana María de San Joseph, a renowned nun from the Convent of the Immaculate Conception in Mexico City, advocated in her writings about Saint Michael and that may have been disseminated through popular channels of communication. Madre Juana María de San Joseph described Saint Michael as so successful in his battles against the Devil, as was proved in the Book of Revelations. This particular saint could also be especially cherished by Isabel, as he was considered in popular Catholicism to be a very prominent healer "and that, in the hour of death, he offered one last chance for redemption and the forgiveness of sins . . . and that his humility would triumph over Lucifer's arrogance and that he would grant the assistance needed to defeat [a] passionate nature" (Cárdenas, *Novena al gloriosissimo Archangel*, qtd. in Curcio-Nagy 2014, 50). Isabel de Montoya would definitely identify with this last point, namely, her need to overcome lust. Furthermore, one could also attribute this devotion to the fact that in September 1644, the archbishop of Puebla instructed his canons and priests to propagate and disseminate the devotion to San Miguel Archangel in his archbishopric.[24]

Nonetheless, one of the most intriguing documents among the two volumes of inquisitorial paperwork written on Isabel's case as part of the second trial conducted between 1662 and 1664 is what is named there as "the prosecutor's propositions for consideration," dating from 10 January 1662. The document highlights, very vividly, the intense mental and ideological conflict that raged among the inquisitors who dealt with this case of the once anonymous healer, Isabel de Montoya. Moreover, examining this discourse, we are able to better understand the more general current of rationality and skepticism that had just begun to ascend within the inquisition, that had turned the punishments of women such as Isabel to be by far more moderate than earlier on. The discourse begins by discrediting Isabel's powers to cure, or even generate evil through her medicine. It goes on to argue that her patients, such as the honorable don Miguel, could have had lost their senses by taking the drugs she prescribed, such as the forbidden peyote, either out of *virtudes naturales* (natural causes) or occult causes; therefore, the prosecutor concludes on this point, it could not have been the natural effect of the peyote and such; thus, it was the work of the Devil. Nevertheless, if those drugs were applied with the intention of causing a supernatural effect, and could not be conceived by means of natural causation, it was indeed witchcraft, which is to say, "at least an implicit pact with the Devil." Thus, the door was left quite open for skepticism.

The same spirit of reservation and doubt is also identified in the prosecutor's interpretation of Isabel's uses of dreams to predict her clients' fortunes. Her dreams were purely divinations, according to his comprehension. If they were true, they could not have originated from God, considering the evil ways she applied, thus leaving still enough room for belief in their existence. Nonetheless, if these dreams "never existed," they were "straightforward witch's swindles," applied only for the sake of reinforcing the recognition of her healing efficacy by her patients. On the margins of his discourse, the prosecutor noted that the deeds, dreams, and cures of which she had confessed proved indeed that she was a witch "and a superstitious person," but, some of the magic she used, such as the dreams themselves, were, actually still in doubt. It was Frat. Juan de Torres, one of the Dominican priests, the tribunal's counselors on theological questions, who advised the prosecutor that magic that was "administered not by means of food or potions" was acceptable and licit and was an inseparable part of the "formal doctrine of the Doctors of the Church." The learned priest clearly referred to the church's uses of charms, blessings, holy water, exorcism, Sacramentals, and so on that were criticized earlier as superstitious and magical by European Reformists. But the priest had also emphasized the already existing concern of the tribunal over a more precise definition of the border line between "diabolism" and "heresy," and the by-then far less sinister "superstitions," some of which would have already been conceived as unreal.

Another point of rationality and skepticism in the prosecutor's "propositions for consideration" is his treatment of a healer's possible blame for not having applied the appropriate means by which the patient could have been cured. As in the case of normative medicine of that time, the prosecutor denies the blame for direct negligence and thus leaves room for natural causation behind the ability of the healer to control. Therefore, don Miguel's death that followed Montoya's treatment of his ailment with a variety of curing procedures in the prosecutor's eyes should not have offered sufficient grounds to denounce her for possible manslaughter. This last point was quite significant with regard to the more general polemic of the church over witchcraft and its malevolent outcomes.

Here are the indictments cited in the document:

1. "Said to have had license from the Holy office to cure *hechizos* [bewitchments], which was a libel for which she was justly tried as a witch."

2. "The said dream (if it was true that she had had it) could not have been a good one, nor from God, considering the evil ways such as the ones she applied. And that is a species of necromancy, and if she had not had this dream it was a pure witch's cheat in order to discredit her healings."

3. Discredits her powers of curing don Miguel or even having poisoned him by her medicine.
[Number 4 intentionally skipped.]

5. "Don Miguel could have had lost his senses by eating the peyote out of virtudes naturales, or occult: hating his wife, whom he had loved earlier, could not be the natural effect of the peyote, and if it was applied with the intention of causing this effect, it is witchcraft, which is to say, at least an implicit pact with the Devil."

6. "These herbs are said and confirmed to be for the usage of sorcery."

7. "The incident with the white stone and the *piedra imán* (fragment of the other magnetic stone) is a witchcraft and a sorcery, and those effects that she had promised could not be retrieved by means of natural causation."

8. "For not having applied the means by which the husband could have been cured, she should not be punished."

9. "It proves that this woman is a cheat and she often recited these words in order to accredit her cures."

10. "Deeds, dreams, cures, potions, which she had confessed of, prove that she is in fact a witch and a superstitious." Fray Juan de Torres confirmed those

propositions but added that bewitchments which are administered not by means of food or potions are the formal doctrine of the Doctors of the Church.

11. In addition, Isabel was accused of having applied when working her magical healings "false visions and untrue divine revelations to which she responded by claiming that the saints commonly communicated with her" ("Processo y causa criminal de Isabel de Montoya, mulata o castiza [llamada la Centella]," fol. 246v.).

Isabel's own deposition about her supernatural powers gravely contested the inquisitors in a number of aspects. On the one hand, Isabel openly acknowledged that all evil "was caused by the Devil"; however, she vehemently insisted that she was able to overcome evil, by "calling forth the saints, whom she knew could easily undo the work of devils." On one occasion, she even went as far as saying that "she was more knowledgeable than the devils themselves." Describing her magical procedures, she also emphasized that prior to curing a patient bewitched by the devils, she would instruct the patient to attend two Masses for the saints. She knew that Masses had the power of curing bewitchments caused by the Devil and that "each day thousands of masses are said all over the world to do away with bewitchments."

EPILOGUE

On 15 May 1664, Isabel entered the Amor de Dios hospital in Mexico City, where she was to serve the poor for three years. On 18 June 1664, a young man from the hospital entered the reception hall of the Inquisition palace and notified the inquisitor, don Pedro de Medina Rico, that Isabel de Montoya had died that day while working, after prolonged suffering from pneumonia.[25] While laying on her deathbed, Isabel uttered a final farewell to her sacred guardian, Saint Michael:

> Most sacred of my soul! A poor woman like myself does not owe
> these pains even to the Holy Virgin, nor to the Virgin of Carmen,
> nor to the Mother of God. My beloved angels keep on
> flying above me and so as not to see me in such pain.
> Nor am I indebted to Jesus . . . nor to St. Gregory, nor to Jesus, nor to Mary, or
> to St. Joseph . . . And for the love of God, that I may die without sin, my
> lords, do not see me escape from this peril lest I
> be indebted to you . . .

Sin, according to Catholic dogma, could cause sickness, and grace could bring about a miraculous cure (Few 2002, 75). That is what Isabel exalts here.

Conclusions

Returning from our journey into the vast landscape of singleness in early to mid-colonial Mexico, could Isabel's life story have taught us about other single women of the lower classes of her time and place? Isabel's life history can, indeed, serve as an apt model for other single plebeian women's life experiences, in so many other ways and in core issues shared by many of them that are of interest here. Let us remind ourselves a number of them: shared experiences of sexual harassment during early childhood and adolescence, immature births and immature motherhood, unwanted and unsuccessful marriage experiences at a young age, channels of mutual assistance among other single women, the shared experience of living in female-headed households, caretaking of single women's children, and foster care and adoption, as well as the otherworldly facet of singleness. All these issues were deeply embedded in the very circumstances that may have, or may not have, led Isabel as well as her "sisters" to deciding or opting to remain single. According to her distant genealogy, Isabel situated herself in both the *república de indios* and *república de españoles* (Spanish and indigenous realms). On the one hand, she associated herself with the Spanish conquistadors and their native allies, while on the other, with the indigenous Cuicatec nobility of southwestern Mexico, traceable back to long before the Spaniards arrived in the area, which may well have inspired her and implanted the will in her to empower herself in so many ways throughout her life history. In all the above examples, and especially so in Isabel's self-description, one may clearly notice the fluidity of casta classifications, and the fact that they could easily be

DOI: 10.5876/9781607329633.c009

transcended, as well as of the social and cultural attributions rendered to them by the various observers, whether coming from the official administrative sectors or from the popular sectors.[26] Juxtaposing the rich and unusually detailed testimony provided in these two separate trials—Isabel de Montoya's own accounts voiced in front of the interrogators in the Inquisition chambers—and the testimony of a great variety of acquaintances who knew her at different phases in her life, as well as parallel data emerging from church records in Mexico City and Puebla (baptisms, marriages, and burials), one is able to almost fully capture the lifelong history of this particular single woman. Isabel's life story also provides us with the rare opportunity of looking in depth into the complex and a multifaceted life stories of single, plebeian women, in general, though most of them had never stood on trial by the Holy Office.

Furthermore, such rich sources allow us to reconsider the whole issue of "singleness" during the early to mid-colonial era, in terms of pervasiveness, empowerment, and life choices, and women's agency and perseverance, whether permanent or temporary. As our records unfold, and as the present study argues, in the same manner as Isabel de Montoya, many of the women studied here were able to mold powerful ways of ignoring and transcending both race and class barriers, as well as operating skillfully outside the bounds of family and marriage, in a multifaceted cultural environment. As debated in this book, single plebeian women relied upon sheltering and a supportive "sisterhoods," namely, actively affiliated to a close circle of mutual assistance so as to be able to maintain their offspring. In spite of being marginal due to "race" and also as an outcome of their loss of sexual honor, their personal histories are, in fact, laden with important insights into their replacement of the conventional family model with forms of alternative kinship. Isabel's life history also represents how some single women in general and poor women in particular living in Mexico City and Puebla during that period made a conscious decision not to marry at all or to dissolve their unhappy marriages and seek alternative lifestyles. Highlighted here is that all the major themes that are identifiable in Isabel's private life story are also representative and reemerging in the life stories of many of the other single plebeian women treated in this book and could serve, in a way, as a "redemptive model."

Nonetheless, in what other ways, then, does Isabel's life story also deviate from the "standard model" of an average plebeian single woman of her era? Her life story does deviate in a number of ways and aspects from its own role model. Although Isabel grew up, and remained most of her lifetime, among humble sorts and racially mixed women from the lower echelons, we also find her on a number of crossroads and periods regular associations with people and clients coming from both "high" and "low" backgrounds, people from up and down the social ladder. Furthermore, some of her close kin and relatives were half Spaniards and succeeded in improving their social standing by marrying middle-class men of Spanish descent and through complex webs of social affiliations with reputed government and court officials, as well as with renowned physicians and other people from the medical profession. Moreover, especially striking are her own personality skills and social assets—her charisma and her audacity, combined with high aspirations and professionalism in midwifery and in popular medicine—all of which, when put together, allowed her to aspire to, and also to fulfill, her different social, economic, and professional goals in a unique form that, alas, other single plebeian women coming from her own racial designation were unable to fulfill during their lifetime.

Utilizing the qualitative methodology allowed me to delve deep into single, plebeian women's issues of concern and to be able to identify major themes and subthemes of concern, in which these women tell of their primordial traumatic and disillusioning experiences during early childhood and adolescence. The first major theme that was identified in plebeian women's discourses was (a) "Being Left on Her Own in This World." Repeatedly articulated is the notion expressed in the women's words: in this theme, one needs to possibly separate the "real" feeling of loneliness (being socially isolated), from the feeling of being "hollow" (being emotionally empty). Lack of trust, as well as early experiences of violence and negligence, may well lead to both states and lingering emotions later in life, and one could become socially connected as she grew up, yet still remain hollow inside, due to enduring childhood traumas and their repeated manifestations. The rest of the themes identified were (b) "I Felt Deceived," (c) "Negligence and Lack of Trust," and (d) "Maltreatment and Cruelty." Initial parental compulsion and coercion to marry the child against her free will played a substantial role in the latter's decision to subsequently dissolve her marriage. Moreover, the significant impact of such early events on these girls' self-image and later womanhood might well have been part of their reluctance to remain married. In this context, also, our first major theme also comes into play here, that is, "a sense of deception" experienced by this girl that served as a catalyst to her strive later in life to remain single. Moreover, the irredeemable circumstances and experiences that these women underwent during early childhood and adolescence are all in the foreground of all these life stories.

The findings also reveal that cross-generational traits and patterns did significantly impact choice making among women of color in a decisive manner; matriarchal patterns, such as those noted in Isabel de Montoya's root family (e.g., the passing on of the healing profession from mother and aunt, to the daughter), as well as repeated experiences of sexual harassment, loss of virginity (and of "honor," as a consequence), or coercion at an early age that many among girls of color underwent—all these factors played a crucial role in their deciding to remain single when reaching adolescence. On the question of "honor," I completely agree with Komisaruk (2013, 153) that it was only a fraction of the myriad overriding considerations that can be traced back to ethnic and cultural backgrounds of the parties involved, thus contradicting Patricia Seed's point of view on the paramount role of honor in women's considerations and choice making in everyday life.

During the peak of the Catholic Reformation, the church norms surrounding marriage and extramarital cohabitation in colonial New Spain brought to the light the insidious image of women living together in "free spirit" and free love. As I wished to highlight here, during the early to mid-colonial era, single plebeian women enacted a practice of free choice, in contrast to contemporaneous church teachings, regarding the ability or choice to forsake matrimony, explore their bodies (and lust), and turn their bodies into a power mechanism. In this context, free choice could be associated with the distinction between body and soul, reality and ideology.

The pervasiveness of the practice of cohabitation among the mixed castas was the most salient phenomenon analyzed here as representative of the counter-reality of the presumed caste system: the fact that the church and state were unable to restrict this activity in actuality. What this present study suggests further in this context and in conversation with Linda Curcio-Nagy is that single *castas*, in effect, represented for Spanish colonial society the contrasting, mirror image of "the perverse Other"—namely, the realities of lust and the moral and bodily freedom of the unmarried, in tension with the discourse on the conquest of lust through the image of a "Marriage-of convenience" and "tamed love," propagated by Spanish elite women and the church. It was actually quite convenient for Spanish colonial society to transfer all of which was considered "perverse" upon single casta women and, consequently, deem their *doncellas* chaste. A close analysis of this reversed image and representation was carried out in chapter 5, by way of the interpretation of the series of popular drawings that enable us to approach popular-cultural views of seduction and lust from "an implicit standpoint."

By the mid-colonial period, at least for the lower echelons of society, and in contrast to Twinam's assertions in *Public Lives, Private Secrets* (1999), at least for the lower echelons of local society the public and private spheres were not entirely divorced from each other, and public and private behaviors were intertwined, more often than not. Women were far from stripped of their abilities to play roles in the public spheres of education, bartering, and popular religion, as well as legal representation in court. Chapter 3, for example, fully explores the ritual and spiritual ways and means by which single plebeian women were able to appropriate public spheres dominated by men. It also highlights how the street becomes a symbolic "battleground" between the sexes, by which women attained power and representation, and the supernatural context attached to this space, mainly because single plebeian women dared transcend their "assigned" roles and place in the household and behind the enclosed gates of the patio, and consequently contested the male's predominance over the street and the market, where commodities of all types were exchanged and circulated by men.

In this very context also, the sections on rituals related to the sphere of nature—in chapters 4 through 7—gender rivalry and challenges took the form of rituals in which these single plebeian women were able to transcend church teachings on morality and chastity and voice power and resourcefulness, in terms of what the church and state, as well as the patriarchy, disenfranchised them from. Also in connection to this subversiveness, this study emphasized that subaltern, racially mixed castas, essentially undermined this "neat" patriarchal model in many ways, and that at least for them the patriarchal model was very much a fictive reality, just like the caste system, and that social barriers presumably based on *calidad* were far from being the social realities of everyday life, in particular from the sixteenth century to the eighteenth. Gauderman's fine and elaborated critique of misconstrued historiographical conventions concerning the patriarchal model in colonial Latin America and her emphasis on nonpatriarchal gender relations are in tune with my own findings.[27] Also along these lines, one is able to identify how Spanish women of the elite class and subaltern women, as I show in various chapters of this book, often met and related to each other, as, for example, through mutual healing practices, midwifery, and the exchanges of ritual knowledge. From yet another vantage point, one is able to attribute single, subaltern women of color's free choice to their boldness of solidly navigating within this fluid and elusive Caste System to their ability to "change hats," namely, play out distinct identities vis-à-vis the church and local authorities, while at the same time, using different hats elsewhere. The changing of hats is also depicted by the interchangeability and elasticity of ethnic identities, such as highlighted in the case study of Isabel de Montoya, which thus allowed the transcendence of single women from one denomination to another, from one caste to another, stretching identities to the limits. As I show, a direct outcome of these phenomena was that women in general, and subaltern women in particular, were far more flexible in their choice making than women of the upper echelons.

Why did subaltern women increasingly resort to the channel of dissolving their marriages during the period under review? I respond to this from a number of angles, all of which are embedded in the qualitative methodology that is utilized here. First, subaltern women were no longer willing to be relegated the "sacrificial"/ victim posture of the wife partnered with negligent husband, were willing to sacrifice their marriage, and were willing to challenge either the claims laid by her husband or by her neighbors. One is able to interpret such a changing position in life as both an intrinsic and an implicit tendency on the part of such women to give up marital life for the sake of claiming their freedom, of becoming voluntarily single, and of finding a path to an alternative household model. Second, the pervasiveness of deserting/absentee husbands led married women to take the initiative within the frameworks of the ecclesiastical or civil courts. A variety of maltreatment, abuse, and violence also played a decisive factor in this direction, as is treated extensively in chapter 2. Economic reasons were also significant in these women's decision to remain single; namely, for many among the unwed blacks, mulatas, and mestizas without pedigree or dowry, the only "better" option was to become a cohabiter.

There is also the caste factor—the exogamous and endogamous customs and patterns, presumably, limited choices of partners—as well as the age factor—women past fertility or average age for marriage were unlikely to find a suitable partner. As demonstrated, utilizing both qualitative and quantitative samples, it was found that the elusiveness of the caste system and the interchangeability of ethnic/racial identities compensated for these factors. With regard to personal background and familial patterning, I argued that individual/personal predispositions—such as competence, resourcefulness, audacity, and stamina—were crucial factors in creating avenues and channels that subaltern women boldly navigated to transcend social/cultural, judicial, and racial obstructions. Part of their strength was in their ability to sustain themselves through their webs of self-assistance and charity and through the assistance and backing of the courts, *without men*.

The findings also draw attention to the importance of sisterhoods and closely knit webs of mutual assistance, in a variety of ways, among single plebeian women, which considerably enhanced their affordability of remaining single, as a conscious choice, either as a single mother or childless. Again, in exploring the nature of reciprocities from the vantage point of what these women recalled, and from the concerns I was able to highlight from the archival contents, about the interactions among these women centering on helping each other in dire straits, as well as in a myriad of aspects, including finding jobs, renting rooms, acquiring municipal licenses for putting up stalls in the marketplace, exchanging goods, provisioning food, assistance in finding a male partner, and childcare. Under circumstances in which single plebeian women could no longer personally raise their sons and daughters, either due to economic reasons, their partners' unwillingness to have the children in their joint household, or ill health and approaching death, single plebeian women were able to trust other single plebeian women to take care of their children. The biological mothers placed their children in the foster care of the woman they selected, paying in advance for the children's upbringing and education. One additional focal point gleaned from the sources was single women's treatment of such foster and adopted children in general, and in particular when the mothers were slaves. Single slave women were eager to have their offspring cared for outside the institution of slavery and they therefore would hand them over to free single plebeian women, to raise them as their own. In this context also, the perseverance and strength of women-headed households, as a new model for a social concordat, especially in urban areas, stood up in sheer contrast to Spanish code of laws' emphasis on patriarchic ideology. Accordingly, men were relegated as heads of the families and filled most of the roles within the family and outside it; the *paterfamilia* was responsible to educating his children, and he was in charge of managing the legal and economic affairs of the family, as well as the transfer of property. A woman who wished to file an appeal in court was bound to her husband's authority and physical presence there, and women were not allowed to serve as guardians of their children. The alternative model of women-headed households created a solid alternative to the paterfamilias and the patriarchal family model, in offering a viable haven to either biological or adopted children, as well as in patterns of inheritance and self-sustenance and women's self-representation in court.

A constructive role played by the ecclesiastical court in Mexico City was to protect single mothers' offspring, harbor them from abuse, reunite them with their single mothers, provide the latter with the ability to be in effect the guardians of their children, and provide the mothers and children with a sense of stability. Furthermore, as Komisaruk notes, the courts "supported property rights for informally divorces women" as well as proper sustenance for the offspring who were placed under the wife's care once the husband was found guilty. Komisaruk's findings, closely coincide with this present study in emphasizing the important role played by the magistrates in defending wives against their abusive husbands (2013, 121, 127, 132). Also, the ecclesiastical court usually favored the processes of legitimization for *hijos naturales*, whereby the two natural parents were acknowledged as the lawful procreators of the child. In this respect also, Karen Graubart, writing on indigenous women in early colonial Peru, highlights that "some indigenous women believed that they could use colonial legal instruments to pressure Spaniards into supporting their illegitimate children" (2007, 109, 119). This present study is also in tune with what Jessica Delgado (2009) emphasizes on the benevolent role of the ecclesiastical court: "The evidence from Toluca suggests that local ecclesiastical courts may have been more accessible to poor women, more flexible and personal in their responses to women's requests, and in some instances more effective in dealing with women's immediate concerns" (102). My own findings demonstrate that while judges showed sympathy for the plight of women, they also reminded women to fulfill their roles as wives; hence judges acted in favor of adhering to the institution of marriage, much more than in favor of other considerations such as curbing family violence. N. E. Jaffary assumes that the magistrates had before them a rigid set of guiding rules, based on the "degree of obedience, humility, and passivity the accused had exhibited, as well as on defendants' record of conforming to contemporary standards of sexual virtue and to social behavior appropriate to their rank and race" (2004, 147). But then, he contradicts this assertion by saying that "in the context of colonial Mexico, as in many other settings, orthodoxy and heterodoxy were not absolute codes that judges simply accessed and applied to the cases before them." (174). My own findings often reaffirms the latter statement. In cases of negligence on the part of parents, as in the case of María Ruiz de las Ruedas, the judge obliged her as mother of María de la Candelaria to provide her daughter with a stable place to live together with the latter's own young daughter, María Josepha, so that the mother and child would be protected from María Ruiz's former cohabiter. In addition, the ecclesiastical judges assisted foster children in obtaining legal representation or volunteer guardian advocates, as well their getting a proper education and upbringing in *depósitos* (guardians' homes). The ecclesiastical magistrates issued specific instructions to those guardians not to allow the entrance of specific persons who might harm these children during visits.

One other major finding in this book, which is explored at length in chapter 6, was the ritualistic facet of gender relations: the rituals crafted by single women reversed, as well as transgressed, the dominant relationships and delegated women to the position of controlling the chaotic male arena. Active participation in religious frameworks within the church, such as lay confraternities, and outside it, formulating their own unique ritualistic practices and networks, allowed single, nonelite women to reaffirm and consolidate mutual interests and common grounds that were formulated outside the realm of religion. This last point is in direct conversation with what Komisaruk has recently shown, how Anna Guerra de Jesús, a very poor single mother and a visionary in eighteenth-century El Salvador and Guatemala, through her own spiritual biography and spiritual networks, as well as through her life of singleness, could redeem herself of the abuse she underwent during her life of marriage. She was able to experience autonomy and a certain independence for the first time; she also "successfully navigated gendered tensions associated with their status as non-elite women living outside both marriage and convent." Furthermore, ritual reversal of the traditional gender order may also be associated with these women's powerful position within the city market's economy and economic networks established by them, similar to the convincing links Komisaruk makes between the persecution of women's ritualistic "heretic" practices in Santiago de Guatemala and their growing role within the illicit market economy (Komisaruk 2013, 38). This hypothesis is further attested to in chapter 6, with the African origins of these rituals and the place of black and mulata single women both as active initiators and practitioners of rites, as well as active, cunning economic entrepreneurs. As argued, for black and mulata women, who were situated in the lowest racial and social rankings of colonial society in Mexico, and even more so when they were still slaves, the subordination of supernatural powers that they brought over with them from their lands of origin in Western Africa provided effective channels to transcend their inferior status and to dominate those of the ruling classes who sought their assistance. As further described, black and mulata single women were able to transfer their faith, ritualistic knowledge, and paraphernalia to other single women coming from different castas and cultural backgrounds in Mexico, which was interpreted here as an endeavor to keep these traditions alive, in spite of the changes, and imbue such traditions with additional vigor as in the case of Isabel's social resourcefulness.

Finally, in a direct response to Silvia Marina Arrom's book *The Women of Mexico City* (1985, 53), I would like to take the opportunity to raise several points of reference and emphasis to the preceding chapters. Arrom writes: "Conversely, where local custom permits, individuals may have more freedom than the laws prescribe." This observation is indeed the essence of this present book, that is, to outline how single plebeian women could, and were able, to transcend the limitations of law and society of their time.

Arrom goes on to write (141):

> Why, though, did so many shun matrimony? Certainly, some did so out of conscious
> choice, since a few wealthy heiresses are known on this loss of liberty, but I tend
> to read these as expressions of male fears rather than of women's opinions. In the
> absence of documents revealing why individual women decided to marry or not, any
> explanation of their motives must remain speculative. We would guess, however, that
> despite the satisfactions available outside of marriage, most women desired it, both
> because they wished to emulate their mothers and because only marriage brought
> opportunities for having licit sexual relations, bearing legitimate children, and, typi-
> cally, becoming mistress of a household.

Contrary to the above citation, in this book I have aimed to bring to light the prominent place of lifestyles that were alternatives to marriage, mainly amongst the subaltern classes, in early to mid-colonial Mexico. Furthermore, I have endeavored to show the significance of such a conscious choice of either never marrying or of dissolving bad marriages among these women. A second point in Arrom's study, which my book contradicts and with which it contrasts:

> A woman or her relatives had to take the initiative in demanding her rights: suing
> for child support, taking a deceitful lover to court for breach of promise, charging a
> husband or father with cruelty . . . soliciting a judge's permission for legal transactions
> the paterfamilias prohibited . . . Moreover, such women were probably unusual. Thus

many women, if they did not waive or lose their right to protection, never enjoyed it because they failed to go to court to enforce it. So it can hardly be said that on balance women's right to protection overcame their restrictions and put them on a par with men (1985, 81).

Correspondingly, Komisaruk, exclaims that women's litigation against their former lovers was not primarily about honor as status, or honor as sexual purity, or marriage. Rather, the suits were mainly about money—specifically, child *support* (see 2013, 147).

In her illuminating study *Domestic Dangers, Women, Words, and Sex in Early Modern London*, Gowing observes the differences between men and women over reasons for ending marriages: "The grounds on which marriages were formally ended were quite different for men and women, and they were founded on the understanding that men and women's sexual behavior had incomparably different meanings. Men sued their wives for adultery; women sued their husbands for extreme cruelty. Effectively, only women could be penalized for extramarital sex and only men could be guilty of violence. The meanings of these two offences were central to the gender relations of marriage" (1996, 180; see also Gauderman 2033, 55; Phillips 1988, ch. 1–2). My own findings also aimed to highlight how deeply and remarkably did the women of the lower classes during this early period become involved in such initiatives as demanding their own rights or the rights of their offspring. The numerous lawsuits filed by women and cited throughout the chapters of this book are solid evidence for such a trend.

My third and final point, in direct conversation with Arrom (1985, 55), refers to her emphasis, earlier on in her book that "Hispanic law accorded considerably more rights to single and widowed women than to married women, if less than to men of the same marital status." This is indeed true for the pre-1811 era also, as shown, in chapter 6 in particular. Either ecclesiastical or civil judges, ruling over demands for alimony or inheritance for their children, were generally speaking, highly favorable toward single plebeian women and their children and in some cases went out of their way to ensure that paterfamilias, and deserting, biological fathers would succumb to their duties toward their deserted female partners and offspring.

Appendix 1

Isabel de Montoya's Genealogy

I begin my journey by trying to establish Isabel's place and date of birth. Within the proceedings of the two separate inquisitorial trials that she underwent, these data are missing. I therefore endeavored to search for these details within the parish of Santa Veracruz's baptismal records. There, in this parish records, I found the following information: "Isabel de Montoya Hernández, female, was baptized in this parish church on 21 March 1593. Her father's name: Diego de Montoya, and her mother's name: Luisa Hernández."[1] Later on the trials' proceedings, I am able to locate an addition: at the age of seven, Isabel was confirmed as a Roman Catholic by a secular priest by the name of Lic. Benavides, who was the very priest of her parish who served as her godfather during her rite of baptism, in Mexico City's cathedral. Her godmother for the act of confirmation was a black woman by the name of Melchora de Fustamante, who, apparently, was a slave of a public notary.[2]

In 1652 Isabel describes her family background as such: On her father's side, Isabel's grandfather, Juan de Montoya, was by profession a weaver, and her grandmother, Ana Rosario, was from the city of Puebla. Isabel was the legitimate daughter of Diego de Montoya y Guzmán, who was, as she recounted, "a Spanish immigrant *gachupín*," "and a shoemaker," who had died in Mexico City in 1622, and Luisa Hernández, his mestiza wife, a baker and a healer by profession.[3] Isabel described her mother, Luisa Hernández, as a mestiza, born in Mexico City, in the Santa Veracruz barrio, where all the rest of this family was deeply rooted. Her parents were married in the church of Santa Veracruz on 22 March 1592.[4] Her grandfather on her mother's side was Miguel

DOI: 10.5876/9781607329633.c010

Hernández, who was a miller in the town of Chalco, and there he had died. Her grandmother was Catalina Martin, a *mestiza blanca* (i.e., pale faced daughter of a male Spaniard and an indigenous woman). She was a healer "who did not practice it" and had died two years after her husband (1624). So if we have faith in her other ancestral tree, then her grandmother Catalina Martin must also have also been born in the same barrio de Santa Veracruz, after her great-grandparents presumably had moved from the Oaxaca area into Mexico City, by the first half of the sixteenth century. We find Catalina Martin and Miguel Hernández present, side by side with Juan de Montoya and Ana Rosario (from the groom's side) at the wedding between Diego de Montoya and Luisa Hernández on 22 March 1592, which also took place at the very same Santa Veracruz Church.[5] Her mother's brother, as she recounted, was Juan López, a castizo, who had been exiled to the Philippines many years earlier for having murdered his wife, and she did not know if he was dead or alive.[6] Her mother's sister, María Hernández Martin, was baptized on 26 June 1583 at the Santa Veracruz Church in Mexico City.[7] Another aunt was Isabel Martin, who married a Portuguese man. They moved to a village where they had some fortune for a time, but afterward Isabel's husband had lost it all and returned to Mexico City, where he had died. Isabel de Montoya added that her aunt, like her own mother, "was also a famous healer in Mexico City." Isabel de Montoya's sister, Juana de Montoya Hernández, who was designated by her as a castiza, like herself, was christened on 30 December 1595 at the same family church in Mexico City.[8] Juana married a cartwright, Gallardo, and died in Mexico City in 1628. They had three children: Nicolás, by profession a tailor of woolen cloth, who died in Puebla at the age of nineteen and did not marry. Juana's third son, Juan, died at the age of three in Mexico City. Isabel de Montoya's younger brother, also Nicolás, was put in prison in 1637 and thereafter married a mestiza named Isabel Renjito, who died a few years earlier in this town, and they did not have children. Isabel's youngest brother, Josephe de Montoya Hernández, was baptized on 21 March 1599 at the very same church of Santa Veracruz in Mexico City,[9] and died in the city of Puebla at the age of eight.

On her mother's side, as Isabel recounted, Pedro Martin de Guzmán, who was supposedly her Spanish great-grandfather, who was married to doña Elvira, an indigenous (Cuicatec) noble woman (during the 1520s?), and who was and in charge of the communities of Teutila (or Dobahucú, in the Cuicatec language, meaning Adobe House; San Pedro Teutila, on the northeastern side of the present State of Oaxaca). Isabel then emphasized that doña Elvira and her daughter, Catalina Martin, Isabel's grandmother, had both received a yearly income from the royal treasury.[10] There is nothing in our compatible sources that authenticates this story, nor is the presumed Spanish conquistador detectable in any historical source for this area.

In 1614, at twenty-one, Isabel was still under the *patria potestad* of her parents. The latter, acknowledging her pregnancy by then from one of Mexico City's treasurers, Juan Serrano, compelled their daughter to marry Serrano in church. Nevertheless, Isabel decided to defy her parents, escaped from the house, and returned to living on her own, subsequently giving birth to her first daughter, Juana.[11] The child later died at young age.[12] Thereafter, Isabel de Montoya gave birth to her only child who survived, the illegitimate daughter, Ana María de Montoya, whose biological father remained unknown but whom Juan Serrano graciously recognized as his daughter. Upon his death, Juan Serrano had bequeathed the house worth 220 pesos to his daughter. Many years later in the archival records, one finds Ana María, a seamstress by then, and also single, living at the age of eighteen in a tiny adobe house or a shack, in a narrow alley behind the San Juan de Dios Convent, several hundred meters from the palace of the Holy Office, between calle Donceles and calle Tacuba, in the Santa Veracruz barrio, in Mexico City, in the very area where her mother, Isabel, was born, back in 1593. Ana María later moved on to live in Las Amilpas.[13]

In 1619, at twenty-six, freed from Puebla's House of Seclusion, Isabel befriended Gaspar de la Péria, who had formerly served as a cabin boy for the Conde de Santiago. She agreed to marry him without further ado, and they moved together to live in Huejotzingo. Their marriage was approved by the local priest (despite his knowledge of her earlier motherhood), but there are no formal records of the ceremony in church. They remained formally married for more than twenty years, but lived together as a couple for only eight days.

Isabel de Montoya' Family Tree

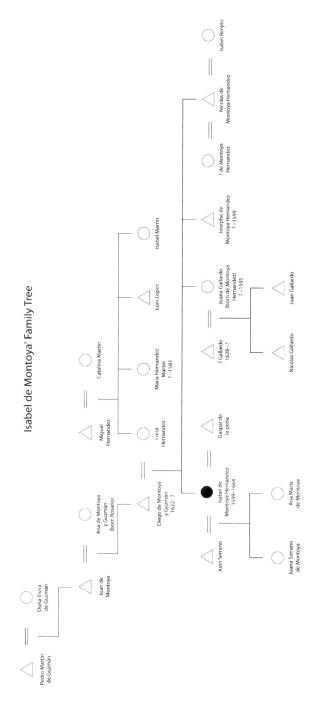

FIGURE A1.1. Isabel de Montoya's family tree.

Appendix 2

The Partial Census of Mexico City, 1670–1695

Grand total of survey: 53,314 inhabitants

Habitaciones = no. of households

Barrios (wards)	Viviendas (houses)	Tiendas (shops) / Obrajes (workshops)	Habitantes (inhabitants)
Barrio de Monserrate	60	5	233
Barrio de Necatitlán	73	4 / 1	272
Barrio del Rastro	99	5	401
Barrio de San Antón	35	2	153
Barrio de San Pablo	236	14 / 1	875
Plazuela de los Gallos	227	5	830
Barrio de Jamaica	95	5	359
Barrio del Hornillo	110	2	398
Puente de la Leña	35	0	134
Barrio de Santa Cruz	105	1	450
Barrio de San Lázaro	175	2 / 1	572
Barrio de Tomaclán	123	1	413
Barrio de San Sebastián	86	1	323
Total	1,459	50	5,413

DOI: 10.5876/9781607329633.c011

Barrios	Viviendas	Habitantes
Desde el patio de los virreyes en el empedradillo	10	149
Portal de los mercaderes	16	96
Calle de San Agustín	92	494
Portal de la Catedral	25	125
Calle de Santo Domingo	126	595
Alcaicería	11	37
Calle de la Palma	72	353
Olla de la Alcaicería	27	105
Frontero de la Casa Profesa	101	548
Hueco frontero San Jerónimo	5	21
La Pila	279	1,241
Calle de don Antonio Vergara Flores	242	1,202
Callejón de los Betlemitas	15	92
Callejón de San Francisco	24	92
Frontero de Santa Isabel	36	155
Total	1,081	5,305

Barrios	Viviendas	Inhabitants
Barrio de la Misericordia	7	35
Barrio de Montserrate	45	265
Barrio de Necaltictlan	58	261
Barrio de San Antonio (Coyoacan)	34	149
Barrio de San Pablo	257	1,191
Barrio del Hornillo	65	345
Barrio de La Merced	57	239
Barrio de Santacruz	33	137
Plazuela de los Gallos	113	437
Callejón de Jamaica	10	44
Callejón de Trapala	27	109
Puente de la Leña	14	58
Callejón Dorado	10	20
Barrio La Trinidad	62	208
Puente de San Lázaro	16	67

Barrio Tomaclán (San Agustín)	66	204
Barrio de San Sebastián	76	217
Puente de Santo Domingo	321	1,444
Calle de Santo Domingo	126	595
Portales de la Catedral	25	125
Cuadra del Empedradillo	44	258
Total	1,466	6,408

Barrios	Viviendas	Habitantes
Barrio de La Merced	30	151
Barrio de la Misericordia	7	35
Barrio de Montserrate	45	265
Barrio de Necaltictlan	58	261
Barrio de San Antón	34	149
Barrio de San Gregorio	10	36
Barrio de San Lázaro	23	105
Barrio de San Pablo	257	1,191
Barrio de San Sebastián	32	163
Barrio de Santacruz	46	198
Barrio del Hornillo	65	345
Barrio La Trinidad	37	201
Barrio Tomatlan	25	102
Callejón de Jamaica	10	44
Callejón de los Loseros	16	96
Callejón de San Antón	7	23
Plazuela de los Gallos	10	58
Plazuela del Rastro	31	136
Puente de la Leña	14	58
Total	757	3,617

Barrios	Viviendas	Tiendas / Obrajes	Habitantes
Puente de Santo Domingo	50	23	323
Portales de la Catedral	16	1	84
Calle de San Agustín	150	35	985
Puente de Almaya	279	20	1,495
Puente de San Lorenzo	198	11 / 1	1,032
Callejón de Sancho Varona	18	1	98

Callejón de Ortiz y cuadra de Santa Isabel	37	0	156
Callejón de Santa Clara	70	0	297
Alcaicería	84	2	411
Callejón de Bilbao	28	0	96
Total	930	94	4,977

Barrios	Viviendas	Tiendas	Habitantes
Alcaicería	29	2	72
Calle de Tacuba	499	22	1,995
Calle de Donceles	440	0	1,500
Calle de la Pila	267	0	1,002
Calle San Lorenzo	199	0	713
Calle de la Misericordia	27	0	82
Calle de las Cocheras	73	0	268
Calle de las Moras	66	0	214
Cerca de la sequía del Carmen	45	0	175
Total	1,645	24	6,021

Barrios	Viviendas	Tiendas	Habitantes
Puente de Santo Domingo	72	6	299
Calle de Santo Domingo	29	19	292
Portales de la Catedral	23	0	101
Calle del empedradillo	44	5	258
Portal de los mercaderes	7	0	43
Calle de San Agustín	202	15	1,007
Alcaicería	74	0	289
Calle de la Palma	41	2	200
Callejón de Bilbao	35	0	126
Puente de Amaya	299	13	1,285
Cerrada de Santa Clara	104	1	400
Puente de San Lorenzo	264	7	1,137
Calle de los Betlemitas y Callejón de Córdova	41	2	183
Callejón de Ortiz	20	0	131
Puente de la Concepción hasta la esquina de San Francisco	32	1	153
Total	1,287	71	5,904

Barrios	Viviendas	Tiendas	Habitantes
Barrio de Monserrate	47	0	163
Plazuela del Rastro	50	0	199
Barrio del Rastro	54	0	171
Callejón de San Antón	38	0	125
Barrio de San Pablo	174	2	584
Plazuela de los Gallos	196	4	716
Callejón de Jamaica	63	2	231
Callejón de Trapala	27	1	109
Barrio del Hornillo	55	1	237
La Merced	57	1	239
Puente de la Leña	29	1	140
Barrio de Santa Cruz	33	1	137
Callejón Dorado	10	0	20
Barrio de la Trinidad	62	0	208
San Lázaro	16	2	67
Barrio de Tomaclán	66	0	204
Barrio de San Sebastián	76	0	217
Total	1,053	15	3,767

Barrios	Viviendas	Tiendas / Obrajes	Habitantes
Barrio de Monserrate	64	4	241
Barrio de Necatitlán	84	3	333
Plazuela del Rastro	31	1	123
Plazuela de los Gallos	113	9	437
Plazuela de San Joseph de Gracia	60	0	258
Plazuela de San Pablo	46	0	196
Barrio de San Antón	95	0	406
Barrio de San Pablo	176	0	896
Barrio de Jamaica	104	0	542
Barrio del Hornillo	57	4	261
Puente de la Leña	101	8	448
Barrio de Santa Cruz	105	7	416
Barrio de San Lázaro	139	6 / 2	502
Barrio de Tomaclán	88	5	312
Barrio de San Sebastián	80	3	315
Total	1,343	52	5,686

Barrios	Viviendas	Tiendas / Obrajes	Habitantes
Puente de Santo Domingo	321	21	1,444
Portal de los mercaderes	96	10	466
Callejón de Bilbao	51	0	171
Calle Alcaicería y la Palma	84	1	367
Callejón de la Olla	36	0	131
Calle de la Pila de santo Domingo hasta el puente de Monsón	366	10 / 1	1,639
Calle de la Pila hasta el puente de Santo Domingo	73	1	295
Calle de Misericordia hasta la de Regina	357	0	1,359
Calle de los Betlemitas junto con Callejón de Córdova	81	1	336
Callejón de la Concepción	13	0	37
Calle de Santa Isabel	50	0	171
Total	1,528	45	6,416

Notes

CHAPTER 1: MISE-EN-SCÈNE

1. About women warriors of Scythia in Greek mythology, see Silverber (1996, 162). See also Blok (1995, 83–93).

2. See, in comparison, Poska's (2012) treatment of this issue of women's position and role in economic activities in Spain and across the Atlantic, as well as Mangan (2005, 134–36, 88–89, 152–54).

3. On this point, see also Komisaruk (2013, 137, 139): "Judicial records suggest that more often than being completely maintained by *amasios*, women may have used unsanctioned sexual relationships as one strategy within a diverse 'portfolio' of financial support mechanisms . . . Factors such as sexual desire, curiosity, and perhaps youthful rebelliousness also played a role."

4. On this point, see Hanjal (1965, 117).

5. "Licencia para tienda. Su excelencia, el conde de salvatierra, aprueba y confirma por otro año mas la licencia que se dio a esteban de quintana para tener una tienda en la plaza del volador, en la que vende: miel, cal y otras menudencias." AGN, fols. Reales Cédulas Duplicadas, vol. 48, exp. 477, fols. 345v–345r, febrero 10 de 1645; Manuel Alfonso de Noriega, dueño de cacahuatería en la plazuela del Volador y vecino de México, pide licencia para venta de prendas empeñadas por no aparecer los dueños. Contiene memoria de prendas. AGN, Instituciones Colonial, caja 97, exp. 5, fol. 6, 1710.

6. On this market and the ensuing riots associated with it, see Arrom (1996, 71–96).

7. AGN, Archivo de la Curia Metropolitana del Arzobispado de México, Proyecto LRO, rollo 1120, ubicación 19-C, Padrones del Sagrario (Catedral), 1672–78.

8. On this strategy see, e.g., Megged (1992, 421–40).

9. Schwaller (2011, 897). My own findings here from the case study of Isabel de Montoya clearly coincide with Schwaller's points.

10. See, e.g., the case in which a single mother to a free mulata, seeks permission from the court to relieve her daughter from all the restrictions pronounced against blacks, free mulatos and mestizos, men and women, due to the fact that she was the offspring of what her mother describes to be "a noble Spaniard": "Francisca de Reynoso, mulata libre, es hija de español, hombre noble y como tal no es del comprehendidas en estando que mande pregonar para que manifestan los negros, mulatos libres y mestizos, hombres y mujeres que no pudiesen traer joyas, mantos ni vestido de seda sino cuero de china ni vivir en casa aparte sin mi licencia." "Sobre la libertad de la esclava María de la Candelaria, 1706," AHJ, doc. 2667.

11. On this point, see especially the conclusions section in the remarkable book by María Elena Martinez, *Genealogical Fictions*, dedicated entirely to this theme (2008).

12. Cope (1994), adds other complementary attributions: "It seems that, side by side with fairly subtle racial distinctions on the individual level (based, as we have seen, on skin color and certain cultural traits), there existed a more general racial identity applied to the family as a whole. This tendency to assign families a single racial label would be reinforced if, as sometimes happened, one of the parents 'passed' into the ethnic category of his or her spouse" (67). See also Komisaruk's discussion on the significance of the word *honra* in comparison with the word *honor*. The former denoted accordingly "hard work and occupational skills," which were not based upon social standing, as opposed to the latter, a meaning definitely in tune with our own definition here (2013, 143).

13. On this theme and within the context of racial identities, see also Miles (2008, 59–80); Burkett (1978, 117–21); Leavitt-Alcantará (2018, ch. 3).

14. See also Schwartz (1995, 185–201). For a discussion of the history and uses of the term, see Kuznesof (1995, 153–68).

15. "Processo y causa criminal de Isabel de Montoya, mulata o castiza (llamada la Centella)," Mexico City, 1652–61, 2 vols., Ms. Lea 160 (Sp.), Philadelphia Special Collections, Van Pelt Library, University of Pennsylvania, Philadelphia (hereafter, "Processo y causa criminal"), fols. 226v, 229v.

16. "Processo y causa criminal," fol. 9v.

17. "Processo y causa criminal," fol. 70v.

18. On this point see also Graubart (2007, 148).

19. Cope (1994, 17–18). See also von Germeten (2006, 75). Bristol provides us with a highly detailed account of the uprising, relying mainly on Chimalpahin's native sources (2007, 98–103).

20. "Para que se pregone que todos los negros y negras, mulatos y mulatas, y zambaigos que hubiere en esta ciudad libres se manifiesten ante el contador de tributos dentro de 15 días para que se haga la lista y padrón de todos a fin de cobrar el tributo que deben pagar." AGN, General de Parte, vol. 7, exp. 520, fols. 340–340v, 1633.

21. On the prohibition see the following ordinances: "Que se vistan de Españolas las mulatas y mestizas con excepción de las que estuvieren casadas con indios. Conde de Coruña." AGN, Ordenanzas, vol. 2, exp. 313, fols. 270, julio 31 de 1582; "Ordenanza que Prohíbe a negras y mulatas que vistan mantos con adornos de oro y plata así como seda." AGN, Reales Cédulas, vol. 3, exp. 181, fols. 156, marzo 30 de 1598; "Para que las licencias sobre el uso de mantos que se den o estuvieren dadas a mulatas y negras libres se cumplan." AGN, Reales Cédulas, vol. 3, exp. 85, fols. 160v, julio 27 de 1598; "Declaración de la ordenanza sobre el uso de mantos a negras y mulatas." AGN, Reales Cédulas, vol. 3, exp. 190, fol. 163v, diciembre 12 de 1598.

22. "Licencia a Francisca de Reynoso, mulata libre para traer manto, oro, plata, perlas y vivir en casa aparte. México." AGN, General de Parte, vol. 8, exp. 103, fols. 67v–68, 1641.

23. See, e.g., royal instructions promulgated in the cities of New Spain in 1584, prohibiting *negras* and mulatas from "dressing like indigenous persons." AGN, Ordenanzas, vol. 2, exp. 313, fols. 270r–270v, 1584. "El virrey aprueba y confirma los mandamientos insertos de los virreyes Conde de Monterrey, Marqués de Salinas y Marqués de Galves sobre la Declaración de no ser comprendidos en la prohibición de la ordenanza que impide que los mulatos y mulatas vivan de por si ni traigan mantos." AGN, General de Parte, vol. 8, exp. 63, fols. 44v–45v, 1641; "Licencia a Francisca de Reynoso, mulata libre para traer manto, oro, plata, perlas y vivir en casa aparte." AGN, General de Parte, vol. 8, exp. 103, fols. 67v–68, 1641. See also Bennett's description: "The Angolan wedding party that entered the parish church Santa Veracruz on 7 May 1635 also manifested a pattern whereby ethnicity spanned barrios and specific streets that linked disparate households. As Ambrosio and Gertrudes petitioned for a marriage license, the couple manifested no concern about a married life without actual cohabitation" (2003, 87).

24. "Escritura de depósito. Ante el licenciado Francisco de Leos alcalde del Crimen en esta corte se presentó una muchacha mestiza llamada Juana, de 12 años, huérfana de padre y madre, dijo que quería asentar al servicio de alguna persona que la tenga honesta y recogida enseñándole buenas costumbres y la doctrina cristiana y el alcalde de corte viendo que estaba desnuda y maltratada la dio en depósito al licenciado Francisco de Figueroa Venegas, relator de la Real Sala del Crimen por 6 años, obligándose a tenerla honesta y enseñándole buenas costumbres, dándole de comer, vestir, calzar, curar sus enfermedades, buen trato y al final de los 6 años le dará 30 pesos para ayuda del estado que tomaré, el alcalde la condenó a que cumpla el servicio y no se ausente o se le obligará a cumplir." Ciudad de México, abril 24 de 1614. AGN, Notaría 374 de Andrés Moreno, vol. 2471, fols. 97–97v, 1614.

25. Pescador (1995, 617–26). See also Graubart (2007).

26. "Proceso y causa criminal contra Isabel de Montoya . . .," AGN, Inquisición, vol. 435, part one.

CHAPTER 2: THE MAJOR THEMES OF CONCERN

1. "Processo y causa criminal," vol. 1, fol. 253v, 11 July 1662.

2. See Graubart's special treatment of the implicit and explicit facets of dress in early colonial Peruvian realities (2007, 123–57).

3. AGN, Indiferente Virreinal, Matrimonios, caja 4520, exp. 37, fol. 6, 1644.

4. "Bríjida de Arteaga, mulata libre, mujer legítima de Joseph de la Cruz, sobre que se declare por nullo el matrimonio entre los susodichos contraído"; solicitud para contraer matrimonio y anulación del mismo por Joseph de la Cruz, mulato sobrey Brígida de Arteaga, mulata de 16 años, AGN, Matrimonios, vol. 135, exp. 46, fols. 1–18, 1666, 33 fols., México Catedral.

5. Brígida de Arteaga, mulata de 16 años, AGN, Matrimonios, vol. 135, exp. 46, fols. 3v–41, 1666, 33 fols., México Catedral.

6. "Ana de San Pedro, mulata pide se declare nulo su matrimonio con Nicolás de Vargas pues se caso como libre y no como esclavo." AGN, Matrimonios, vol. 193, exp. 13, fols. 8, 1690, Ciudad de México.

7. "Processo y causa criminal," vol. 1, fol. 89v, 251r.

8. "Processo de divorcio e impotencia de Catalina Martin contra Juan Martin Herrero, su marido." AGN, Indiferente Virreinal, Matrimonios, caja 6625, exp. 1, fol. 43, 1564.

9. "Processo de divorcio e impotencia de Catalina Martin contra Juan Martin Herrero, su marido." AGN, Indiferente Virreinal, Matrimonios, caja 6625, exp. 1, fol. 43, 1564.

10. AGN, Indiferente Virreinal, caja 5568, exp. 25, fol. 3, 1566. Provisorato y Vicario General del Arzobispado de México. See also Gauderman (2003, 54).

11. AGN, Matrimonios, vol. 101, exp. 2, fols. 229v–300r, 1617.

12. "María de Xérez pide que su esposo Joseph de Reinoso la alimente correctamente o pedirá el divorcio. Cd. de México." AGN, Matrimonios, vol. 193, exp. 12, fol. 14, 1690. See also Grupo Documental Matrimonios, vol. 194, exp. 83, fol. 25, 1686. See also "Solicitud de divorcio por malos tratos . . . Sebastián Cordero y Margarita de Porras. Cd. de México." AGN, Matrimonios, vol. 194, exp. 83, fol. 25; "Juana de Rivera demanda divorcio contra Lorenzo Yánez por malos tratos. Cd. México." AGN, Matrimonios, vol. 213, exp. 20, fol. 2, 1651.

13. AGN, Matrimonios, cajas, vol. 255, exp. 16, 3 fols., 1690. See, by comparison, doña María Rencife's testimony in, Mangan (2005, 157).

14. AGN, Matrimonios, vol. 75, exp. 121, fols. 431–49, 1648.

15. "Diego, negro esclavo solicita que Clara, mulata libre haga vida matrimonial." AGN, Matrimonios, vol. 127, exp. 2, fols. 8–9, 1604, Cd. de México.

16. AGN, Matrimonios, vol. 82, exp. 81, fols. 366–69, 1690.

17. AGN, Matrimonios, cajas, vol. 317B, exp. 218, 2 fols., 1688.

18. "Sebastián López, marido de Juana de la Cruz, contra la dicha su muger, sobre que coabite y haga vida maridable con el." Civil Litigation before the Ecclesiastic Court of the Cathedral—Proceedings of the Ecclesiastical court of the Archbishopric of Mexico City. AGN, Matrimonios, vol. 19, exp. 5, fols. 28–33, June 1673.

19. On the imprisonment of abusive husbands see Delgado (2009, 114).

20. "Processo y causa criminal," vol. 1, fol. 90r.

21. "Autos de divorcio que pretenden a Leonor de Toro por malos tratamientos y por estar amancebado Juan Gonzales su marido." AGN, Indiferente Virreinal, caja 5410, exp. 28, 1573.

22. On the conditions of single women in the mines of Zacatecas, see also Murillo (2013, 3–32).

23. During the sixteenth and seventeenth centuries, adultery was considered a criminal act by the ecclesiastical courts across Spanish America. See Gauderman (2003, 55).

24. AGN, Matrimonios, vol. 61, exp. 34, fols. 154–154v.

25. "Gertrudis de Vargas, muger legítima de Miguel Martinez, vecino de esta ciudad, contra Al dicho su demanda sobre que se haga separación y divorcio de su matrimonio por malos tratamientos que dije le ha hecho y lo demás contenido en su demanda." AGN, Matrimonios, vol. 172, exp. 181, fols. 1–150, 1649.

26. AGN, Matrimonios, Divorcio de Miguel y Gertrudis Vargas. México, vol. 172, exp. 181, fol. 15v., 1649.

27. "Francisca Magdalena, india, mujer de Juan de San Pedro, sobre que se haga separación y divorcio del matrimonio que contrajeron, 1678." AGN, Indiferente Virreinal, Matrimoniales, caja 2218/7297–23, exp. 23.

28. See, in parallel, similar accounts of friends and neighbors coming to the rescue of abused wives in colonial Quito, in Gauderman (2003, 58).

29. "Francisca Magdalena, india, mujer de Juan de San Pedro, sobre que se haga separación y divorcio del matrimonio que contrajeron, 1678." AGN, Indiferente Virreinal, Matrimoniales, caja 2218/7297–23, exp. 23.

30. "Margarita de Porras mujer legítima de Sebastián Cordero dice que su esposo la mal tratado con amenazas y el hizo correr en la casa por miedo." AGN, Matrimonios, vol. 194, exp. 83, 1686.

31. On the close scrutiny by neighbors within such closely knit private and public spaces, see also Komisaruk (2013, 135).

32. "Margarita de Porras mujer legítima de Sebastián Cordero." AGN, Matrimonios, vol. 194, exp. 83, fol. 5v, 1686.

33. On a similar methodology of utilizing such court proceedings in litigations for divorce, see Komisaruk (2013, 129–32).

34. AGN, Matrimonios, volumen 172, expediente 181, foja 15v., año 1649. Divorcio de Miguel Martínez y Gertrudis Vargas. México, fol. 14r.

35. See, in parallel, Gauderman (2003, 58–59).

36. Dávila Mendoza (2005, 187). By comparison also is García Peña's survey from the nineteenth century, in which the total number of appeals found for the entire century is merely 380 (2006, 74, table II.1).

37. Dávila Mendoza (2005, 58). On this significant colonial institution, see van Deusen (2001); Penyak (1999, 93, 94, 95). See also Komisaruk (2013, 24); Holler (2001, ch. 4).

38. On the difference between the two institutions, see Penyak (1999, 93, 94).

39. AGN, Indiferente Virreinal, caja 4941, exp. 028, 1691.

CHAPTER 3: FEMALE-HEADED HOUSEHOLDS

1. On the overwhelming majority of plebeian, female-headed households, see, e.g., Ramos (1991, 261–82).

2. See, in parallel, Komisaruk (2013, 29) on Santiago de Guatemala.

3. On the issue of sexual honor in Spanish colonial society and the social consequences of its loss, see Seed (1998a, esp. 63–69). On the contemporary Spanish concept of honor, and its ideological legitimation for the forced appropriation of women, see Maravall (1979, 41).

4. "Proceso y causa criminal contra Isabel de Montoya . . .," fol. 63r.

5. Bosch (1999). Also, partial censuses of Santiago de Guatemala, in 1796 and 1824, show 51 percent as female-headed households, of which 38 percent were single, and a majority of households in which there was no patriarchal family. However, in 11 percent of these women-headed households, the husband was present. Komisaruk (2013, 122).

6. AGN, Mapas y Planos, 210100/5077, image no. 04792.

7. "Processo y causa criminal." vol. 1, fol. 289v.

8. "Processo y causa criminal," fol. 240v, Catalina de Arcila's testimony, 29 October 1663.

9. AGN, Archivo de la Curia (Metropolitana) del Arzobispado de México, Proyecto LRO, rollo 1120, ubicación 19-C, Padrones del Sagrario (Catedral), 1672–78 (1678), Cura Antonio de la Torre y Arellano.

10. Lipsett-Rivera (2001, 231–47). "Tuvo en Donceles unas casas valoradas en 20.000 p. el rico hacendado Mateo de Mauleón, que vendió en 1594 al regidor Jerónimo López el Mozo." See also González Rodríguez (2004, 32–49).

11. On the private and public lives of domestic servants, see the magnificent study by Lauderdale Graham, *House and Street* (1992, esp. ch. 3).

12. Ana María Vázquez (morena), natural de Santiago de Guatemala y recién llegada a la ciudad de México, fue a vivir a casa de una mujer mestiza llamada Josepha donde le roba con sus pertenencias, una negra de nombre Adriana de Cabrera le ayudaría a saber quién si está

guardaba secreto. México, 28 de noviembre, 1650. AGN, Inquisición, vol. 1602, exp. 1, 260 fols., 1650–56.

13. See, e.g., Kinkead (2009, 13, 390). See also AGN, Tribunal Supremo de Justicia, alcalde del crimen/procesos civiles, vol. 8, fols. 1r–8v, 1673.

14. AGN, Real Junta, vol. 1, fol. 41, n.d. See also "Pretensión de la Congregación de San Francisco Javier para fundar un recogimiento de doncellas y viudas en la Cd. de México." AGN, Reales Cédulas, vol. 26, exp. 211, fol. 198, 1670. On the Santa Mónica penitentiary, see also Holler (2001, 25–26).

15. E.g., "Razón de los arrendamientos de la casa de vecindad de la Calle de Tacuba, y su accesoria, que se le entregó en la administración al contador d. José de contreras, que quedaron por muerte del alferez Jerónimo de Guzmán, y la relación jurada que de ellos presenta da. Antonia de Castro, viuda, albacea, tenedora de bienes y heredera de dicho contador." Mexico. AGN, Bienes Nacionales, vol. 1080, exp. 9, 1704.

16. Bailey-Glasco (2010, 39).

17. The church insisted on freedom of choice in marriage. On this issue, see Seed (1988a, 24–25).

18. AGN, Archivo de la Curia (Metropolitana) del Archobispado de México, Proyecto LRO, rollo 1120, ubicación 19-C, Padrones de Sagrario (Catedral), 1672–78.

19. On the traditional *compadrazgo* system in the state of Tlaxcala, see the classical study of this institution by Nutini, *Ritual Kinship, Ideological and Structural Integration of the Compadrazgo System in Rural Tlaxcala* (1980).

20. Bosch (1999); Boyer (1989, 252–86); Calvo (1973; 1984, 149–74; 1989); Gonzalbo Aizpuru (1987, 2005); McCaa (1994, 11–43); Morin (1972, 389–418; 1977, 301–12; 1987, 75–87); Porras (2010, 27–66); Rabell (1990); Valdés (1978). By comparison with other areas of Latin America, Poska (2012), e.g., cites the figure that 15 percent of all households for Buenos Aires, in 1767, were single women's households.

21. Morin (1972, 389–418; 1997); Valdés (1978); Calvo (1973, 1984); Thomas Calvo (1989, 292–93); Gonzalbo Aizpuru (1987, 2005); Boyer (1989, 252–86); Rabell (1990); McCaa (1994, 11–43); Bosch (1999); Porras (2010, 27–66).

22. AGN, Sagrario Metropolitano baptism of castas, 1653–89.

23. "Padrón exacto del Arzobispado de México," AGN, *Varios*, vol. 38; *Primer Censo de población de la Nueva España, 1790. Censo de Revillagigedo, un censo condenado*, Mexico City, 1977, 16–18.

24. Within the European family history, see, e.g., Boswell (1988); Fuchs (1984); Gavitt (1990); Kertzer (1993); McClure (1981); Ransel (1988); and Sherwood (1988). Recent Works by Latin American historians include Cadet (1998); Cardoso (1984); Fonseca (1998); Guy (1994); Kuznesof (1998, 225–39); Mannarelli (1993); Meznar (1994, 499–515); Milanich (2002a, 2002b, 2004, 311–40); Nazzari (1998); Marcílio (1998); Moreno (2000, 663–85); Pinto Venâncio (1999); Salinas Meza (1991, 315–29).

25. Komisaruk (2013, 91), in particular on the case of the adopted orphan and a *doncella*, María Antonia Matamoros, who herself raised or, more precisely, adopted a girl with whom she shared her lodgings and allowed to remain in the house after her death.

26. Blum (1998, 240–71). See also Sá (1995); and the contributions to Panter-Brick and Smith's edited volume *Abandoned Children* (2000).

27. "Inventario y sequestro de bienes de Isabel de Montoya, 5–25 Julio 1662." AGN, Inquisición, vol. 447, exp. 8, fols. 308–26.

28. See, e.g., Isabel de Pinzón in Santiago de Guatemala, who "like other poor single mothers," "may have placed one or more of her children in the care of others." Komisaruk (2013, 78).

29. See, e.g., "Para que Francisco de Herrera albacea de Lorenzo Moreno entregue una niña huérfana a pedimento de la mulata Menchaca." AGN, Tierras, vol. 2946, exp. 573, fols. 129–129v, 1667.

30. "Declaro que he tenido en mi compañía y he criado a María de la O y a María Ventura, indíquela que sus padres me las dieron para sus enseñanzas y educación y por el amor y buena voluntad que les he tenido mando que a María de la O den mis bienes mis papeles de oro de China, y ha traído y un colchón el mayor que yo tuviera y una colcha blanca de confitillo y alabada, y otro azul, y dos sábanas y alabadas, y una almohada blanca y dos pulseras de corales gordos viejos y es mi voluntad que ambas, las dos muchachas tengan . . . un santo ecúmeno, y una Santa Rosa pequeña, y unas naguas de saraja nuevas, un San Francisco de bulto pequeño, una sábana de ruan de china, y un huipil a damascado amarillo, una Nuestra Señora de Bulto a poco más de media vara, con su tabernáculo y el corazón de la Limpia Concepción." "Cotejo de testamento que otorgó Juana de las Vírgenes, natural de las minas de Pachuca." AGN, Bienes Nacionales, leg. 489, exp. 3, 1691.

31. "Cotejo efectuado en 1691 del testamento que otorgó María de Armenta en 7 de febrero de 1670." AGN, Bienes Nacionales, vol. 258, exp. 1, fols. 5–6. Cotejo efectuado en 1691 del testamento que otorgó María de Armenta en 7 de febrero de 1670.

32. "Testamento de Juana María de la Cruz, india, viuda del capitán Felipe de Monzón Mojica, pardo libre." AHJ, doc. 2463, 1688.

33. On this point, see Poska (1996, 879).

34. AGN, Tribunal Supremo Judicial, DF, Colonial, caja 43, exp. 9, fol. 3, 1784.

35. AGN, Indiferente Virreinal, Pachuca, Clero Regular y Secular 5594-032, fol. 19, 1786.

36. "Libro de matrimonios de castas." AGN, Archivo de la Curia (Metropolitana) del Arzobispado de México, Proyecto LRO, rolls 518–19, vol. 3, fol. 1r.

37. See, e.g., "Para que Francisco de Herrera albacea de Lorenzo Moreno entregue una niña huérfana a pedimento de la mulata Menchaca." AGN, Tierras, vol. 2946, exp. 573, fols. 129–129v, 1667.

38. See, e.g., doña Beatriz de la Mirabal's will, in which she instructs that "the sum of 500 pesos should be granted to Diego de Mirabal, an orphan child, and he should be deposited

in the household of Alonso de Herrera until he reaches maturity ... Juan, criollo, 13-year-old Juan, Creole, my slave, should be handed over to Lic. Andrés de Aguirre, my nephew." "Cotejo de testamento socura disposición falleció doña Beatriz de Mirabal, 9 de agosto de 1653." AGN, Matrimonios, vol. 164, exp. 57.

39. "Cotejo efectuado en 1693 del testamento y renuncia que otorgó la madre María Antonia de Santa Theresa, religiosa del Convento de Jesús María de la ciudad de México que en el siglo se nombraba María Antonia Pardo de Lagos, en marzo 12 de 1685 ante Juan Marchena, escribano real." AGN, Bienes Nacionales, vol. 678, exp. 31, fols. 3–4.

40. "Cotejo hecho en 1700 del testamento otorgado en México, julio 4 de 1682 por María Estupiñán, vecina de esta ciudad y originaria de Puebla de los Ángeles, viuda de Juan de la Gala Moreno, no tuvieron hijos." AGN, Bienes Nacionales, volumen 678, exp. 32, fols. 33–36.

41. AGN, Tribunal Supremo Judicial, DF, Colonial, caja 77, exp. 3, fol. 79, 1638. Convento de San Juan Bautista de Coyoacán, Mexico.

42. Graubart (2007$, 108) comments that "the courts usually favored fathers over mothers in questions of custody, and in many cases the perceived benefit of raising a child in more privileged circumstances must have been considerable."

43. "Causa seguida entre María Magdalena Bueno y Caytano Vargas, sobre la pertenencia sobre una hija que este pretendía y aquella negaba, señalando otro padre, 1740." AGN, Instituciones Coloniales, civil, vol. 1277.

44. AGN, Geneología y Heráldica, vol. 2386, Santa María de la Natividad, Atlixco, "Defunciones de Mestizos," 1704–14. For comparison, see Calvo (1984, 203), in which he quotes the ratio of more than 2:1 of burials of single women versus single men, according to the burial records of the Sagrario parish of Guadalajara, between 1685 and 1699.

45. *Escritura de servicio* a favor de Catalina de Chávez." AGN, Notaría 374 de Andrés Moreno, Bienes Nacionales, vol. 2469, fols. 311.–312, 1612. See also AGN, Indiferente Virreinal, caja 5980, exp. 044, fol. 1, 1645. "Joseph Beltrán, Ana María Despinosa. Oficio de Ana María despinosa que pide al provisor juez y vicario, que otorgue censuras por una india huérfana que estaba cuidando desde hace tiempo y ha desaparecido sin saber en donde o quien la tiene. México. [1645]. Ramo asignado: Clero Regular y Secular 5980-044."

46. *Escritura de depósito*. María de Chávez." Notaría 374 de Andrés Moreno, AGN, Bienes Nacionales, vol. 2469, fols. 144–144v.

47. *Escritura de depósito*, "María de Chávez." AGN, Notaría 374 de Andrés Moreno, Bienes Nacionales, vol. 2469, fol. 204v.

48. "Catalina de la Cruz, negra libre, soltera, madre de Bernardino Adame, mulato, contra Tomasa Ruiz, mujer de Alonso Rodríguez, maestro de zapatero, para que exhiba la escritura de obligación de enseñar el oficio de zapatero, por no cumplir con ella y darle mal trato al menor." AJ, Fondo Tribunal Superior de Justicia del Distrito Federal, sección alcalde ordinario, serie civil, vol. 4, exp., 7, 4 fols., 1632.

49. AGN, Tierras, vol. 2946, exp. 573, fol. 1, 1667.

50. Testamento otorgado el 9 de febrero de 1700 por Pascuala de San Juan de Dios, mulata libre, viuda, originaria de la ciudad de Guadiana y vecina de la ciudad de México. AGN, Bienes Nacionales, vol. 678, exp. 32, fols. 26–30, 1700–1701.

51. AGN, Bienes Nacionales, vol. 678, exp. 32, fols. 26–30, 1700–1701.

52. "Marta Rodríguez, negra libre, inventario de bienes, 1633." AHJ, doc. 1622, 1667.

53. AHJ, Puebla, doc. 1640, 1635.

54. "Cotejo y testamento de Lorenzina de la Cruz, residente de Texcoco, 5 March 1695." AGI, Bienes Nacionales, vol. 489, exp. 3, fols. 1r–15v.

55. "Cotejo de testamento de Francisca Gómez, Mulata, vecina de Coyoacán." AGN, Matrimonios vol. 164, exp. 57.

56. "Cotejo efectuado en la ciudad de México, año 1691, del testamento que otorgó Juana de las Vírgenes, natural de las Minas de Pachuca, vecina de esta ciudad, en enero 13 de 1689 ante Joseph de Ulloa y Callejas, escribano real. Nombró por su albacea, tenedor de bienes y heredero al Lic. Alonso de Encinas, presbítero." AGN, Bienes Nacionales, vol. 258, exp. 1, fols. 46–47. See also Graubart's treatment of the material facet of dress in indigenous women's wills in early colonial Peru (2007, 141–46).

57. "Cotejo efectuado en la ciudad de México, año 1691, del testamento otorgado por Josepha de Santillán . . ." AGN, Bienes Nacionales, vol. 258, exp. 1, fols. 54–55.

58. Through a close study of their wills, Komisaruk explores in depth the associations of single women in Santiago de Guatemala with local priests, and the benefices that such relationships offered to these women, as well as impacted their bequeathing of property and devotional objects to the church (2013, 95).

59. "Marta Rodríguez, negra libre, inventario de bienes, 1633." AHJ, Puebla, doc. 1622. On the donation of devotional objects by single women in Santiago de Guatemala, see Komisaruk (2013, 88–89).

60. "Cotejo de testamento que otorgaron María de Vargas y Leonor de Vargas conjuntas, vecinas de la villa de Coyoacán, a la otra se dejaron por herederas . . . 1633." AGN, Matrimonios, vol. 164, exp. 57.

61. "Cotejo de testamento de Francisca Gómez, Mulata, vecina de Coyoacán." AGN, Matrimonios vol. 164, exp. 57. Also, of the same person, AGN, Bienes Nacionales, leg. 489, exp. 2, 1653.

62. "Cotejo efectuado en la ciudad de México, año 1691, del testamento otorgado por originaria de esta ciudad, en junio 17 de 1681 ante Antonio Negrete, escribano real. Nombró por sus albaceas a Agustina Gallegos, Antonio de Santillán y Juan de Abrego y por su heredera a la primera." AGN, Bienes Nacionales, vol. 258, exp. 1, fols. 54–55.

63. "Testamento otorgado el 9 de febrero de 1700 por Pascuala de San Juan de Dios, mulata libre, viuda, originaria de la ciudad de Guadiana y vecina de la ciudad de México." AGN, Bienes Nacionales, vol. 678, exp. 32, fols. 26–30, 1700–1701.

64. "Cotejo efectuado en 1700 de la memoria simple que otorgó Thomasa de San Juan, mestiza, vecina de la ciudad de México, en marzo 12 de 1696." AGN, Bienes Nacionales, vol. 678, exp. 32, fols. 31–32, 1700.

65. AGN, Indiferente Virreinal, caja 2224, exp. 028, fol. 1, 1604.

CHAPTER 4: RAISING CHILDREN

1. "Processo y causa criminal contra Isabel de Montoya." "Inventario y sequestro de vienes de Isabel de Montoya, 5–25 Julio 1662." AGN, Mexico City, Inquisición, vol. 447, exp. 8, fols. 308–26,

2. "Juliana de la Cruz mulata madre de María de Monroy y Juan de Monroy pidase reciba información de ser hijos naturales del Capitán Alonso de Segura y Monroy alcalde mayor de Cuautitlan para obtener su libertad una parte de su herencia. Ciudad de México 1689." AGN, AJ, vol. 11, exp. 23, fol. 48, exp. 25, 7 fols.

3. "Información por María de Segovia para que se entrega a Juana de Aguilar, su hija natural." AHJ, doc. 2250, 1666.

4. AGN, Tribunal Supremo Judicial, DF Colonial, caja 175, exp. 31, fols. 3, 1677.

5. "En nombre de María de la Candelaria, mulata, vecina de San Juan de los Llanos, como madre de María Josefa, en la ocasión del fallecimiento de doña Isabel Martinez Carellosa, mujer legítima que fue de Antonio de los Reyes, en 7 de junio del año pasado de 1702, dejó la dicha María de Candelaria libre de cautivera, 1706." AHJ, doc. 2667. María Ruiz de las Rueda's testimony, and Sebastián Flores Perla's testimony, fol. 29v.

6. The same fate was that of Juana Nicolasa, Antonio, and a baby named Juan, all of whom were under the age of ten when they were sold by their respective mothers into slavery in the town of Jalapa (Veracruz); Juana was sold by her mother in 1635, Antonio, in 1641, and the baby, Juan, in 1667 (Carroll 2001, 84).

7. "En nombre de María de la Candelaria, mulata, vecina de San Juan de los Llanos, como madre de María Josefa, en la ocasión del fallecimiento de doña Isabel Martinez Carellosa, mujer legítima que fue de Antonio de los Reyes, en 7 de junio del año pasado de 1702, dejó la dicha María de Candelaria libre de cautivera, 1706." AHJ, Puebla, doc. 2667 (hereafter, "En nombre de María de la Candelaria . . ."). María Ruiz de las Ruedas's testimony, and Sebastián Flores Perla's testimony.

8. "En nombre de María de la Candelaria . . . ," fol. 13r.

9. "En nombre de María de la Candelaria . . . ," fol. 31r.

10. "Cotejo del testamento que otorga en esta ciudad doña Damiana Osorio, 1653." AGN, Matrimonios, vol. 164, exp. 57, fol. 40r. Conditions for manumission would often include the naming of a precise price that the parents or a benefactor should pay in order to set the children free. As, e.g., "ordena que a Joseph Viveros, mulato esclavo se le de carta de libertad, lo mismo que a Michaela, mulata blanca por lo bien que le sirvieron; también ordena que a la

hija de ésta llamada Blaza, mulata blanca de 6 años su esclava se le de carta de libertad cuando su padre u otra persona paguen 100 pesos mientras tanto quede por esclava al igual que los hijos que tuviese; la misma disposición da con respecto a Isabel mulata su esclava quien deberá pagar 200 pesos por su libertad. México." "Cotejo hecho en 1700 del testamento otorgado en México, julio 4 de 1682 por María Estupiñán, vecina de esta ciudad y originaria de Puebla de los Ángeles," AGN, Bienes Nacionales, vol. 678, exp. 32, fols. 33–36.

11. "En Real Fisco declara que Josepha de los Angeles, mulata e hija natural de Diego Tinoco y de María negra esclava suya indica que su hijo es libre." AGN, Tierras, vol. 3099, exp. 34, fols. 347v–349v, 1643.

12. Juan de la Cruz, e.g., a grown-up mulato, the son of the late Francisco Beloso, *chino libre* (a free person, Filipino, many of whom came to New Spain on returning Manila ships) and of the late Juana de la Cruz, *negra*, was the slave of Juana Gutiérrez de Mesa when he went to court for the sake of claiming part of his late father's bequest. "Juan de la Cruz mulato, esclavo de Juana Gutiérrez de Mesa, hijo de Francisco Beloso, chino libre y de Juana de la Cruz, negra difunta. Información de legitimación para recibir herencia a la muerte de su padre." AJ, Fondo Tribunal Superior de Justicia del Distrito Federal, sección alcalde ordinario, serie civil, vol. 10, exp. 32, 13 fols., 1664.

13. AJ, Fondo Tribunal Superior de Justicia del DF, sección alcalde del crimen, Procesos Civiles, 1538–1799.

14. As, e.g., "Luisa de Rivera contra Pedro Cortés de la Torre, su marido, para que le pague la alimentación de ella y á su hija, Antonia Cortés. Ciudad de México, 1648." AGN, AJ, vol. 5, exp. 19, 15 fols.

15. As, e.g., "Agustín Juan de Almogueda, vecino de la Villa de Coyoacán. Información de su hijo natural de Francisco Amoguede e Isabel Sánchez." AGN, AJ, vol. 15, exp. 16, fol. 65. See also Komisaruk (2013, 78, 149).

16. AGN, Indiferente Virreinal, caja 957, exp. 17, Civil, fol. 11, 1663.

17. Twinam (1999, 143, 173).

18. AGN, Indiferente Virreinal, caja 5286, exp. 34, Bienes de Difuntos, año, fol. 8, 1732.

19. On this point, see Graubart (2007, 103–4).

20. "Información por parte de Nicolás Benítez Cabello vecino de la ciudad de México, de ser hijo natural de Felipe Cabello, difunto, vecino que fue del pueblo de San Jacinto, jurisdicción de la Villa de Coyoacán, y de mujer soltera" (hereafter, "Información por parte de Nicolás Benítez Cabello"). AGN, Tribunal Superior de Justicia, 1538–1799, Alcalde del crimen, procesos civiles, vol. 8, exp. 1, fols. 1–12, fol. 10r, 1693.

21. "Información por parte de Nicolás Benítez Cabello," fol. 9r.

22. "Información por parte de Nicolás Benítez Cabello," fol. 9r.

23. "Información por parte de Nicolás Benítez Cabello," fol. 3r, 22 June 1693.

24. "Información por parte de Nicolás Benítez Cabello," fol. 6r, 25 June 1693. See also Seed's treatment of how from the 1670s, the growing involvement of black women and

women of mixed race in marriage brought about the decrease of pressures exerted upon Spanish women, prior their marriage, to defend their honor, and, in parallel, the church's involvement in premarital arrangements shrunk (1998a).

25. "Información por parte de Nicolás Benítez Cabello," fol. 4r.

26. Finally, Nicolás Benítez admitted for the first time that María Espinosa was the wife of his late father but still claims to be the sole, legitimate heir of his father and his property. "Información por parte de Nicolás Benítez Cabello," fol. 17r, 27 July 1693.

27. "Información por parte de Nicolás Benítez Cabello vecino de la ciudad de México." Fols. 38r–39v. Compare those circumstances with Twinam's description of "Do Joseph and doña Gertrudis of Zimapan publicly but informally accepted the infant Joseph Francisco as their son and that they openly took him into their household," "rather than arranging for the child to be cared for by someone else. Or, with the story from Santiago de Chile of doña Gabriela's raising her baby all alone, but thereafter, the child's close ties of great affection with her father and her relatives within the private circle" (1999, 143, 175).

28. See also a very similar case, discussed earlier: "Nicolás Cabello Benítez, vecino de esta ciudad, hijo natural de Felipe Cabello, natural de San Jacinto, Coyoacán, pide informe de legitimidad y que se le notifique a Nicolás de Heredía persona a quien deja encargado y en cuyo poder paran los bienes de su padre. Contiene pleito de Nicolás de Heredía y María Calvo de Espinoza, mujer legítima de Cabello, sobre que se declare por testamento nuncupativo la memoria que se otorgó." AGN, Tribunal Supremo Judicial DF Colonial, caja 92, exp. 60, fol. 19, Mexico City, 1693.

29. "Información de legitimación de Beatriz de Carvajal, mulata libre, hija natural de Isabel de la Cruz, mulata libre y de Juan Carvajal, español, difunto, para la posesión de casas que fueron del finado, en el barrio de Santiago." AJ, Fondo Tribunal Superior de Justicia del Distrito Federal, sección alcalde ordinario, serie civil, vol. 9, exp. 13, 22 fols.

30. AGN, Tribunal Supremo Judicial DF, Colonial, caja 178, exp. 43, fol. 37, 1726.

31. "María de Villalobos solicita Real Provisión para que la hija de Sebastiana, mulata no tenga derecho a los bienes del padre." AGN, Tierras, vol. 2945, exp. 417, fol. 1, 1632.

32. "Información de legitimación de Beatriz de Carvajal, mulata libre, hija natural de Isabel de la Cruz, mulata libre y de Juan Carvajal, español, difunto, para la posesión de casas que fueron del finado, en el barrio de Santiago." AJ, Fondo Tribunal Superior de Justicia del Distrito Federal, sección alcalde ordinario, serie civil, vol. 9, exp. 13, 22 fols.

33. "Andrea de Rivera, madre soltera del niño contra el capitán Pedro Álvarez de Hinostroza, albacea y tenedor de bienes de Agustín de Useda, difunto, y padre natural del niño, por 500 pesos que le dio el finado por la entrega del menor." AJ, Fondo Tribunal Superior de Justicia del Distrito Federal, sección alcalde ordinario, serie civil, vol. 7, exp. 13, 5 fols., 1648.

34. "Información dada por Barbola del Moral [Barbara de Morales], madre natural de Juana María y María, niñas, para que declaren que son hijas naturales de Lucas Gonzales

difunto, her mother-in-law María de Contreras." AGN, Tribunal Superior de Justicia, Alcalde del Crimen, procesos civiles, vol. 9, exp. 15, fols. 1–70v, 1675.

35. "Información dada por Barbola del Moral," fol. 12v.

36. "Información dada por Barbola del Moral," fol. 32v.

37. "Información dada por Barbola del Moral," fol. 15v.

38. "Doña Patrona Bravo de Agüero, tutor y curadora de la persona y bienes de doña Juana Lorenza y mi hija adoptiva, digo que como el escrito que tengo dice, Clara Rosa, mulata libre, como madre legítima de María Micaela asimismo mulata, de edad de quince años, a quien he criado desde la edad de tres años, y que en una de las clausuras del testamento dicha difunta deja por esclava a la dicha María Micaela para que le sirve a doña Juana Lorenza, con la calidad de que sea la esclavitud por los días que viviese dicha doña Juana, y ahora, por parte de Clara Rosa en el escrito que presento informa a Vuestra de que se le dan a la dicha su hija malos tratamientos que no se ha mirado como a esclava, sino como a hija, como pudiera dar información de la buena vida y tratamientos que le he dado, supuesto que para querer la libertad y sacarla de cautiverio, no era necesario de dar quejas sino es decir la verdad pudiera dicha mi hija empadrarlo y conseguir su intenta y así habiendo entrado en mejor acuerdo desde luego consiente, doña Juana, como su ama, a quien pertenece, y yo, en su nombre, como su tutora y curadora, el que la saque de su cautiverio exhibiendo la cantidad de dos cientos pesos a que la valen, a los corredores de Lonja haciendo juramento legalmente." "Diligencias hechas para la libertad de María Micaela, mulata esclava por los días de la vida de doña Juana Loayza, legataria de doña Gertrudis Bravo de Agüero, de pedimento de Clara Rosa, mulata libertina de la dicha doña Gertrudis, como madre de la dicha María Micaela, contra doña Patrona Bravo de Agüero, como madre adoptiva de la dicha doña Juana Lorenza, 1726." AGN, Bienes Nacionales, caja 488 (2), exp. 36.

39. AGN, Instituciones Coloniales, Matrimonios, vol. 78, fols. 91–93r, 1663.

CHAPTER 5: SINGLENESS AND SEXUALITY

1. Decrees of Trent, vol. II, 754–55; *El sacrosanto y ecuménico Concilio de Trento* (1785).

2. Martin Schnucker (1988, 244). On women's roles and obligations, see also Vives ([1528] 1936, 9–14); de León ([1583] 1943, 14, 129); de la Cerda (1599, 323); de Cordoba ([1542] 1974).

3. On the lack of recogimientos for reeducating wayward women in Santiago de Guatemala, see Komisaruk (2013, 30).

4. In the Archivo General de Indias in Mexico City, there are at least thirty-two entire expedientes registered dealing with single women of the lower castas living together during the seventeenth century. AGN, Bienes Nacionales, vol. 442, exps. 3–17, 19–24, 35, 36, 38, 41–48; vol. 465, exps. 24–25, 28, 29, 31, 32, 34, 35–40, 42, 44–46, 48–53; vol. 497, exps.

36–40, 1605 y 1609. Stern, in contrast to Seed, has argued recently that subaltern women and men in fact developed their own ideas about legitimate gender authority, and therefore there was no single code of honor and shame in colonial Mexican society. (1995; Seed 1988a).

5. On Farfán's treatise, as well as on Boerhaave's tract, "Of the Diseases of Women and Children," see also Jaffary (2004, 148–49).

6. "Juan de Espinosa y María de Rivera, viuda, por amancebados, 1639." AHJ, Puebla, doc. no. 1737, "Proceso criminal contra Juan de Espinosa y María de Rivera, viuda, por amancebados, 1639."

7. See, e.g., "Denuncia contra Juan Martin mulato libre soltero por estar amancebando con Luisa Hernández, mulata libre soltera." AHJ, Puebla, doc. 1989, fol. 2, 1646.

8. Mateo de Herrera, neighbor, and Bartolomé de Venones, shoemaker, fol. 65r; Gaspar de los Reyes also denounces her for having used foul words against his son, fol. 69r.

9. "Autos criminales contra Maríana de Ojeda, mulata, soltera." AHJ, Puebla, doc. 793, 1606–14, Proceso judicial; criminal, 155 fols.

10. "Autos criminales contra Maríana de Ojeda," fols. 12v–12r.

11. "Autos criminales contra Maríana de Ojeda," fol. 56r.

12. On a similar wording concerning sexual promiscuity among Spanish doncellas in Cartagena, Colombia, see von Germeten (2013, 28–29).

13. "Autos criminales contra Maríana de Ojeda," fol. 18r.

14. AGN, Bienes Nacionales, vol. 465, exp. 40, fols. 1–3, 1606.

15. *Papel del Pulque, en favor de sus virtudes medicinales y singulares, propiedades . . .* See also AGN, Ordenanzas, s. XVl–XVlll. Pulques, 1769–1810, Real Acuerdo, 1569–1821; "Superior decreto del Virrey prohibiendo el uso de la bebida del pulque y encargando al Corregidor la vigilancia sobre este punto, 1693." AGN, Pulquerías, "Libro en que se asientan las pulquerías y casilloas que hay en ésta capital." vol. 3719.

16. On parallel accounts from the city authorities of Puebla see, e.g., "Catalina de Aguilar, negra libre, que vive en la calle que vuelve de Los Herreros, vende pulque amarillo." AHJ, Puebla, 2, image 0733. The room where she sold the liquor was full of indigenous persons drinking. "Proceso criminal contra Juana de la Cruz, mestiza, por vender pulque Amarillo de trapiche, 1672": "She is single, lives alone in a room in the city, and is 30 years old. She sells the pulque to indigenous persons, blacks and mulatoes." AHJ, Puebla, doc. 2346.

17. *Papel del Pulque,* 1748.

18. On this point, see Ortega's (1985) supportive stance that not all of "Mexican society" agreed with the church's teachings on sexual/matrimonial matters.

19. "Causa criminal promovida por Pedro Juárez, alcalde de los Indios del barrio de San Francisco, contra Luisa e Inés, viudas, que visten en ropas de Indios, por causar escándolo y vender públicamente pulque de tepache en sus casas y estar amancebadas." El Archivo Judicial, INAH, Puebla, exp. 1538, 1629.

20. *Ordenanzas sobre la bebida del pulque*: 24 de agosto de 1529, Toledo; 24 de agosto de 1540, Valladolid; 3 de octubre de 1607, don Felipe III, 1654, los corregidores de la Ciudad de México, "Ordenanzas sobre la reformación de la bebida por el obispo de Puebla, julio 1674."

21. "María de Abendaño, como prima de Inés de Perea vecina de San José del Parral, contra Pedro de Heredía, vecino de esta ciudad, sobre palabra de casamiento." AGN, Instituciones Coloniales, Matrimonios, tomo 19, vol. 78, 1663.

22. On the language of seduction/solicitation, see Curcio-Nagy (2014, 57); see also Delgado, on lawsuits over the loss of virginity in eighteenth-century Toluca (2009, 99–121).

23. "Agustina de San Jerónimo, mestiza y mujer legítima de Pascual de los Reyes, mestizo, como madre legítima de Marta de San Pedro, mestiza, contra Juan de los Reyes, indio, por haber estuprado y llevado su virginidad a la dicha Marta de San Pedro." AHJ, Puebla, doc. 2348 (1673).

24. AGN—Archivo Judicial del Tribunal Superior del Distrito Federal, Mexico, caja 62, exp. 105, fol. 5, 1763.

25. "Luisa María, india, casada, vecina del pueblo de San Bernabé y Juana de la Cruz, india, de edad de 16 años, soltera, Vecina del pueblo de San Bernabé, contra Lucas Miguel, indio, soltero, vecino de México, cargador, natural del pueblo de Santa María Masatla y otros acusados ausentes." AGN, Tribunal Supremo Judicial DF, Colonial, caja 217, exp. 11, fols. 31, 1714.

26. See, e.g., "Permiso a Agustina Hernández, mulata libre para vivir con una hija suya y usar manto." Reales Cédulas, Duplicadas, AGN, Bienes Nacionales, vol. 16, exp. 398, fols. 202–202v, 3 September 1620.

27. For comparisons, see Poska (1996, 874); see also Gauderman (2003, 64–66). On the case of María de la Candelaria's letter of appeal to the Audiencia on grounds of her coerced defloration see above.

28. AGN, Indiferente Virreinal, Clero Regular y Secular, caja-exp. 5529-001, fol. 11r, año 170.

29. AGN, Matrimonios, vol. 75, exp. 52, fols. 219–35, año 1648.

30. AGN, Indiferente Virreinal, Clero Regular y Secular, caja 6005, exp. 91, fol. 1, 1632.

31. AGN, Indiferente Virreinal, caja 5529, exp. 001, fol. 11, 1701.

32. AGN, Indiferente Virreinal, caja 5217, exp. 31, fol. 2, 1663.

33. "Provisorato Oficial y Vicariato General. Carta de edicto para el matrimonio, porque hay muchos feligreses, que viven amancebados en la Catedral de la México." AGN, Matrimonios, vol. 265, exp. 68, 1 fol., 1674.

34. AGN Matrimonios, vol. 64, exp. 38, fols. 134–135v, 1628.

35. AGN Matrimonios, vol. 64, exp. 38, fols. 134–135v, 1628.

36. AGN Matrimonios, vol. 256, exp. 82, 4 fols., 1672.

37. AGN, Indiferente Virreinal, Clero Regular y Secular, caja-exp. 2860-029, año 1611, fol. 3.

38. Mateo de Herrera, neighbor, and Bartolomé de Venones, shoemaker, fol. 65r; Gaspar de los Reyes also denounces her for having used foul words against his son, fol. 69r.

39. AGN, Indiferente Virreinal, Criminal, caja 5069, exp. 21, fol. 23, 1692.

40. See Komisaruk's treatment of the wording used in Guatemala to denote illicit relationships and their significance: "As far as the wording used to name these relationships, contemporaries did not distinguish between affairs that were adulterous and those that were illicit simply because the couple was not married" (2013, 133).

41. According to Perry, by the end of the sixteenth century, one-quarter of the births in the parish of San Martin in Seville were illegitimate (1990, 58).

42. Schwartz (2008, 32–33). See my own estimates of illegitimacy, in chapter 1, above.

43. "Contra Diego Ruiz, hombre casado, y Maríana Sánchez, mestiza, soltera, por amancebados." Proceedings of the Ecclesiastical court of the Archbishopric of Mexico City in the Cathedral. AGN, Bienes Nacionales, vol. 465, exp. 44, 1606, 1–8, fols.

44. "Jeronimo de León y María de Miradeles, por amancebados." Proceedings of the Ecclesiastical court of the Archbishopric of Mexico City, in the Cathedral. AGN, Bienes Nacionales, vol. 225, exp. 24, fols. 1–11v, 1606.

45. "Ana López, mujer soltera, vecina de México." AGN, Inquisición vol. 117, exp. 6, 1574.

46. AGN, Inquisición, vol. 304, exp. 7, fols. 1r–3v, 1626.

47. Astorga, sínodo, 1553, c. 5.1.1 n.30, y Oviedo, sínodo, 1553, c. 5.1.1 n.24. Sigüenza, sínodo, fol. 13v, 1553. Cf. Cárcel Ortí (1999, 9–135); E. Hall (1997); Seidel (1995).

48. "Declaran ser amancebados. Contrayentes: Diego Márquez 26 años; Maríana Pérez, mestiza, 34 años." AGN, Matrimonios, vol. 64, exp. 38, fols. 134–135v.

49. AGN, Matrimonios, vol. 49, exp. 121, fols. 332–336v, 1628.

50. AGN, Matrimonios, vol. 49, exp. 107, fols. 296–301r, 1628.

51. AGN, Matrimonios, vol. 11, exp. 19, fol. 68, 1701.

52. Cf. Bennett (2003, 154–57): "Beatriz eventually developed a romantic attachment to one of the cowboys, known as el Indio, with whom she subsequently cohabited. Unsatisfied with this arrangement, the couple requested Antonio de Savedra's permission to be married . . . The relationship soon soured; years later, Beatriz informed the inquisitors that Diego 'gave me a bad life . . . beating me where and whenever he wanted.'" The insufferable abuse prompted Beatriz to flee for Guanajuato, ending their two-year marriage.

53. AGN, Matrimonios, vol. 11, exp. 19, fol. 4r.

54. "Información por parte de Nicolás Benítez Cabello vecino de la ciudad de México, de ser hijo natural de Felipe Cabello, difunto, vecino que fue del pueblo de San Jacinto, jurisdicción de la Villa de Coyoacán, y de mujer soltera." AGN, Tribunal Superior de Justicia, Alcalde del crimen, procesos civiles, vol. 8, exp. 1, fols. 1–12, 1693.

55. See Ferraro (2001, 74–101), in which she treats in-depth comparable attitudes toward cases of impotence in late Renaissance Venice. See also Poska (1996).

56. AGN, Indiferente Virreinal, caja 1120, exp. 5, fol. 3, 173.

57. "Antonio de Añas, tirador de oro, contra su mujer, Francisca Rosillo, sobre que se anule el matrimonio contrayendo." AGN, Indiferente Virreinal, Clero Regular, caja 6208, exp. 28, fol. 6, 1609. See comparable cases of impotence resulting in the woman partner's seeking annulment of marriage, in Ferraro (2001, 77).

58. "El fiscal del Santo Oficio contra una mestiza llamada Magdalena, que vive en casa de fulano, Sáenz, médico." AGN, Inquisición, vol. 518, fols. 351r–415v (Puebla, 1674).

59. Similarly, in the Republic of Congo, *bilonga* is a medicine bundle, *nganga* a healer (Jules-Rosette 1981).

60. AGN, Mapas y Planos, 04903.

61. AGN, Mapas y Planos, 04904.

62. "Processo y causa criminal," vol. 1, fols. 11r, 286r.

63. AGN, Mapas y Planos, No. 04904.

64. See also Gomes de Melo (2012). Santo Antônio de Jesus, Bahia, Setembro/2012. See also Giuseppe Marcocci, "uma reprodução de uma curiosa e interessantíssima 'carta de tocar', destinada a proteger o seu portador. Illustration No. 30," in Paiva (2013); Lahon (2004, 9–70). On the practices of love magic in seventeenth-century Cartagena de Indias, see von Germeten (2013, ch. 2).

65. On the usage of holy water as ritual means by poor women, see Graham (1992, 64–65).

66. "Testificaciones y deposiciones voluntarias." AGN, Inquisición, vol. 435, part I, fols. 36r–67v.

67. "Testificaciones y deposiciones voluntarias." AGN, Inquisición, vol. 435, part I, fols. 218r–221v.

68. Sánchez Ortega (1992, 196–215): case files of 28 men and 92 women; among the women: 37 amorous magic, 24 denounced as having cast spells, 19 specialists in curative practices, 7 amorous spells, and 4 possible witches. Lewis, *Hall of Mirrors*, Introduction.

69. Few, *Women Who Live Evil Lives* (2002, 77); Alberro (1992, 290–91). On the role of the intermediary in this context, see also Ginzburg (1986, 190).

70. *An interim translation of Manuel Alvares S.J. "Etiópia Menor e Descripção Géografica da Província da Serra Leoa" [c. 1615]* (1990, ch. 24).

71. Boilat (1853, 461–62). AGN, Inquisición, vol. 435, "Testificaciones y deposiciones voluntarias remitidas a este tribunal de diferentes partes del distrito de esta Inquisición-en virtud de los edictos generales de la fe, que se publicaron dicho año 1650," fol. 44r. See also "Testificaciones y deposiciones voluntarias," Sixth Case, 9.8, fol. 418r, 1650.

CHAPTER 6: SHELTERING SISTERHOOD

1. AHJ, exp. 2017, doc. 13, 1648. Holy Week of 1648 was followed by many days of blustering rains: the streets were flooded by water, mud, and garbage. The worst situation occurred near the Saint Catherine's Baths and the San Pedro Hospital, next to the Río San Francisco. At the end of August that year a terrible epidemic struck Puebla, causing numerous deaths. The local hospitals and hospices were filled with the sick and dying. Under Bishop Palafox's instructions, Isabel and the rest of the populace who had escaped the catastrophe proceeded to the now-renovated cathedral, carrying the image of the city's patron saint, St. Joseph, and holding special prayers to counteract the plague.

2. Sánchez (2013). See also Lara (2010, 19). On the substantial role of mulato and black slaves in disseminating love-magic substances, see also Bristol (2007, 165–72).

3. "Processo y causa criminal," vol. 1, fols. 95r–109r.

4. "Processo y causa criminal," vol. 1, fols. 11r, 286r.

5. "Processo y causa criminal," vol. 1, fols. 18r and 98v. During the act of confiscation of Isabel's belongings in 1652 by the city authorities in Puebla, they found three or four glasses belonging to María de Rivera, who gave them to her for safekeeping.

6. "Processo y causa criminal," vol. 1, fols. 19r, 25v, 34r, 297r.

7. "Processo y causa criminal," vol. 1, fol. 98v.

8. "Testificaciones y deposiciones voluntarias . . . 1650," fol. 63r; AGN, Inquisición, vol. 435, part 1.

9. "Testificaciones y deposiciones voluntarias . . . 1650," fol. 81r.

10. "Processo y causa criminal," vol. 1, fol. 100r.

11. In 1620 the Inquisition made public an edict stressing that the peyote fell under the category of superstition and warned the indigenous populace against the intervention of the Devil in its practices (Bristol 2007, 162).

12. "Processo y causa criminal," vol. 1, fol. 103r.

13. "Processo y causa criminal," vol. 1, fol. 34r.

14. "Testificaciones y deposiciones voluntarias." AGN, Inquisición, vol. 435, part I, fols. 218r–221v.

15. See Overmayer-Velazquez (1998, 1–28). See also Heyden (1989): "En Chalma, se colocan los cordones umbilicales de los recién nacidos en dos cuevas, una de la parte baja del cerro y otra en la parte alta; esto les asegura la buena suerte al principiar la vida" "In Chalma the umbilical cords of the recently born are hung inside two caves, the one on the lower side of the mountain, and the other, on the upper side; this act assures their good fortune during the beginning of their lives" (J. Hobgood, personal communication).

16. McCafferty and McCafferty (2008): art historian Milbrath (1988) has found iconographic linkages between caves (as entrances to the earth) and the vagina (as the entrance to the womb and especially at the point of the emergence for newborn infants).

17. De Fonseca (1606). In sixteenth- and seventeenth-century Friuli, Italy cauls were also associated with fertility, believed to belong to the witch-hunting *benandanti*, who were born wrapped in their membrane (*camiscia,* or "shirt"; Ginzburg 1966, 160–65, 179n36).

18. Resnick (2002), unpublished paper. I am grateful to the author for allowing me to cite this study.

19. Duvernoy (1978, I, 260–290). During the second decade of the fourteenth century, in Béatrice de Planissoles's trial in Pamiers, conducted by Jacques Fournier, this accusation becomes a central issue discussed by the judges (1978, 1:260–90); in Italy, during the late sixteenth century and early seventeenth, the Venetian Inquisition was also much concerned about these "love-magic" practices. See, e.g., Martin (1989); Ruggiero (1993). On sixteenth-century Spain: Sánchez Ortega (1992, 196–215); Alberro (1987, 79–94); Alberro (1998, esp. 180–192, 456–72); Aguirre Beltán (1955); Franco (1989, 55–79); Behar (1986, 34–54).

20. Sullivan (1966). On the growing limitations placed upon midwives in seventeenth-century Europe, see also Forbes (1966, 144–47); Hernández Sáenz (1997, 204–5).

21. Hernández Sáenz, ibid.

22. Alonso de las Ruyezses de Fonseca, *Diez privilegios . . .* , fols. 107v–111r.

CHAPTER 7: REPRESENTATIONAL SPACES

1. AGN, Indios, vol. 32, exp. 69, fols. 72v–74r.

2. AGN, Instituciones Coloniales, caja 171, exp. 14, fol. 4, 1625.

3. AGN, Indiferente Virreinal, Cofradías y Archicofradías, caja-exp. 4767-076, fol. 301, 1593–99; AGN, Indiferente Virreinal, caja 0932, exp. 17; Indiferente Virreinal, Cofradías y Archicofradías, caja-exp. 3871-030, fol. 1, 1758; AGN, Indiferente Virreinal, Cofradías y Archicofradías, caja-exp. 1988-011, fol. 15, 1712–18.

4. "Antonio de Castro, fiscal de este arzobispado, contra Pedro Bravo y Manuel de Figueroa, y contra Maríana Pérez, mestiza, por amancebados y ella está acusada por blásphama contra el nombre de Jesús y de los santos." Proceedings of the Ecclesiastical court of the Archbishopric of Mexico City, in the Catedral. AGN, Bienes Nacionales, vol. 465, exp. 53, 1606–7, fols. 1–38.

5. "Autos criminales contra Maríana de Ojeda, mulata, soltera." AHJ, doc. 793, 1606–14, p. 155, Proceso judicial, criminal, fols. 12v–12r.

6. AGN, Archivo de la Curia Metropolitana del Arzobispado de México, Proyecto LRO, rollo 1120, ubicación 19-C, Padrones del Sagrario (Catedral), 1672–78.

7. AGN, Mapas y Planos, 210100/5503.

8. "Autos criminales contra Maríana de Ojeda," fol. 56v.

9. "Autos criminales contra Maríana de Ojeda," fol. 12r.

10. "Autos criminales contra Maríana de Ojeda, mulata, soltera," fol. 16v.

11. "Processo y causa criminal de Isabel de Montoya." AGN, Inquisición, vol. 447, exp. 8, fol. 286r, Mexico City.

12. "Processo y causa criminal de Isabel de Montoya," fol. 29r.

13. "Processo y causa criminal," vol. 1, fol. 14v.

14. "Processo y causa criminal de Isabel de Montoya." AGN, Mexico City, fol. 16v. See also a similar description in Few (2002, 55).

15. On women's diverse emotional forms of jealousy, see also Lipsett-Rivera (2014, 66–84).

16. AGN, Inquisición, vol. 308, exp. 72, fol. 394, 1615. "Testificación en contra de María Vasquez, por superstición para cometer adulterio (ponía tierra de muerto y le daba a su marido sesos secos de burro y sangre menstrual). Querétaro."

17. "Processo y causa criminal," fol. 118v.

18. "Processo Criminal Contra Leonor de Isla, Mulata, Vecina de la Ciudad de Nueva Veracruz y Natural de la Ciudad de Cadiz que vive en la calle de Farfan en la casa donde vivia Beatriz la pastelera, por que yo he oido decir que es buena hechicera y que sabe la oración de Santa Marta y de la anima sola y porque arte lo sabe preguntarle por bien quien son sus amigas y aunque sean españolas con don traiganlas tambien a preguntarles." AGN, Inquisición vol. 341, exp. 2, fol. 27r.

19. "Processo y causa criminal," fol. 95r. See Cirac Estaponán (1942).

20. "Processo y causa criminal," fol. 95r.

21. "Processo y causa criminal," fol. 23r. Rivera testified before the inquisitors that she had known the prayer ever since she was a child, "together with other prayers for the saints." See also Campos Moreno (2001, 119–26); versión H in this compilation of the different versions of the Santa Marta prayers is identical to that recited by Isabel de Isla.

22. On this important point, see also Poska (2012).

23. AGN, Inquisición, vol. 447, exp. 8, fol. 89v.

24. "Inés de Osario, mujer de Francisco de Villanueva, corredor, vive en el tianquiz de San Juan, en casas de Gaspar Osario, su padre." AGN, Inquisición, vol. 360, exp. 55, fol. 159r, 18 March 1627.

25. AGN, Inquisición, vol. 360, exp. 159, fols. 464r–466v.

26. See also the important study on this theme by Masferrer León and Verónica (2011, 83–103).

27. "María Ramírez, mulata esclava de doña Catalina Chamazero y Abendaño, viuda, vezina de esta ciudad contra el Lic. Miguel de Pedroza, presbítero, sobre el entrego de unas cajas de ropa y otras cosas." AGN, Bienes Nacionales, vol. 630, exp. 11, fols. 1–65v.

28. "Processo y causa criminal," fol. 253v.

29. "Marta Rodríguez, negra libre, inventario de bienes, 1633." AHJ, Puebla, doc. 1622. Von Germeten (2003, 24–30).

CHAPTER 8: COMFORTING RITUALS

1. Major contributions to this debate are books and essays such as Pearce, Millett, and Struck (2000); Williams (2003b); Morris (1992). See also J. Pearce (1998, 99–111); Parry ([1995] 2010, 612–30); Weekes (2001, 73–82).

2. "Processo y causa criminal contra Isabel de Montoya." AGN, Inquisición, vol. 435, pt. 1.

3. Alberro found that women did not exceed 30 percent of the suspects in any year between 1571 and 1700, and women were defendants in only 16 percent of suspects during this period. Alberro, *La actividad del Santo Oficio*, 130.

4. "Testificaciones y deposiciones voluntarias remitidas a este tribunal de diferentes partes del distrito de esta Inquisición—en virtud de los edictos generales de la fe, que se publicaron dicho año 1650." Proceso contra Clara Trujillo, María Altamirano, Bernardina, mestiza y María india por hechiceras y brujas. AGN, Inquisición, Puebla, vol. 435, part 1, fol. 291 (30.3.1650), fol. 292 (29.4.1650). See also AGN, Inquisición, vol. 179, exp. 4, fol. 15, 1646.

5. "Testificaciones y deposiciones," fol. 410v.

6. "Testificaciones y deposiciones," fol. 410v.

7. "Testificaciones y deposiciones," fol. 410v. "María de Roelas se acusa ante el Santo Oficio por haber empleado la ayuda de un indio herbolario para que le diese unas yerbas para que los hombres quisieran bien a su hija, consultando después a una mulata de nombre Cathalina y a doña Antonia la Chupona." AGN, Inquisición, vol. (cajas) 1602, exp. 1, 260 fols., 1650–56.

8. "Processo Criminal contra Leonor de Isla," fol. 125.

9. "Processo Criminal contra Leonor de Isla," fol. 95r.

10. "Processo Criminal contra Leonor de Isla," fol. 130r.

11. Luis Garcia-Ballester (1985, 246–70). On the amalgamation between Old World and New World popular medical practices in sixteenth-century Spain, see Fragoso's famous treatise, *Discurso de las cosas aromáticas . . . de las Indias . . . para uso de medicinas* (1570). See also Risse (1987, 32–54).

12. "Processo criminal contra Isabel de Montoya," fol. 303v.

13. "Processo criminal contra Isabel de Montoya," fol. 268r.

14. See, e.g., Garcia-Ballester (1985, 246–70); Fragoso (1570). See also Risse (1987, 32–54); Garcia-Ballester (1984, 114–18); Madrid, Biblioteca Nacional, MS 18.586–587, IV, No. vi; Sánches Granjel (1972, 407–20); Herrero (1955–56, 173–90); Yañez Polo and Zaragosa Rubira (1976, 2:1287–93); Parrilla Hermida (1977, 475–515); Malvido (November–December 1975, 793–802); Lanning (1985); León (1918, 210–86; 1921, 3–48); *Hospitales de la Nueva España* (1956–60, 1:36–48); Quezada (1978, 51–68); Jarcho (1976, 431–39); Comas (1954, 327–61); Farfán ([1592] 1944).

15. "Processo criminal contra Isabel de Montoya," fol. 83r.

16. *Martin* "Cacica, señora de los pueblos de Teutila, y que ella y su hija Catalina Martinez, abuela de esta confesante, por ser principales, comían renta de la Real caja, circunstancias de quenas toda atención." "Proceso y causa criminal," fol. 152v.

17. "Proceso y causa criminal," fols. 248v–249v: *Habeas Corpus* and act of Confiscation (printed form, official form, filled up with the culprit's name and address). Compare also with Teresa de Losada's list of devotional objects in Bristol (2007, 109). See, in parallel, Komisaruk (2013, 88).

18. On the alliances between priests and single women, see, e.g., Leavitt-Alcantará (2018, ch. 2).

19. "Processo y causa criminal," fol. 218v, Juana de Ochoa's Testimony, 13 January 1663.

20. "Processo y causa criminal," fols. 83v–84r.

21. "Processo y causa criminal," fol. 24v.

22. "Processo y causa criminal," fol. 91v.

23. "Processo y causa criminal," fol. 199r.

24. "Visitación del obispado de Puebla," Biblioteca Nacional de España, Mss. 8865, September 1644.

25. "Processo y causa criminal," fol. 349r: Isabel de Montoya's Notice of Death (18 June 1664): "At noon entered the reception hall of the Inquisition a man from the hospital and notified the Inquisitor don Pedro de Medina Rico that Isabel de Montoya had died at the hospital that same day."

26. See, e.g., Chance (1978, 126–7); Patrick Carroll's classical study of late-colonial Jalapa, "Estudio sociodemográfico de personas de sangre negra en Jalapa, 1791" (n.d., 111–25), in which he highlights the significant presence of indigenous African intermarriages during the seventeenth century.

27. Gauderman remarks that by the eighteenth century, women faced greater legal restrictions than earlier on, and this may also be true to social realities (2003, 23–24).

CONCLUSIONS

1. "Mexico, Baptisms, 1560–1950," Index, *FamilySearch*, accessed 12 Nov. 2012, https://familysearch.org/pal:/MM9.1.1/N5CX-M32, Ysabel de Montoya Hernández, 21 Mar 1593, Reference ID: 2:KDJMBD, FHL microfilm 35818.

2. "Processo y causa criminal," fol. 91v.

3. "Processo y causa criminal," fol. 253v, 11 July 1662.

4. "Mexico, Marriages, 1570–1950," Index, *FamilySearch*, accessed 13 November 2012, https://familysearch.org/pal:/MM9.1.1/JHPS-WC6, Catalina Martin, in entry for "Diego De Montoya and Luiza Hernández, 22 Mar 1592" (Familysearch [The Church of Jesus Christ

of Latter-Day Saints] MM9.1.1/N5CX-M32 KDJMBD, FHL microfilm No. 35818). In 1578 the church was elevated to the status of a parish church. Hernando Cortés first founded there the Arch-confraternity de la Cruz, an organization composed of noblemen whose aim was to comfort, in their last hour, and bury criminals condemned to execution. A papal bull of January 1573 conceded to this privileged brotherhood the name of Santísimo Cristo de San Marcelo, and a hundred days' indulgence to the faithful who would visit the sacrosanct image to which the arch-confraternity was dedicated. The image, which is highly venerated, was brought to Mexico City by the conquistadors. It was always covered with seven veils and was known as El Señor de las Siete Velas.

5. "Mexico, Marriages, 1570–1950," *FamilySearch* (The Church of Jesus Christ of Latter-Day Saints) M61903-1, System Origin: Mexico-VR, GS Film number: 35848, Reference ID: 2:147MN2H.

6. "Mexico, Marriages, 1570–1950," *FamilySearch* (The Church of Jesus Christ of Latter-Day Saints) M61903-1, System Origin: Mexico-VR, GS Film number: 35848, Reference ID: 2:147MN2H.

7. "Mexico, Marriages, 1570–1950," *FamilySearch*, Indexing Project (Batch) Number: C03794-8, https://familysearch.org/pal:/MM9, System Origin: Mexico-EASy, Reference ID: vol. 2, p. 61, GS Film number: 35818.

8. "Mexico, Marriages, 1570–1950," *FamilySearch*, Indexing Project (Batch) Number: C03794-8, System Origin: Mexico-ODM, GS Film number: 35818.

9. "Mexico, Marriages, 1570–1950," *FamilySearch*, Indexing Project (Batch) C61900-8, System Origin: Mexico-VR, Reference ID: 2:KDL31T, GS Film number: 35818.

10. "*Cacica, señora de los pueblos de Teutila, y que ella y su hija Catalina Martinez, abuela de esta confesante, por ser principales, comían renta de la Real caja, circunstancias de quenas toda atención.*" "Processo y causa criminal," fol. 152v.

11. "Processo y causa criminal," fol. 253v, 11 July 1662.

12. "Processo y causa criminal," fol. 90r.

13. "Processo y causa criminal," fol. 251r.

References

ARCHIVES, MUSEUMS, AND LIBRARIES

Archivo Histórico Judicial, INAH, Puebla (AHJ)

Archivo General de la Nación, Mexico (AGN)

    Archivo de la Curia (Metropolitana) del Arzobispado de México, Proyecto LRO, Padrones de Sagrario

    Archivo Histórico de Hacienda

    Archivo Judicial (AJ), sección alcalde ordinario, serie civil

    Archivo Histórico del Tribunal Superior de Justicia

    Bienes de Difuntos

    Bienes Nacionales

    Civil

    Escribanos

    Geneología y Heráldica

    General de Parte

    Indiferente Virreinal

    Indios

    Inquisición

DOI: 10.5876/9781607329633.c012

Instituciones Coloniales

Jesuitas

Mapas y Planos

Matrimonios

Notaría

Ordenanzas

Real Junta

Reales Cédulas

Sagrario Metropolitano

Tierras

Tribunal Supremo Judicial

Bibliotéca Nacional, Madrid

Bibliothèque Nationale (Richelieu), France, Rare Manuscripts

FamilySearch. https://familysearch.org/pal:/MM9

Musée Quai Branly, Paris

Rich Collection, University of California, Berkeley

Van Pelt Library, University of Pennsylvania, rare manuscript collections

SOURCES

Abu-Lughod Lila. 1990. The Romance of Resistance: Tracing Transformations of Power through Bedouin Women. *American Ethnologist* 17. no. 1 (February): 41–55.

Adair, Richard. 1996. *Courtship, Illegitimacy and Marriage in Early Modern*. Manchester, England: Manchester University Press.

Aguirre Beltrán, Gonzalo. (1946) 1972. *La población negra en México: Estudio etnohistórico*. México: Fondo de Cultura Económica.

Aguirre Beltrán, Gonzalo. 1955. *Medicina y magia: El proceso de aculturación y el curanderismo en México*. Mexico City: Instituto Nacional Indigenista.

Ajofrín, Fray Francisco. [1726] 1959. *Diario de viaje que por orden de la sagrada congregación de la propaganda fide hizo a la América Septentrional en el siglo XVIII*. 2 vols. Mexico City: Archivo Documental Español.

Alberro, Solange. 1981. *La actividad del Santo Oficio de la Inquisicion en Nueva España*. Mexico City: INAH.

Alberro, Solange. 1987. "Herejes, brujas y beatas: Mugeres ante el Tribunal del Santo Oficio de la Inquisición en la Nueva España." In *Presencia y transparencia: La muger en la historia de México*. Mexico City: Colegio de México.

Alberro, Solange. 1991. "El amancebamiento en los Siglos XVI y XVII: Un medio eventual de medrar." In *Familia y poder en Nueva España*, 155–66. Mexico City: Instituto Nacional de Antropología e Historia.

Alberro, Solange. 1992. *Del gachupín al criollo: O de cómo los españoles de México dejaron de serlo*. Mexico City: El Colegio de México.

Alberro, Solange. 1998. *Inquisición y sociedad en México 1571–1700*. Mexico City: Fondo de Cultura Económica.

Ames, David. 1959. "Belief in Witches among the Rural Wolof of the Gambia." *Africa* 29, no. 3 (July), 263–73.

Andrén, Anders. 1993. "Doors to Other Worlds: Scandinavian Death Rituals in Gotlandic Perspectives." *Journal of European Archaeology* 1, no. 1: 33–56.

Arrom, Silvia Marina. 1976. *La mujer mexicana ante el divorcio eclesiástico (1800–1857)*. Mexico City: SepSetentas.

Arrom, Silvia Marina. 1985. *The Women of Mexico City, 1790–1857*. Stanford, Calif.: Stanford University Press.

Arrom, Silvia Marina. 1996. "Popular Politics in Mexico City: The Parián Riot, 1828." In *Riots in the Cities: Popular Politics and the Urban Poor in Latin America, 1765–1910*, ed. Silvia M. Arrom and Servando Ortoll, 71–96. Wilmington: Scholarly Resources.

Bailey-Glasco, Sharon. 2010. *Constructing Mexico City: Colonial Conflicts over Culture, Space, and Authority*. New York: Palgrave Macmillan.

Beattie, Cordelia. 2006. "Single Women, Work, and Family: The Chancery Dispute of Jane Wynde and Margaret Clerk." In *Voices from the Bench: The Narratives of Lesser Folk in Medieval Trials*, ed. Michael Goodich, 177–202. Palgrave Macmillan.

Behar, Ruth. 1986. "Sex and Sin, Witchcraft and the Devil in Late-Colonial Mexico," *American Ethnologist* 14, no. 1:34–54.

Bell, Rudolph M. 1999. *How to Do It. Guides to Good Living for Renaissance Italians*. Chicago: University of Chicago Press.

Bennett, Herman L. 2003. *Africans in Colonial Mexico: Absolutism, Christianity, and Afro-Creole Consciousness, 1570–1640*. Bloomington: Indiana University Press.

Berndt, Ronald M. 1951. *Kunapipi: A Study of an Australian Aboriginal Religious Cult*. New York: International Universities Press.

Blaisdell, Charmarie J. 1988. "Calvin's and Loyola's Letters to Women: Politics and Spiritual Counsel in the Sixteenth Century." *Calviniana: Ideas and Influence of Jean Calvin*, ed. Robert V. Schnucker, 10. Kirksville, MO: Sixteenth Century Journal Publishers.

Blok, Josine H. 1995. *The Early Amazons: Modern and Ancient Perspectives on a Persistent Myth*. Trans. Peter Mason. Leiden, Netherlands: Brill.

Blum, Ann, S. 1998. "Public Welfare and Child Circulation in Mexico City, 1877 to 1925." *Journal of Family History* 23, no. 3:240–71.

Boilat, L'Abbe P. D. 1853. *Esquisses sénégalaises, physionomie du pays, peuplades, commerce, religions, passe et avenir, récits et légendes*. Paris: P. Bertrand.

Borah, Woodrow, and Sherburne F. Cook. 1966. "Marriage and Legitimacy in Mexican Culture: Mexico and California." *California Law Review* 54, no. 2:946–1008.

Bosch, Miguel Marín. 1999. *Puebla neocolonial, 1777–1831, casta, ocupación y matrimonio en la segunda ciudad de la Nueva España*. Mexico City: Colegio de Jalisco.

Boswell, John. 1988. *The Kindness of Strangers: The Abandonment of Children in Western Europe from Late Antiquity to the Renaissance*. Chicago, IL: University of Chicago Press.

Boubacar Barry. 1972. *Le royaume du Waalo, le Senegal avant la conquete*. Paris: Francois Maspero.

Boyer, Richard. 1989. "Women, la *mala vida* and the Politics of Marriage." In *Sexuality and Marriage in Colonial Latin America*, ed. Asunción Lavrin, 252–86. Lincoln: University of Nebraska Press.

Boyer, Richard. 1995. *Lives of the Bigamists: Marriage, Family, and Community in Colonial Mexico*. Albuquerque: University of New Mexico Press.

Boyer, Richard. 1989. "Women, la *mala vida* and the Politics of Marriage." *Sexuality and Marriage in Colonial Latin America*, ed. Asunción Lavrin, 252–86. Lincoln: University of Nebraska Press.

Boyer, Richard. 1995. *Lives of the Bigamists: Marriage, Family, and Community in Colonial Mexico*. Albuquerque: University of New Mexico Press.

Brading, David. 1971. *Miners and Merchants in Bourbon Mexico 1763–1810*. Cambridge: Cambridge University Press.

Brading, David. 1978. *Haciendas and Ranchos in the Mexican Bajío-Leon 1700–1860*. Cambridge: Cambridge University Press.

Bramly, Serge. 1975. *Macumba, forces noires du Brésil: Les enseignements de María-José, mère des dieux*. Paris: Seghers.

Bristol, Joan Cameron. 2007. *Christians, Blasphemers, and Witches: Afro-American Ritual Practice in the Seventeenth Century*. Albuquerque: University of New Mexico Press.

Brumana, Fernando G., and Elda G. Martinez. 1991. *Marginália Sagrada*. Campinas: Ed. da Unicamp.

Burkett, Elinor C. 1978. "Indigenous Women and White Society: The Case of Sixteenth-Century Peru." In *Latin American Women: Historical Perspectives*, ed. Asunción Lavrin, 117–21. Westport, CT: Greenwood Press.

Butler, Judith. 1988. "Performative Acts and Gender Constitution: An Essay in Phenomenology and Feminist Theory." *Theatre Journal* 40, no. 4 (December): 519–31.

Cacciatore, Olga G. 1977. *Diccionario de cultos afro-brasileiros*. Minas Gerais, Brazil: Editora Forense Universidade.

Cadet, Jean-Robert. 1998. *Restavec: From Haitian Slave Child to Middle-Class American*. Austin.

Calvo, Thomas. 1973. *Acatzingo: Demografía de una parroquia mexicana*. Mexico City: Instituto Nacional de Antropología e Historia.

Calvo, Thomas. 1984. "Concubinato y mestizaje en el medio urbano: El caso de Guadalajara." *Revista de Indias* (Spain) 61, no. 173: 203–12.

Calvo, Tomás. 1984. "Familles mexicaines au XVIIe siècle: Une tentative de reconstitution." *Annales de démographie historique* 3: 149–74.

Calvo, Tomás. 1989. *La Nueva Galicia en los siglos XVI y XVII*. Guadalajara: El Colegio de Jalisco and Centro de Estudios Mexicanos y Centroamericanos.

Calvo, Thomas. 1989. "The Warmth of the Hearth: Seventeenth-Century Guadalajara Families." In *Sexuality and marriage in colonial Latin America*, ed. Asunción Lavrin. Lincoln: University of Nebraska Press.

Calvo, Tomás. 1992. *Guadalajara y su región en el siglo XVII: Población y economía*. Guadalajara: Centro de Estudios Mexicanos y Centroamericanos and H. Ayuntamiento de Guadalajara.

Campos Moreno, Araceli. 2001. *Oraciones, ensalmos y conjuros mágicos del Archivo Inquisitorial de la Nueva España*. Annotated edition and preliminary study. Mexico City: El Colegio de México.

Cárcel Ortí, M. M. 1999. *Hacia un inventario de visitas pastorales en España de los siglos XVI—XX. Memoria Ecclesiae* 15 (Oviedo):9135.

Cardoso, Ruth C. L. 1984. "Creating Kinship: The Fostering of Children in Favela Families in Brazil." In *Kinship Ideology and Practice in Latin America*, ed. Raymond T. Smith, 196–203. Chapel Hill: University of North Carolina Press.

Caro Baroja, Julio. 1965. *The World of the Witches*. Chicago: University of Chicago Press.

Carroll, Patrick, J. n.d. "Estudio sociodemográfico de personas de sangre negra de Jalapa, 1791."

Carroll, Patrick J. 2001. *Blacks in Colonial Veracruz*. Austin: University of Texas Press.

Castañeda García, Carmen. 1989. *Violación, estupro y sexualidad: Nueva Galicia, 1790–1821* Guadalajara, Mexico: Editorial Hexágono.

Chance, John. 1978. *Race and Class in Colonial Oaxaca*. Stanford, CA: Stanford University Press.

Cirac Estaponán, Sebastián. 1942. *Los procesos de hechicería en Castilla la Nueva, Tribunales de Cuenca y Toledo*. Madrid: Consejo Superior de Investigaciones Científicas-Instituto Gerónimo Zurita.

Cohen, Elizabeth, and Thomas V. Cohen. 1993. *Words and Deeds in Renaissance Rome. Trials before the Papal Magistrates*. Toronto: University of Toronto Press.

Comas, Juan. 1954. "Influencia indígena en la medicina hipocrática en la Nueva España del Siglo XVI." *América Indígena* 14:327–61.

Cope, R. Douglas. 1994. *The Limits of Racial Domination: Plebeian Society in Colonial Mexico City*. Madison: University of Wisconsin Press.

Covarubias y Leiva, Diego de. 1734. *Opera omnia*. Geneva: Fratrum de Tournes.

Crawford, Patricia. 1982. "Attitudes to Menstruation in Seventeenth-Century England." *Past and Present* 91, no. 2:47–73.

Curcio-Nagy, Linda A. 2014. "The Language of Desire in Colonial Mexico." In *Emotions and Daily Life in Colonial Mexico*, ed. Javier Villa-Flores and Sonya Lipsett-Rivera, 44–61. Albuquerque: University of New Mexico Press.

Dávila Mendoza, Dora. 2005. *Hasta la muerte nos separe: Divorcio eclesiástico en el arzobispado de México 1702–1800*. Mexico City, El Colegio de México.

Davis, Natalie Zemon. 1987. *Fiction in the Archives: Pardon Tales and their Tellers in Sixteenth-Century France*. Stanford, CA: Stanford University Press.

De Almada, Andre. 1982. *A Brief Treatise on the Rivers of Guinea*. University of Liverpool.

De Cordoba, Martin. [1542] 1974. *Jardin de nobles donzellas*. Ed. Harriet Goldberg. Chapel Hill: University of North Carolina Press.

Dedieu, Jean-Pierre. 1989. *L'Administration de la foi: L'Inquisition de Tolède (XVIe–XVIIIe Siècle)*. Madrid: Casa de Velazquez.

De Fonseca, Alonso de las Ruyezses. 1606. *Diez privilegios para mugeres preñadas*. Biblioteca Nacional, Madrid, Rare Manuscripts Section, No. R/27415, fols. 107r–108v, 128v.

Dehouve, Danièle 2003. "La segunda mujer entre los Nahuas." In *El matrimonio en Mesoamerica, ayer y hoy, unas miradas antropológicas*, cord. David Robichaux cord, 94–106. Mexico City: Universidad Iberoamericana.

De la Cerda, Juan.1599. *Vida Política de todos los estados de mujeres*. Alcalá.

De León, Fray Luis. [1583] 1943. *La perfecta casada*. Trans. Alice P. Hubbard. Denton, TX: Texas State College for Women.

Delgado, Jessica. 2009. "Sin temor de Dios: Women and Ecclesiastical Justice in Eighteenth-Century Toluca." *Colonial Latin American Review* 18, no. 1:99–121.

De Moor, Tine, and Jan Luiten Van Zanden, 2010. "Girl Power: The European Marriage Pattern and Labour Markets in the North Sea Region in the Late Medieval and Early Modern Period." *Economic History Review* 63, no. 1:1–33.

De Sandoval, Alonso. 1647. *De instauranda Aethiopum salute: Naturaleza, policia sagrada i profana, costumbres i ritos, disciplina i catechismo evángelico de todos etíopes*.

Diccionario de Autoridades (1732).

Denevan, William M. 1992. "The Pristine Myth: The Landscape of the Americas in 1492." *Annals of the Association of American Geographers* 82, no. 3: 369–85.

Detienne, Marcel, and Jean Pierre Vernant. 1978. *Cunning Intelligence in Greek Culture and Society*. London: Harvester Press.

Didier Lahon. 2004. "Inquisição, pacto com o demônio e 'magia' africana em Lisboa no século XVIII." *TOPOI* 5, no. 8 (January–June): 9–70.

Doenges, Catherine Elspet. 1993. "A Regional Society in Colonial Mexico: Eighteenth-Century Celaya, Perspectives from the Household." Unpublished PhD dissertation, Syracuse University.

Donelha, André. 1977 [1625]. Descriçao da Serra Leoa e dos rios de Guiné do Eabo Verde. Lisboa: Junta de Investigacioes Cientificas do Ultramar, Centro de Estudios de Cartografia Antiga.

Dore, Elizabeth. 1997. "The Holy Family: Imagined Households in Latin American History." In *Gender Politics in Latin America: Debates in Theory and Practice*, ed. Elizabeth Dore, 101–17. New York: Monthly Review Press.

Douglas, Mary. 1975. *Implicit Meanings: Essays in Anthropology*. London: Routledge and Kegan Paul.

Duby, Georges. 1978. *Medieval Marriage: Two Models for Twelfth Century France*. Trans. Elborg Forster. Baltimore: The Johns Hopkins Symposia in Comparative History-Johns Hopkins University Press.

Duvernoy, Jean. 1978. (Trans. and ed.). *Le Registre D'Inquisition de Jacques Fournier 1318–1325*. 3 vols. Paris: Mouton.

Elena Martinez, María 2004. "The Black Blood of New Spain: Limpieza de Sangre, Racial Violence, and Gendered Power in Early Colonial Mexico." *William and Mary Quarterly*, 3rd ser., 61, no. 3:479–520.

El sacrosanto y ecuménico Concilio de Trento. 1785. Trans. Ignacio López de Ayala. 2. ed. Madrid, La Imprenta Real.

Estaponán, Sebastián Cirac. 1942. *Los procesos de hechicería en Castilla la Nueva, Tribunales de Cuenca y Toledo*. Madrid: Consejo Superior de Investigaciones Científicas-Instituto Jerónimo Zurita.

Farfán, Agustín. [1592] 1944. *Tractado Breve de medicina*. Obra impressa en México, por Pedro Ocharte, en 1592; rpt. Madrid: Edición Cultura Hispánica.

Fernandes, Valentim. 1506–7. *Relação de Diogo Gomes* and *Descripcam*. De prima inuentione Guinee, De insulis primo inventis in mare Occidentis e De inventione insularum de Açores.

Ferraro, Joanne M. 2001. *Marriage Wars in Late Renaissance Venice*. Studies in the History of Sexuality. Ed. Guido Ruggiero. Oxford: Oxford University Press.

Few, Martha. 2002. *Women Who Live Evil Lives: Gender, Religion, and the Politics of Power in Colonial Guatemala*. Austin: University of Texas Press.

Finlay, Linda. 2015. *Relational Integrative Psychotherapy: Process and Theory in Practice*. Chichester: Wiley.

Flandrin, Jean-Louis. 1979. *Families in Former Times: Kinship, Household and Sexuality*. Cambridge: Cambridge University Press.

Fletcher, Lea. 1994. *Mujeres y cultura en la Argentina del siglo XIX*. Buenos Aires: Feminaria Editora.

Fonseca, Claudia. 1998. *Caminos de adopción*. Buenos Aires: EUDEBA.

Forbes, T.R. 1966. *The Midwife and the Witch*. London: Yale University Press.

Fragoso, Juan. 1570 (reprint 2018). *Discurso de las cosas aromáticas . . . de las Indias . . . para uso de medicinas*. Madrid: Forgotten Books.

Franco, Jean. 1989. *Plotting Women, Gender and Representation in Mexico*. New York: Columbia University Press.

Froide, Amy M. 2005. *Never Married: Single Women in Early Modern England*. Oxford: Oxford University Press.

Fuchs, Rachel. 1984. *Abandoned Children: Foundlings and Child Welfare in Nineteenth-Century France*. Albany: SUNY Press.

Gal, Susan. 1993. "Language and the Arts of Resistance." *Cultural Anthropology* 10, no. 3 (August): 407–35.

Gal, Susan. 2008. "Language Ideologies Compared." *Journal of Linguistic Anthropology* 15 (1): 23–37.

Gal, Susan, and Kathryn Woolard, eds. 2001. *Languages and Publics: The Making of Authority*. Manchester: Manchester University Press.

Gamble, David P. 1957. *The Wolof of Senegambia*. London: International African Institute.

Garcia-Ballester, Luis. 1985. "Academicism versus Empiricism in Practical Medicine in Sixteenth-Century Spain, with regard to Morisco Practitioners." In *The Medical Renaissance of the Sixteenth Century*, ed. A. Wear et al., 246–70. Cambridge: Cambridge University Press.

Garcia-Ballester, Luis. 1984. *Los moriscos y la medicina, Un capitulo de la medicina y la ciencia marginadas en la España del siglo XVI*. Barcelona: Labor.

García Peña, Ana Lidia. 2004. "Madres solteras, pobres y abandonados: Ciudad de México, siglo XIX." *Historia Mexicana* 53, no. 3 (January): 647–92.

García Peña, Ana Lidia. 2006. *El fracaso del amor, genero e individualismo en el siglo XIX mexicano*. Mexico City: El Colegio de México / Universidad Autónoma del Estado de México.

Gauderman, Kimberly. 2003. *Women's Lives in Colonial Quito: Gender, Law, and Economy in Spanish America*. Austin: University of Texas Press.

Gavitt, Philip. 1990. *Charity and Children in Renaissance Florence: The Ospedale degli Innocenti, 1410–1536*. Ann Arbor: University of Michigan Press.

Gerhard, Peter. 1993. *A Guide to the Historical Geography of New Spain*. Rev. ed. Norman: University of Oklahoma Press.

Giladi, Avner. 2010. "Liminal Craft, Exceptional Law: Preliminary Notes on Midwives in Medieval Islamic Writings." *International. Journal of Middle East Studies* 42 (2010): 185–202.

Ginzburg, Carlo. 1966. *The Night Battles, Witchcraft and Agrarian Cults in the Sixteenth and Seventeenth Centuries*. London: Johns Hopkins University Press.

Ginzburg, Carlo. 1986. "The Dovecote Has Opened Its Eyes: Popular Conspiracy in Seventeenth-Century Italy." In *The Inquisition in Early Modern Europe*, ed. G. Henningsen and John Tedeschi. Dekalb: Northern Illinois University Press.

Gomes de Melo, Jaqueline Souza. 2012. "Praticantes e usuários de magia na primeira visitação do santo ofício à Bahia (1591–1593): Apreciações sobre relações sociais." Universidade do Estado da Bahia, Departamento de Ciências Humanas—Campus v Programa de Pós-Graduação em História Regional e Local Mestrado Acadêmico.

Gonzalbo Aizpuru, Pilar 1987. *Las mujeres en la Nueva España: Educación y vida cotidiana*. Mexico City: El Colegio de México.

Gonzalbo Aizpuru, Pilar. 2005. *Familia y orden colonial*. Mexico City: El Colegio de México.

Gonzàles, Rhonda M. 2012. "Potions, Power, and Persecution: African Women and Religion in Seventeenth-Century Mexico City." Unpublished paper, CLAH, Chicago.

González Rodríguez, Jaime. 2004. "El plano de México a través de la sección capellanías del Archivo General de la Nación." International Congress of Americanists, 32–49. Accessed 24 December 2012. http://www.americanistas.es/biblo/textos/cu04/cu04-05 .pdf.

Goody, Jack. 1984. *The Development of the Family and Marriage in Europe*. Cambridge: Cambridge University Press.

Gowing, Laura. 1996. *Domestic Dangers, Women, Words, and Sex in Early Modern London*. Oxford: Clarendon Press.

Grajales Porras, Agustín, and José Aranda Romero. 1991. "Hijos naturales del Sagrario Angelpolitano a mediados del siglo XVIII." In *Segundo Coloquio: Balances y prospectivas de las investigaciones sobre Puebla*, 21–32. Puebla: Colección V centenario.

Graubart, Karen B. 2007. *With Our Labor and Sweat: Indigenous Women and the Formation of Colonial Society in Peru, 1550–1700*. Stanford, CA: Stanford University Press.

Guevara Sangines. 2005. "El proceso de liberación de los esclavos en la América virreinal." In Pautas de convivencia étnica en la América Latina colonial. (Indios, mulatos, negros, pardos y esclavos), ed. Juan Manuel de la Serna Herrera, 111–59. Mexico City: CCyDEL-UNAM / Universidad de Guanajuato.

Gutiérrez, Ramón A. 1991. *When Jesus Came, the Corn Mothers Went Away: Marriage, Sexuality, and Power in New Mexico, 1500–1846*. Stanford, CA: Stanford University Press.

Gutmann, Matthew C. 1993. "Rituals of Resistance: A Critique of the Theory of Everyday Forms of Resistance." *Latin American Perspectives* 20, no. 2:74–92.

Guy, Donna. 1991. *Sex and Danger in Buenos Aires: Prostitution, Family, and Nation in Argentina*. Lincoln: University of Nebraska Press.

Guy, Donna. 1994. "Niños abandonados en Buenos Aires (1880–1914)." *Mujeres y cultura en la Argentina del siglo XIX*, ed. Lea Fletcher, 217–26. Buenos Aires: Seminaria.

Hall, E. 1997. *The Arnolfini Betrothal: Medieval Marriage and the Enigma of Van Eyck's Double Portrait*. Los Angeles: University of California Press.

Hallgren, R. 1983. "West African Childbirth Traditions." *Jordemodern* (Nov) 96:11: 311–316.

Hanawalt, Barbara A. 1986. *The Ties that Bound: Peasant Families in Medieval England*. Oxford: Oxford University Press.

Hanjal, J. 1965. "European Marriage Patterns in Perspective." In *Population in History*, ed. D. V. Glass and D. E. C Eversley, 101–43. London, Edward Arnold Publishers.

Hanley, Sarah. 1989. "Engendering the State: Family Formation and State Building in Early Modern France." *French Historical Studies* 16, no. 1 (Spring): 4–27.

Hanson, Ann Ellis. 1995. "Uterine Amulets and Greek Uterine Medicine." *Medicina nei secoli* 7, no. 2:281–99.

Harper, Kyle. 2013. *From Shame to Sin: The Christian Transformation of Sexual Morality in Late Antiquity*. Cambridge, MA: Harvard University Press.

Haslip-Viera, Gabriel. 1999. *Crime and Punishment In Late Colonial Mexico City, 1692–1810*. Albuquerque: University of New Mexico Press.

Hernández Sáenz, Luz María. 1997. *Learning to Heal: The Medical Profession in Colonial Mexico, 1767–1831*. London: Peter Lang.

Herrero, Manuel. 1955–56. "Tipología social del siglo XVII: Ensalmadores y saludadores." *Hispania* 15:173–90.

Heyden, Doris. 1989. "Aspectos mágicos religiosos de las cuevas." In *Las máscaras de la cueva de Santa Ana Teloxtoc*, ed. Ernesto Vargas, 91–96. Mexico City: UNAM.

Holler, Jaquelline. 2001. *Escogidas Plantas: Nuns and Beatas in Mexico City, 1531–1601*. New York: Columbia University Press.

Holler, Jacqueline. 2010. "The Holy Office of the Inquisition and Women." In *Religion and Society in Latin America: Interpretive Essays from Conquest to Present*, ed. M. Penyak and Walter J. Petry, 115–37. New York: Orbis Books.

Hospitales de la Nueva España. 1956–60. 2 vols. Mexico City: Edición Jus.

Hutchinson, Thomas Joseph. [1858] 1970. *Impressions of Western Africa*. London: Frank Cass.

INSAD (Investigación en salud y demografica s.c.). 2019. http://insad.com.mx/portafolio/investigacion/2017/.

An interim translation of Manuel Alvares S.J. "Etiópia Menor e Descripção Géografica da Província da Serra Leoa" [c. 1615]. 1990. Transcription from an unpublished manuscript by the late Avelino Teixeira da Mota and Luís de Matos on behalf of the Centro de Estudos de Cartografia Antiga, Lisbon; translation and introduction by P. E. H. Hair. Department of History, University of Liverpool, 1990.

Irigaray, Luce. 1985. *This Sex Which Is Not One*. Ithaca: Cornell University Press.

Israel, Jonathan. 1975. *Race, Class and Politics in Colonial Mexico, 1610–1670*. London: Oxford University Press.

Israel, Jonathan. 1980. *Razas, clases sociales y vida política en el México colonial 1610–1670*. Mexico City: Fondo de Cultura Econòmica.

Jaffary, N. E. 2004. *False Mystics: Deviant Orthodoxy in Colonial Mexico*. Lincoln: University of Nebraska Press.

Jarcho, Saul. 1976. "Medicine in Sixteenth-Century New Spain." In *Essays on the History of Medicine: Selected from the Bulletin of the New York Academy of Medicine*, ed. Saul Jarcho, 431–39. New York: Science History Publications, No. 49.

Johnson, Paul Christopher. 2002. *Secrets, Gossip, and Gods: The Transformation of Brazilian Candomblé*. Oxford: Oxford University Press.

Jones, A. 2003. "'Technologies of Remembrance': Memory, Materiality and Identity in Early Bronze Age Scotland." In *Archaeologies of Remembrance. Death and Memory in Past Societies*, ed. Howard Williams, 65–88. New York: Springer.

Jules-Rosette, Benetta, 1981. "Faith Healers and Folk Healers: The Symbolism and Practice of Indigenous Therapy in Urban Africa," *Religion* 11 (2), 127–149.

Jutte, Robert. 1981. "Poor Relief and Social Discipline in Sixteenth-Century Europe." *European Studies Review* 11:25–52.

Kertzer, David. 1993. *Sacrificed for Honor: Italian Infant Abandonment and the Politics of Reproductive Control*. Boston: Beacon Press.

Kinkead, Duncan T. 2009. *Pintores y doradores en Sevilla: 1650–1699, Documentos*. Bloomington IN: Author House.

Kicza, John E. 1988. "The Social and Ethnic Historiography of Colonial Latin America: The Last Twenty Years." *William and Mary Quarterly* 45, no. 3 (July): 453–88.

Knight, Chris. 1983. "Lévi-Strauss and the Dragon: Mythologiques Reconsidered in the Light of an Australian Aboriginal Myth." *Man*, new ser., 18, no. 1 (March): 21–50.

Knight, Chris. 1997. "The Wives of the Sun and the Moon." *Journal of the Royal Anthropological Institute* 3, no. 1:133–53.

Komisaruk, Catherine. 2013. *Labor and Love in Guatemala: The Eve of Independence*. Stanford, CA: Stanford University Press.

Korth, Eugene H., S.J., and Della M. Flusche. 1987. "Dowry and Inheritance in Colonial Spanish America: Peninsular Law and Chilean Practice." *Americas* 43:395–410.

Kuznesof, Ann. 1989. "The History of the Family in Latin America: A Critique of Recent Work." *Latin America Research Review* 24, no. 2:168–86.

Kuznesof, Elizabeth Anne. 1995. "Ethnic and Gender Influences on 'Spanish' Creole Society in Colonial Spanish America." *Colonial Latin American Review* 4:153–68.

Kuznesof, Elizabeth Anne. 1998. "The Puzzling Contradictions of Child Labor, Unemployment, and Education in Brazil." *Journal of Family History* 23:225–39.

Lanning, John Tate. 1985. *The Royal Protomedicato: The Regulations of the Medical Professions in the Spanish Empire*, ed. John J. Tepaske. Durham, NC: Duke University Press.

Lara, Eva. 2010. *Hechiceras y brujas en la literatura española de los siglos de oro*. Valencia: Ed. Parnaseo-Universidad de Valencia.

Lavrin, Asunción 1978. "In Search for the Colonial Woman in Mexico: The Seventeenth and Eighteenth Centuries." In *Latin American Women, Historical Perspectives*, ed. Asunción Lavrin Westport, CT: Greenwood Publishing Group.

Lavrin, Asunción, ed. 1989a. *Sexuality and Marriage in Colonial Latin America*. Lincoln: University of Nebraska Press.

Lavrin, Asunción. 1989b. "Sexuality in Colonial Mexico: A Church Dilemma." In *Sexuality and Marriage in Colonial Latin America*, ed. Asunción Lavrin, 47–95. Lincoln: University of Nebraska Press.

Lavrin, Asunción, and Edith Couturier. 1979. "Dowries and Wills: A View of Women's Socioeconomic Role in Colonial Guadalajara and Puebla, 1640–1790." *Hispanic American Historical Review* 59, no. 2:280–304.

Lauderdale Graham, Sandra. 1992. *House and Street: The Domestic World of Servants and Masters in Nineteenth-Century Rio de Janeiro*. Austin: University of Texas Press.

Lefebvre, Henry. 1991. *The Production of Space* Blackwell: Oxford.

León, Nicolás. 1918–1921. "Apuntes para la historia de la enseñanza y ejercicio de la medicina en México desde la conquista hispana hasta el año de 1833." *Gaceta de Medicina Mexicana* 3, no. 11 (1918): 210–86, and 14 (1921): 3–48.

Leavitt-Alcantará, Briana. 2018. *Alone at the Altar: Single Women and Devotion in Santiago de Guatemala, 1670–1870*. Stanford, CA: Stanford University Press.

Lewis, Laura A. 2011. *The Hall of Mirrors: Power, Witchcraft, and Caste in Colonial Mexico*. Durham, NC: Duke University Press.

Lipsett-Rivera, Sonya. 1997. "The Interaction of Rape and Marriage in Late Colonial and Early National Mexico." *Colonial Latin American Historical Review* 6 no. 4 (Fall): 559–90.

Lipsett-Rivera, Sonya. 2001. "La casa como protagonista en la vida cotidiana de México (1750–1856)." In *Casas, viviendas y hogares en la historia de México*, ed. Rosalva Loreto López, 231–47. Mexico City: El Colegio de México.

Lipsett-Rivera, Sonya. 2012. *Gender and the Negotiation of Daily Life in Mexico, 1750–1856*. Lincoln: University of Nebraska Press.

Lipsett-Rivera, Sonya. 2014. "If I Can't Have Her, No One Else Can." In *Emotions and Daily Life in Colonial Mexico*, ed. Javier Villa-Flores and Sonya Lipsett-Rivera, 66–84. Albuquerque: University of New Mexico Press.

Livingstone, E. A. 1982. *Concise Dictionary of the Christian Church*. Oxford: Oxford University Press.

Low, Setha. 1996. "Spatializing Culture: The Social Production and Social Construction of Public Space in Costa Rica." *American Ethnologist* 23, no. 4 (November): 861–79.

Luis Vives, Juan. 1536. *Instrucción de la mujer cristiana*. Valencia.

Lutz, Christopher H. 1994. *Santiago de Guatemala, 1541–1773: City, Caste, and the Colonial Experience*. Norman: University of Oklahoma Press.

Madajczak, Julia. 2014. *Nahuatl Kinship Terminology as Reflected in Colonial Written Sources from Central Mexico: A System of Classification* PhD dissertation, University of Warsaw.

Malvido, Eduardo. 1975. "Efectos de las epidemias y hambrunas en la población colonial de México." *Salud Pública de México, Epoca V* 17:793–802.

Mangan, Jane E. 2005. *Trading Roles: Gender, Ethnicity, and the Urban Economy in Colonial Potosí*. Durham, NC: Duke University Press.

Mannarelli, María. 1993. *Pecados públicos: La ilegitimidad en Lima, siglo XVII*. Lima: Ediciones Flora Tristán.

Maravall, José Antonio. 1979. *Poder, honor y elites en el siglo XVII*. Madrid: Siglo Veintiuno Editores.

Marcílio, María Luiza. 1998. *História social da criança abandonada*. São Paulo: Siglo XXI.

Márquez Morfín, Lourdes. 1993. "La evolución cuantitativa de la población novohispana: Siglos XVI, XVII y XVIII." In *El poblamiento de México*, 36–63. Vol. 2. Mexico City: Consejo Nacional de la Población.

Martin, R. 1989. *Witchcraft and the Inquisition in Venice, 1550–1650*. Oxford: Oxford University Press.

Martinez, María Elena. 2008. *Genealogical Fictions: Limpieza de Sangre in Colonial Mexico*. Stanford, CA: Stanford University Press.

Martinez-Alier, Verena. 1974. *Marriage, Class and Colour in Nineteenth-Century Cuba: A Study of Racial Attitudes and Sexual Values in a Slave Society*. Cambridge: Cambridge University Press.

Masferrer León, and Cristina Verónica. 2011. "Por las ánimas de negros bozales: Las cofradías de personas de origen africano en la ciudad de México (siglo xvii)." *Cuicuilco* 18, no. 51 (May–August): 83–103.0, 2011, pp

Mauss, Marcel. [1924] 1997. "Gift, Gift." In *The Logic of the Gift: Toward an Ethic of Generosity*, ed. Alan D. Schrift, 28–31. Routledge.

McCaa, Robert. 1989. "La viuda viva del México Borbónico: Sus voces, variedades y veja-ciones." In *Familias Novohispanicas*, ed. Pilar Gonzalbo Aizpuru, 299–325.

McCaa, Robert. 1991. "Introduction," "Female and Family in Nineteenth-Century Latin America," special issue, *Journal of Family History* 16, no. 3 (July): 211–14.

McCaa, Robert. 1994. "Marriageways in Mexico and Spain, 1500–1900." *Continuity and Change* 9, no. 1 (1994): 11–43.

McCaa, Robert. 2003. "The Nahua Calli of Ancient Mexico: Household, Family and Gender." *Continuity and Change* 18:23–48.

McCafferty, Sharisse D., and Geoffrey G. McCafferty. 2008. "Back to the Womb: Caves, Sweatbaths and Sacred Water in Ancient Mesoamerica." In *Flowing Through Time*, ed. L. Steinbrenner, B. Cripps, M. Georgopoulos, and J. Carr. Chacmool. Proceedings of the 36th Annual Chacmool Conference. The Archaeological Association of the University of Calgary, Calgary, AB.

McClure, Ruth. 1981. *Coram's Children: The London Foundling Hospital in the Eighteenth Century*. New Haven, CT: Yale University Press.

Megged, Amos. 1992. "The Rise of Creole Identity in Early Colonial Guatemala, Differential Patterns between Town and Countryside" *Social History* 17:421–40.

Megged, Amos. 2014. "Between History, Memory, and Law: Courtroom Methods in Mexico." *Journal of Interdisciplinary History* (ERS INT1) 45, no. 2 (Autumn): 163–86.

Melé, Patríce. 2006. "Un tipo de vivienda símbolo de los centros antiguos: La vecindad." In *La producción del patrimonio urbano*, ed. Patríce Melé. Mexico City: CIESAS.

Meza, René Salinas. 1991. "Orphans and Family Disintegration in Chile: The Mortality of Abandoned Children, 1750–1930." *Journal of Family History* 16, no. 3:315–29.

Meznar, Joan. 1994. "Orphans and the Transition to Free Labor in Northeast Brazil: The Case of Campinas Grande, 1850–1888," *Journal of Social History* 27:499–515.

Milanich, Nara. 2002a. "Historical Perspectives on Illegitimacy and Illegitimates in Latin America." In *Minor Omissions: Children in Latin American History and Society*, ed. Tobias Hecht. Madison, WI: University of Wisconsin Press.

Milanich, Nara. 2002b. "The Children of Fate: Family, Class, and the State in Chile, 1857–1930." Unpublished PhD dissertation, Yale.

Milanich, Nara. 2004. "The *Casa de Huerfanos* and Child Circulation in Late-Nineteenth-Century Chile." *Journal of Social History* 38, no. 2:311–40.

Milbrath, Susan. 1988. "Birth Images in Mixteca-Puebla Art," in *The Role of Gender in Pre-Columbian Art and Arcitecture*, Virginia Miller, ed., pp. 153–177. Lenham: University Press of America.

Miles, Tiya. 2008. "The Narrative of Nancy: A Cherokee Woman." *Frontiers: A Journal of Women Studies* 29 no. 2/3:59–80.

Molina, Alonso de. [1571] 2001. *Vocabulario en lengua castellana y mexicana y mexicana y castellana*. Mexico City: Editorial Porrúa, S. A.

Moreno, José Luis. 2000. "El delgado hilo de la vida: Los niños expósitos de Buenos Aires, 1779–1823." *Revista de Indias* 60:220, 663–85.

Morin, Claude. 1972. "Los libros parroquiales como fuente para la historia demográfica y social Novohispana." *Historia Mexicana* 21:389–418.

Morin, Claude. 1977. "Démographie et différences ethniques en Amérique latine coloniale." *Annales de démographie historique*, 301–12.

Morin, Claude. 1987. "Des terres sans hommes aux hommes sans terres: Les paramètres agraires de l'évolution démographique dans l'Indoamérique (Mexique-Pérou)." In *Évolution agraire et croissance démographique*, ed. Antoinette Fauve-Chamoux, 75–87. Liège, Belgium: Ordina Editions.

Morin, C. 1997. "Age at Marriage and Female Employment in Colonial Mexico." Paper read at Women's Employment, Marriage-Age and Population Change, New Delhi.

Mörner, Mangus, ed. 1970. *Race and Class in Latin America*. New York: Columbia University Press.

Morris, Ian. 1992. *Death-Ritual and Social Structure in Classical Antiquity*. Cambridge: Cambridge University Press.

Murillo, Dana Velasco. 2013. "Laboring Above Ground: Indigenous Women in New Spain's Silver Mining District, Zacatecas, Mexico, 1620–1770." *Hispanic American Historical Review* 93, no. 1:3–32.

Murray, Tim. 2002. Review of *Landscapes, Rock-art and the Dreaming: An Archaeology of Preunderstanding* by Bruno David (London: Leicester University Press, 2002), *Australian Archaeology* 66 (June 2008): 79–81.

Myers, Kathleen A. 1993. "A Glimpse of Family Life in Colonial Mexico: A Nun's Account," *Latin American Research Review* 28, no. 2:63–87.

Nazzari, Muriel. 1996. "Concubinage in Colonial Brazil: The Inequalities of Race, Class, and Gender." *Journal of Family History* 21, no. 2 (April): 107–24.

Nazzari, Muriel. 1998. "An Urgent Need to Conceal." In *The Faces of Honor: Sex, Shame, and Violence in Colonial Latin America*, ed. Lyman L. Johnson and Sonya Lipsett-Rivera. Albuquerque: University of New Mexico Press.

Neuwinger, H. D. 1996. *African Ethnobotany, Poisons and Drugs*. London: Chapman and Hall.

Nutini, Hugo Gino. 1980. *Ritual Kinship, Ideological and Structural Integration of the Compadrazgo System in Rural Tlaxcala*. 2 vols. Princeton: Princeton University Press.

Ortega Noriega, Sergio. 1986. *De la santidad a la perversión: O de porqué no se cumplía la ley de Dios en la sociedad novohispana*. Mexico City: Grijalbo.

Ortiz, Néstor R. 1976. *Macumba: Culturas africanas en el Brasil*. Colección Ensayos. Buenos Aires: Plus Ultra.

Ortner, Sherry B. 1995. "Resistance and the Problem of Ethnographic Refusal." *Comparative Studies in Society and History* 37, no. 1 (January 1995): 173–93.

Overmayer-Velazquez, R. 1998. "Christian Morality Revealed in New Spain: The inimical Nahua Woman in Book Ten of the Florentine Codex." *Journal of Women's History* 10, no. 2:1–28.

Paiva, José Pedro. 2013. *História da Inquisição Portuguesa 1536–1821*. Lisbon: Esfera dos Livros.

Palmer, Colin. 1970. "Negro Slavery in Mexico: 1570–1650." Unpublished PhD dissertation, University of Wisconsin, Madison.

Panter-Brick, Catherine, and Malcolm T. Smith, eds. 2000. *Abandoned Children*. Cambridge: Cambridge University Press.

Papel del Pulque, en favor de sus virtudes medicinales y singulares, propiedades, escrito por el Bachiller don Caytano Francisco María de Torres, médico en la ciudad de Puebla de los Angeles y lo dirige al Doctor don Pedro Ruiz de Palma, presbítero, cura proprio por el partido de Santa María Acaxete, y médico del ilustrísimo Doctor Domingo Pantaleón Alvarez de Abreu, obispo de la dicha ciudad de Puebla, Año de 1748.

Parrilla Hermida, Manuel. 1977. "Apuntes históricos sobre el protomedicato." *Anales de la Real Academia Nacional de Medicina–Madrid* 64:475–515.

Parry, J. [1995] 2001. "Death and Digestion: The Symbolism of Food and Eating in North indigenous Mortuary Rites." *Man* 20: 612–30.

Pearce, J. 1998. "From Death to Deposition: The Sequence of Ritual in Cremation Burials of the Roman Period." In *TRAC 97. Proceedings of the Seventh Annual Theoretical Roman Archaeology Conference, Nottingham 1997*, ed. C. Forcey, J. Hawthorne, and R. Witcher, 99–111. Oxford: Oxford University Press.

Pearce, J., M. Millett, and M. Struck, eds. 2000. *Burial, Society and Context in the Roman World*. Oxford: Oxford University Press.

Penyak, Lee M. 1999. "Safe Harbors and Compulsory Custody: *Casas de depósito* in Mexico, 1750–1865." *HAHR* 79, no. 1 (February): 84–99.

Perry, Mary Elizabeth. 1990. *Gender and Disorder in Early Modern Seville*. Princeton: Princeton University Press.

Perry, Mary Elizabeth. 2007. *The Handless Maiden: Moriscos and the Politics of Religions in Early Modern Spain*. Princeton, NJ: Princeton University Press.

Pescador, Juan Javier. 1992. *De bautizados a fieles difuntos: Familia y mentalidades en una parroquia urbana: Santa Catarina de Mexico, 1568–1820*. Mexico City: El Colegio de Mexico.

Pescador, Juan Javier. 1995. "Vanishing Women: Female Migration and Ethnic Identity in Late-Colonial Mexico City." *Ethnohistory* 42, no. 4 (Fall): 617–26.

Peters, C. 1997. "Single Women in Early Modern England." *Continuity and Change* 12:325–45.

Phillips, Kim M. 2003. *Medieval Maidens: Young Women and Gender in England, 1270–1540*. Manchester: Manchester University Press.

Phillips, Roderick. 1980. *Family Breakdown in Late Eighteenth-Century France, Divorces in Rouen, 1792–1803*. Oxford: Oxford University Press.

Philips, Roderick. 1988. *Putting Asunder: A History of Divorce in Western Society*. Cambridge: Cambridge University Press.

Polo, Inés Yañez, and Juan Ramón Zaragosa Rubira. 1976. "Spanish Folk Medicine of the XVIIth Century." In *Acta Congressus Internationalis XXIV: Historiae Artis Medicinae*. 2 Vols., 2:1287–93. Budapest: Semmelweis Museum.

Poska, Allyson M. 1996. "When Love Goes Wrong: Getting Out of Marriage in Seventeenth-Century Spain." *Journal of Social History* 29, no. 4 (Summer): 871–82.

Poska, Allyson, M. 2012. "An Ocean Apart: Reframing Gender in the Spanish Empire." In *Women of the Iberian Atlantic*, ed. Jane E. Mangan, and Sarah E. Owens, 37–56. Baton Rouge: Louisiana State University Press.

Potter, Jonathan 2001. "Wittgenstein and Austin." In *Discourse Theory and Practice: A Reader*, ed. M. Wetherell, S. Taylor, and S. Yates, 39–46. London: Sage Publications.

Quezada, Naomi. 1978. "La herbolaria en el México colonial." In *Estado actual del conocimiento en plantas medicinales mexicanas*, ed. Xavier Lozaya, 51–68. Mexico City: Instituto Mexicano para el Estudio de las Plantas Medicinales.

Rabell, C. 1990. *La población novohispana a la luz de los registros parroquiales (advances y perespectivas de investigación)*. Mexico City: FCE/CONAPO.

Raby, Dominque. 1999. "Xochiquetzal en el Cuicacalli: Cantos de amor y voces femeninas entre los antiguos nahuas." *Estudios de Cultura Nahuatl* 30:203–29.

Ramos, Donald. 1991. "Single and Married Women in Vila Rica, Brazil, 1754–1838." *Journal of Family History* 16, no. 3 (July): 261–82.

Ransel, David. 1988. *Mothers of Misery: Child Abandonment in Russia*. Princeton: Princeton University Press.

Resnick, Irvin M. 2002. "On Roots of the Myth of Jewish Male Menses in Jacques de Vitry's *History of Jerusalem*." Unpublished paper.

Reyes, J. M. 1912. "Estudios históricos sobre el ejercicio de la medicina 1646–1800." *Anales de la Escuela de Medicina* (Mexico) 1:511–73.

Risse, Guenter B. 1987. "Medicine in the New World." In *Medicine in the New World: New Spain, New France, and New England*, ed. Ronald L. Numbers. Knoxville: University of Tennessee Press.

Rosenwein, Barbara H. 2015. *Generations of Feeling: A History of Emotions, 600–1700*. Cambridge: Cambridge University Press.

Ruggiero, Guido. 1993. *Binding Passions, Tales of Magic, Marriage, and Power at the End of the Renaissance*. Oxford: Oxford University Press.

Sá, Isabel dos Guimarães 1995. *A circulação de crianças na Europa do Sul: O caso dos expostos do Porto no século XVIII*. Lisbon: Fundação Calouste Gulbenkian.

Sahagún, Fray Bernardino de. 1950–63. *Florentine Codex: General History of the Things of New Spain*, trans. C. E. Dibble and A. J. O. Anderson. Salt Lake City: University of Utah Press.

Sahagún, Fray Bernardino de. 1982. "De las calidades y condiciones de las personas conjuntas por parentesco. De los grados de afinidad. De las personas que difieren por edad y de sus condiciones buenas y malas," *Nueva Antropología* vol. 5:18 (Enero): 13–40.

Sahagún, Fray Bernardino de. 1989. *Historia general de las cosas de la Nueva España (Códice Florentino)*. Introduction. and notes by Alfredo López Austin and Josefina García Quintana. México: Consejo Nacional para la Cultura y las Artes-Alianza Editorial Mexicana.

Skaria, Ajay. 1997. "Women, Witchcraft and Gratuitous Violence in Colonial Western India." *Past and Present* 155:108–37.

Sahlins, Marshal. 1997. "The Spirit of the Gift." In *The Logic of the Gift, Toward an Ethic of Generosity*, ed. Alan D. Schrift, 71–72. London: Routledge.

Salinas Meza, René. 1991. "Orphans and Family Disintegration in Chile: The Mortality of Abandoned Children, 1750–1930." *Journal of Family History* 16, no. 3:315–29.

Sánches Granjel, Luis. 1972. "Medicina y brujeria," *Cuaderno de Historia de la medicina Española*, 11: 407–20.

Sánchez Ortega, María Elena 1988. *La Inquisición y los gitanos*. Madrid: Taurus.

Sánchez Ortega, María Helena. 1992. "Women as a Source of 'Evil' in Counter-Reformation Spain." In *Cultural Encounters*, ed. Ann Cruz and Mary Elizabeth Parry. Berkeley: University of California Press.

Sánchez Ortega, María Helena. 1992. "Woman as Source of 'Evil' in Counter-Reformation Spain." In *Cultural Encounters . . . ed.* Ann Cruz and Mary Elizabeth Perry, 196–215. Minneapolis, MN: University of Minnesota Press.

Sánchez, Tania Romero. 2013. "La sexualidad y los estereotipos de la bruja." Presentation at El Coloquio de Magia, Brujería y Herejía en La Nueva España (siglos xvi–xix), Escuela Nacional de Antropología e Historia, Mexico City.

Sarró, Ramon. 2009. *The Politics of Religious Change on the Upper Guinea Coast: Iconoclasm Done and Undone*. Edinburgh: Edinburgh University Press.

Savage-Smith, Emilie. 1996. "Medicine." in *Encyclopedia of the History of Arabic Science*, ed. R. Rashid. 3:947. London: Routledge.

Schnucker, Robert V., ed. 1988. *Calviniana: Ideas and Influence of Jean Calvin*. Vol. 10. Kirksville, MO.: Sixteenth Century Journal Publishers.

Schrift, Alan D., ed. 1997. *The Logic of the Gift: Toward an Ethic of Generosity*. London: Routledge.

Schwaller, Stuart. 2011. "'Mulata, Hija de Negra e India': Afro-Indigenous Mulatoes in Early Colonial Mexico." *Journal of Social History* 44, no. 3 (Spring): 889–914.

Schwartz, Stuart. 1995. "Colonial Identities and the Sociedad de Castas." *Colonial Latin American Review* 4:185–201.

Schwartz, Stuart. 2008. *All Can Be Saved: Religious Tolerance and Salvation in the Iberian Atlantic World*. New Haven, CT: Yale University Press.

Seed, Patricia. 1982. "Social Dimensions of Race: Mexico City, 1753." *HAHR* 62, no. 4:569–606.

Seed, Patricia. 1985. "The Church and the Patriarchal Family: Marriage Conflicts in Sixteenth- and Seventeenth-Century New Spain." *Journal of Family History* (Fall): 284–93.

Seed, Patricia. 1988a. *To Love, Honor, and Obey in Colonial Mexico*. Stanford, CA: Stanford University Press.

Seed, Patricia. 1988b. "Marriage Promises and the Value of Woman's Testimony in Colonial Mexico." *Signs: Journal of Women in Culture and Society* 13/2:253–76.

Seidel, L. 1995. *Jan Van Eyck's Arnolfini Portrait: Stories of an Icon*. Cambridge: Cambridge University Press.

Sherwood, Joan. 1988. *Poverty in Eighteenth-Century Spain: The Women and Children of the Inclusa*. Toronto: University of Toronto Press.

Sherzer, J. 1983. *Kuna Ways of Speaking: An Ethnographic Perspective*. Austin: University of Texas Press.

Schuler, Sidney Ruth. 1987. *The Other Side of Polyandry, Property, Stratification and Nonmarriage in the Nepal Himalayas*. Boulder: Westview Press.

Silverber, Robert. 1996. *The Golden Dream: Seekers of El Dorado*. Athens: Ohio University Press.

Skaria, Ajay. 1997. "Women, Witchcraft and Gratuitous Violence in Colonial Western India." *Past and Present* 155 (May): 108–37.

"Slave Voyages." n.d. *Trans-Atlantic Slave Trade Database*. Accessed 6 March 2017. http://www.slavevoyages.org/voyages/TJOFj4pc.

Snelgrave, William. 1733. *A New Account of Some Parts of Africa and the Slave Trade*. London: Jame Johns and Paul Knapton.

Snoep, Nanette Jacomijn. 2014. "Deriere le miroir, la magie du mond intangible." In *Bois Sacre initiation dans les forets guineennes*. Paris: Musee du Quai Branly.

Socolow, Susan Migden. 2000. *The Women of Colonial Latin America*. Cambridge: Cambridge University Press.

Soto, Juan de. 1619. *Obligaciones de todos los estados, y oficios, con los remedios y consejos mas eficaces para la salud espiritual, y general reformación de la costumbres*. Alcala.

Stern, Steve J. 1995. *The Secret History of Gender: Women, Men, and Power in Late Colonial Mexico*. Chapel Hill: University of North Carolina Press.

Stone, Lawrence. 1993. *Broken Lives: Separation and Divorce in England, 1660–1857.* Oxford: Oxford University Press.

Sullivan, Thelma D. 1966. "Childbirth, Pregnancy, and the Deification of the Women Who Died in Childbirth: Texts from the Florentine Codex, Book VI, Folios 128v–143v." In *Estudios de Cultura Nahuatl* 6: 63–95. México.

Symonds, Leigh. 2009. "Death as a Window to Life: Anthropological Approaches to Early Medieval Mortuary Ritual." *Reviews in Anthropology* 38: 48–87.

Sweet, James H. 2014. "Reimagining the African-Atlantic Archive: Method, Concept, Epistemology, Ontology." *Journal of African History* 55:147–59.

Szoblik, Katarzyna. 2008. "La *Ahuiani, ¿*Flor preciosa o mensajera del Diablo? La visión de las ahuianime en las fuentes indígenas y cristianas." *Itinerarios* 8:196–215.

Tanner, Norman P., ed. 1989. *Decrees of the Ecumenical Councils.* Vol. 1. Washington, DC: Georgetown University Press.

Tannenbaum, Frank. 1947. *Slave and Citizen: The Negro in the Americas.* New York: Vintage Books.

Thomas Gage's Travels in the New World. 1969. Ed. J. Eric Thompson. Norman: University of Oklahoma Press.

Thornton, John. 1998. *Africa and Africans in the Making of the Atlantic World, 1400–1800.* Cambridge: Cambridge University Press.

Thornton, John. 2003. "Cannibals, Witches, and Slave Traders in the Atlantic World," *William and Mary Quarterly* 60, no. 2:273–94.

Tine de Moor, and Jan Luiten Van Zanden. 2010. "Girl Power: the European Marriage Pattern and Labour Markets in the North Sea Region in the Late Medieval and Early Modern Europe." *Economic History Review* 63, no. 1:1–33.

Torales Pacheco, María Cristina. 1990. "A Note on the Composiciones de Tierra in the Jurisdiction of Cholula, Puebla (1591–1757)." In *The indigenous Community of Colonial Mexico, Fifteen Essays on Land Tenure, Corporate Organizations, Ideology and Village Politics*, ed. Arij Ouweneel and Simon Miller, 84–101. Amsterdam: University of Amsterdam Press.

Torquemada Juan de. 1723. *Monarchia Indiana.* Madrid: Nicolás Rodríguez Franco.

Townsend, Camilla. 2006. "'What in the World Have You Done to Me, My Lover?': Sex, Servitude, and Politics among the Pre-Conquest Nahuas as Seen in the *Cantares Mexicanos*." *Americas* 62, no. 3:347–89.

Turner, Victor. 1974. *Dramas, Fields, and Metaphors: Symbolic Action in Human Society.* Ithaca: Cornell University Press.

Twinam, Ann. 1999. *Public Lives, Private Secrets: Gender, Honor, Sexuality and Illegitimacy in Colonial Spanish America.* Stanford, CA: Stanford University Press.

Twinam, Ann. 2015. *Purchasing Whiteness: Pardos, Mulattoes, and the Quest for Social Mobility in the Spanish Indies*. Stanford: Stanford University Press.

Valdés, D. N. 1978. "The Decline of the *sociedad de castas* in Mexico City." Unpublished PhD dissertation, University of Michigan, Ann Arbor.

Van Deusen, Nancy. 2001. *Between the Sacred and the Worldly: The Institutional and Cultural Practice of Recogimiento in Colonial Lima*. Stanford, CA: Stanford University Press.

Vaughan, Genevieve. 2004. "Feminist Semiotics for Social Change: The Mother or the Market." *Mimesis* 1–17. http://www.gift-economy.com/articlesAndEssays/motherOr Market.pdf.

Vázquez Valle, Irene. 1975. "Los habitantes de la ciudad de México vistos a través del censo del año de 1753." Unpublished MA thesis, Mexico, Colegio de Mexico.

Venâncio, Renato Pinto. 1999. *Famílias abandonadas: Assistência à criança de camadas populares no Rio de Janeiro e em Salvador, séculos XVIII e XIX*. Rio de Janeiro: Papirus Editora.

Vieira Powers, Karen. 2002. "'Conquering Discourses of 'Sexual Conquest': Of Women, Language, and *Mestizaje*." *Colonial Latin American Review* 11, no. 1:9–32.

Vigil, Mariló. 1986. *La vida de las mujeres en los siglos XVI y XVII*. Madrid: Siglo XXI.

Villa Sánchez, Juan. (1746) 1972. *Puebla sagrada y profana*. Centro de Estudios Históricos de Puebla. Puebla: MAXTOR.

Vincent, Ann. 2012. "Singleness and the State: Unmarried and Widowed Women in Colonial Guadalajara, Mexico, 1821–1910." Unpublished PhD dissertation, University of Minnesota.

Vives, Juan Luis. [1528] 1936. *Libro llamado instrucción de la mujer cristiana*. Trans. Juan Justiano. Madrid: Signo.

Von Germeten, Nicole. 2003. "Corporate Salvation in a Colonial Society: Confraternities and Social Mobility for Africans and Their Descendants in New Spain." PhD dissertation, University of California, Berkeley.

Von Germeten, Nicole, 2006. *Black Blood Brothers: Confraternities and Social Mobility for Afro-Mexicans*. Gainesville: University of Florida Press.

Von Germeten, Nicole. 2013. *Violent Delights, Violent Ends: Sex, Race, and Honor in Colonial Cartagena de Indias*. Albuquerque: University of New Mexico Press.

Von Nettesheim, Heinrich Conelius Agrippa. 1531. *Of Occult Philosophy*.

Weekes, J. 2001. "Acculturation and the Temporal Features of Ritual Action." In *TRAC 2000. Proceedings of the Tenth Annual Theoretical Roman Archaeology Conference, London 2000*, ed. G. Davies, A. Gardner, and K. Lockyear, 73–82. Oxford: Oxford Universitiy Press.

Williams, Howard. 2003a. "Material Culture as Memory: Combs and Cremation in Early Medieval Britain." *Early Medieval Europe* 12, no. 2 (July): 89–128.

Williams, Howard, ed. 2003b. *Archaeologies of Remembrance: Death and Memory in Past Societies.* New York: Springer.

Zamora, Romina. 2010. "Lo doméstico y lo público: Los espacios de sociabilidad de la ciudad de San Miguel de Tucumán a fines del siglo XVIII y comienzos del siglo XIX." In "Espacios urbanos, lugares domésticos convergencias y divergencias," ed. Osvaldo Otero. Sección Debate, *Nuevo mundo, mundos nuevos.* OpenEdition Journal, CNRS.

Index